Created and Directed by Hans Höfer

WILDWEST

Edited by John Gattuso
Managing Editor: Martha Ellen Zenfell

Editorial Director: Brian Bell

Houghton Mifflin

APA PUBLICATIONS

"**E**astward I go by force; westward I go free," wrote Henry David Thoreau. To Americans, the West has always represented freedom and never more than in the latter half of the 19th century. It was an era of larger-than-life characters and epic events, of cattle drives and gold rushes, Indian wars and outlaws.

Insight Guide: Wild West chronicles the people and places of the Old West and its modern-day legacy. It is just one of nearly 200 guides in the series founded by **Hans Höfer**. The first title, *Insight Guide: Bali*, was published in 1970 and became the seminal work for this widely acclaimed series.

The book's project editor is **John Gattuso**, editor of Stone Creek Publications in Milford, New Jersey, and project editor of several Insight titles, including *Insight Guide: National Parks West*, *Insight Guide: National Parks East*, *Insight Guide: Philadelphia* and most tellingly *Insight Guide: Native America*.

Trained in anthropology, Gattuso was interested in exploring the relationship between the real and mystic West, "to explode the stereotypes, misconceptions and out-and-out lies about the Wild West, but also understand its romantic appeal." He was aided in the overall direction of the book by **Martha Ellen Zenfell**, Apa Publications' editor-in-chief of US titles.

"The Old West has been turned into a national epic," Gattuso says, "a sort of modern myth that's been reworked by writers and filmmakers to suit the thinking of the day." For his part, Gattuso penned chapters on the Indian wars and the myth of the West and co-wrote several pieces in the "Places" section of the book. "Western lore has become so ingrained in American culture that it's virtually impossible to

avoid. Whether it's pop icons like the 'Marlboro Man' or the cowboy posturing of public figures like the former president Ronald Reagan, it's become a cultural touchstone, a shorthand we use to define ourselves."

One of the contributors, **Tony Hillerman**, needs no introduction. The author of more than a dozen books, including a series of bestselling mystery novels featuring Navajo Tribal Police officers, Hillerman has been writing about the West for more than 35 years. He lends his vast experience to "They Sang It Like It Was," a look at western song and folklore.

Among the first people Gattuso recruited for the project was **Peter Alexander**, a California based writer who specializes in both western history and travel. Alexander covered the historic and contemporary West, with chapters on railroads, rodeo, literature, fashion and several other topics, including that most emblematic of western figures, the cowboy – "the West's own Odysseus, Don Quixote and Sir Galahad all rolled into one."

Anyone familiar with cowboy poetry will have heard of **Hal Cannon**, director of the Western Folklife Center and founder of the well-known Cowboy Poetry Gathering in Elko, Nevada. The editor of several books on western folk arts, for this book Cannon turns his attention to "buffalo soldiers," Chinese immigrants and other non-Anglo Westerners in "We Were There Too." He also covered northern Utah and his home state of Nevada.

Chapters on Wyoming, Montana and Idaho were penned by **Thomas Schmidt** in Victor, Idaho. Arizona was covered by two writers from Flagstaff, **Nicky Leach** and **Rose Houk**; Leach

Hillerman

Höfer

Gattuso

Zenfell

Schmidt

Leach

Houk

also wrote about southern Utah. The former publisher of *El Palacio*, the magazine of the Museum of New Mexico, **Beverly Becker** wrote about the early days of *ranchos* and *vaqueros* in the Spanish Southwest as well as issues facing the West today; she also covered New Mexico and Colorado. She now lives in California.

Also in California, **Matthew Jaffe**, a staff writer at *Sunset Magazine*, took a look at Western movies and southern California. **Bill O'Neal**, author of seven books about the Old West, covered his native Texas and neighboring Oklahoma. **Nan Siegel**, an editor at *Wild West* magazine, wrote "Western Women." **Mark Trahant**, an award-winning journalist and member of the Shoshone-Bannock Tribe, takes a revealing look at the Old West from "The Indian Point of View."

Gregory Lalire, editor of *Wild West* magazine in Leesburg, Virginia, profiled some of the Old West's most colorful figures, from trailblazers like Lewis and Clark to legendary gunfighters like Billy the Kid. His personal favorite is Henry Plummer, a Montana sheriff who was hanged – perhaps unjustly – for leading a secret band of highwaymen. "He's the classic western gunslinger," Lalire says, "a man who walked on both sides of the law, with deadly results."

The chapter on powwows was written by **George Horse Capture**, a curator at the National Museum of the American Indian in New York City and a member of the Gros Ventre Tribe; **Peter Anderson** in Salt Lake City covered "Art of the West;" freelance writer **Yvette LaPierre** worked on "The Dakotas;" and **John Grossman** contributed "Outhouses."

The book's rich imagery is the work of an extraordinary team of photographers. "I want the cowboy to be considered a great American hero," says **David Stoecklein**, who has photographed cowboys throughout the West. Based in Sun Valley, Idaho, Stoecklein has published two books, *The Idaho Cowboy* and *Cowboy Gear*.

Stoecklein

The Santa Fe photographer **Jack Parsons** says he's interested in the connection between "the landscape and the many cultures of the American West," particularly the Hispanic culture of northern New Mexico, "with its deep sense of history and strong ties to the land." Parsons' work has appeared in three highly successful books on western style: *True West*, *Santa Fe Style* and *Native America*.

Both **John Running** and **Stephen Trimble** are well-known for their compelling pictures of Native Americans. Trimble lives in Salt Lake City and is the author and photographer of several books, including *The People*, about the Indians of the Southwest. Running is based in Flagstaff, Arizona; his work appears around the world. **Tom Till** in Moab, Utah, and **Larry Ulrich** in Trinidad, California, are among the best-known landscape photographers in the US. Their images have appeared in countless calendars, books and magazines.

Tom Stack & Associates, located in Colorado Springs, Colorado, provided an assortment of vivid images. Additional photography was provided by **Catherine Karnow, Kerrick James, Olivier Laude, Scott Rutherford**, and **Jack Hollingsworth**.

In Insight Guides' London editorial office, the manuscript was proofread and indexed by **Pam Barrett**. Special thanks go to **Edward Jardim** in the US for invaluable editorial help.

O'Neal

Trahant

Horse Capture

Running

Trimble

Till

CONTENTS

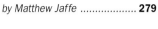

Maps

TRAVEL TIPS

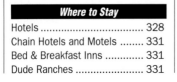

MYTH OF THE WEST

In 1893, a young professor named Frederick Jackson Turner presented a paper in Chicago that would influence the way Americans think about the West and themselves right up to the present day. The United States, he said, is a frontier nation. Its most cherished values – democracy, freedom, individualism – were forged on the ever-receding border between wilderness and civilization. Pioneers. Mountain men. Cowboys. These are the figures that embody the true character of the nation. In spirit if not in fact, Americans are the heirs of the Wild West.

"To the frontier the American intellect owes its striking characteristics. That coarseness and strength combined with acuteness and inquisitiveness; that practical, inventive turn of mind... that masterful grasp of material things... that restless, nervous energy... that dominant individualism working for good and evil... that buoyancy and exuberance that comes with freedom – these are the traits of the frontier."

It's a stirring notion. But is it true? Many latter-day historians have come to think otherwise. For one thing, big corporations were at least as important in the settling of the West as Turner's "rugged individual." And while the frontier was certainly brimming with a scrappy, freedom-loving spirit, so too were millions of poor European immigrants flooding into eastern cities.

No matter. Turner's "frontier thesis" was always more significant as ideology than as history. And still is. For many Americans, the Old West is more than a time and place, it's part of American legend. Its open prairies and shining mountains sprawl across what Archibald MacLeish called the "country of the mind." Its larger-than-life figures – Wyatt Earp, Billy the Kid, George Armstrong Custer, Crazy Horse – are players in a national mythology.

Ironically, on the very same evening that Turner delivered his landmark speech, a man of a very different sort was presenting his own ideas about the western frontier. William Frederick Cody, better known as Buffalo Bill, was dazzling a packed arena across town with his enormously popular Wild West Show – a sort of circus-on-the-hoof with whooping cowboys, "wild" Indians and a host of other western cliches, many of which are still being worked over in Western books and movies.

It was a telling coincidence, because in their own way, both Turner and Cody were doing the same thing: elevating the frontier into an abstraction, an epic saga about the "winning of the West," the triumph of civilization over wilderness, and the fulfillment of the nation's destiny.

Myth-making had been a part of the Old West right from the very beginning. Whether it was cowboys spinning yarns around a campfire or dime-novel writers churning out frontier fantasies, it

Preceding pages: cattle drive; Idaho cowboy; silver spurs; Arizona cowgirls; welcome to the Wilson Ranch; fiddlin' time; Shoshone-Bannock powwow. **Left**, "Ride 'em cowboy."

was often difficult to know where fact ended and fiction began. Stretching the truth just seemed to come naturally in a land so vast and stunning. "[A] man in the states might have been a liar in a small way," said cowboy artist Charlie Russell, "but when he comes west he soon takes a lesson from the prairies where ranges a hundred miles away seem within touching distance, streams run uphill, and nature appears to lie some herself."

Lying could pay pretty well, too. Real-life figures like Calamity Jane, Wild Bill Hickok and Pat Garrett were only too happy to peddle their legends to an adventure-starved public. Even Sitting Bull, the defiant chief of the Hunkpapa Sioux, signed on for a stint with Buffalo Bill's Wild West Show, though not before negotiating a steady supply of oyster stew and an exclusive right to sell photographs of himself.

But, as always, reality has a way of bleeding through the hype. For every myth that's been told about the winning of the West, there is an equally vivid reminder of the true nature of conquest. Depleted forests. Exhausted soil. Ghost towns where thousands of men came in a fruitless search for the mother lode.

Other voices break through, too, those of ordinary folk long ignored by history books, many of whom spent their lives chasing dreams in the West only to come up empty-handed. Unlucky prospectors. Farmers gone bust. Cowboys put out of work by barbed wire and achy bones.

There are the compelling but often overlooked stories of Chinese laborers who helped build the first transcontinental railroad, Spanish *vaqueros* who planted the seeds of "cowboy culture" in North America, black cavalrymen – buffalo soldiers – who patrolled some of the toughest outposts in the West, and the thousands of nameless men and women who did the hard work of raising families and building communities on the frontier.

For Indians, of course, the Wild West means something entirely different – not the settlement of an "untamed" wilderness but an invasion of their homeland. "Only to the white man was nature a 'wilderness' and only to him was the land 'infested' with 'wild' animals and 'savage' people," observed Luther Standing Bear, a Lakota writer who was a veteran of Buffalo Bill's Wild West Show. "Not until the hairy man from the East came and with brutal frenzy heaped injustices upon us and the families we loved was it 'wild' for us. When the very animals of the forest began fleeing from his approach, then it was for us the 'Wild West' began."

The mythic West of Turner and Cody, with its heroic frontiersmen bringing the blessings of "civilization" to a savage land, is only a starting point. Like all mythology, it says less about who Americans really are than who they imagine themselves to be. Look beneath the surface and you begin to see something far more complex and interesting – an explosive, often violent encounter of many races and cultures in a land more vast and wondrous than anyone could have imagined. And it all happened in the Wild West.

Right, *The Morning Shower* by Frank Tenney Johnson, 1927.

THE SPANISH WEST

A generation before the Pilgrims landed in Massachusetts, Spanish settlers were tending herds on the piñon-covered hills of northern New Mexico. By the early 17th century, a combination of *conquistadores, vaqueros* and Franciscan *padres* had transplanted their culture to the dusty Southwest. It took two more centuries for Anglo pioneers to make their own discovery of the Wild West.

The story of the Spanish West begins in 1528. Hoping to find gold in North America, Spanish adventurers got as far as Florida, where they were done in by a combination of inclement weather and poor judgment. Their ships, their supplies and most of their crew were lost. Of some 600 men, only four survived: two soldiers, an African slave named Esteban and, most famous of all, the expedition's second-in-command, Alvar Núñez Cabeza de Vaca.

Strange power: For seven years they lived among the natives of the Gulf Coast, first as slaves, then as sages after they began to cure ailing Indians. Determined to find Mexico, the four Spaniards headed west, helped along by thankful natives who believed in the strangers' power to heal. The Indians' solicitude convinced Cabeza de Vaca that converting them to Christianity was simple: "they must be won by kindness."

In 1535 the survivors reached northern Mexico. A small group of astounded Spanish soldiers escorted them to Mexico City where the equally amazed viceroy heard their story, including reports of Indians with emerald arrowheads (probably malachite). Cabeza de Vaca declined the viceroy's request to find this tribe, but his slave, Esteban, was willing.

Esteban headed north in 1539 accompanied by a Jesuit missionary, Fray Marcos de Niza. But this time the African wasn't so lucky. He was killed by Zuni Indians at the Hawikuh pueblo. Not one for tempting fate, Niza beat a retreat to Mexico, where he came across Francisco Vásquez de Coronado, the governor of a northern province.

Preceding pages: the sandstone buttes of Monument Valley, Arizona. **Left**, an idyllic view of a California *rancho*.

Cities of gold: Upon hearing Niza's story, Coronado sought permission to lead a huge expedition in search of the Seven Cities of Cibola, the fabled cities of gold thought to lie somewhere to the north. In 1540, Coronado and a band of conquistadors rode into Hawikuh and quickly subdued the Zuni. Finding no gold, they continued north to the pueblos of the Rio Grande and then east onto the plains. Although he had penetrated farther north than any other Spaniard, the expedition was a failure. Coronado returned to Mexico empty-handed in 1542, leaving a few missionaries and a trail of carnage behind him.

In 1598, settlers, not soldiers, made the first permanent inroads into the Southwest when Juan de Oñate led 149 colonists from Mexico to a spot just north of present-day Santa Fe.

Oñate's expedition was the first American trail ride: 7,000 cattle and 4,000 sheep were herded by *vaqueros* mounted on treasured cow ponies. The Spaniards knew their business: they'd been roping, branding and rounding up cows on ranches in Spain for centuries. The compact, hardy Spanish Barb horses and the rangy, longhorn cattle were the cornerstones of Spanish prosperity in Mexico.

Villages, missions and ranches sprang up in New Mexico, Texas and Arizona. Last to be colonized was California, separated from Mexico by hostile deserts and Indians. It had only 600 colonists by the late 1700s, but the spread of European diseases was already having a devastating effect on the Indians. While expeditions explored California's interior, Spanish colonists led by Gaspar de Portola and Fray Junípero de Serra built *ranchos* and missions along the coast.

California's mission priests kept herds of cattle that thrived in the region's temperate climate. Cowboy culture took root with the Indians, whom the Franciscans taught to ride, rope and brand. It was a good life for the rancheros if they didn't mind the isolation.

San Francisco was established in 1776, followed five years later, in 1781, by the founding of Los Angeles. By now, however, a weakened mother country was losing hold of its maturing colonies.

While Spanish California grew slowly, New Mexico's settlements were doing quite well. For most people, however, life was austere. Although the elite had access to trade goods like silk, porcelain, jewelry and books, the *peónes* were self-reliant and dirt poor. But out of their hardscrabble existence came what many regard as the golden age of Spanish colonial folk art. As churches were built and settlements grew in the 18th century, artisans laid the groundwork for traditions in textiles, furniture and religious art that are enjoying a renaissance today.

Consider Santa Fe-style architecture. Without sawmills or brick kilns, settlers could use only mud and unmilled lumber. Influenced

Cabeza de Vaca's belief in treating the Indians kindly. Many Indians were killed, tortured, enslaved or otherwise abused in the name of salvation. But it is worth noting that Spain was the only European invader to write laws protecting the Indians, although they were often ignored in the far-off colonies.

By 1680, the Pueblo Indians had had enough. Under the leadership of a San Juan medicine man named Pope, they revolted, slaughtering priests and administrators, destroying missions and laying siege to the capital at Santa Fe. Badly outnumbered, the Spanish beat a quick retreat south to El Paso.

Freedom for the Indians was all too brief. Twelve years after their expulsion, Spanish

by both the Spanish Moors and the Pueblo Indians, they built adobe brick buildings with dirt roofs and ceilings of *latillas* (hewn planks or narrow aspen trunks) supported by massive log beams known as *vigas*.

Faith was the glue that held these small frontier communities together, and villagers crafted their own religious art such as *bultos* (carved saints), *retablos* (painted wooden panels) and altar screens. And nearly every home had a creaky Spanish treadle loom used to weave the long-fleeced wool of the hardy *churro* sheep into serapes and rugs.

As the Spanish settled in with priests and plows, it became clear that not all shared

soldiers marched back into Santa Fe under the command of Diego de Vargas, who spent the next four years re-establishing colonial rule. The Indians rose up again in 1696 but were quickly put down. The Spanish remained in power for more than a century, forging an uneasy but influential link with the Indians of the Rio Grande Valley.

To this day, Catholic churches stand near sacred *kivas* (ceremonial chambers). On feast days, Pueblo people honor their patron saints at Mass as well as at traditional Indian dances. At Christmas, villages celebrate with turtle, buffalo and deer dances and even a Spanish-Moorish dance called *Los Matachines*.

Of course not everyone lived happily ever after. The Spanish treated Indians as little more than indentured servants. Indians attacked and enslaved members of other tribes. Both the Pueblo Indians and the Spanish were raided by nomadic Apaches, Navajos and Comanches. And wherever Europeans settled, *de facto* germ warfare was more fatal than any army.

Anglo invasion: When Mexico won independence from Spain in 1821, borders that had been closed for centuries were suddenly opened. Americans began trickling into the Southwest, first as traders along the Santa Fe Trail, then as settlers after the Civil War.

In 1845 the United States annexed Texas, touching off the Mexican War. American soldiers captured Mexico City only two years later and, under the terms of the Treaty of Guadalupe Hidalgo, the United States took possession of New Mexico (including present-day Arizona) and California and solidified its hold on Texas. After more than three centuries, Hispanic dominance in the Southwest was ended.

Everything about the conquering Americans was different: their language, religion, food and, perhaps most significantly, their laws. Suddenly Spanish-speakers were second-class citizens. Anglo cattlemen, traders and prospectors poured into the region and displaced long-time residents; land claims dating back to the Spanish colonial period were often dismissed by American courts.

The discovery in 1849 of gold in the Sacramento Valley hammered the final nail in the coffin of California's Spanish *ranchos*. With the arrival of thousands of '49ers, food prices went through the roof. To meet demand, cattle were slaughtered indiscriminately and herds dwindled. A drought delivered the *coup de grace*, and within 10 years California's *ranchos* – and *vaqueros* – were little more than a romantic memory. Change was more gradual in New Mexico and Arizona, but the outcome was much the same.

Despite these overwhelming changes, the influence of Hispanic culture in the American West remains profound. Much of cowboy culture, for example, has Spanish origins, from the names of cowpunching gear like

jáquima (hackamore), *chaparrejos* (chaps) and *la reata* (lariat) to old-time cowboy traditions like the roundup, rodeo and *mesta*, the Spanish precursor of the stockowners association. All cowboys worth their salt can dally a rope (a special way of tying a rope to the saddle horn after lassoing a cow), but most cowboys don't know that the term is derived from the Spanish *dar la vuelta* – to turn around.

The abundance of Spanish place names testifies to centuries of Spanish exploration. In Arizona and especially in New Mexico, Spanish folk art is still created by people whose families have lived on "American" soil for nearly four centuries. Mission

churches and humble chapels are found throughout the Southwest. And Spanish colonial architecture, with its graceful Moorish and Indian touches, has been emulated by designers around the world.

As the population of Spanish-speakers grows, so too does their influence over life in the modern West. Hispanic arrivals work on ranches and farms, in small towns and cities; they are doctors and nurses, mechanics and cooks. And like Hispanic immigrants before them – including the 16th-century sons and daughters of Spain – they come to the West seeking opportunity, abandoning a life they know in favor of a life they dream.

Left, *Sangre de Cristo Mountains* by **Ernest Blumenschein depicts Hispanic culture. Right, Spanish inscription in New Mexico, *circa* 1709.**

What a deal: for a paltry $15 million, Thomas Jefferson picked up New Orleans and a vast piece of real estate to be named later. "You have made a noble bargain for yourselves," said Napoleon's foreign minister, Talleyrand, "and I suppose you will make the most of it."

It was, of course, the Louisiana Purchase of 1803, the Franco-American deal which with one stroke of the pen – or quill – doubled the size of the US. The map of the nation was redrawn to shift its western boundary from the mighty Mississippi to the redoubtable Rockies. Thrown wide open was the gate leading to largely uncharted territory.

The first surveyors whom President Jefferson sent through that gateway were Captains William Clark and Meriwether Lewis, along with 43 other hardy souls. They formed the Corps of Discovery – we know it as the famed Lewis and Clark Expedition. Up the Missouri River they went in May 1804. Not until November of the following year would they reach the Pacific Ocean, returning to St Louis in September 1806.

Lewis and Clark did not discover an uninterrupted water route to the Pacific (the so-called Northwest Passage), but their topographical sketches showed the government and its people at least one good way to reach that great western ocean. The two captains also achieved several other goals that Jefferson had set, including the collection of scientific data on plant and animal life and the establishment of friendly ties with many western Indians. Only one member of the expedition died – probably from a ruptured appendix – during the two years, four months and nine days in the backcountry.

Growing pains: The high-adventure, high-risk work of blazing trails in the vast trans-Mississippi West would continue throughout the first half of the 19th century and beyond, but perhaps no other expedition would go so smoothly or be as productive as the Corps of Discovery. During the work ahead, blunders and tragedy would often accompany the discoveries, but that was

inevitable. Call them a nation's growing pains. The work would attract a wide assortment of intriguing characters – explorers, mountain men, trappers, traders, prospectors, soldiers, scientists and solo adventurers. And even before the first official map of Lewis and Clark Country was published in 1814, one thing must have seemed certain to the trailblazers: there was more than enough work for everybody.

While Lewis and Clark were still far off in the wilds, Lieutenant Zebulon Montgomery

Pike completed an expedition to find the source of the Mississippi River (he failed), and before Lewis and Clark's triumphant return, he left on an even more ambitious expedition – to find the headwaters of the Red River. The real purpose of Pike's second expedition in 1806 may have been to spy on the Spanish in Santa Fe as part of a conspiracy to carve a personal empire out of the Spanish-controlled Southwest. Indeed, the Spanish arrested Pike near Santa Fe after he had "found" the Rio Grande instead of the Red River. In the summer of 1807, he was deposited back in US territory after being escorted through Chihuahua and Texas.

Left, Glacier Point, high above California's Yosemite Valley. **Right**, John Wesley Powell, one-armed explorer, with a Paiute guide.

Before his arrest, Pike had wandered in the southern Rockies and had seen the mountain that would come to be called Pikes Peak and symbolize the nation's westward migration. Pike called it "Grand Peak" and did not climb it; he mistakenly ascended a smaller, adjacent summit. Colorado's most famous mountain was finally climbed in 1820 by the naturalist Dr Edwin James and other members of Major Stephen Long's expedition.

Despite the impressive ground covered by Pike, and later by Long, and the geographical knowledge of Louisiana Territory that their respective expeditions provided, the two men actually served to inhibit settlement in the Southwest. Pike spoke of "sandy deserts"

to St Louis with the others. Colter trapped successfully with his partners along the Yellowstone River that winter and then hooked up the following year with free-wheeling Manuel Lisa, who had set up a fort at the mouth of the Bighorn River and formed the Missouri Fur Company. Colter, a 6-foot Virginian who never learned to read or write, set off from Lisa's Fort in the winter of 1807–08 on an amazing solo exploration. Most likely he was the first white man to explore the land that became Yellowstone National Park. He traversed the Absaroka Mountains and the Teton Range, taking in Jackson's Hole and Pierre's Hole. When he returned with tales of a land laden with

that reminded him of the Sahara and suggested that the inhospitable, unfarmable land was best left to Indians and wild animals. The myth of the "Great American Desert" was born, and Long reinforced that myth, saying that the southern plains were "almost wholly unfit for cultivation."

Hell on earth: The outlook toward the new Northwest was completely different. Men were inspired to go there, not to cultivate the land but to trap beaver and trade the valuable furs. A member of the Lewis and Clark Expedition, John Colter, actually turned around in August 1806 and went back up the Missouri with two trappers rather than return

gurgling mud, demonic fire pots and gushing geysers, he was told, "You've been in the wilderness too long, Colter." His discovery was given the derisive name "Colter's Hell."

Only a couple of years later, employees of John Jacob Astor's newly formed Pacific Fur Company found their own hell. In September 1810, Astor sent 33 men aboard the brig *Tonquin* to sail around Cape Horn to the Oregon coast, and soon afterward he had Wilson Price Hunt lead 63 men overland from St Louis to meet the sailing party at the mouth of the Columbia River. The *Tonquin* reached its destination on March 22, 1811, and Fort Astoria was built on the river's south bank. But in April, Salish Indians stormed onto the ship, killing all but one of the crewmen. The ship was blown to bits when the surviving crewman set fire to the powder magazine. Hunt's party had only slightly better success, losing 19 men before finally reaching Fort Astoria in 1812.

Hunt's overland expedition did prove that the coast could be reached by a route through the Rockies south of the one Lewis and Clark had taken. More significant was the route blazed by one of Astor's men, Robert Stuart, on a trip back to St Louis in 1813. Stuart's small party covered ground that the Oregon Trail would largely follow 30 years later. Their most important discovery was South Pass, at the southern end of the Wind River Range, which made crossing the Continental Divide much easier.

Not long after Stuart left the coast, Fort Astoria was surrendered to the British when Canadian-based North West Company employees broke the news about the War of 1812. American fur trading, though, would continue to flourish farther inland for 25 more years. Manuel Lisa died in 1820, but former partner Andrew Henry and William Henry Ashley formed a business (forerunner of the Rocky Mountain Fur Company) that reaped even greater profits in the beaver trade. Lisa had had the services of John Colter, the first mountain man, but Henry and Ashley, after advertising in newspapers for "enterprising young men," recruited a veritable Who's Who of mountain men – Jim Bridger, Jim Beckwourth, James Clyman, Hugh Glass, Thomas "Broken Hand" Fitzpatrick, Edward Rose and Jedediah Strong Smith, men who would be known for their feats of daring in the wilderness and their hell-raising at the annual fur traders' rendezvous, but they would also contribute heavily to western exploration.

Jedediah Smith (1799–1831), for example, achieved an extraordinary number of firsts in the West. Smith, who carried a Bible along with a butcher's knife and collected 668 beaver pelts in a single season, was the first white man to traverse the Rocky Mountains to California, the first to cross the Sierra Nevada from west to east, the first to cross the Great Salt Lake Desert and the first

Mountain man Jim Bridger (right) made this inscription (left) near La Barge, Wyoming.

to hike from southern California to the Pacific Northwest. Smith's far-reaching treks in the second half of the 1820s showed that the Rio Buenaventura, a mythical river flowing all the way to the Pacific, did not exist, but that Oregon and California were prime spots for settlement. Smith was one of only two people (the other being Canadian-born explorer Peter Skene Ogden) during the "mountain-man" era to glimpse the whole West north to south. The modest, ever-curious Smith was killed by Comanche Indians in 1831 while making his first trip on the Santa Fe Trail, which had been blazed a decade earlier by trader William Becknell.

Jim Bridger (1804–81), just 19 when he

joined Ashley's first expedition to the Rockies, may have been the first white man to see the Great Salt Lake. He would continue to roam the mountains as a trapper, trader, scout and Indian fighter until his arthritis and failing eyesight forced him to retire shortly after the Civil War. Emigrants knew "Old Gabe" Bridger well because of Fort Bridger, a trading post he built on the Oregon Trail in 1843. As late as the 1860s, he laid out the "Bridger Cut-off" to help prospectors reach Virginia City in the gold-rich Montana Territory, since the Sioux were a menace to travelers on the Bozeman Trail.

Another trapper-trader who became one of

the leading trailblazers was a tall, good-looking Tennessean named Joseph Reddeford Walker (1798–1876). Like Bridger, he had a long career on the western frontier. In 1826, Walker was part of an official US government survey party that was laying out the Santa Fe Trail. In 1833, as field lieutenant for Captain Benjamin Bonneville, Walker led an expedition from the Great Salt Lake, down the Humboldt River and across the formidable Sierras to California. He may have been the first white man to view the falls and sequoias, or "big trees," in what is now Yosemite National Park. On the way back he discovered what became known as Walker Pass, soon to be a popular gateway

rivers and through the Grand Canyon.

Kit Carson (1809–1868), the mountain man whose name is best known today, was another free spirit who helped Fremont find a few paths. The small but sturdy Carson ran off with a traders' caravan to Santa Fe at age 16. He left on his first trapping expedition from his Taos, New Mexico, base in 1829, and for two decades he hunted beaver and fought Indians all over the Rockies. Carson guided Fremont on an expedition in 1842 whose principal objectives were to make the first reliable map of the Oregon Trail and to encourage western expansion. Carson served as Fremont's guide twice more in the 1840s before becoming an Indian agent and an

through the southern Sierras. The first transcontinental railroad would follow his route along the Humboldt River 36 years later. In the 1840s, he twice served as guide for Lieutenant John C. ("The Pathfinder") Fremont. Two decades later, while prospecting for gold in Arizona, he struck pay dirt at a site that would become Prescott. Walker's dream was to explore the Green River through the mysterious high plateaus and canyons of Utah Territory. He never made the dream come true, but he did live to see one-armed Major John Wesley Powell accomplish that feat in May 1869, when Powell led the first expedition down the Green and Colorado

Indian fighter again (he led the roundup of both the Navajos and Apaches in the 1860s).

Artists and adventurers: Mountain men and US Army officers were not the only explorers during the first half of the 19th century. It could be argued that every person who stepped foot in the Rockies during that time blazed one trail or another. In a book about his colorful life as a mountain man, Jim Beckwourth – his father was a Virginia plantation overseer and his mother was a slave – wrote that "civilized man can accustom himself to any mode of life when pelf (treasure) is the governing principle – that power which dominates through all the ramifications of social life, and gives expression to the universal instinct of self-interest." There were men, however, who came to explore the West for reasons that had little to do with treasures or territorial control or, in some cases, even self-interest. These were the artists, scientists and adventurers.

Best known of the artist-explorers was George Catlin, who spent six years in the 1830s documenting Indian life and customs. In 1834, he accompanied Colonel Henry Leavenworth's reconnaissance mission in the Arkansas River valley and became the first white man to do portraits of Comanche, Kiowa and Wichita Indians. In 1833–34 a talented young Swiss artist named Karl

from 1833 to 1838, and then had one last grandiose expedition in 1843.

John J. Audubon arrived in the 1840s to paint western birds and other animals. Some of his drawings were based on skins collected by naturalist Thomas Nuttall, who gathered thousands of specimens while traveling to Oregon with another naturalist, John K. Townsend, on fur trader Nathaniel Wyeth's expedition in 1834. Nuttall, who used his rifle for digging up plants, not for shooting, could put up with every sort of hardship in the name of science. His name lives on with Nuttall's woodpecker. Another ardent collector was Frederick Paul Wilhelm, Duke of Wurttemberg. The duke ventured

Bodmer traveled up the Missouri with German explorer Prince Maximilian of Wied Neuwied to capture the Indian way of life. In 1837, Alfred Jacob Miller became the first artist to travel the Oregon Trail and also became the only white artist to picture firsthand the mountain men at the annual fur traders' rendezvous. Miller had been brought west by Sir William Drummond Stewart, a Scottish baronet who chased buffalo and other western dreams in grand, high style

Left, a wagon from the King Expedition of 1867 crosses Nevada's Carson Desert. Above, members of the party at Shoshone Canyon, Idaho.

into the western frontier on five expeditions, the first one coming in 1822 after he had read naturalist Edwin James's reports from the Major Long expedition.

Trailblazing continued with the railroad surveys of the 1850s, and the government surveys by John Wesley Powell and others. The era of the true trailblazer that had begun with Lewis and Clark was rapidly coming to an end. Still, the urge to explore and re-explore the West – whether as individuals in the mountain-man tradition or as part of large caravans in the Army-expedition tradition – would continue through the century and still be going strong into the next.

It was not an experience for the faint of heart. "To enjoy such a trip," said an overland pioneer, "a man must be able to endure heat like a salamander; mud and water like a muskrat, dust like a toad, and labor like a jackass." Still, more than one city-bred tenderfoot attempted the great trek. So did Ohio farmers, English mill workers, Danish peasants. The overland pioneers sought God and gold, salvation and rich topsoil, and if their respective visions of the Promised Land varied, they all seemed to know where that land could be found: in the American West.

The heyday of the overland routes to the West – the Oregon Trail, the California Trail, the Mormon Trail – was relatively brief, but these dust-ridden thoroughfares changed the face of the nation. In roughly 20 years, the United States went from a country still tied to its Atlantic roots to a transcontinental power that laid claim to the shores of the Pacific. The prairies and mountains in between had been transformed from terra incognita to a frontier still raw and rough but filled with infinite promise.

Hope and destiny: There had long been an urge to strike out for the West. As early as the 1780s, Benjamin Franklin had encouraged Americans to fill the continent. In 1803 Thomas Jefferson made that process possible by his Louisiana Purchase and by sending Lewis and Clark to survey the territory's grand dimensions. Beginning in the 1820s and accelerating in the 1830s, the Santa Fe Trail, running from the state of Missouri 900 miles (1,450 km) southwest to New Mexico, had opened up the Spanish southwest.

But it was in the 1840s that migration into the West truly gained momentum. News began filtering back of the rich lands of the Willamette Valley in the Oregon Country. This information fell on receptive ears, and a newspaper editor named John Lewis O'Sullivan coined the phrase that would echo across American history to this day: "Our manifest destiny is to overspread and to possess the whole of the continent."

The destiny was certainly fulfilled, but it wasn't easy. Much of the lands west of the Missouri River were unknown. The Great American Desert, a vast blankness on the map, was presumably filled with peril. Many trails had not been scouted. "Our ignorance of the route was complete," wrote an Ohio schoolteacher, John Bidwell, of his party's plans to reach the Pacific Ocean. "We knew that California lay west, and that was the extent of our knowledge." Nevertheless, good fortune smiled on Bidwell and his band, who

were the first party to arrive overland in California, in 1841.

For much of the 1840s, it was the rich lands of the Oregon Country that were the primary goal of American settlers, many of them farmers from the Mississippi Valley. In 1843 an estimated 875 men, women and children made the journey on the Oregon Trail; by 1845 that number had increased to perhaps 3,000. The usual route took travelers up the Missouri River by steamboat from St Louis to Independence. Here the hopeful travelers would outfit themselves for the nearly 2,000-mile (3,220 km), six-month journey west.

From Independence, the Oregon Trail ran

along the North Platte River ("too thick to drink, too thin to plow"), and then past landmarks that became famous across the nation: the mighty eroded spire of Chimney Rock, visible for days ahead, and Register Cliff, where the members of one wagon train after another marked its passage by scrawling their names into rock.

South Pass, in the shadow of Wyoming's Wind River Range, marked the halfway point of the journey; the trail then ran across the wilderness of present-day Idaho, crossed the Boise and Snake rivers, then plumbed the Columbia River Gorge.

For trail pioneers, the vehicle of choice was generally a simple midwestern farm

touch via the "roadside telegraph" (or the "Bone Express," as one called it): messages and even advertisements scrawled on rocks and bones at trail junctions.

The promised land: At the same time that farmers were moving toward Oregon Country, another smaller, more tightly organized group was also seeking refuge in the West. Joseph Smith's Church of Jesus Christ of Latter-day Saints had sought homes in Ohio, then Missouri, and then in Nauvoo, Illinois. But, mistrustful of the saints' polygamous ways, other Americans would not let them live in peace. Fearing the worst, Joseph Smith commanded his scouts to search the West and find a place where they could

wagon, usually pulled by two or three yoke of oxen, with other livestock – cows, sheep, goats – trailing behind. Loaded up with wheat flower, corn meal, hard tack, dried fruit to prevent scurvy, and driver and passengers, the wagons lumbered along, making perhaps 25 miles (40 km) on a good day, next to no miles on a bad one.

It was rarely a solitary journey. Overlanders needed to start late enough for spring grass to be available to feed their stock, but not so late that they risked early-winter snows. This relatively narrow window of opportunity meant that there were usually lots of wagons on the trail at the same time. Pioneers kept in

"get up in the mountains, where the devil cannot dig us out, and live in a healthy climate where we can live as old as we have a mind to."

Smith himself would not find that refuge, nor live as long as he had a mind to: a mob dragged him and his brother from a jail in Carthage, Illinois, in 1844 and shot them. It was left to his successor, Brigham Young, to lead the saints on their epic journey. Leaving Nauvoo in 1846, they traveled 1,400 miles (2,250 km), following the Oregon Trail as far as South Pass and then branching south to Fort Bridger and across the Wasatch Mountains. On July 27, 1847, they descended what is now called Emigration Canyon and glimpsed the Great Salt Lake. "This is the right place," said Brigham Young. And over the next decades, some 60,000 saints would follow the Mormon Trail.

Throughout the 1840s, the numbers of Americans heading west on the trails increased. And yet it was not until the end of that decade that the steady stream swelled to a deluge. In January of 1848, a man named John Marshall discovered gold on the banks of the South Fork American River in California, at a spot called Sutter's Mill. Within a few months a San Francisco newspaper would complain, "The whole country, from San Francisco to Los Angeles, and from the sea-

westward across the Humboldt Sink of Nevada, then climbed the eastern face of the Sierra Nevada before dropping west into the gentle, gold-rich California foothills.

In 1851 some 45,000 argonauts attempted this trail; the next year that number rose to 52,000. Unlike travelers on the Oregon Trail, who were mostly land-seeking farm families, California-bound pioneers were mainly single young men, hoping for gold strikes that would quickly return them rich to the East. Some of them did strike pay dirt. Others did not. "I have made up my mind that I have got enough of California and am coming home as fast as I can," wrote William Swain, failed argonaut, in 1851.

#357. "We have It Rich." - Washing and panning gold. Rockerville. Dak. Old: timers, Spriggs. Lamb and Dillon at work. Photo and copyright by Grabill, 1889.

shore to the base of the Sierra Nevada, resounds with the sordid cry of 'Gold! Gold! Gold!'" The rush of 1849 had started.

The fever soon spread east. By 1850, one westward-bound argonaut would write, "The road is closely lined with emigrants. We can count one hundred wagons ahead of us and behind us." Treasure-seekers from other countries and continents came as well.

The California Trail, which was the gold-seekers' preferred route, slid off from the Oregon Trail at South Pass to head south-

Left, pioneer family on the Nebraska plains. **Above**, panning for gold in the Dakota Territory.

Whether they came seeking farmland or the mother lode, overland travelers faced privations that ranged from irksome to dire. Wagon wheels dried and splintered; axles broke. Oxen ailed or were struck dead by rattlesnakes. Indians were perhaps the most feared hazard, and it was true that wagon trains were attacked and settlers killed, although also true that the death toll was probably far higher among Native Americans. But some Indians were friendly to the newcomers. One party struggling up the Sierra Nevada received guidance from a brave named Truckee; out of gratitude they named a river for him.

Far more dangerous than Indians were other hazards, natural and man-made. Stream crossings were invariably treacherous, drownings common. Trigger-happy travelers killed each other, or themselves, accidentally shooting off firearms. Disease was no stranger: some maladies, like cholera, were apparently brought west with the pioneers, other ailments, like mountain fever, seemed endemic to the new lands.

The Donner party: Perhaps most terrible of all were the threats posed by the elements. In 1846 Illinois farmers George and Jacob Donner led a party bound for California. At Fort Bridger, the group decided to break off from a larger band of emigrants and take a

short-cut, the Hastings Cut-off, toward the Great Salt Lake. It was a disastrous detour.

The Donners wandered, lost, in the Wasatch Mountains for a month, and did not reach the Great Salt Lake until autumn. They bickered their way across Nevada. By the time they began to climb the steep eastern slope of the Sierra Nevada Mountains, it was late October. And winter set in a month early.

The next few months witnessed one of the great tragedies of American history. Holed up in lean-tos as unusually severe winter storms roared around them, the Donner party froze, starved, and eventually attempted survival by cannibalizing their dead. By the

time rescue came, nearly half of the party had died – and the name Donner became synonymous with the perils of the promised land.

Terrible as their fate was, the Donners were not alone in hardship. Two bands of Mormon immigrants, pushing their possessions in handcarts, were caught in blizzards along the Sweetwater River in Wyoming; some 200 died. Nor was cold the only foe. In 1849, the William Manley and Jayhawker parties attempted a southerly short-cut to the California gold fields. They wandered across a waterless wasteland that cost life after life. At the end of the ordeal Manley cursed the land and gave it a name. "We took off our hats, and then overlooking the scene of so much travail, suffering and death spoke the thought uppermost in our minds, saying, 'Good-bye, Death Valley.'"

Yet it is important not to overstate the dangers of the trail. The truth is that the majority of overlanders who attempted the trip made it safely. Some historians even doubt that death rates among overlanders were higher than their friends and families who stayed back east. By the 1860s, the great overland migrations were slowing. The trails were soon made partly obsolete by the transcontinental railway in 1869. Yet as late as the 1880s some settlers still attempted the overland route across the plains and mountains. The epitaph for the entire period of western expansion was written in 1893 by Frederick Jackson Turner, who noted that all the blank spaces on the map had been filled and that the frontier had passed into posterity.

The days of the trails live on, though, in the Oregonians and Californians and Utahans who trace their roots back to ancestors who made the overland journey. It's possible even now, in places like Black Rock Springs in Nevada or Coffee Creek in Wyoming, to stand in the stillness, trace wagon ruts across the prairie, and imagine wagon wheels creaking along and the call of "Gee" and "Haw" imploring balky horses to move on – the sounds of America heading West.

A map of America's Westward Expansion can be found on page 78–79.

A map of America's Westward Expansion can be found on page 78–79.

Left, painting depicting the Donner party, who were trapped in the mountains and attempted to survive by cannibalism. **Right**, Frederic Remington's *The Old Stagecoach of the Plains*.

Geronimo Head War Chief Chiricahua Apaches now raiding.

The confrontation of Indians and whites in the American West was as much a conflict of cultures as of guns and arrows. For the Indians, the land was an ancient and sacred home, source of their livelihood and center of their spiritual life. "The earth and myself are of one mind," said Chief Joseph of the Nez Perce. "The measure of the land and the measure of our bodies are the same."

But to the pioneers who crossed the Great Plains, the land was something to be exploited, a commodity to be bought and sold, and they felt justified in pushing aside Indians in order to possess it. The Indian "requires a greater extent of territory... than is compatible with the progress and just claims of civilized life... and must yield to it," President James Monroe proclaimed in 1817.

When Europeans touched on North American shores in the late 15th century, there were perhaps 2 million Indians in what is now the continental United States. By 1900, only 250,000 were left.

Disease was the biggest killer. Old-world illnesses like smallpox and measles swept through the population like wildfire, wiping out entire villages in only a few months. Sometimes the victims had never even seen a white person. Those who survived faced the hardships of conquest – hunger, dispossession, warfare.

In the end, Indian tribes were left with a single, terrible dilemma – either give up the land they loved or risk extermination. For many, confrontation was the only option. "I mean to keep this land," said Chief Red Cloud of the Lakota Sioux. "The Great Father sent his soldiers out here to spill blood... If they disturb me, there will be no peace."

By the time the first wagon trains set out on the Oregon Trail, conflicts between western tribes and whites were already starting to erupt. As early as 1835, Comanche and Kiowa raiders were harassing travelers on the Staked Plains of Texas. In Oregon country, the Cayuse War of 1847 triggered hostilities that lasted more than 10 years. And in California,

public funds were disbursed to freelance Indian hunters who, as one official put it, were serving "the great cause of civilization, which, in the natural course of things, must exterminate Indians."

As always, violence was preceded by years of bad blood. Whites invaded hunting grounds, peddled liquor, harassed and kidnapped Indian women and children. Indians raided homesteads, stole livestock and attacked travelers. By the time soldiers were called out, both sides were so poisoned by

resentment that almost nothing could hold back the bloodshed. All too often it was the ambitious soldier, hotheaded warrior or unscrupulous trader who drew first blood, and the innocents who suffered the consequences.

First blood: Among the first tribes to feel the brunt of the new American presence were the Apaches, particularly the Chiricahua band of Apaches who made their home around the mountains of the same name in southeastern Arizona. Unlike nearby Pueblo Indians, the Apaches had remained largely unfettered by the Spanish. They were a wild and free-roaming people, predominantly hunters and gatherers, who had honed their considerable

Left, Geronimo and his small band of followers were the last Apaches to surrender to the Army. **Right**, Cheyenne girl at home.

fighting skills against the Spanish for some 200 years and against the Pueblo Indians for centuries before that.

Relations between Apaches and whites had never been very good. The age-old practice of kidnapping and enslaving Apache children had survived well into the era of American rule, as did the Apaches' taste for revenge. Despite a few friendly overtures between Apaches and Americans, neither side trusted the other. Violence broke out in 1861 when an American military officer wrongly accused a Chiricahua leader, Cochise, of kidnapping a rancher's son. The bungled arrest led to bloodshed on both sides, setting off a terrible cycle of revenge.

flected, "that they carry their lives on their fingernails?" Growing old and weary of fighting, Cochise requested a reservation in the Chiricahua Mountains. After much negotiation, the request was finally granted. Cochise died there in 1874.

But two years later, the Chiricahuas were again forced to leave their homeland. The government wanted them to go to the San Carlos reservation where other western Apaches were confined. A few Chiricahuas complied for the sake of peace. Others, like Victorio, Nana and Geronimo, fled to the mountains and for the next 10 years fought an intermittent war of resistance. One by one, they surrendered or were killed.

For the next 10 years, Cochise and his Mimbreno Apache ally, Mangas Colorado, plagued the frontier with deadly hit-and-run tactics. In response, the Americans launched an all-out war of extermination, encouraging soldiers and citizens to kill Apaches however they saw fit. In some parts of Arizona, a fresh Apache scalp fetched a $250 reward.

The madness came to a head in 1871 with the massacre of 85 Apaches by a mob of Tucson vigilantes. The victims were neither Chiricahuas nor Mimbrenos but Aravapais – a peaceful band of Apaches that had settled near a military fort for protection. "Why is it that the Apaches wait to die," Cochise re-

Geronimo was the last. By the time he surrendered in 1886, the entire country knew his name, and many people, including the president, wanted him hanged. Instead, he and the Chiricahuas were shipped to Fort Marion in Florida as prisoners of war. In 1894 the surviving Chiricahuas were allowed to go to Fort Sill in Indian Territory, now Oklahoma. Geronimo died there in 1909, still a prisoner of war.

The Long Walk: While Cochise was terrorizing the border country, a second Southwestern tribe, the Navajo, was also being pursued by the US Army.

The Navajos and Apaches are both of

Athabascan stock, their common ancestors having migrated into the Southwest about 600 years earlier. Culturally, however, the two groups were miles apart. The Navajos – or, as they call themselves, the Dine (the People) – had long since followed a different path, borrowing from the Pueblo Indians and the Spanish. They took up sheepherding and various elements of Pueblo religion, creating a life that was distinctly their own.

Like their Apache cousins, the Navajos had a fierce reputation. They were like "wolves that run through the mountains," an American general said, and in his estimation they needed to be removed by force. (It hadn't escaped the general's attention that

to starve them out. Under Carson's orders, the Navajos' sheep and horses were seized or killed; crops were burned; hogans destroyed; even the beloved peach orchards of Canyon de Chelly were cut down.

The Navajos were slowly starved into surrendering. By 1865, more than 8,000 had been sent on the "Long Walk" – 300 miles (500 km) to Bosque Redondo. Some 400 died on the trail. There the Navajos suffered more hardships: scarce supplies, undrinkable water, poor soil, disease, crop failure. Finally, in 1868, after thousands of Navajos had died under extreme circumstances, and conditions at the Bosque were publicly condemned, the Navajos were free to go home.

the Navajos were likely to be sitting on a fortune in mineral wealth.)

In 1863, the US Army commissioned Christopher "Kit" Carson to round up the Navajos and ship them to a camp in eastern New Mexico at a place called Bosque Redondo. Carson was a former mountain man, trader and Indian fighter. He knew the Navajos, their willingness to fight and the sheer impossibility of defeating them on their own rugged terrain. He chose, instead,

Left, Charles Schreyvogel's *A Sharp Encounter*. **Above**, *Custer's Last Stand*, Edgar S. Paxson's improbable depiction of Custer's final moments.

Prairie fire: The crimson flower of war was blooming on the Great Plains, too. Gold strikes in Colorado, California, Montana and Dakota Territory sent white people sweeping across the plains like a prairie fire, engulfing the Plains tribes and igniting their passion for war. "When the white man comes into my country he leaves a trail of blood behind him," Chief Red Cloud told a council of military men. For the major tribes of the Great Plains – the Sioux, Cheyenne, Crow, Blackfoot, Arapaho, Comanche and Kiowa – these trails were many, tangled and very bloody indeed.

The Plains Indians hold a special place in

the American imagination. The mounted Plains warrior – eagle feathers streaming from his hair, bow and arrow in his hand – has become a Wild West icon, the quintessential American Indian. And yet, ironically, the horse-and-buffalo culture that blossomed on the Great Plains in the 19th century was impossible before European contact. Until the Spanish brought their herds to the New World, wild horses hadn't roamed American soil since the Ice Age. By the time Indian-white hostilities broke out in the mid-1800s, most Plains tribes had been mounted for only 80 or 90 years. In only three or four generations, Plains Indians had created an individual culture of raw and vital beauty.

By the late 1850s, white encroachment had already triggered a number of bloody engagements on the Great Plains, and several tribes, including the Santee Sioux of Minnesota – easternmost branch of the great Sioux tribe – had made enormous land cessions to the federal government. The Santees felt swindled by their treaty, and after 10 miserable years of reservation life they had nothing to show but hunger, hopelessness and an explosive hatred of whites. In 1862, under the leadership of Chief Little Crow, they rampaged across the countryside, killing 800 settlers and soldiers before the army drove them back. More than 35 Santees were

hanged and 250 imprisoned. Little Crow escaped, only to be shot by a white settler a few months later.

Two years after the Santee uprising, violence broke out again, this time in the Colorado hunting range of the Southern Cheyenne and Arapaho tribes. Gold had been discovered in the Rocky Mountains and, with thousands of whites flooding the area, authorities were pressured to open Indian land to settlement. In 1864, a campaign was launched to harass the Cheyennes and Arapahos into submission. Villages were burned to the ground, skirmishes were fought, Indian raids were answered with cavalry and cannons, but with little success.

Itching for a decisive victory and dead-set on killing Indians, an American commander, Colonel John Chivington, unleashed his men on a peaceful group of Cheyennes camped at Sand Creek near Fort Lyon in southern Colorado. The camp was led by Chief Black Kettle, a long-time advocate of peace who had brought his people to the fort in order to protect them from hostilities.

When Chivington's soldiers appeared around the camp, Black Kettle flew an American flag and a white flag over his tepee, confident that the bluecoats wouldn't attack their steadfast friend. But Chivington's orders had been brutally clear: "Kill and scalp all, big and little." His "boys" were instructed to take no prisoners, not even women and children. The reason, in Chivington's own words: "Nits make lice."

By all accounts, the Sand Creek Massacre was an orgy of murder and mutilation. Of perhaps 270 Indians killed, 200 were women and children. Even Kit Carson, the man who sent the Navajos on their Long Walk, described Chivington's men as "cowards and dogs." Nevertheless, "the boys" received a hero's welcome in Denver, displaying fresh scalps like badges of honor. Terse as ever, Chivington's official report commended their behavior: "All did nobly."

Miraculously, Black Kettle survived. But still he did not make war against the whites. Hoping to spare his people further suffering, he led them into Indian Territory, thinking they would be safe. But four years later, the nightmare happened again. This time the bluecoats were led by a rash young officer, Lt. Col. George Armstrong Custer. It made no difference to Custer that Black Kettle had personally sued for peace or that he had never led a raid against white settlers. Custer ordered his men to charge at dawn. They rode into the sleeping camp with the strains of *Garry Owen*, Custer's favorite battle theme, blaring in the background. The Indians responded as best they could, killing 20 soldiers and wounding many others, but they were badly outnumbered. The Battle of Washita, as it came to be known, claimed more than 100 Cheyenne lives. This time, Black Kettle did not survive.

Red Cloud's War: While the Southern Cheyennes were fast losing ground on the Southern Plains, the Sioux and Northern Cheyennes, led by Red Cloud, Sitting Bull

William J. Fetterman, who only weeks earlier had boasted that with 80 men he could ride through the entire Sioux nation.

After two years of hard fighting, the Americans withdrew. In 1868, Red Cloud signed a treaty supposedly guaranteeing the Powder River country, including the sacred Black Hills, to the Indians. Red Cloud promised never to lift his hand against whites again, and kept his word until the day he died. He was the only Indian leader in the West to have won a war against the US Army.

The treaty lasted eight years. Almost from the day it was signed, rumors of gold in the Black Hills proved too enticing for prospectors to ignore. In 1874, the Army dispatched

and Dull Knife, were driving soldiers out of the rich Powder River country of Montana and Dakota territories. At stake in the fighting was one of the white people's roads, the Bozeman Trail, which cut a path across the Indians' best hunting ground toward the gold fields of Montana. The confrontation came to a climax in December 1866, when warriors led by a daring young Sioux named Crazy Horse wiped out 81 soldiers. The troopers were commanded by Captain

Left, Custer led the Seventh Cavalry to certain death at the Battle of Little Bighorn. Above, Chief Big Foot lies dead at Wounded Knee, 1891.

its own gold-hunting expedition under the command of Lt. Col. Custer. It was to be Custer's last major transgression.

The Army's brazen disregard for the treaty brought war back to the Great Plains, and under the leadership of Sitting Bull, Gall and Crazy Horse, the Sioux, Cheyennes and Arapahos frustrated the soldiers again and again. A major campaign was launched against the Indians, with Custer commanding the Seventh Cavalry. On June 25, 1876, he located a large Indian camp on the Little Bighorn River in present-day Montana and ordered an immediate attack. Custer rode into the valley and never returned. In the legendary engagement remembered as "Custer's Last Stand," the impetuous young officer and his elite corps of Indian-fighters were wiped out to a man.

But the engagements that followed were bitter defeats for the Indians. In the hard winter of 1877, the flush of victory at the Battle of Little Bighorn was worn away by constant harassment, heavy losses, chronic hunger and biting cold. By the following spring, even the young mystic, Crazy Horse, was ready to surrender. He was stabbed to death soon after during a fight with military guards. Seeing the hopelessness of life in the United States, Sitting Bull escaped to Canada.

Ghost Dance: Elsewhere in the West, other

tribes were approaching a climax to years of struggle. On the plains of Texas and Oklahoma, the Kiowas, led by chiefs Satank and Satanta, and the Kwahadi Comanches, led by Quanah Parker, were meeting bitter defeat in their efforts to save the southern buffalo range. In 1872, Captain Jack and the Modocs made a last desperate attempt to save themselves in the rugged lava beds of northern California. In the Northwest, Nez Perce Chief Joseph led his people on a four-month flight through Idaho and Montana territories only to be captured a mere 30 miles (50 km) from freedom in Canada.

Sitting Bull, meanwhile, was having little success convincing the Canadian government to grant him a reservation. When a commission was sent to coax him back to the United States, he responded defiantly. "What have we done that you should want us to stop?… I have ears. I have eyes to see with. If you think me a fool, you are a bigger fool than I am." But not even Sitting Bull could stem the tide of history, and in 1881 he relented. "My followers are weary of cold and hunger… therefore I bow my head."

The final blow in the wars for the West came in 1890 as the last of the Sioux "hostiles" were being confined to reservations. Demoralized and desperate, many Sioux sought refuge in a new religious movement known as the Ghost Dance, which promised the dawning of a new age when the buffalo would return to the prairie and whites would be swept away.

Reservation officials were frightened by the ecstatic dancing and, fearing a new uprising, ordered the capture of all off-reservation bands. An order went out to arrest Sitting Bull, too, and a contingent of Indian policemen was sent to do the job. As the officers led Sitting Bull away, a group of his followers surrounded them. A policeman was shot, a fight broke out, and Sitting Bull was killed.

Another of the so-called "hostiles" was Chief Big Foot, whose ragged band of Miniconjou Sioux were intercepted by the army and ordered to make camp near Wounded Knee Creek on the Pine Ridge reservation. The soldiers set up their own camp around the Indians, positioning artillery on an overlooking bluff. The following morning, a small group of soldiers entered the camp and began rifling through tepees looking for weapons. What happened next is not entirely clear, but somewhere, somehow, a shot was fired into the line of soldiers guarding the Sioux men. And thus began a frenzy of killing. The artillery cut down everything that moved. Soldiers swept into the camp and murdered the survivors, chasing them into ravines and gullies.

By the end of the day, nearly 300 Indians and 25 soldiers lay dead. It was the last tragic episode of a courageous but desperate struggle. The Indian wars were over.

<u>Left</u>, Chief Red Cloud was the only Indian leader to win a war against the Army. <u>Right</u>, Sitting Bull in a publicity photo with Buffalo Bill, *circa* 1885.

WHEN CATTLE WAS KING

I woke up one morning on the Old Chisholm
  Trail,
Rope in my hand and a cow by the tail,
Feet in the stirrups and seat in the saddle,
I hung and rattled with them Longhorn cattle.

South of Abilene, as cowboys sat around a campfire, that song could be heard above the bellows of longhorns settling in for the night. Life on the cattle trail was hard and dangerous; sometimes only a song made it easier.

It was also a life that changed the face of the West. The rise of the cattle kingdom was one of the fastest transformations of a land in the history of the world. In 1860 the plains from Texas to the Dakotas were thought to be mostly worthless, "the Great American Desert." By 1870 they were a profitable empire where ranchers were kings and beef on the hoof was money in the bank.

The era of the great cattle drives and ranches began in Texas after the Civil War, when Confederate veterans returned to a homeland utterly impoverished. About the only creatures thriving were Texas longhorn cattle – hybrids of Spanish criollo cattle and English longhorns. Long-legged, long-tailed, long-bodied, fertile and full of fight, the Texas longhorn roamed the Lone Star State some 5 million strong.

Were they good for anything? Possibly, a few ranchers figured. They noticed that a steer that brought $3 or $4 in Texas might bring $40 in Chicago and $80 in New York. But how could they get that Lone Star beef onto eastern tables?

From ranch to rail: An entrepreneur named Joseph McCoy came up with an answer: move the cattle north from Texas to Kansas to meet the advancing railroad, which could then ship them east. In 1867, McCoy got Texans to drive some 35,000 cattle on the Chisholm Trail from San Antonio to Abilene, Kansas. The town of Abilene was barely civilized: "A small dead place consisting of about one dozen log huts," as McCoy described it. But he had vision and faith: he bought land for a stockyard and built the

Drovers Cottage, the finest hotel on the plains, to house the cattle aristocracy he was sure his enterprise would nurture.

The first drives were not profitable, but that would change. Over the next 20 years, some 2 million cattle would shuffle and sometimes stampede along the Chisholm Trail. Millions more would do the same along the Western Trail, which ran to Dodge City, Kansas, and the Goodnight Loving Trail, which went to Fort Sumner, New Mexico, and then north to Colorado.

Beef on the hoof: There were, however, continuing obstacles to this migration of beef on the hoof. First, many northern farmers were anything but happy to see Texas cattle arrive in their vicinity. Longhorns carried a tick that caused Texas fever, an ailment to which they seemed immune but which often proved fatal to other breeds. Texans were often met with quarantines (and sometimes violence) when they tried to bring their herds into settled farm country.

As a result, as the line of settlement moved west, the cattle trails had to keep one step ahead. For that reason, Abilene's reign as queen of the cattle trails lasted only a couple of years. It was succeeded by Ellsworth, Kansas, and then by Dodge City.

The Texas longhorn also had some major failings as a consumer product. "Eight pounds of hamburger on eight hundred pounds of bone and horn," one critic carped. Longhorns produced beef that was stringy and tough – a far cry from the marbled, tender steaks for which Easterners paid top dollar. By the late 1870s, longhorns had mainly been abandoned for "American" cattle like Herefords and Shorthorn bulls.

By that time, cattle ranchers had fully mastered their yearly routine. The season began in spring, when cowboys would fan across the ranches' open range, rounding up cattle until a herd of thousands was assembled. They would then ride through the herd, separating out cattle, marking young calves: it was here that a genuine western folk art – the cattle brand – developed.

And then the cattle drive would begin. Most ranchers did not participate. Instead they depended on drovers – contractors hired to move cattle between ranch and railhead. The drovers in turn depended on the trail boss, the key man of the drive. The boss would ride out in front of the herd (along with the cook and chuck wagon). Directly at the herd's head would ride two point riders, whose job it was to lead the cattle, often with the help of a lead steer. Riding on either side of the cattle were two swing riders and behind them two flank riders; eating dust at the very end were three drag riders. Off to one side would be the *remuda*, the herd of horses – about five per cowboy – supplied for the drive and overseen by the horse wrangler. In general, the trail boss would try to keep cattle moving 20 to 25 miles a day at the start of the

drive so as to break them and make them tired enough to lie down at night. Then he would slow them down to 10 or 15 miles a day for the duration of the drive.

Trail and town: A cattle drive could last two or three months, and these could be hard months indeed. Famed cattleman Charles Goodnight recalled a drive along the trail that bore his name. "In my first drive across the 96-mile desert, I lost 300 head of cattle. We were three days and nights in crossing and during that time we had no sleep or rest, as we had to keep the cattle moving constantly in order to get them to water before they died of thirst. I rode the same horse for three days and nights and what sleep I got was on his back."

Hazards were numerous. Drovers would pay a toll – generally 10¢ to a dollar per head of cattle – to pass through Indian territory, but Indian attacks occurred nonetheless. Another great danger was crossing rivers swollen by spring rains; still another was sun so fierce the cattle could go blind. Spooked by lightning, or a simple broken twig, the cattle could stampede: a terrifying and uncontrollable menace. All in all, it was an arduous journey. Andy Adams, in *Log of a Cowboy,* wrote of "outfits that had eagerly started north, only to reach their destination months later with half of their cattle gone, some of their men lying in shallow graves along the trail or lost in the water of angry rushing rivers."

No wonder the cowboy was ready to blow off some steam when he finally reached Abilene or Ellsworth or Dodge. As one cowboy said, "It was our intention and ambition to paint the town a deep red color and drink up all the bad whiskey in the city." First stop would be a barber for a shave, haircut and bath, then it was on to some local emporium to buy new clothing. Next stop might be for a dinner that wasn't biscuits and sowbelly (the usual trail fare), after which the cowboy might head to a tavern like Abilene's finest, the Alamo, a gilded delight whose walls were decorated with paintings of Renaissance nudes. And for some there were visits with the local "soiled doves" – women like Squirrel Tooth Alice or Big Nose Kate Elder – for other kinds of pleasure.

The cattle towns, too, quickly acquired the reputation of being among the most dangerous places in the US. In its first year in the cattle trade, Dodge City experienced the violent deaths of nine men. In Ellsworth, Kansas, a feud between town lawmen and Texas cowboys ended with dead cowboys, dead sheriffs, and Texans threatening to burn the whole town down. The towns' violent ways were spectacular enough to earn their local lawmen – like Abilene's Sheriff Wild Bill Hickok and Dodge City's Wyatt Earp – international fame. Yet the towns were in a bind. The more proper citizenry wanted to clamp down on the cowboy shenanigans. But if authorities clamped down too hard, the cowboys might take their business elsewhere, depriving the town of its livelihood.

The end of empire: By the 1880s, the cattle kingdom had spread north from Texas and Kansas into the northern plains, as ranchers expanded onto newly opened public land in the Dakotas, Wyoming and Montana. The ranchers' enthusiasm for expansion was understandable: given the apparently insatiable American appetite for beef, cattle ranching could be an extremely profitable business. European and eastern investors began to pour considerable sums of money into the business, and the holdings of many cattle kings grew enormously. John Iliff ran more than 50,000 head of cattle on land along the South Platte River in Colorado. Alexander Hamilton Swan's company owned thousands

The Johnson County War signaled that the days of the cattle kingdom were drawing to a close. Already it had seen considerable change. The arrival of barbed wire – the "devil's hatband," some called it – initially threatened the great ranches, which were accustomed to letting their cattle graze on open range. But they learned to make use of it, fencing out competitors, stringing it across public land and even across public roads. But the cattle kings could not hold out against larger economic forces. Farmers were pushing west across the plains; where they moved in, ranching was often edged out. As one Kansas farmer said, "The cowmen look upon us the same as the Indians do the white man,

of acres stretching from Ogalala, Nebraska, to Fort Steele, Wyoming. And in south Texas, Richard King began a ranch that would eventually encompass 1.27 million acres.

With such wealth came power – sometimes displayed in the territorial legislatures, sometimes in vigilante hangings. The most famous battle was the Johnson County War of 1892, in which a Wyoming county was rocked with violence between large ranchers and the homesteaders they accused of rustling.

Left, dinner at the Box T Ranch, Texas, *circa* 1890. **Above**, cowboys knew how to spend their earnings quickly.

driving them off their hunting grounds."

And then came the winter of 1886–87. Across the cattle kingdom, animals died by the thousand, frozen to death, starved to death, their carcasses piled up against the barbed wire. A grim Granville Stuart looked at his ranch and said, "I wanted no more of it. I never wanted to own again an animal that I could not feed and shelter." There were some ranchers who were able to hang on – but many of these later descended into bankruptcy during the financial panics of the early 1890s. Granville Stuart's words became an epitaph not just for his own career but for an entire way of life across the West.

Promontory Summit in Utah doesn't look like the kind of place where history was made. It's a barren rise just north of the Great Salt Lake. But here a great crowd of workmen and dignitaries assembled on May 10, 1869, to celebrate the completion of the transcontinental railway.

The final rails were in place. One iron spike remained to be hammered. The job fell to Leland Stanford, once a grocer, now partner in the Central Pacific Railroad.

Stanford swung – and missed. But a telegraph operator sent out a triumphant message anyway. *"Dot. dot. dot. Done."* A Central Pacific locomotive crept forward from the west, a Union Pacific engine from the east. Their cowcatchers kissed. Recently sundered by the Civil War, the United States was now united by rail.

It was a long-awaited consummation. As early as the 1830s, visionaries proposed linking Pacific and Atlantic coasts by rail. The advantages were obvious. To travel by wagon from St Louis to California required six months. The sea route from New York to San Francisco took a month, including a trek across the fever-infested Isthmus of Panama; the longer sea route around Cape Horn took a storm-tossed six months. Once gold was discovered in California, the pull of the Pacific was all the greater. The editor Horace Greeley exclaimed, "Men and brethren! Let us resolve to have a railroad to the Pacific – to have it soon."

But obstacles loomed even larger than visionary enthusiasm. There was the matter of the 1,600 miles (2,570 km) of plains and prairie, mountains and desert between the Missouri River and the Pacific – a vast swath of continent only partly surveyed. Steam locomotives required water for boilers, wood for fireboxes and relatively gentle grades to ascend and descend. Where in the wilderness would these essentials be found? As the nation edged toward civil war, the debate became embroiled in sectional arguments. Northerners proposed northerly routes. The powerful Secretary of War, southerner

Jefferson Davis, demanded a Texas-to-Pacific route that would firmly link California's fortunes to the South.

Slow starters: Searching for a scientific answer to these arguments, the federal government commissioned railroad survey expeditions to plot possible passages. The route chosen roughly followed the Emigrant Trail over which many wagon trains had already rolled. Starting at Omaha, it moved west through the Platte River Valley, crossed South Pass in what is now Wyoming, traversed the

ROCK CUT, NEAR ASPEN.

Wasatch Mountains, and then skirted the Great Salt Lake. After braving the Nevada deserts, it ascended the Sierra Nevada just north of ill-fated Donner Pass, and then dropped down into the California gold fields and the Sacramento Valley.

Construction began in 1862, with the Central Pacific Railroad building east from Sacramento, the Union Pacific working west from Omaha. But the job went slowly indeed. By now the nation was at war. Financiers preferred to invest in munitions rather than squander money on such a high-risk enterprise. Contractors had to compete with the Union Army for manpower and blasting

Left, the first train to reach the Grand Canyon, 1901. **Right**, cuts were blasted into the mountains.

powder. By 1863, the Central Pacific had completed a grand total of 20 miles (32 km) of track. The Union Pacific did not yet extend beyond the Omaha city limits.

At war's end, work sped up considerably. Even then crews were faced with the most daunting obstacles. Central Pacific crews may have had the harder time of it. Most supplies – ties and track and locomotives – had to come to them via the Isthmus of Panama or Cape Horn. And they had to grapple with one of the most formidable topographical obstacles in North America: the steep, blizzard-ridden Sierra Nevada. In the terrible winter of 1866, crews worked among snowdrifts 60 feet (18.3 meters) deep,

tacks by Cheyenne and Sioux Indians. Still, it was here that railroad-building reached a pinnacle of efficiency. Roustabouts would grade road cuts as much as 300 miles (480 km) in front of the advancing tracks. Twenty miles ahead, workers would erect trestles. And then, a little in front of the work train weighed down with materials and men, tracks would be laid with astonishing speed. "Four rails go down to the minute!" a journalist reported. "It is a grand Anvil Chorus playing across the plains."

The faster this chorus was played, the more money and land the railroads earned. The government rewarded the railroads with 20-square-mile (52 sq km) parcels laid out in

and hunkered down as avalanches roared down the slopes. They blasted grades and tunnels out of solid granite: hard-driving construction chief James Strobridge lost an eye when blasting a cut through the mountains. Soon the Central Pacific began losing workers to the easier life in the California gold fields. In desperation the company looked across the Pacific for workers, importing boatloads of Chinese laborers.

As for the Union Pacific, the prairie it traveled was gentler than the Sierra Nevada. But workers faced their own sets of worries: torrential thunderstorms, flash floods, prairie fires, buffalo stampedes, occasional at-

a checkerboard pattern along the route – one of the most fantastic giveaways in the history of the nation. Eager to grab as much land as possible, the Central and Union Pacific actually worked past each other, their survey parties overlapping for 200 miles (320 km) before the federal government ordered them to link up at Promontory Summit.

Joined by steel: The joining of the Central and Union Pacific was only the beginning of the West's age of rail. Still to come were the Great Northern and Northern Pacific from the Great Lakes to Puget Sound, the Southern Pacific from New Orleans to California, the Atchison, Topeka and Santa Fe from

Chicago southwest to Los Angeles. In 1852 there were 5 miles (8 km) of track west of the Mississippi. By 1890 there would be 72,000.

It is impossible to overstate the impact the railroads had on the West and on the nation. On the negative side, they contributed mightily to the Gilded Age's corrupt politics: the Central Pacific's Collis Huntington spent an estimated $200,000 to $500,000 buying votes during every session of Congress. But without the trains the West would not have been settled. New cities sprang up along railroad right-of-ways; existing settlements prayed for the day when the tracks would reach them. When Pueblo, Colorado, learned that the Atchison, Topeka, and Santa Fe would

Nor can tourists be forgotten. Almost as soon as the tracks were laid, wealthy Easterners clamored to experience the wonders of the West by train. These journeys mixed hardship and luxury. Travelers could recline in paneled Pullman parlor cars and dine on food that was the equal of that served by the best restaurants of Chicago or New York. On the other hand, there was always the slim chance that they might lose some valuables to a train robber. They would almost certainly find themselves choking on the clouds of dust that rolled through the first-class cars. Such conditions undermined attempts at fashionable dressing. One traveler advised women passengers to bring "an entire change of

soon steam into town, the local newspaper crowed, "The biggest drunk of the present century will occur here on the 7th of March." The railroads made industries: without railheads at Abilene or Dodge City to ship cattle east, there would have been no Texas cattle drives. And, anxious to profit from their holdings of western lands, the railroads became the West's biggest boosters, advertising to immigrants all over the world. And the immigrants came – by train, of course.

Left, rail men on the Montana frontier. **Above**, celebrating the completion of the transcontinental railroad at Promontory Summit, Utah, in 1869.

linen in a hand valise to be carried in the sleeping coach. Dresses should be of gray or brown worsted – never black. A linen duster of ample size is essential."

Today, western railroads have been substantially replaced by airlines and the interstate highway system. But it's not so hard to return to the glory days of the western train. Just ride the Durango & Silverton Narrow Gauge out of Durango, Colorado, or the Yosemite Mountain-Sugar Pine in California. You'll see the steam plume rising, hear that lonesome whistle blow, and know that in the West the Iron Horse will never entirely be put out to pasture.

Cole
Younger

Bob
Younger
(rear)

Jesse
James

Frank
James

The James Boys and the Younger Brothers

On an August day in 1895, a lawman in El Paso, Texas, named John Selman walked into a saloon and shot the notorious gunman John Wesley Hardin in the back of the head. At his trial, Selman said it was a fair fight – Hardin could have seen him coming if he had only looked in the mirror above the bar.

Heroes and villains: This is pretty much how things went in the Wild West. There were plenty of heroes and villains. But the line between gunmen who used weapons to break the law and gunfighters who resorted to them to uphold the law was often thinner than a hair-trigger.

Selman himself, before becoming a popular El Paso lawman, probably gunned down more than a dozen men before putting on the badge of a constable and swearing, presumably, to uphold law and order.

Two decades earlier, Kansas was home to William "Buffalo Bill" Brooks (not to be confused with the more famous "Buffalo Bill," William Cody). With or without a badge on his chest, Brooks was a bully. He kept the peace, to a degree, as a lawman in Newton and then Dodge City before he was caught stealing horses, for which he was hanged in 1874. Also in Kansas was one Henry Brown, who became an assistant marshal in Caldwell in 1882 even though he had killed in cold blood alongside the notorious Billy the Kid four years earlier. Brown was soon promoted to marshal, and with the help of Deputy Ben Wheeler he "cleaned up" the tough cattle town.

In 1884, however, Brown and Wheeler were far less successful when they tried to rob the bank in Medicine Lodge. The two lawmen, along with a pair of associates, killed two bank employees and fled empty-handed. All four gang members were swiftly captured and put in jail, which was not always a safe place to be. That night, a mob broke into the jailhouse with a necktie party in mind. Three of the four prisoners were indeed strung up, while lawman-outlaw Brown was shot down trying to make a run for it.

Left, legendary outlaw Jesse James – and to a lesser extent his brother Frank – became heroes because of dime-novel writers.

No one person symbolizes the western gunfighter's dichotomous nature more than soft-spoken, well-mannered Henry Plummer, who operated in Montana in 1863. The miners in the booming gold town of Bannack elected him sheriff in May, and he proved to be an efficient lawman. The charismatic Plummer patrolled the streets diligently and saw to it that a jail house was built. But on January 10, 1864, the Montana Vigilantes hanged him. He had, it was thought, directed a secret band of murderous road agents. Some historians believe that no such band existed and that Plummer was basically a good sheriff who killed only in self-defense. As with many other gunfighters of the Old West, Plummer has become immortalized in folklore, and the truths behind the myths and fables will never be completely known.

Jesse and Billy: The most legendary of all gunmen, and the most mythical, was Jesse Woodson James. While he never adopted a lawman's badge, Jesse James did get good press in certain circles and was variously described as "chivalrous," "a devout Christian," "loyal," "brave," "good-humored" and "a good family man." Nevertheless, between 1865 and 1882, the James-Younger gang killed at least a dozen innocent citizens and pulled off about two dozen robberies involving banks, trains and stagecoaches. Still, this blue-eyed bandit was perceived by some as an American Robin Hood who, after being forced into a life of crime by vindictive Yankees and vicious Pinkerton detectives, stole from the rich (the robber barons who controlled the railroads and banks) and gave to the poor.

Jesse and his older brother Frank had in fact been Confederate guerrillas who found it impossible to live peacefully on their family farm in postwar Missouri. And on January 26, 1875, Pinkerton agents did attack the James farmhouse near Kearny, Missouri, accidentally killing their young stepbrother and injuring their mother, Zerelda Samuel. But was that reason enough to keep riding the Outlaw Trail? The James gang of reality stole for themselves and their families, not for the poor, and they weren't hesitant about eliminating anyone who got in their way.

Contrary to common belief, Jesse James did not call all the shots for the gang. Cole Younger, who had been a guerrilla friend of Frank James, and brothers Jim and Bob Younger considered the James boys to be their partners in crime. The partnership ended with a botched bank job in Northfield, Minnesota, on September 7, 1876. Frank and Jesse managed to outride a pursuing posse and make it back to Missouri, but the three Youngers were captured and sentenced to life terms in the Minnesota State Penitentiary. Undeterred, the James boys brought in new gang members and continued their outlaw ways; a $10,000 reward was put up for

BAT MASTERSON

each brother. Then, on April 3, 1882, two new gang members, Robert and Charles Ford, betrayed Jesse in St Joseph, Missouri, where he was living under an assumed name, Tom Howard. Charles watched as Robert gunned down 34-year-old Jesse from behind.

Nearly as many myths surround that other legendary Old West badman, Billy the Kid – also known as William Bonney. Certainly, the Kid did not gun down 21 men in 21 years, as the legend has it, but even eight or 10 in 21 years would seem to justify his reputation as an efficient killer. While most people consider him a clear-cut exception to the "only the good die young" adage, there are others who argue that he had been a misguided youth who probably would have gone "straight" if only he had received amnesty after the bloody Lincoln County War. In any event, his boyish "rebel" image has a certain appeal. And even though he did not rob trains or banks and did not have a gang of his own the way Jesse James did, Billy the Kid has on occasion also been called a Robin Hood who fired his revolver only in self-defense or for a cause he believed in.

Natural-born killers: Nobody, on the other hand, ever thought of John Wesley Hardin as a Robin Hood. Homicidal maniac is more like it. He did become a lawyer, after studying hard in the state penitentiary, but that's the best thing that could be said about this mean-spirited desperado. Named after John Wesley, the father of the Methodist movement, Hardin methodically sent 40 men (by his own count) to Boot Hill by the time he turned 21. His first victim was a former black slave who "shook a stick" at him in November 1868. When three US Cavalry troopers came to arrest Hardin, he killed all three in an ambush.

Although he was a wizard at spinning and twirling a six-shooter, Hardin seldom gave the other guy a chance. At a hotel in Abilene in 1871 he stopped a man from snoring… with a bullet; then he high-tailed it out of town to avoid a confrontation with the town marshal, Wild Bill Hickok. Captured by Texas Rangers in 1877, Hardin spent 16 years in the state penitentiary at Huntsville. He set up a law practice upon his release in 1894, but he soon was spending far more time gambling and drinking in saloons than practicing his profession in courtrooms. Hardin was shot dead by El Paso Constable John Selman the following year. Selman was acquitted of any wrongdoing. Case closed.

Other unquestionably nasty gunmen who killed hard to gain a relatively high degree of infamy included William "Wild Bill" Longley, who is reputed to have killed 32 men before being hanged at age 27 on October 11, 1878; Clay Allison, a psychopath who took at least 15 lives – and yanked a tooth from a dentist who had drilled him the wrong way – before dying in a wagon accident in 1887; and John King Fisher, a first-class Texas rustler who beat a half-dozen murder raps (he was implicated in 20 others), only to be shot down along with another well-known gunman, Ben Thompson, in a San Antonio theater on March 11, 1884.

Deadman's Hand: Gangs continued to operate after the James gang was put out of business – most notably the Daltons and the Wild Bunch. The Daltons, much influenced by the James and Younger boys, tried to top their predecessors by robbing two banks at once in their hometown of Coffeyville, Kansas, on October 5, 1892. The net result was worse then the James-Younger fiasco in Minnesota. Bob and Gratton Dalton and two other gang members were shot dead. Emmett Dalton was another story; despite being struck by two bullets, he survived the wrath of the Coffeyville citizenry and eventually went Hollywood before dying of natural causes.

The Wild Bunch, featuring Butch Cassidy and the Sundance Kid, began robbing banks and trains in 1897. Their favorite hideout was a remote area in Wyoming known as the Hole-in-the-Wall, but their wide-ranging operations extended from Montana to New Mexico. When the law closed in on the gang early in the 20th century, Cassidy and Sundance retreated all the way to South America. Butch Cassidy, who had been the leader of the Bunch, was reportedly a likeable, happy-go-lucky fellow who was not keen on killing. The Robin Hood label that various people had applied to Jesse James and Billy the Kid was now passed on to him, and it probably suited Butch better.

Just as some of the West's villains were not all bad, many of the so-called heroes were not all good. Legendary lawman James Butler Hickok, better known as Wild Bill, was unquestionably a top-notch gunfighter, but he was also a notorious liar. He claimed to have shot down more than 100 bad men, but it was more like 10 – and some of them weren't all that bad. Hickok was tried for murder but acquitted in 1861 after a gunfight at Rock Creek Station in Nebraska Territory; he killed a drunken 7th Cavalry trooper during a saloon fight in Hays City, Kansas, in 1870; and in the process of dispatching a Texas gambler named Phil Coe in Abilene in 1871, he accidentally killed a friend of his named Mike Williams. "I never allowed a

man to get the drop on me," Wild Bill once said, but while playing poker in the #10 Saloon in Deadwood, Dakota Territory, on August 2, 1876, a cross-eyed drifter named Jack McCall shot him in the back. Hickok was holding a pair of aces and a pair of eights at the time – destined to be known as the "Deadman's Hand."

The O.K. Corral: Wyatt Earp is the only other Old West lawman who can match Wild Bill's legendary status. Like Hickok, Earp started life in Illinois, wore his first badge in Kansas, was fond of gambling, and occasionally stood on the wrong side of the law. In 1871, Earp was charged with stealing horses in Indian Territory; he bolted to Kansas

before his trial. Three years later he began serving as a policeman in Wichita, but in May 1876, shortly after the city council decided not to rehire him, Wyatt and brother Virgil were charged with vagrancy. Wyatt then became an assistant marshal in Dodge City, where he befriended a dentist-gambler named John "Doc" Holliday.

Wyatt's real claim to fame, though, can be attributed to one event – the gunfight near the O.K. Corral in Tombstone, Arizona, on October 26, 1881. The West's most famous shootout has been widely portrayed as an epic event pitting the good guys against the bad ones, but more accurately it was an

Left, Masterson was reputed to have gunned down 27 men but actually killed only one. **Right**, Earp was a lawman in Wichita and Dodge City before the O.K. Corral incident.

economic and political struggle coming to a head. On one side were the so-called cowboys, a loosely organized band of free-ranging ranchers and gunmen, supported by politically ambitious Sheriff John Behan. On the other side were the law-and-order-minded Earp brothers, supported by Doc Holliday, who Wyatt called "the nerviest, fastest, deadliest man with a six-gun I ever saw."

The actual gunfight, which lasted all of 30 seconds, pitted Deputy US Marshal Virgil Earp, his deputies Wyatt and Morgan Earp and Doc against Ike and Billy Clanton, Tom and Frank McLaury and a young tough named Billy "the Kid" Claiborne, who fled before the lead flew. Who fired the first shot has

ance on an untold number of "cowboys." Tuberculosis did in Holliday at age 35 in 1887. After nearly two months in bed, he supposedly smiled and said "This is funny," just before dying. Wyatt engaged in numerous occupations, including boxing referee, saloon-keeper and real estate agent – before dying of natural causes at age 80 in 1929.

Another of Wyatt's friends from both the Dodge City and Tombstone days, sometimes-lawman Bat Masterson, also lived well into the 20th century. The distinguished William Bartholomew Masterson apparently became "Bat" because he used a cane to club recalcitrant lawbreakers. He must have been effective with his cane – he managed to kill

been much debated, but Holliday certainly proved his worth with both shotgun and revolver. When it was over, Billy Clanton and both McLaurys were dead; loudmouth Ike Clanton, like Claiborne, had made a hasty retreat to safety. Virgil and Morgan were both wounded but recovered, Doc Holliday was grazed in the hip, and Wyatt emerged unscathed.

The O.K. Corral business did not settle things between the two factions. Two months later Virgil Earp was critically wounded in an ambush; the following March, Morgan Earp was shot down while playing billiards; and then Wyatt Earp and Doc wreaked venge-

only one man while upholding the peace. Bat put the West behind him and moved to New York City in 1902. He became a sportswriter there for nearly two decades, dying at his desk on October 25, 1921.

By then, the Golden Age of the gunslinger had long since set in the West. Well, maybe it wasn't golden. But it certainly was thrilling and unforgettable, even if it lasted only 30-odd years and even if the players wore hats that were neither black nor white, but various shades of gray.

Above, Butch Cassidy (far right) and the Sundance Kid (far left) with members of the Wild Bunch.

THE GREAT EQUALIZER

"**G**od made some men big and some small, but Colonel Sam Colt made them equal all." So went a popular saying down Texas way, where the Colt revolver made its mark early on.

Firearms went by many names back then: six-shooters, six guns, persuaders, hog legs, peace-makers, belly guns, lead chuckers, equalizers. Whatever the name, they were an essential piece of equipment in the shoot-'em-up West.

In the early days, guns weren't terribly effective for either hunting or protection. An Indian could unleash several arrows in the time it took to reload a single-shot firearm.

And then came Sam Colt.

In the 1830s, Colt patented and manufactured revolving pistols and rifles capable of firing several shots without reloading. Their impact was almost immediate. At Plum Creek in 1841, Texas Rangers armed with five-shot Paterson Colts overcame four-to-one odds against 100 Comanche warriors. Other types of firearms, such as long-range rifles, were being improved, too. At the Second Battle of Adobe Walls on the Texas Panhandle in 1874, less than 30 besieged hide hunters used buffalo guns to drive off hundreds of Indians. The decisive blow was Billy Dixon's famed "long shot" with a Sharps rifle, which killed an Indian at 1,500 yards.

By the 1850s, the Colt revolver was the gun-of-choice of many westerners, although the most popular Colt of the frontier era, the .45-caliber Peacemaker, didn't appear for another two decades, about 10 years after Samuel Colt's death.

But then, not every gunman preferred a Colt. After surrendering in 1882, the notorious outlaw Frank James called his Remington "the hardest and surest shooting pistol made." Lt. Col. George Armstrong Custer was said to be carrying a pair of Webley "British Bulldog" revolvers when he fell at Little Bighorn. Wyatt Earp probably drew a Smith & Wesson at the O.K. Corral. And Mark Twain packed a little .22-caliber pistol known as a "suicide special" which he claimed had just one fault: "You could not hit anything with it."

Because low-caliber guns were used in much of the Wild West's "gun play," it usually took more than one shot to disable an opponent. That's why shootists came to prefer a revolver of at least .44 caliber, which was often enough to drop a man with one hit. But even the best firearm was worthless without the nerve and skill to use it. The trick was balancing a draw with enough presence of mind to aim accurately, which, according to Wyatt Earp,

Right, a quick draw and sharp eye were essential in a shoot-out.

meant "going into action with the greatest speed of which a man's muscles are capable, but mentally unflustered by an urge to hurry... "

Most Westerners also owned a rifle or carbine because they were far more accurate at long range than handguns. The Winchester rifle was called the "gun that won the West" – an exaggeration, certainly, although it was one of the finest and most popular. The rifle was standard-issue among Texas Rangers, who put it to use against outlaws and Indians. As the manufacturer, Oliver F. Winchester, liked to say, "It has become a household word, and a household necessity on our western plains and mountains. The pioneer, the hunter and trapper, believe in the Winchester, and its possession is a passion with every Indian."

Lever-action repeating rifles were just the thing to give a man confidence even if he was only a fair

shot. More than 300,000 Spencer rifles were issued to Union soldiers during the Civil War (Abraham Lincoln tested the weapon personally before recommending it to the Army) and were often used by former soldiers who moved out West. The powerful Henry rifle was popular, too. Its magazine held 15 rounds, leading some to say that "you could load it on Sunday and fire it all week."

But not everyone favored a repeating rifle. Buffalo hunters preferred the more powerful single-shot Remington or Sharps, and many other frontiersmen stuck with older models because it wasn't always easy to obtain metal-case ammunition. A shotgun was sometimes chosen for the same reason, although some men liked the shotgun because it was deadly at close range and it didn't have to be aimed carefully. ∎

THE NORMAN FILM MFG. CO.
PRESENTS

BILL PICKETT
WORLD'S COLORED CHAMPION —IN—
'THE BULL-DOGGER'
Featuring The Colored Hero of the Mexican Bull Ring in Death Defying Feats of Courage and Skill.
THRILLS! LAUGHS TOO!
Produced by NORMAN FILM MFG. CO.
JACKSONVILLE, FLA.

The history books often overlook it, but the West actually had a good deal of the multiculturalism we hear so much about these days. Spaniards, of course, were trailblazers in the Southwest and California. Chinese immigrants played a big part in hammering together the transcontinental rail lines. Europeans came by the boatload to farm the prairies and mine the hills. And like so many of their white counterparts, African-Americans were out there putting into practice the admonition popularly ascribed to Horace Greeley: "Go West, young man, and grow up with the country."

Mountain men: Every schoolboy has heard of white frontiersmen such as Kit Carson and Daniel Boone, but what about a character like Jean Baptiste Pointe Du Sable. He was born in the Caribbean, probably in Haiti, of French and African parentage, and in 1779 he established a trading post on a river bank near Lake Michigan – which was pretty far "out west" in those days. Du Sable's post was the first permanent settlement at the place we now call Chicago, making him in effect the city's founder.

Another frequently-overlooked figure from the mountain-man era is James Beckwourth, known to the Crow Indians as "Morning Star." Beckwourth was born in 1798 in St Louis, Missouri, of Afro-European parentage. Restless by nature, he picked up and went west at an early age.

Beckwourth soon became one of the most feared Indian fighters on the frontier. In 1824 he was adopted by the Crow Indians and later became a tribal leader. A rough-and-ready character who was always on the move, Beckwourth worked as a trapper, prospector, Indian fighter, army scout, and plain wanderer. He is remembered best, however, for establishing a route through the Sierra Nevada Mountains that still bears his name: Beckwourth Pass.

Ironically, Beckwourth's first biographer didn't even mention his African-American heritage. Perhaps such "oversights" aren't

Left, celebrated African-American cowboy Bill Pickett. **Right**, Beckwourth was a fur trader, scout and war leader of the Crow Indians.

surprising. After all, Horace Greeley was rather blunt about which men he had in mind when he dispensed his famous advice. The West, he said, "shall be reserved for the benefit of the white Caucasian race." Of course, Greeley was already too late; blacks had been a part of the West for decades. As early as 1790, a Spanish census indicated that 18 percent of California's population was of African descent.

Exodus: Before the Civil War, blacks moved west along with the general population of the

JIM BECKWOURTH

fledgling nation. For some who had escaped bondage on the underground railroad, farflung western settlements were a safe haven from slave-hunters and persecution. For others, like an ex-slave named Clara Brown, the frontier offered a chance to restore their lives and reunite their families.

"Aunt Clara" was born in 1803 in Virginia. As a slave she saw her husband, two daughters and son sold to different slaveholders. She had been sold several times herself before purchasing her own freedom in 1859 and taking a job as a cook on a wagon train to Central City in Colorado.

Upon arriving in the mining camp she

opened a laundry, worked as a nurse, and established the first Sunday school in town. By 1866 this resolute and charitable lady had managed to save $10,000. She spent much of it in efforts to locate her family in the South and succeeded in finding 34 relatives as well as sponsoring wagon trains to transport former slaves to Colorado. Just before her death she was reunited with her daughter.

After the Civil War, freed slaves searched for places where they might better their status. Poverty and oppression had become so severe by the 1870s that a host of destitute freedmen found themselves compelled to move on to the plains. One of them was Benjamin "Pap" Singleton, a charismatic

figure who encouraged thousands of former slaves to walk along or boat up the Mississippi River in search of fertile farmland. Known as the Exodus of 1879, as many as 40,000 black homesteaders followed Singleton's lead to Kansas and other western states.

Buffalo soldiers: Other men found opportunity in the Army. Black soldiers made up the rank-and-file of the Ninth and Tenth Cavalries that were formed after the war to preserve law and order on the western frontier – not always an easy thing to do. Mostly exslaves, these troopers proved to be effective fighters whom their Indian adversaries dubbed "buffalo soldiers," because their hair

and dark skin reminded them of the great beasts. The soldiers accepted the name proudly and placed a symbol of a buffalo on their regimental crest.

From the Canadian border south into Mexico their mission was to make peace – and sometimes war – with the Indian tribes and track down desperadoes like Pancho Villa. They did a good job at it, too, yet were not often accorded fair treatment, as the historian William H. Leckie noted. "Their stations were among the most lonely and isolated to be found anywhere in the country... Discipline was severe, food usually poor, recreation difficult, and violent death always near at hand. Prejudice robbed them of recognition and often of simple justice."

Despite hardships, the buffalo soldiers remained loyal, tallying up some of the highest re-enlistment rates and lowest desertion rates in the Army. Frederic Remington recorded his impressions after joining a black unit on patrol: "They may be tired and they may be hungry, but they do not see fit to augment their misery by finding fault with everybody or everything. In the particular, they are charming men with whom to serve."

There were plenty of black cowboys, too. Some historians estimate that African-Americans constituted as many as a quarter of the cowboys who rode the cattle trails in the latter half of the 19th century. One of the most flamboyant and intrepid was Nat Love, better known as Deadwood Dick (one of several men who laid claim to the name).

In his memoir, Love remarked on the absence of a color barrier among cowboys; men were judged on their skill as horsemen and cowpunchers. Toughness helped, too, in an occupation as dangerous as this one. Love bragged about his own prowess as a cowpoke: "I carry the marks of 14 bullet wounds on different parts of my body, most any one of which would be sufficient to kill an ordinary man, but I was not even crippled."

A different kind of notoriety was achieved by Bill Pickett, famous for his contributions to the sport of rodeo. Around the turn of the century he was regarded as the finest cowboy on the crew of the renowned 101 Ranch in Oklahoma. While sporting with his comrades, he invented a competition known as bulldogging in which a cowboy jumps off his horse and wrestles a steer to the ground. The name comes from Pickett's way of subduing the animals by biting their lower lips much as a bulldog does.

The Chinese experience: Perhaps more than any other single event, the discovery of gold in California in 1849 altered the population of the West. Fortune-hunters poured into the territory from the eastern United States, Europe, China and Latin America. Within only four years, the non-Indian population of California had grown spectacularly from 14,000 to almost 224,000, a third of whom were foreign-born compared to 10 percent in the rest of the United States.

The treatment of Chinese immigrants in California was particularly harsh. Word spread quickly in China that a man could

in with American society, the Chinese were unwilling to give up traditional ways. Their different culture, language and appearance made them targets of racial enmity. The situation was only made worse by the intense competition for jobs, often blamed on the glut of inexpensive Chinese labor. At its worst, anti-Chinese sentiment turned to violence; homes were looted and men harassed or beaten. Organizations like the California Workingman's Party called for the removal of Chinese immigrants or, at least, the termination of Chinese immigration. The party's slogan during the 1876 campaign: "Treason is better than to labor beside a Chinese slave."

In actual fact, many Chinese immigrants

travel to California and make a fortune mining gold. A system quickly developed in which agents lent money for steamship passage at high rates of interest. For most men, the dream of coming back rich and respected never materialized. No one knows how many Chinese traveled to the United States during the Gold Rush, although at least 200,000 came between 1876 and 1890. About half returned to their homeland, most still poor.

Unlike other immigrants who tried to blend

Left, Chinese railroad laborers. **Above,** members of the 10th Cavalry in 1894; buffalo soldiers were stationed at the toughest outposts in the West.

were recruited by American companies, particularly the railroads. Unable to find enough men in California, the Central Pacific brought in laborers directly from China. Chinese workers were regarded as expendable by the railroad (records were not kept of deaths or injuries) and were often given jobs considered too dangerous or demeaning for whites. According to company president Charles Crocker, "you would take 75,000 white men from an elevated class of work and put them down to doing a low class of labor that the Chinamen are now doing, and instead of elevating you would degrade white labor to that extent."

Despite harsh conditions, Chinese workers proved their mettle again and again, blasting and pickaxing their way across some of the most rugged terrain in the West. On April 28, 1869, the Central Pacific's Chinese crew laid more than 10 miles of track in only 12 hours, a feat that the largely Irish crew of the Union Pacific was never able to match.

Promised land: Completion of the transcontinental railroad made all parts of the West more accessible. The railroads advertised extensively for settlers to move west and purchase company-owned lands. In fact, in 1882, the Northern Pacific distributed more than 600,000 leaflets printed in several languages, including English, Dutch, Norwe-

gian, Danish and Swedish. They promised favorable terms and fertile soil – a surefire way to get rich on the prairie. Once word-of-mouth started rolling, entire families – and sometimes whole communities – were convinced to move out west.

A typical example of a planned community in the West is the town of New Sweden, Idaho. When an irrigation company built canals running from the Snake River to the edge of an ancient lava field, the deep topsoil was transformed into fertile farmland. Developers advertised in Swedish newspapers, mostly in the upper Midwest, and in Sweden itself. Sweden was undergoing a period of

political turmoil at the time, making the offer of cheap, arable land virtually irresistible to ambitious young men and their families.

In other countries, like Norway, antiquated inheritance laws prompted some men to cash in their meager inheritances and head for Norwegian communities in places like Minnesota or North Dakota. For others the attraction was religious freedom and the promise of a wholesome life in utopian communities like the Old Russians in Oregon or the Mormon settlements in Utah. In many countries that were not well off, villages were virtually emptied by the promise of a better life in the United States.

Mining companies advertised for immigrants, too. In the early 20th century, for example, Greeks, Slovenes and Italians were recruited to work in newly opened coal mines in Utah and Wyoming. As a result, towns like Price, Utah, and Rock Springs, Wyoming, today have telephone directories full of names like Papadakis or Kokal or Martini. Other mining operations like those in Park City, Utah, or Butte, Montana, were owned by Irish-Americans, who advertised in Irish newspapers back east. At one time, more Irish lived in Butte, per capita, than in any other city in the United States. In what is perhaps the West's first case of reverse discrimination, Montana's copper baron, Marcus Daly, commissioned signs that boldly stated, "English Need Not Apply."

Other immigrants came and practiced centuries-old skills. Most of the wonderful stone buildings on ranches in northern Nevada were built by Italian stone masons. Portuguese farmers carried on agricultural traditions in California. Italian fishermen plied the waters off San Francisco and Monterey. Basque herders came to raise sheep and cattle and now run many of the large ranches in Nevada.

And new immigrants continue to pour into the West. Many rural towns in the region have more residents who speak Spanish than English. Asians have made a major impact on commerce in western cities, and a growing number of South Sea Islanders now live there too.

The new West, like the old, is still looked on as a place of promise. And where promise lies, diversity is never far behind.

Left, Italian workers. **Right**, enjoying a smoke.

Chapter 3
"THE HORROR
IN THE DARK"

Nat Levine
presents

TOM TYLER
IN

"The PHANTOM OF THE WEST"

with a
Great Supporting Cast including
WILLIAM DESMOND · TOM SANTSCHI · DOROTHY GULLIVER
JOE BONOMO · TOM DUGAN AND OTHERS

An ALL-TALKING   SERIAL IN 10
THRILLING CHAPTERS

Directed by
ROSS LEDERMAN

MASCOT
SERIAL

The West will welcome the 21st century looking quite different than it did a century ago. Progress brings change – some good, some questionable. But one thing is certain: the West can't change its past. Nor should it. The same brawling spirit, boundless optimism and grand landscapes that made the West a unique part of American history will also help it rise to the challenges of the next millennium.

In the early 1890s, the Superintendent of the Census declared that the American frontier was closed: "At present the unsettled area has been so broken into by isolated bodies of settlement that there can hardly be said to be a frontier line." The Old West was dead; a new era had begun.

The dawn of the New West is evident in evolving attitudes about the arid lands west of the 100th meridian. As the old Hollywood sentimentality wears thin, a more realistic picture of the West is beginning to emerge. That new picture is colored by two enduring legacies. The first is a belief in nature's limitless bounty, a faith that encourages exploitation of natural resources with little regard for long-term consequences. The second is the "Great Migration," the vast wave of humanity that started to pour into the West in the 1840s and never really ended.

Myth and history: The Wild West isn't merely the raucous boom towns, rutted trails, roguish gunmen, free-riding Indians and ragged forts strung along the frontier. It didn't begin with the journey of Lewis and Clark or with the cowboys who drove herds of cattle north from Texas.

The West is bigger than this. It's an idea, a promise, a seed of hope. "Eastward I go only by force; westward I go free," wrote Henry David Thoreau, summing up America's faith in the frontier. And as that frontier was pushed farther west, from Christopher Columbus to Daniel Boone to Lewis and Clark, its place in the national psyche grew in significance.

Today, the myth of the Wild West has become part and parcel of America's na-

Left and **right**, two images of the cowboy: matinee idol and buckaroo.

tional identity, and anyone who tries to challenge it is in for a difficult time.

A case in point: in the early 1990s, the National Museum of American Art in Washington, DC, opened an exhibit called "The West As America: Reinterpreting Images of the Frontier." Various curators suggested that masterworks by Remington, Russell, Catlin and other legendary artists were worth another look.

Perhaps these visual icons weren't as faithful to history as was once thought. Nice

Cow Boy Throwing Lariet.

pictures, yes. Accurate history, no. The exhibition drew public and private criticism that reverberated through the marble halls of the museum for months. Bedeviled curators finally changed a few labels, and their exhibition, which was scheduled to tour museums around the country, closed without ever leaving the nation's capital.

Such are the struggles as the Old West gives way to the New. But the hour has come. The frontier long ago receded into history. It's time to reexamine the image of the West as a boundless Eden. The New West is hearing a wake-up call. Resources are not infinite; the Land of Plenty has a fence around it.

There may be no end to the fascination with all things western, but there are limits to the West's resources.

The transition is slow. It will take time to reshape popular attitudes about a region where, in the early 1800s, mountain-man James Clyman joined a buffalo hunt that killed "a thousand or upwards" in one afternoon. To early pilgrims like Clyman, the Old West was vast beyond comprehension, and there seemed to be no end to the wildlife, rivers, timber and precious metals.

The riches were there for the taking, and those who came, took. Within 20 years of the Lewis and Clark expedition, about 3,000 trappers killed so many beaver and otters that

ago, "The West begins where the average annual rainfall drops below twenty inches. When you reach… the one hundredth meridian – you have reached the West." In wetter climates where vegetation reclaims the land quickly, it's easier for the wounds of development to heal.

But the lack of water has never stopped progress in the West, where diverting water is a long-standing practice. As far back as the 1500s, Spanish engineers built irrigation ditches in their far-flung *villas* just as the Hohokam Indians did hundreds of years earlier. Hundreds of years after the Spanish, emigrant Mormons organized entire settlements around their irrigation systems.

even now, after decades of conservation, the population of these animals is only a fraction of what it used to be.

All over the West, rust-colored rivers and creeks, filled with the waste of old mines, run clear but lifeless, undrinkable and inhospitable to aquatic life. On lands where cattle was once king, overgrazed soils have been eroded by rain and wind, and trampled streambeds have been turned into muddy shallows in which no fish can survive.

Water works: Most of the western environment is naturally dry and easily scarred by the exertions of civilization. As historian Bernard DeVoto noted more than 60 years

In this century, irrigation projects have been engineered on a monumental scale. After World War II, water flowing through concrete-lined irrigation channels transformed California's Central Valley into the nation's food basket. But within a few decades, farmers realized that irrigated soils – naturally saline and difficult to drain – became less productive.

When it comes to the environment, the proverbial chickens have come home to roost. It's time to clean up the mess. Instead of hacking through forests, contemporary trailblazers must find ways to cleanse the rivers, conserve wilderness, reclaim overgrazed and overirrigated lands, and save the fragile western environment from further degradation.

This is a challenge that from time to time exhibits all the characteristics of an old-fashioned Wild West showdown. A current brouhaha in rural Catron County, New Mexico, is like similar conflicts in many other western counties. Ranchers and officials are fighting over grazing rights on public lands. The ranchers say they're fighting to preserve a way of life. The officials claim the ranchers want to run too many cattle on public lands, thus bringing ruin to designated wilderness areas.

The dispute is no longer confined to the civilities of courtrooms or public hearings.

11 western states is held by the federal government. Drive for an hour in any part of the West and you'll probably cross public land. That's an awful lot of resources, and the squabbles over their management are far from over.

The West continues to grow. Since the early 1500s, pioneers have come in search of their own personal Eden. Later, they followed Horace Greeley's exhortation to "Go West... and grow up with the country." If their dreams went sour, they hitched up the wagon and headed for the sunset.

As a land is shaped by its people, so the increase in population is reshaping the West. Since 1890 the West's population has grown

In fact, Catron County officials took the extraordinary measure of passing a gun-control law that *requires* the heads of most households to hold or own firearms in order to defend their rights. Who says the Wild West is dead?

This New Mexico example hearkens back to the Sagebrush Rebellion of the 1980s, when advocates of states' rights tried to assert control over lands held by the Bureau of Land Management, Forest Service and other federal agencies. Half of the land in the

Left, Utah's canyonlands under threat. Above, a cowboy cut-out and the modern world.

faster than that of any other region of the United States. It is still a magnet for refugees from other parts of the country and the world who, like their pioneering predecessors, believe they'll find a better life in the West's open spaces.

As the 20th century draws to a close, Westerners face a number of challenges, not the least of which is learning to live together on a shrunken frontier. But then, Westerners have always been optimists. They believe in the promise of the coming day. And, together with an acceptance of nature's limits, that native optimism will help define the New West in the future.

'S WILD WEST
RIDERS OF THE WORLD.

COPYRIGHT 1899

Courier
LITHO. CO.
BUFFALO

COL. W. F. CODY
"BUFFALO BILL"
WILL APPEAR
AT EVERY PERFORMA

E REAL ROUGH RIDERS OF THE WORLD WHOSE DARING EXP
VE MADE THEIR VERY NAMES SYNONYMOUS WITH DEEDS OF BR

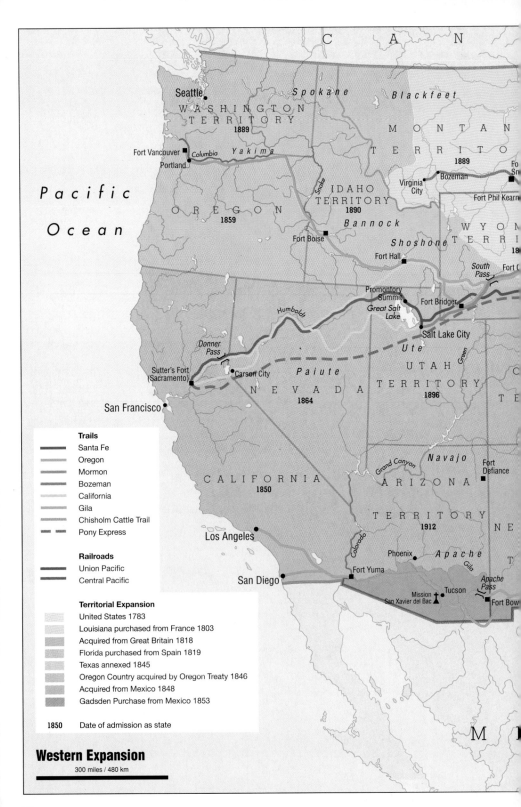

Seattle

Spokane

Blackfeet

W A S H I N G T O N
T E R R I T O R Y
1889

M O N T A N

T E R R I T O

1889

Fo
Sn

Fort Vancouver ■ *Columbia* *Yakima*
Portland

Virginia
City

Bozeman ●

Fort Phil Kearn

Pacific

Ocean

Snake

I D A H O
T E R R I T O R Y
1890

Bannock

W Y O M

T E R R I

1?

O R E G O N
1859

Fort Boise ■

Shoshone

Fort Hall ■

*South
Pass* Fort (

Promontory
Summit

*Great Salt
Lake*

Fort Bridger ■

Humboldt

*Donner
Pass*

Sutter's Fort
(Sacramento) ■

Carson City ●

Paiute

N E V A D A
1864

Salt Lake City

Ute

U T A H
T E R R I T O R Y
1896

Green

T E

San Francisco ●

Trails
— Santa Fe
— Oregon
— Mormon
— Bozeman
— California
— Gila
— Chisholm Cattle Trail
– – Pony Express

C A L I F O R N I A
1850

Navajo

Grand Canyon

Fort
Defiance ■

A R I Z O N A

Railroads
— Union Pacific
— Central Pacific

T E R R I T O R Y
1912

N E

Los Angeles ●

Colorado

Phoenix ●

Apache

Gila

T

San Diego ●

Fort Yuma ■

Mission ✝
San Xavier del Bac ▲

Tucson ●

*Apache
Pass*

Fort Bow

Territorial Expansion
United States 1783
Louisiana purchased from France 1803
Acquired from Great Britain 1818
Florida purchased from Spain 1819
Texas annexed 1845
Oregon Country acquired by Oregon Treaty 1846
Acquired from Mexico 1848
Gadsden Purchase from Mexico 1853

1850   Date of admission as state

Western Expansion

300 miles / 480 km

C A N

M

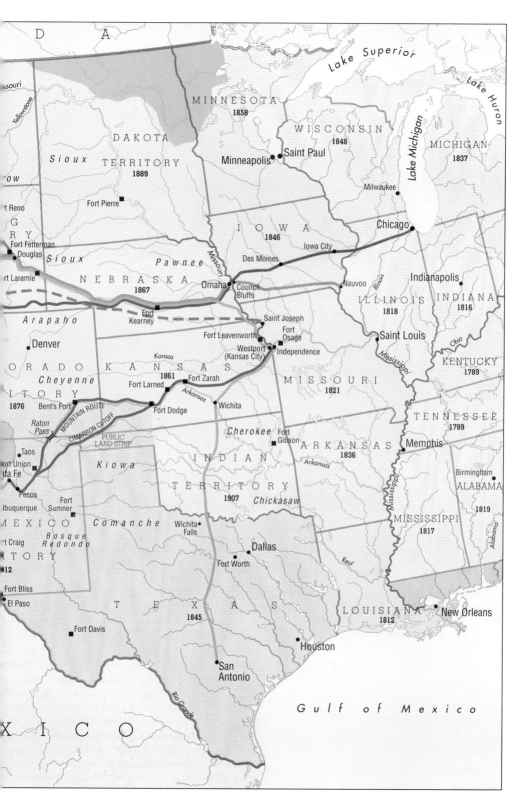

D A K O T A

Lake Superior

Lake Huron

ssouri

Yellowstone

MINNESOTA
1858

WISCONSIN
1848

MICHIGAN
1837

DAKOTA

Sioux   TERRITORY
1889

Minneapolis   Saint Paul

ow

Milwaukee

Lake Michigan

t Reno

Fort Pierre

Chicago

G
R Y   Fort Fetterman
Douglas

Sioux   Pawnee

IOWA
1846

Iowa City

Indianapolis

t Laramie

NEBRASKA
1867

Des Moines

Omaha   Council
Bluffs

Nauvoo

Illinois

ILLINOIS
1818

INDIANA
1816

Arapaho

Fort
Kearney

Saint Joseph

Fort Leavenworth

Westport
(Kansas City)   Independence
Fort
Osage

Saint Louis

Mississippi

Ohio

KENTUCKY
1789

Denver

ORADO   K A N S A S
Cheyenne

Kansas

Fort Zarah

MISSOURI
1821

TENNESSEE
1789

TORY
1876

Fort Larned
1861   Fort Dodge

Arkansas

Wichita

Bent's Fort

MOUNTAIN ROUTE

Raton
Pass

CIMARRON CUTOFF

PUBLIC
LAND STRIP

Cherokee   Fort
Gibson

ARKANSAS
1836

Memphis

Arkansas

Taos
rt Union
ta Fe

Kiowa

INDIAN

Birmingham

Pecos

Fort
Sumner

TERRITORY
1907

Chickasaw

Mississippi

ALABAMA

buquerque
Albuquerque

Comanche

Wichita
Falls

MISSISSIPPI
1817

Alabama

MEXICO
rt Craig
TORY
12

Bosque
Redondo

Dallas

Fort Worth

Red

LOUISIANA
1812

Fort Bliss
El Paso

T   E   X   A   S
1845

Houston

New Orleans

Fort Davis

San
Antonio

Rio Grande

Gulf   of   Mexico

X I C O

79

Come autumn, Rod McQueary rides the range north of Elko, Nevada, hiring himself out to the ranches that spread across this still lonesome country. His work day is a long one. He and his fellow cowboys gather at four in the morning to head up toward the mountains, there spending the next 13 or 14 hours in the saddle as they cajole ornery cattle from the summer range toward winter pastures.

It's not an easy life, but it is a life that McQueary loves – and one that he feels lucky to be leading. Northeastern Nevada is one of the few corners of the West where cattle ranching remains an economically viable activity, and cowboying a possible career path. Even here, though, McQueary warns that the going is tough for many a cowpoke. "You can make it if you don't have a family," he says, explaining that a cowboy's pay is $400 a month plus board, "and all the horses you can ride." But if you acquire a wife or children, you need to diversify. That's what McQueary has done. He's a published author, a humorist who has appeared on national television: these other careers enable him to continue cowboying.

The legend endures: That just goes to show the draw that cowboy life has on Americans, whether they're working wranglers like Rod McQueary or the millions of others who have never been closer to the open range than their last Clint Eastwood movie. The cowboy's heyday was brief indeed – roughly the 25 years from 1865 to 1890 – but it doesn't look as though the American West will ever see the last of him.

He got his start in Texas in the days after the Civil War. The Lone Star State lay defeated and impoverished. But it did hold vast herds of longhorn cattle roaming its open range. Farsighted ranchers realized that they might make money sending Texas cattle to the beef-hungry cities of the East, if only they could get the cattle to the railheads in Kansas. They also saw that Texas had a ready work force of young men able to help.

Preceding pages: Buffalo Bill Cody's Wild West Show; flying the flag, Montana's Rocky Boys Reservation; cow skulls in Taos, New Mexico. Left, cattle branding. Right, coffee break.

And so it was in the scrub country south of San Antonio that an American archetype was born. The early cowboy was a hybrid creature. He drew some of his gear and many of his skills, notably roping, from the *vaqueros* of Mexico. Traces of Spain echoed in his cowboy palaver (itself a term derived from the Spanish, *palabra*). *Cincha* became cinch, *la reata* lariat, *rancho* ranch; the *vaquero* himself became the buckaroo. Yet other aspects of the cowboy world had roots deep in the United States. The roundup, for

example, can be traced back to the Appalachian Mountains.

Who were these cowboys? They were not great in number – historians estimate that between 1866 and 1896 some 35,000 men rode the cattle trails between Texas and Kansas, or worked on ranches elsewhere on the plains. They were young, generally in their teens or twenties. And, according to Montana cowboy E. C. "Teddy Blue" Abbott, they tended to be "medium-sized men, as a heavy man was hard on horses, quick and wiry, and as a rule good-natured: in fact it didn't pay to be anything else." Chiefly Texans at first, they were eventually joined by men from other regions – midwestern boys seeking better pay than could be found on the farm, East Coast remittance men seeking excitement. And although decades of dime novels and movie westerns portrayed only cowboys with Anglo-Saxon features, some historians estimate that as many as one-third of cowboys were black or Hispanic.

Horse sense: Whoever he was, wherever he came from, the cowboy had one chief distinguishing feature – his horse. The horse was not just his preferred form of locomotion, it was his rite of passage, his source of pride. As Teddy Blue said, there were only two things a cowboy was afraid of: "a decent woman and being set afoot." Over the years

stragglers missed in spring. But probably the cattle drive itself was the high point of the cowboy's work life. Each drive attempted to steer 2,500 or so cattle 1,200 miles (1,930 km) from Texas to the railheads in Kansas, a journey that could take up to four months. It was on these epic journeys that the cowboy carved his legend. Among the cattle trail's petty hardships were lice and a monotonous diet of biscuits and sowbelly that practically invited scurvy. Among its more serious threats were occasionally hostile Indians, river crossings, rattlesnakes and the menaces peculiar to working with horses and cattle: fingers sliced off by poorly tied ropes, legs crushed beneath fallen horses, wounds in-

this cowpoke-pony relationship has perhaps been romanticized. Many cowboys did not own their own horses (some trail bosses discouraged it), and in the course of a cattle drive, a cowboy might often switch mounts. As one historian wrote, "More sweat than sentiment passed between horse and rider." Nevertheless, an intelligent, responsive horse was greatly respected, and a cowboy who could gentle a wild horse into such a mount was equally respected.

The cowboy's ranch tasks were numerous. The spring roundup separated out cattle to be branded and castrated for that year's trail drive; a fall roundup caught new calves and

flicted by the horns of maddened steers.

Even when calamity did not intervene, the work could seem Sisyphean. "We worked every day," one cowboy recalled. "There was no Sunday. Often we would not know what day of the week it was. It would just be daylight and night." Fourteen-hour days were commonplace, and night was not much easier, as cowboys stood guard over uneasily sleeping cattle praying that they would not stampede. It was there, on those prairie nights, that one of the art forms of cowboy life grew up, for one way of calming the cattle was to sing to them, perhaps a low, gentle lament like "The Kansas Line":

The cowboy's life is a dreadful life
He's driven through heat and cold
I'm almost froze with water on my clothes
A-ridin' through heat and cold

Good and reckless: Music was one compensation for the hard life of the trail. More compensations lay at the trail's end, in the cattle towns of Abilene or Dodge City. Here the cowboy could take the $90 he had earned on the drive and buy himself a bath and some new duds and a meal of oysters brought on ice from New Orleans – and then get into who knew what kind of trouble at dance halls like Dodge City's Longbranch Saloon.

The brawling nature of the cowboy's foray into these cattle towns may have been overstated; many young cowboys may have tried to appear fiercer than they were in order to get a rise out of gullible townspeople. Nonetheless, they garnered a wild reputation. One matron recalled about the Miles City, Montana, of her youth: "Nice people in Miles City would as soon as thought of inviting a rattlesnake into their homes as a cowboy." And even though cowboys were in some ways the lifeblood of the local economy, the *Cheyenne Daily Leader* printed this criticism of the breed: "As you mingle with these boys you find them a strange mixture of good nature and recklessness. Morally, as a class, they are foulmouthed, blasphemous, drunken, lecherous, utterly corrupt. Usually harmless on the plains when sober, they are dreaded in towns, for then liquor has the ascendancy over them."

Yet by the 1870s these blasphemous and corrupt figures rode throughout the plains, as the cattle kingdom spread north from Texas into the newly opened lands of the Dakotas, Wyoming and Montana. And what's more, the cowboy was well on his way to becoming an American folk hero. Walt Whitman caught the spirit as he traveled through Kansas in 1879: cowboys, the poet wrote, were "a strangely interesting class, bright-eyed as hawks, with their swarthy complexions, and their broad-brimmed hats – apparently always on horseback, with loose arms slightly raised and swinging as they ride."

Whitman was not the only one to admire this new figure. Newspaperman Ned Buntline came out and made Buffalo Bill Cody famous in the New York press. Dime novelists thrilled readers throughout America with cowboy exploits, although the nature of these feats were so far-fetched that some observers felt compelled to complain. One wrote that the cowboy's "admirers are investing him with all manner of romantic qualities; they descant upon him his manifold virtues and his pardonable weaknesses as if he were a demi-god," while "the true character of the cowboy has become obscured, his genuine qualities are lost in fantastic tales of impossible daring and skill…"

Cowboy culture: But criticism could not stem the tide of admiration Americans came to feel for the cowboy. There was something

about him that stirred the country deeply indeed: a pattern of conduct that was in some ways so rigorously demanding it could be called the cowboy code. Cowboy-turned-author Eugene Manlove Rhodes detailed some aspects of this code. The cowboy was physically courageous, he explained, and always uncomplaining, even if tired or sick. He was a stranger to excuses and alibis, always doing his job well, not for the satisfaction of his boss – who might well be a New York or London joint stock company – but for the job itself. By displaying such qualities, Rhodes wrote, the cowboy had earned the independence that was the hall-

Left and **right**, off-duty. Walt Whitman called cowboys "a strangely interesting class."

mark of the job. "I worked on the range twenty-five years," he recalled, "and in that time I did not hear any man told what to do."

It was by taking on these noble qualities that the cowboy began his ascendance into myth. Easterners like Owen Wister wrote that the American cowboy was a direct descendant of the knights of Camelot. Teddy Roosevelt, who had encountered the cowboy during his sojourn in the Badlands, praised him thus: "A cowboy will not submit tamely to an insult, and is ever ready to avenge his own wrongs; nor has he an overwrought fear of shedding blood… He does possess, to a very high degree, the stern, manly qualities that are invaluable to a nation."

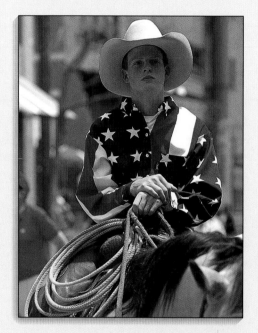

But the cowboy's pride and independence came at a price. Compared to other manual laborers – workers on factories or farms – he was paid well enough by the standards of the time: about a dollar a day. But the work was notoriously backbreaking, the career notoriously short. Wrote cowboy Andy Adams, "No harder life is lived by any working man." Another warned, "For a man to be stove up at thirty may sound strange to some people, but many a cowboy has been so banged up that he has to quit riding that early in life… My advice to any young man or boy is to stay at home and not to be a rambler, as it won't buy you anything. And above every-thing stay away from a cow ranch, as not many cowpunchers ever save any money and 'tis a dangerous life to live."

Cowboys tried to fight back. Despite their independent nature, some of them banded together to strike in Texas in 1883 and in Wyoming in 1886. But they weren't successful. And while many cowboys tried to save enough of their pay to secure a small ranch of their own – become "nesters," in the parlance of the day – few succeeded.

Numbered: For in truth the West itself was changing. As railroads brought new settlers, as barbed wire divided up miles of prairie, the cattle kingdom's days were numbered. And with it went the cowboy. Some would be able to find work; some find work even today. But they no longer ruled the open range, as there was no open range to rule.

Yet the cowboy did not go quietly into that American night. As America urbanized, it felt an increased need for a hero who embodied a wilder, more independent past. The cowboy was ready. By the turn of the century he was being celebrated in best-selling fiction (Wister's *The Virginian*) and best-selling fact (the works of cowboys-turned-authors Andy Adams and Charles Siringo). Remington and Russell immortalized him in oil and bronze. And when the gaudy new motion pictures began flickering across the American screen, he found a new home at the Saturday matinee: Western stars like William S. Hart and stunt man Yakima Canutt, began their careers as cowboys.

Indeed, 20th-century American culture is nearly unimaginable without this heroic figure in boots and big hat. Think *Red River* and *She Wore a Yellow Ribbon,* think *Bonanza* and *Blazing Saddles,* Aaron Copland's *Billy the Kid* and Waylon Jennings' "My Heroes Have Always Been Cowboys." Think John Wayne and Clint Eastwood, and the host of *Death Valley Days* – Ronald Reagan – who carried the aura of simple frontier virtue all the way to the White House. The cowboy shows no sign of heading towards that last roundup. Driven from the prairies and canyons of the real West, he rides, triumphant, across the more spacious range of the American imagination.

Left and right, on parade and on the range: the best in the West. Historians suggest some 35,000 cowboys hit the trails in the late 1800s.

There are so many misconceptions about American Indians, it's difficult to know where to start correcting them. Needless to say, the Wild West looks a whole lot different from the Indian point of view.

It all seems to have started with Christopher Columbus. He reported his discovery of a simple people – they were the same color as Canary Islanders, he said – who lived in an idyllic state of nature. He made his first big mistake when, thinking he had landed in the East Indies, he named them Indians. And like so many other explorers, he talked about them as if they were all the same. One Indian people. One Indian culture.

"Once unleashed, the idea of 'the Indian' used in the singular, as if there were one standard character involved, showed a remarkable power to flatten reality," notes historian Patricia Nelson Limerick. "The difference between the sedentary, farming Pueblo Indians, and nomadic, buffalo-hunting Plains Indians... would seem to have the power to shake the term Indian permanently into pieces."

It would indeed. And yet, Indians are still commonly perceived as members of a single, monolithic society. The fact is, when Columbus arrived there were some 500 tribes in North America. They spoke hundreds of distinct languages and practiced very different ways of life. And, despite the influence of modern-day living, they still do.

Civilized savage: There's a similarly persistent belief that Indian people and cultures will gradually become extinct. But the so-called "vanishing Red Man" has hardly vanished. True, some old-time traditions (and particularly languages) have fallen by the wayside, but then cultures are always in the process of change. As far as population goes, however, there are probably more Indians now than there were before European contact, and many more than 100 years ago.

The idea picked up steam some time in the 18th century when it was strongly felt that indigenous people had to become "civilized" or face extermination. Both George Washington and Thomas Jefferson urged Indians to acculturate for their own good and the country's. Washington predicted that it would take only 50 years. By 1839, he said, the Indian would be civilized.

But civilization wasn't all that it was cracked up to be. "You here behold an Indian," said Elias Boudinot, a Cherokee, in Philadelphia in 1826 – more than a decade before Washington's deadline. "I stand before you delegated by my native country to seek her interest, to labor for her respectabil-

ity, and ... in raising her to an equal standing with other nations of the earth."

Boudinot argued that it was time for white Americans to accept the Christian and democratic communities of the country. "The shrill sound of the Savage yell shall die away as the roaring of far distant thunder; and heaven wrought music will gladden," he said.

Boudinot was a bilingual Cherokee educated in New England. In 1828, he was editor of the Cherokee Nation's first newspaper and, judging by the standards of the day, a successful, civilized gentleman. He was not alone. The Cherokees met any measure of civilization. They were economically self-

Left, Paiute tribal leader, Utah. **Right**, Tohono O'odham women gather saguaro cactus fruit.

sufficient, had a democratic and independent government and a high literacy rate.

To prove their loyalty to the United States, the Cherokees joined General Andrew Jackson in the war against the Seminole Indians in Florida. Two Cherokee leaders, Major Ridge and John Ross, served as Jackson's officers.

But civilization wasn't enough for the government. Removal or extermination were the only acceptable alternatives. Elected to the nation's highest office in 1828, President Jackson turned on his Cherokee allies by making the Indian Removal Act his top priority. The law evicted the Cherokees and other eastern tribes from their homelands

talgia. So-called "wild Indians" were imbued with a mystical, romantic power, while those who had become "tamed" or "civilized" were no longer regarded as "real Indians." The notion persists to this day.

In the writings of lawyer and author C.E.S. Wood, for example, Indians are portrayed as the country's last hope of moral redemption: "We seem to have utterly lost the powers of imagination. The North American Indians are still imaginative and poetical" and as morally "fresh as the scent of fir woods." Wood dismissed all Indian writers, arguing that when they learned English they forgot the truth. Some historians contend that Wood even wrote Chief Joseph's famous "I Will

and forced them on the Trail of Tears to Indian Territory (now Oklahoma). Jackson, the founder of the Democratic Party, ignored a Supreme Court ruling in favor of the Cherokees and declared Indian treaties "absurd." If this was "civilization," maybe the Indians were better off without it.

"Real" Indians: Around the turn of the century, as the last Indian wars were winding down and tribes were being confined to reservations, a new and equally damaging myth was born. Western writers, ignoring voices from within the Indian community, redefined the "authentic" nature of tribal people. It was a misconception born of nos-

Fight No More Forever" speech. Ironic when you consider that Wood was an army officer who fought against Chief Joseph in the Nez Perce War, then sent his children to the chief for a "true" education. It's a no-win situation. And when it comes to the perception of the public, that's pretty much where Indian people find themselves today. They're damned if they try to fit into society and damned if they don't.

What is missing from these two very different stories is a simple truth: Native Americans ought to shape their own identities and draft their own histories. Indians know who they are and where they come from. They ought to be allowed the freedom to define themselves as they wish.

In his manifesto, *Custer Died For Your Sins*, Vine Deloria, Jr, writes: "The primary goal and need of Indians today is not for someone to feel sorry for us and claim descent from Pocahontas to make us feel better." Instead, Deloria argues for cultural sovereignty, "a leave-us-alone agreement, in spirit and in fact."

Reexamination: And the best place to start is a reexamination of Indian history from an Indian point of view. It's no wonder that most traditional history books depict Indians as merely an impediment to western settlement, or that they portray the defeat of Indian

material written by obviously biased men is readily accepted as reality."

If there is to be a new American Indian history, it must reflect the experiences of Indians as distinct nations akin to those of Europe; it must draw on the memories and lore of Indian people themselves; and it must incorporate the definition that Indian people create for themselves. What's more, Indian history needs to be brought up to date. Most people assume that the Indian story ended with the frontier – that Indians have just been hanging around the reservation for the last hundred years.

Except in native communities, Indian history after the turn of the century is almost

tribes as the "taming" or "winning" of the West rather than as territorial conquest. Most American history is written from the perspective of the conquerors – for what historian Donald Worster calls "my people." A record of what "we" accomplished.

"Our stories are frequently discredited by Western historians as 'merely myth,'" says Wilma Mankiller, chief of the Cherokee Nation. "I have always found [this] fascinating. An entire body of knowledge can be dismissed because it was not written, while

never taught. But history matters to native people. While most Americans see treaties as dusty old documents, Indian children are taught that the words have power and that the US Constitution calls treaties "the supreme law of the land." Their people's stories don't start with history books, but with Mother Nature and the stories she can tell.

In the end, we have to realize that the history of the West belongs to all of us. It is not a one-sided story about how white Americans "civilized" the frontier, but the record of an encounter between people of many races and cultures and the impact their actions continue to have on the present day.

Left, *Land O'Bucks* by David Bradley. Above, Comanche dance at San Juan Pueblo.

They called her "Skipper" and thought of her as the quintessential western woman – strong, capable and fiercely independent. Her real name was Anna Lucylle Moon Hall, and she managed her own 700-acre (280-ha) ranch near Cody, Wyoming, for roughly half a century, rearing a daughter and supporting a (largely absentee) husband in the process. She also wrote a newspaper column titled "Sage Brush Savage," and she had her own radio program.

When Anna Hall died in October 1993, just a few days short of her 90th birthday, her passing evoked remembrances of Cody's past. She had always taken great pride in the fact that her grandfather, Laban Hillberry, had been partly responsible for bringing the legendary scout and buffalo hunter William F. Cody – for whom the town was named – to the Bighorn Basin. Known in her younger years for being able to ride all day in a rodeo and then dance the night through, Hall was a woman so secure in her own abilities and place in the community that she found an element of the ridiculous in the feminist movement of the 1960s. Her daughter Chaska Hall Reitz recalls that when her mother heard about "women's lib," she was not the least bit impressed. "She said, 'Huh – guess they'll expect us to shoe our own horses next.' "

Most of the hard working women of the frontier West would have shared Skipper Hall's reaction to modern rhetoric on the subject of women's equality. It's hard to envision women like Sacajawea, the Shoshone teenager who led Lewis and Clark to the Pacific Northwest, or taciturn stagecoach driver Charlotte "Charley" Parkhurst on the feminist lecture circuit. Yet they – and others who lived and died in relative obscurity – were pioneers in the American feminist movement. Like Skipper Hall, they probably would have ridiculed the notion of fighting for equality with men – but that was because a struggle for sexual equality was beside the point. On the frontier, the day-to-day struggle for survival was the main concern.

Left, dime-novel heroine Martha "Calamity Jane" Cannary was a real-life bullwhacker, teamster and occasional prostitute. **Right**, Annie Oakley.

Pathfinders: Skipper Hall grew up on a remote Wyoming ranch. In fact, she never even made it into the nearest town until she was all of nine years old. Infected early on with a love of literature and learning by her mother, who was a teacher, she eventually went off to finishing school and college. But very soon Hall hankered for the open range and a horse to ride, and she borrowed enough money from relatives to buy a ranch on Rattlesnake Creek. Her holdings prospered, and she acquired more land, more farms.

Until late in her life, she persisted in doing much of the outdoor work she had always enjoyed – including irrigating her own land. Hall's legendary status as a rancher, horsewoman and community spokesperson was honored in her lifetime. She was chosen Ranchwoman of the Year by the Cody Country Cow Belles in 1979, and also nominated for the National Cowgirl Hall of Fame.

Like Hall, the Indian woman Sacajawea was a native of the West. But it was her fate to prove her worth as an interpreter and guide while she was virtually a hostage – a Shoshone woman taken prisoner by the Hidatsa tribe during a raid, and subsequently sold as a wife to French-Canadian guide Toussaint Charbonneau. For the 15-year-old, heavily pregnant Sacajawea, the westward journey she embarked on in 1805 with Meriwether Lewis and William Clark was not a matter of choice. Like many other women who would soon follow in her footsteps, Sacajawea set out on her cross-continent journey at her husband's insistence.

She joined the expedition as it passed through Fort Mandan, in what is now North Dakota. Sacajawea ("Bird Woman") was signed on by Charbonneau to serve as an interpreter for the party in their dealings with the Shoshone as well as a visible symbol that these white men meant no harm to the native

tribes. She gave birth to a son at Fort Mandan and then set out with the expedition on what remained of their grueling journey, carrying her newborn in a cradleboard on her back.

Sacajawea's contribution to the expedition soon proved invaluable. In addition to her ability to communicate with the Indians and obtain food and horses for the party, Sacajawea's quick-wittedness and calm purposefulness got the travelers out of many sticky situations. Lewis would later recall that she managed to save much of the expedition's equipment when her husband, the "worst steersman of the party," caused their pirogue to overturn. Lewis described her as

"The Indian woman to whom I ascribe equal fortitude and resolution, with any person onboard at the time of the accident," who "caught and preserved most of the light articles which were washed overboard." As was said by Abigail Scott Duniway during the 1905 dedication of a statue in Portland, Oregon, "This woman was an Indian, a mother and a slave. And as she pointed out the devious way in the wilderness that led at last to the home of her people, a man-child on her back, little did she know that she was helping to upbuild a Pacific empire."

In the 50 years following Sacajawea's journey, many hundreds of women would benefit from her leadership. The wagon trains were filled with families who felt that the West offered tremendous promise. Some women, however, came West on their own – hoping to own their own farm or have a career for the first time. Of course, not all of those who traveled west survived the trek or found life in the harsh landscape of the West as fulfilling as they had thought; many gave up their land or moved to cities or returned to the East. But by 1910, about 10 percent of the homesteaders west of the Rockies were women. And they were not just tolerated by the territories and frontier states they settled in. By that time, the government had realized that women settlers made good, permanent farmers and businesswomen, and they welcomed them with open arms.

Charley the wise: Many of the women who had traveled west on the wagon trains lived to celebrate when the first women's suffrage laws were passed in Wyoming in 1869 and when Utah gave women the vote in 1870. And at least one woman, Charlotte Parkhurst, found a way to exercise her democratic rights even before it was strictly legal to do so.

Parkhurst traveled west on her own, following the great Gold Rush to California. She had been disguising herself as a man since her teens, when she had dressed as a boy to escape from an orphanage in Massachusetts in the 1840s. She came west as "Charley" in the 1850s and soon established herself as an expert driver for the California Stage Company on some of the most treacherous coach routes in the world to rough frontier towns like Georgetown, Hangton and Coloma.

Parkhurst – who seldom spoke, in order to disguise her harsh, high-pitched voice – soon established a reputation as a capable and unflappable driver. Her silence and courageous handling of her teams earned her the nickname El Sabre, "The Wise One." Parkhurst took runaway horses, hysterical passengers, robbers and tumble-down bridges in her stride. By the time she finally hung up her whip and retired from driving in 1864, she had lost an eye while shoeing a horse, but she was ready to take on a second career: farming. She bought land in the Rancho Soquel Augmentation, where she raised cattle and grew vegetables.

Despite her colorful career as a stagecoach driver, it was not until 1867 – long after she had stopped riding the dusty roads to mining

Her death unleashed a storm of speculation in the press about the reasons for the deception. The subsequent publicity even inspired treasure-hunters to invade her land, searching for any wealth she might have squirreled away or buried. None was found.

Today Parkhurst's successful career as a stagecoach driver is largely forgotten. The significance of Charley Parkhurst's lonely life is summed up in a plaque in Soquel, California, that reads: "On this site on November 3, 1868, was cast the first vote by a woman in California. A ballot by Charlotte (Charley) Parkhurst who disguised herself as a man."

Send for Jane: Unlike Charley Parkhurst,

towns – that Parkhurst made the move that would earn her a place in history. That year she registered and voted in a local and state election – the first female (however well disguised) to do so in California, which would not grant female suffrage until 1911. The next year she voted in a federal election, becoming the first female to vote in such an election since women in New Jersey had lost their vote in 1807.

It wasn't until she died in December of 1879 that it was discovered she was a woman.

Western women on the range (left) and home on the ranch (above).

who claimed the public eye only after her death, Martha "Calamity Jane" Cannary was well known in her own lifetime. In fact, she openly courted publicity, telling a variety of colorful lies that put her in the spotlight throughout the last 25 years of the 19th century. But when the facts are separated from the many fictions that embellish the story of Cannary's life, it's clear that she was more notorious than admirable.

Martha Cannary was born in 1852 (or thereabouts, depending on who was telling the story) near Princeton, Missouri. She claimed to have come west with her family to the gold fields near Virginia City, Montana, in 1865, gaining experience along the way in handling guns and horses. After her parents died, Cannary became a camp follower of the Union Pacific Railroad crews working in what is today southwestern Wyoming.

What she did for the next eight years is anyone's guess, but Cannary had a variety of stories to tell about the interval – including tales of serving as a scout for George Custer at Fort D.A. Russell in 1870 (he never served there) and stories about helping Generals Nelson Miles, Alfred Terry and George Crook fight the Nez Perce in 1872 (also an impossibility, since they were nowhere near each other and the Nez Perce outbreak didn't happen until 1877). We do know that Cannary

August 2, 1876, Cannary was probably genuinely heartbroken. She later claimed to have captured his killer, Jack McCall, but that was nowhere near the truth, either.

The following years found Cannary wandering the Black Hills, working as a sometime letter carrier, bullwhacker, teamster and prostitute in the mining towns. Her hobbies were apparently drinking and fighting. But during the smallpox epidemic of 1878, Cannary earned the respect and gratitude of the whole Black Hills community as well as the nickname "The Black Hills Florence Nightingale" and, perhaps, her better-known sobriquet, Calamity Jane.

As Dora Dufran wrote in her memoirs,

was a scout for General Crook during the 1876 Sioux campaign and that she probably did so dressed as a man.

Most of Cannary's notoriety came about because of her romantic passion for James Butler "Wild Bill" Hickok, whom she met near Abilene, Kansas, around 1870. It seems clear that the two worked together as outriders for a wagon train of prostitutes headed toward the Black Hills mining camp of Deadwood, in what is now South Dakota. But the rumors Cannary spread – that they were lovers, that they had married – were for the most part recognized as falsehoods at the time. When Hickok was gunned down on

Cannary did her best to ease the miners' suffering, nursing them in very primitive conditions: "Her only medicines were epsom salts and cream of tartar... But her good nursing brought five of these men out of the shadow of death, and many more later on, before the disease died out."

According to Dufran, Cannary went wherever in the region there was sickness: "If anyone was sick in camp, it was 'send for Jane'; where Calamity was, there was Jane; and so she was christened Calamity Jane."

There are other, far less flattering explanations given for her new name, however, including the one by historian Watson Parker, who said that many of the men who consorted with Cannary became infected with a type of venereal "calamity."

Followed by the press since her days as the self-proclaimed soul-mate of Wild Bill Hickok, Calamity Jane was soon a dime-novel heroine. At the turn of the century, millions of Americans were reading of her western "adventures" in stories with titles like *The Beautiful Devil of the Yellowstone*. But Calamity Jane never managed to profit from the publicity.

Toward the end of her life, by now a chronic alcoholic who was out of work, Calamity Jane was induced to travel to Buffalo, New York, to participate in a Wild West

than any man. Her name was Annie Oakley, and her skill as a "dead shot" made her a star in Buffalo Bill Cody's Wild West Show. Nellie Cashman, the so-called Angel of Tombstone, was celebrated for her care of down-and-out miners as well as for her own adventures as a prospector. Sarah Winnemucca, a Paiute Indian, became the spokeswoman for her people in their struggle to regain tribal land.

Clara Brown, an ex-slave, used the money she made as a laundress in a Colorado mining town to help other freed slaves start a new life in the West. Narcissa Whitman built a mission in Oregon with her husband, Marcus, and was killed at his side during an Indian

show at the Pan American Exposition. She was a hit in the show for a short time, but then her continual drinking and carousing put a quick end to her career in show business. She returned to the Deadwood area, where she died in 1903 and was buried next to Hickok, as she had requested.

Countless other women left their mark on the Old West – some famous, others virtually unknown. There was an Ohio farm girl, for example, who showed the world that a woman could shoot as well – Hell! much better –

Left, bringing a stray calf back to the herd. **Above**, soon to be born under a wandering star.

attack. And notorious figures like Belle Starr and Cattle Annie proved that women outlaws could raise hell as well as any male desperado.

The American West has always been a proving ground. Over the years, western women have found themselves faced with challenges they never expected – coyotes in the chicken coop, wolves at the door, hostile Indians and inhospitable climates. For most, forging a life in the West was hard, thankless work – establishing homes, raising children, tending crops, and building a sense of community. The kind of work that Skipper Hall of Cody loved.

In John Ford's *The Man Who Shot Liberty Valance,* a senator played by James Stewart confesses to a newspaper editor that for decades he has lived a lie. The senator admits that 30 years earlier he did not actually gun down the sadistic outlaw, an act that launched his political career. Having heard the whole story, the editor tosses away his notes and declares, "This is the West, sir. When the legend becomes fact, print the legend."

Duels in the sun: By the time the film *Liberty Valance* came out in 1962, the makers of Western movies had instinctively followed that creed for nearly 70 years. The West they portrayed was the West of duels in the sun, cavalry charges across desert dreamscapes and savage Indians lined up on ruddy buttes. These films offer little sense of everyday life, just an idealized world where things usually go according to plan: the bad guy embodies evil, while the hero upholds all that is good, reluctantly resorting to violence to right a world gone wrong. It's a simple scheme, one that prevailed in countless B Westerns, the second-billed feature at old-time movie houses. Wildly popular, B movies both influenced the public's image of the West and cemented a perception of the Western as light entertainment.

That perspective disregards the artistry of leading filmmakers from silent-movie star William S. Hart to John Ford and Clint Eastwood. Traditional elements run through their work, but all three take the Western beyond simple formula, an achievement long ignored: Ford won six Academy Awards but none for his Westerns.Only recently, during a minor Western revival, has the genre earned greater respect, especially Kevin Costner's *Dances with Wolves* and Eastwood's *Unforgiven.* Both won Academy Awards for best film – the first Western winners since *Cimarron* 60 years earlier.

Western mythologizing was well under way by the time movies flickered into the public consciousness. Even before the Old West rode off into the sunset for good, 19th-century novels, stage plays and Wild West shows had reshaped it. Film just offered a new medium for an already popular genre.

One of the first movies filmed in Hollywood was also a Western, Cecil B. DeMille's *The Squaw Man* (1913). Originally produced for the stage, *The Squaw Man* played another pivotal role in film history. It launched the film career of actor-director William S. Hart, who won Broadway acclaim in the play as a cowboy named Cash Hawkins.

Hart knew and loved the West. Born in

New York State in 1865, he ventured with his family to the Midwest and grew up playing with Sioux Indian children in the frontier towns where his father worked setting up gristmills. He traveled with his father deep into Sioux Country as well as Kansas and Texas before the family returned east.

After *The Squaw Man,* Hart began getting more Western roles, such as the lead in *The Virginian,* enhancing his cowboy reputation. None other than Bat Masterson touted Hart's portrayal as "a true type of that reckless nomad who flourished on the border when the six-shooter was the final arbiter of all disputes between man and man."

Left, John Wayne, James Stewart and director John Ford on the set of *Liberty Valance.* **Right,** Henry Fonda in *My Darling Clementine,* 1946.

Committed to an honest depiction (and chronically in need of money), Hart had a revelation while watching a Western movie in 1913. Horrified at its inaccuracies, he likened the film to burlesque. But he also recognized that if this movie succeeded, then his truer vision of the West would surely capture movie audiences.

By the time Hart arrived in Hollywood, producers were sounding a death knell for Westerns, one of several times the genre seemed to be on its way to the last roundup. Under film pioneer Thomas Ince's guidance, he began his career, and many credit Hart with reviving the Western. His sober face and hunched, two-gun stance (picture Richard

Nixon with six-shooters) became as famous as Charlie Chaplin's Little Tramp.

Unlike the glossy Tom Mix movies, Hart didn't depict a rhinestone West. His had dust and grit. Wild West shows had popularized flashy western duds, more Liberace than Laramie. Hart righted that image with a plaid shirt, simple kerchief and a vest. He prided himself on his vision and in his autobiography wrote, "My pictures of the West in the early days will make that colorful period of American life live forever."

Western expert William K. Everson agreed with Hart and wrote, "His films were raw, unglamorous, and gutsy... the ramshackle

Western towns and their inhabitants like unretouched Matthew Brady photographs, the sense of dry heat ever present (panchromatic film stock, developed in the 1920s, softened and glamorized the landscapes in later Westerns), and the clouds of dust everywhere." Other directors had wetted the ground for a cleaner look. Considered Hart's masterpiece, *Tumbleweeds* (1925) has a documentary feel, especially the depiction of Oklahoma's Cherokee Strip Land Rush. The pioneers race across the screen with a sense of urgency and danger, on horseback, in wagons, even on bicycles. Filmed by a semi-buried camera, ground-level shots of thundering hooves and wagon wheels mesmerized audiences and became Western classics.

Hart's character declares, "Boys, it's the last of the West," and indeed *Tumbleweeds* proved to be Hart's final film. Hart pioneered the Western hero as a loner, the austere good-bad man who finds purpose and redemption in riding to the rescue. That strict moralistic quality appealed to World War I audiences but seemed heavy-handed by the Roaring Twenties.

Clashing with the studios, Hart retired to his ranch north of Los Angeles. Over the years, a steady stream of notables, including Charles Russell and Will Rogers, visited him at his Spanish-style home. Hart died in 1946 and gave the Newhall estate to Los Angeles County for a museum. In typical Two-Gun Bill fashion, he explained, "While I was making pictures, the people gave me their nickels, dimes, and quarters. When I am gone, I want them to have my home."

Ford Country: There are statues of John Wayne in California; they even named an airport after him. To the public, John Wayne is the Western. But no man dominated the genre like director John Ford. Within the film community, Ford's legend is as big as Wayne's. Ingmar Bergman called him the world's greatest film maker. Orson Welles watched Ford's 1939 *Stagecoach* 40 times and declared his three great influences "John Ford, John Ford, and John Ford."

Born in Maine of Irish immigrants, Ford headed west following the Hollywood acting success of his brother Francis. As he explained in an interview with Peter Bogdanovich, he got his chance when a director failed to show for a big scene the same morning that Universal Studios chief

Carl Laemmle visited the lot. Someone needed to look in charge, so Ford took control of the action, ultimately burning down the street in a scene he described as "more pogrom than Western." Later, when a new film needed a director, Laemmle said, "Give Jack Ford the job. He yells good."

Yelling good and using his sharp eye for composition, Ford first directed silent two-reelers, then moved on to some of the earliest Western epics, most notably *The Iron Horse* (1924). Like Hart, Ford sought authenticity. He often consulted old-timers and eschewed quick-draw duels and showy costumes. Ford met Wyatt Earp on the back lot a few times and based his 1946 O.K. Corral tale *My*

grown into a kind of holy trinity of the classic Western. But the West they portrayed was one of considerable complexity. The early Wayne is as different from the icon Duke of later years as Hound Dog Elvis is from Vegas Elvis. Jane Tompkins in *West of Everything* writes, "The expression of the young John Wayne is tender… Pure and sweet…"

Ford cast Wayne in the roles of men with clashing emotions and loyalties, such as the cavalry officer who is torn between obedience to his commanding officer and his better judgment in *Fort Apache*. And the classic Monument Valley films often ended ambiguously, allowing audiences to reach conflicting conclusions, something that could

Will Rogers ~

Darling Clementine on Earp's accounts, although by that time the old gunfighter was definitely printing the legend, not the facts.

Ford rode out to locations and slept under the stars during shooting. In 1938, he headed out to a more distant location, Monument Valley, to film his first sound Western, *Stagecoach*, starring John Wayne. Dubbed "Ford Country," the valley and its towering red rock formations evolved into a trademark.

Ford, Wayne and Monument Valley have

"When the legend becomes fact, print the legend." Left, silent-film star Tom Mix. Above, cowboy philosopher and film star Will Rogers.

never happen in good guy-bad guy Westerns.

In *Fort Apache*, Henry Fonda plays the commanding officer, a martinet who leads his troops on a suicidal charge against Apaches. Based on Custer's last stand, the film feels almost like a Vietnam-vintage attack on military incompetence. But as the movie closes, Wayne, whose advice Fonda disastrously ignored, tells myth-seeking reporters of the officer's heroism and eulogizes, "No man died more gallantly."

Critics chastise Ford for his depictions of Indians as bloodthirsty marauders. Certainly in *Stagecoach* they appear as anonymous killers, while in *The Searchers* (1956), the white women captured by Indians have gone insane. Wayne's character is even ready to shoot his captive niece, the one he spent seven years searching for, declaring, "Living with Comanches ain't being alive." Yet in *Fort Apache*, Cochise appears as the man of reason, and it is Fonda who displays the bloodlust and bigotry that draw the Indians into reluctant battle.

"Let's face it," Ford told Bogdanovich, "we've treated them very badly – it's a blot on our shield; we've cheated and robbed, killed, murdered, massacred and everything else, but they kill one white man and, God, out come the troops."

Certainly, if you've seen one Ford film,

the social pressures of the 1960s, Westerns underwent major changes. The lilting cavalry song that accompanied an Indian surrender in *The Searchers* was used to ironic effect behind a scene of slaughter in *Little Big Man* (1969). And the new Western man had as much Liberty Valance in him as he did John Wayne.

He smoked a foul little Italian cigar, wore a poncho, sported stubble and a scowl. He was Clint Eastwood as The Man With No Name in a trilogy of mid-1960s Westerns shot in Spain by Italian director Sergio Leone.

The low-budget Spaghetti Westerns helped revive the genre at a time when big-money American epics had bombed. Eastwood told

you haven't seen them all. Ford's West was one of shadings, not unlike the changing play of natural light and shadow found in his movies. It reflects the man himself, who could charm his actors or, as he did to Wayne, reduce them to tears. As James Stewart said of the director, "Take everything you've heard, everything you've ever heard and multiply it about a hundred times – and you still won't have a picture of John Ford."

The Man With No Name: Ford filmed his final Western in 1964. John Wayne continued making Westerns until 1976 and won an Oscar for his portrayal of Marshal Rooster Cogburn in *True Grit* (1969). But reflecting

Kenneth Turan of the *Los Angeles Times,* "When I first went and did *A Fistful of Dollars*, there were a lot of predictions in the trade papers that Westerns were through. And I said, 'Swell, now that I'm doing one they're through,' but that film turned out to have its place in the world."

Eastwood is not exclusively a Western actor, but his career follows some of the genre's trends. His break came in the modern equivalent of a B picture, the television show *Rawhide,* where he played the amicable Rowdy Yates. His appearance in the musical *Paint Your Wagon* evoked the heyday of Roy Rogers and the singing cowboys.

But The Man With No Name had no Hollywood precedent. He subscribed to no moral code like William S. Hart's characters. He and his cohorts did what they had to do in order to survive in a moral and physical desert. In *The Good, The Bad, and The Ugly*, the Eastwood character kills three men before the audience even sees his face – then takes the man he saved captive so he can collect the bounty.

Cynical loner: In an essay on Eastwood the actor, writer Jim Miller describes the character as "a cynical loner at a time when the mood of the country was shaped in much the same line of thought… he brought a whole new look at the Western hero as a lone

Wolves, a kind of New Age eco-Western, stunned Hollywood with its success and launched a revival that had everyone from rapper Tone Loc to party girl Drew Barrymore back in the saddle again. And after years of waiting, Eastwood decided that he had aged enough to portray reformed killer William Munny in *Unforgiven.*

Now a widower and hog farmer, Munny tries to convince himself that he is truly a changed man, even as he heads out again as a bounty hunter. He struggles with almost everything – his past, his horse and his shooting – and looks as weary as The Man With No Name looked invincible. When his young partner asks him about what the Old-

wolf, anti-hero that was totally different than characters John Wayne played."

Westerns declined steadily during the 1970s and 1980s; Eastwood went nearly 10 years without making one after he directed and starred in the modern classic *The Outlaw Josey Wales* (1976). In 1980, one of the biggest movie bombs of all time, *Heaven's Gate*, convinced Hollywood that, finally, Westerns were truly dead.

In the early 1990s, Costner's *Dances with*

West days were like, Munny replies, "I can't remember. I was drunk most of the time."

Every murder has its consequences, and Eastwood demythologizes killers and sheriffs alike by exposing the fictions of a reporter who would twist their exploits into the kind of dime novels that inspired Westerns in the first place. As in *Liberty Valance*, the genre has turned in on itself, exposing its own false origins. In 1992, Eastwood told a *Los Angeles Times* reporter that *Unforgiven* would be his final Western. "Maybe that's why I didn't do it right away. I was kind of savoring it as the last of that genre, maybe the last film of that type for me."

<u>Left</u>, Monument Valley, seen here in *Stagecoach*, is the backdrop in countless Westerns. <u>Above</u>, Clint Eastwood as The Man With No Name.

THE WRITER AND THE WEST
SPONSORED BY LEVI STRAUSS & Cº
JULY 5 – 8, 1978
AT THE SUN VALLEY CENTER
FOR THE ARTS & HUMANITIES
SUN VALLEY, IDAHO

"When you call me that, smile." That laconic expression won literary immortality upon its publication in 1902. The words were spoken by a slim young giant of a man who could lasso a horse and charm a woman with equal ease. He was called, simply, The Virginian. And once he had ridden into the literature of the American West, that literature would never be the same.

Written by Owen Wister – no frontier scribe but a Harvard-educated lawyer who, like his friend Teddy Roosevelt, ventured west to escape personal troubles – *The Virginian* was an immediate best-seller, going through sixteen printings in its first year. And it helped establish what later became hoary Western clichés. Its hero is unlettered but possessed of natural wisdom, courage and eloquence. This sagebrush Galahad finds his Guinevere in a schoolmarm newly arrived from the East; she is standoffish at first but quickly won over to western ways. *The Virginian* has it all: a conniving villain, a showdown at sundown, and a happy ending in which Virginian and schoolmarm marry to form the new aristocracy of a tamed but still noble West.

Cowboys, but no cows: *The Virginian* was the first Western to garner both mass popularity and critical respectability. But for decades, Western stories had been popular if raffishly unrespectable. Starting in the 1860s, publisher Erastus Beadle began churning out dime novels – 30,000-word books clad in orange bindings that sold for a princely 10¢. Beadle and his fellow dime-novel publishers took Industrial Revolution concepts of mass production and applied them to literature. Writers cranked out a thousand words an hour on twelve-hour shifts; one Beadle writer produced some 600 books over the course of his career. Needless to say, such assembly-line methods created little in the way of lasting literature. Nor did works like *Deadwood Dick of Deadwood* or *Calamity Jane, The Heroine of Whoop-Up* have much to say about the actual ways people made a living in the frontier West. As Texas writer J. Frank Dobie once noted, these cowboy stories are notable for their absence of cows. Why should characters spend time driving cattle when there were sinister Indians to be battled in hand-to-hand combat and mysterious underground cities of gold to seek?

In the universe of the dime novel, fiction was stranger than truth – and in some cases, strange fiction became even stranger truth. William F. Cody was a 23-year-old stagecoach driver and occasional buffalo hunter,

no more noteworthy than a thousand other young men set loose on the western plains after the Civil War. But in 1869 a writer named Ned Buntline came to Kansas from New York looking for material for newspaper articles, and he found it in Cody. Soon "Buffalo Bill" Cody's exploits were thrilling Manhattan readers, and before long Cody himself was the star of his own Wild West show. By the end of his life, Cody had been the hero of 200 dime novels, and it was said that even he could no longer determine where his real life ended and his myth began.

Nor was Cody the only ne'er-do-well transformed into a Western legend. Martha

Left, the fastest fingers in the West. **Right**, Dustin Farnum in a stage version of Owen Wister's classic book *The Virginian*.

Cannary was a washerwoman and sometime prostitute who liked to ride, shoot and drink. But as the dime novelist's Calamity Jane, she was a virtuous Amazon whose hard-bitten exterior concealed a heart of gold. Like Cody, Jane starred in Wild West shows and came to believe her own publicity, although by the end of her life she had wearied of the role: she demanded that the world "leave me alone and let me go to hell my own route."

The era of the dime novels ended in the 1920s. But readers' fascination with the Old West did not. An Ohio dentist named Zane Grey (his given name was Pearl, but he wisely changed it) traveled west and came back with the phenomenally successful *Rid-*

ers of the Purple Sage. By the end of his life Grey had published 78 books, and his readership numbered in the tens of millions. His successor, Max Brand (the pen name of Frederick Schillder Faust), was nearly as prolific: the creator of *Destry Rides Again* published some 30 million words.

Americans weren't the only people who lapped up Western stories like cattle at a water hole. Europeans loved a good cowboy story, too, although they put their own continental spin on the tales. German author Karl May's hero, Old Shatterhand, appeared in 20 novels and became a favorite of Germans from Albert Einstein to Adolf Hitler. In France, the Western novels of Gustave Aimard featured a hero, Valentine Guillois, whose Parisian savvy proved more than a match for the uncouth Yanks and Mexicans and Indians he battled in the Southwest.

Asking big questions: Whether written in English or French or German, these printed horse operas set many readers' pulses racing. But an awful lot of the real-life West and Westerners' lives were ignored or reduced to cliché or stereotype.

Where was western writing that might prove to be enduring literature? As early as the 1870s, humorists Bret Harte and Mark Twain showed that the West could be mined for humor as profitably as it could be mined for gold. Twain's "The Celebrated Jumping Frog of Calaveras County" and Harte's "The Outcasts of Poker Flat" remain rollicking good reads today. Serious fiction took longer to develop. Hamlin Garland depicted the harsh lives of prairie farmers in his 1891 work, *Main-Travelled Roads.* Two decades later, Willa Cather painted a more hopeful picture of prairie life in *O Pioneers* and *My Antonia*, although her last great novel – *Death Comes for the Archbishop* – takes place in Spanish New Mexico.

California supplied the setting for two vivid depictions of clashing ethnic groups and economic classes. Helen Hunt Jackson was a popular novelist passionately stirred by the mistreatment of Southern California's Indians; her response was the 1884 best-seller *Ramona.* It became the *Gone with the Wind* of its day, although Jackson lamented that readers concentrated too much on her sentimental descriptions of California rancho life and ignored her pleas for better treatment of Native Americans. More tough-minded was Frank Norris's 1901 novel, *The Octopus,* a fierce account of warfare between California wheat growers and the powerful Southern Pacific Railroad.

Once 20th-century writers began looking seriously at the western past and present, even the clichés – cowboys and Indians, fur trappers and cattle barons – got a good going-over. In *The Ox-Bow Incident*, Nevada writer Walter Van Tilburg Clark turned the idea of frontier justice on its head, as a western posse hangs three innocent men. But more traditional stories also retained their appeal. When author Louis L'Amour died, for example, nearly 200 million copies of his works were in print. Unlike most of his predecessors, L'Amour prided himself on accuracy. He also demanded that the Western novel be taken seriously as a genre.

Probably no 20th-century western writer had a more distinguished career than novelist and essayist Wallace Stegner. Proud that his collected fiction – more than a dozen novels and numerous short stories – contained no more than one or two cowboys, Stegner nonetheless populated his work with a varied collection of western characters, from the hardscrabble family portrayed in *Big Rock Candy Mountain* to the well-bred artist Susan Ward who is the tragic heroine of *Angle of Repose*. And in essays like *The Sound of Mountain Water*, Stegner asked and tried to answer the big questions about his region. What is the West? What makes it different? What makes it valuable?

Today's writers on the American West are still pondering those questions. Texas-born Larry McMurtry has ventured all over the territory with novels that range from sardonic accounts of ranch life (*Horseman, Pass By* – later filmed as *Hud*) to a rootin'-tootin' western saga, *Lonesome Dove*, which won a Pulitzer Prize. In recent books, McMurtry explores the gap between dime-novel legend and western reality: in *Anything for Billy*, he takes on Billy the Kid; in *Buffalo Girls*, Calamity Jane, Wild Bill Hickok and Buffalo Bill are shown as aging has-beens.

Other contemporary writers have also spurred fresh horses over familiar trails. In *Desperadoes* and *The Assassination of Jesse James by the Coward Robert Ford*, Ron Hansen paints the world of the Dalton Gang and the James Brothers with an elegant prose reminiscent of Fitzgerald. In *All The Pretty Horses* and *The Crossing*, Cormac McCarthy has written two Western novels whose complexity rivals that of William Faulkner.

Perhaps the most heartening development in contemporary Western writing is the inclusion of voices not often heard around the literary campfire before. These new writers of the purple sage include Native Americans, Latinos and women. Thomas Sanchez's *Rabbit Boss* is a harrowing novel that follows the misfortunes of California's Washoe

Indians. Kiowa author N. Scott Momaday earned a Pulitzer Prize for his *House Made of Dawn*, a fictionalized account of the tribe's historic passage from Yellowstone to the Great Plains and its decimation at the hands of the US Cavalry. Leslie Marmon Silko's *Ceremony* depicts a half-breed World War II veteran struggling to make a life for himself on the Laguna reservation. A member of the Blackfoot and Gros Ventre tribes, writer James Welch has focused on Indian life in *Winter in the Blood*, *The Death of Jim Loney*, *Fool's Crow* and *The Indian Lawyer*. And New Mexico writer Tony Hillerman triumphantly combines both Western and detective genres in novels featuring Navajo Tribal

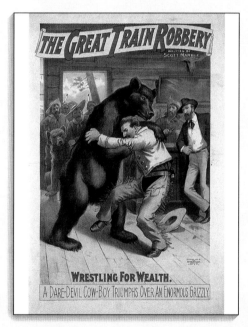

WRESTLING FOR WEALTH.
A Dare-Devil Cow-Boy Triumphs Over An Enormous Grizzly.

Police officers Joe Leaphorn and Jim Chee.

With these writers the literature of the West has galloped a long way from the world of *The Virginian*, and even farther from the dime-novel exploits of Buffalo Bill Cody. The West no longer looks as simple as it once did. Villains who once glowered in black hats may now be the good guys wearing white. But the best of today's writers still know the power of a good yarn. They still portray a handsome, outsized land where an individual's destiny, heroic or tragic or both, counts for more than it might in some crowded eastern city. The literature of the American West still has the power to awe and entertain.

Tony Hillerman, author of this chapter, is the best-selling writer of more than a dozen books, including a series of popular mystery novels featuring Navajo Tribal Police officers.

When I was a boy, the neighbor we called Old Man Mann was already very old. And the song he most liked to sing in his cracked, breathy old voice was much older. He'd learned it, so he said, when he was a boy himself from his daddy's older brother in the Wyoming cow country.

All year o'er the prairies alone I do ride,
Not even a hound-dog to run at my side.
My fire I do kindle from chips gathered round
To boil up my coffee from beans that ain't ground.
My ceiling's the sky, my carpet's the grass
My music's the sound of the herds as they pass.
My books are the creeks, and my sermons the stones,
My parson's a wolf on a pulpit of bones.

There were a dozen other verses and a dozen other songs. But the messages were pretty much the same. They were songs of self-reliance and loneliness; of a hard life and a free one; of men who were crude, tough and unlettered, but nevertheless unfailingly chivalrous.

Old Man Mann's songs were cowboy songs, for he'd spent much of his 78 years in the cow business. My mother's repertoire represented the other side of the frontier coin. Her family had come to Oklahoma when the last of the great American land rushes opened Indian Territory to settlement; and as a girl she had held her own homestead in Beaver County. Hers were the songs of the sodbusters.

My clothes are all ragged, my bedding is rough.
My bread is corn dodgers, rock solid and tough;
But yet I am happy, and live at my ease
On sorghum molasses, sowbelly and cheese.

Left, Thomas Eakins' *Home Ranch*, 1888. **Right**, where the buffalo roam and the deer and the antelope play.

Goodby to Greer County, where blizzards arise
Where the sun never sinks and a flea never dies,
And the wind never ceases, but always remains
Till it starves us to death on our government claims.

Different as they were, both were the genuine songs of the West. In their different ways each represented the sort of poetry that the frontier produced – a folk music that re-

flected the harsh, grim, hungry reality of an inhospitable land.

The gorgeous lie: The same might well be said of the folklore of the American West. The folktales usually represent ways found to live with discomfort either by exaggerating deprivation to the point of humor or defying it with tall-tale heroes twice as romantic as Ivanhoe and ten times as powerful.

Some folklore grew out of fun in a country where the gorgeous lie became an art form. And some of it grew out of reality – the metamorphosis of real people and real events into giants and mythic adventures. There was Davy Crockett, real enough to serve in

Congress when he lived in Tennessee. When he moved west into Texas and died at the Alamo, however, he and Jim Bowie became nine feet tall and full of magic.

Crockett helped build his own legend with his books of frontier humor, but other flesh-and-blood figures became word-of-mouth myths long before writing men discovered them. Some were good men, some were – by any sane man's definition – genuinely bad. And some, like Kit Carson, were human enough to be both.

Pecos Bill, who was purely a product of imagination and who could put his saddle on a tornado, was not much less potent in legend than Sam Bass, who started his career as a

cowboy, ended it as a bank and train robber, and lives on in western song as a sort of Robin Hood in chaps.

Even Black Jack Ketchum, a bandito of monumental stupidity, became glamorized by the myth-makers. They don't mention that he was captured because he persisted in robbing exactly the same train at exactly the same hill outside Folsom, New Mexico. After he was hanged at Clayton (with a drop so long that his head popped off) the guitar pickers of the day promptly converted him into an Anglo-Saxon Zorro.

The land, the weather and the animals were all equally subject to this myth-making

process. There are tales of the Montana wind which blew so persistently from the north that it rolled up an entire county like a rug. North of El Paso where the shifting dunes of the Chihuahua Desert spread northward into New Mexico, one hears a legend of two cowboys who rode out of town after a sandstorm, stopped to pick up a hat from a sand dune, and found a man's head under it. When they brushed the sand away from his face, he's reputed to have said: "Get a shovel. I'm horseback."

Gusty tales: Windwagon Thomas, on the other hand, was real enough, as are the newspaper reports of his organizing the Overland Navigation Company at Westport Landing, Missouri, to manufacture "sailing wagons" to haul freight over the Santa Fe Trail. Thomas purportedly sailed a small experimental wagon almost 300 miles from Westport to Council Grove in 1853 with no power but the wind. He then built a mammoth freight wagon (480 km) with a 20-foot (6-meter) mast and a tiller which turned its back wheels. The demonstration of this prairie schooner reportedly suffered because Thomas was too drunk to navigate.

His bankers thereupon withdrew their financing and Thomas, legend tells us, sailed away alone across the prairie with only his jug. He became a sort of Flying Dutchman of the sea of grass – turning up now and then in the tales told by startled Plains Indians but seen no more by white men.

Other wind tales vary from the slightly plausible to the downright gusty. They range from the flight of snow geese hung suspended in the sky over North Dakota from daylight to dusk, unable to gain an inch against the headwind, to the "crowbar holes" beside the back doors of Nebraska farm homes. Folklore has Nebraskans sticking an iron bar through the hole to serve as a wind gauge. If it only bends, the wind isn't too strong for a safe exit.

In the northern climes, the cold, too, is the subject of folklore. One hears of fur-bearing trout in the headwaters of the Yellowstone, and of lakes freezing so fast that frogs are left to spend the winter with their heads stuck out of the ice. Behind even this sort of hyperbole lie some dramatic facts. Temperatures as low as 60 degrees below zero (-51° C) have been recorded in the high Rocky Mountain valleys; 76 inches of snow actually fell in a single day at Silver Lake, Colorado; in 1921, Coffeyville, Kansas, weighed out a pound-and-a-half hailstone; and 1,014 inches of snow (enough to cover an eight-story building) fell on Mount Rainier in Washington in the winter of 1970–71.

It is also supposed to be dead-true that the Number 3 freight of the Denver & Salt Lake Railroad managed to get lost in a blizzard between Denver and points west – the eastbound Number 2 freight completing the journey without meeting it. Number 3, it seems, left the ice-coated rails near Granby, Colorado, and skidded three quarters of a mile up a frozen highway before coming to a halt, all traction gone, on the main street of living room with the other furnishings left undisturbed inside the house.

Blessed rain: The drought, of course, was always a natural part of the West. And folk songs celebrate it.

My cornmeal is weevily, my sorghum's gone bad
Kinfolks have ate up what little I had.
That God has forgot me has give me some pain,
But now he's forgot how to make it to rain.

In Nebraska there's the tale of a settler determined to grow a vegetable garden. He planted it in a wagon bed filled with topsoil and wore out a dozen teams of horses chasing rain clouds all summer. The mythology

the town. Tracks had to be built to get the train back on the main line.

Tornadoes form their own body of folklore and songs across the old buffalo plains, with some of the most incredible incidents being true. One hears of wheat straws driven through bricks, of babies being sucked out of their nurseries and discovered miles away still tucked neatly in their cribs, of fish being whirled out of ponds, of chickens being denuded of feathers but left otherwise unharmed, of carpets being whipped out of a

Left, Spanish-style songstress. **Above**, spinning yarns near Matador, Texas, *circa* 1907.

of the dry country is full of signs, portents and symbols that foretell the coming of the blessed thunderstorm. The early-morning howling of coyotes is a good sign, as is the misty "ring around the moon." Throughout the West, farmers and cattlemen alike know that flies swarming around the doors of their houses mean a storm is coming, as does the sight of chickens "oiling" their feathers, rising moisture levels in the dry sand of a creek bed, dirt around the mouth of a prairie-dog den, or unusually large numbers of fireflies glowing in the nocturnal woods.

Farmers, of course, were most directly affected by the endless drought. But ranchers were not immune. A song entitled "The Cowman's Prayer," current in the 1880s, included a plea that the Lord "water the land" and "provide a little snow," in addition to stopping the drought-caused range fires. The prayer, the very model of materialism, also has the cowman telling the Lord: "I think at least five cents a pound, Should be the price of beef year round."

There is a similar body of folklore and song about the fauna of the West. The buffalo, not surprisingly, provided a mass of legends. What is surprising is that so many of them were so obviously erroneous. For example, it was widely believed that bison were dangerous animals. As a matter of fact,

they tended to be less dangerous than range cattle – having a sensible fear of men and a tendency to attack only if desperate after flight had failed.

Among other popular buffalo beliefs: That they were afraid of white men but tended to congregate around Indian encampments. (As a matter of fact, Indians tended to congregate around buffalo.) That buffalo steak, heart, liver, etc. would cure rheumatism (or tuberculosis, jaundice, cancer, etc.) That buffalo bulls gallantly formed patrols to guard the rear of moving herds. And that buffalo were migratory animals – like the arctic caribou – moving south for the winter and north for the

summer. It's said that a homesteader in the Oklahoma Panhandle tamed two buffalo cows and trained them to pull his plow. When migration time arrived, they headed north, plowing a furrow all the way across Kansas and Nebraska.

The folktales of the West also involve a myriad of other animals. The rattlesnake, naturally, is the hero of hundreds of legends and bits of lore – ranging from the ridiculous (that he sets aside his poison sacs before taking a drink of water to avoid poisoning himself) to the sublime (that, when injured, enraged or tired of life, he will commit suicide by biting himself). Thomas Hart Benton reported being told by a cowboy that when shooting at rattlers one always hits the snake in the head because they strike at the approaching bullet.

Wolves, and their cousins the coyotes, are legendary in the West for their intelligence. Jim Bridger, the famous real-life mountain man and yarn-spinner, is credited with reporting that he once escaped a pack of timber wolves by climbing an aspen. The wolves left a guard to watch Bridger and went away. A little later they returned with a beaver which set about cutting down the aspen. It's a matter of legend that a wolf, locally known as Old Reddy and credited with killing several thousand sheep, was publicly executed in the town square at San Marcos, Texas, after being snared.

Cunning coyote: A whole literature has grown up around the coyote, who has proven himself even smarter than big brother wolf by flourishing while the lobo was decimated. The Indians almost universally admire him for his cunning, and the Navajos – who, like him, have thrived while other tribes vanish – rate Coyote as one of the Holy People. He emerged from their underworld with equal status with First Man and First Woman and a better reputation for brains.

Non-Indian westerners, including such literary types as Charles Loomis, credit him with the powers of ventriloquism – insisting that he's the only animal on earth with the ability to make his voice seem to come from where he is not.

Folklore also credits him with the ability to communicate complex messages, warnings and summons, not just by his famous warbling voice, but through such devices as leaving scents at predesignated places, and through message relays from one coyote to another.

But no animal rates the attention western song gives to the horse. For example, there's the Zebra Dun, which like most genuine folk-song horses is named for the pattern and color of its coat.

Old Dunny was a rocky outlaw that had grown so awful wild
That he could paw the white out of the moon every jump for a mile.
Old Dunny stood still – as if he didn't know
Until he was saddled and ready for to go.
When the stranger hit the saddle, old Dunny quit the earth
And traveled right straight up for all that he was worth.

picture with Hollywood movies. About as close to affection as one can find in the genuine article is that universal favorite named "Old Paint," which used to be sung to waltz music.

Goodby, Old Paint, I'm a-leavin' Cheyenne,
Goodby, Old Paint, I'm a-leavin' Cheyenne,
Old Paint's a good pony, he paces when he can;
Good morning, young lady, my hosses won't stand...

and so forth.

In general the attitude of the genuine cowboy toward his several horses was similar to that of the truck driver toward his trucks – it depended solely upon performance. And he

A-pitching and a-squealing, a-having wall-eyed fits,
His hind feet perpendicular, his front one by the bit.

One can search both folklore and song without finding a trace of sentiment – unless frustration, respect and hostility are classed under that word – of a cowboy for his mount. The business of cowboys talking to horses (except in oaths and imprecations) and having a palsy-walsy relationship entered the

Left, old time fiddler, northern New Mexico. **Above**, bluebonnets and a belle strumming a Texas tune.

knew the animal, its notorious neuroses and stupidities, far too well to credit it with the sort of unnatural intelligence western folklore sometimes granted to more mysterious animals. The superhorse was a product of show business, the medicine tent, and the age in which ponies became pets.

There was, of course, at least one exception to the rule. The Superhorse of western folk myth was either all white, or white with black ears. He was first reduced to print by Washington Irving, who reported the tales he had heard on the Cimarron River in his *Tour of the Prairies*. The same sort of tales about a mystical white horse were noted by the other famous reporter of the early frontier, Josiah Gregg, in his classic *Commerce of the Prairies*.

Gregg reported hearing various accounts of the more or less phantom stallion told from the northern Rockies all the way down to Texas. Like Irving's, Gregg's white horse was a fabulous pacer – easily able to outdistance flesh-and-blood nags running at full gallop without breaking out of his disciplined stride.

Three race horses were once brought to his grazing ground to pursue him in relays, but the Phantom Pacer was too fast to be captured by anything but the western imagination.

But the horses of western story and song

that ate barbed wire and drank nitroglycerin, there were a thousand nameless animals like the "old gray hack padded down with a gunny sack" which caused the hero of a ballad called "The Horse Wrangler" to offer his classic advice:

Before you try cow-punching, kiss your wife,
Take a heavy insurance on your life,
Then cut your throat with a barlow knife.

The gritty, hardscrabble life of the cowboy, logger, miner and settler is reflected in the best of this oral tradition. They came, many of them, out of the Civil War: refugees from the ruins of the Confederacy or uprooted Yankees looking for something better

were more typically like "Freckles" who, the folk song tells us, "was little and peaked and thin," and notable only "for single and double cussedness and for double fired sin." In other words, the myths tended to be based on real life.

Rebels and ramblers: Exactly the same could be said for the central subject of it all, the human male. There were the supermen – the Paul Bunyans (he seems to have been created to promote a timber company) and the Pecos Bills (another late-comer of doubtful authenticity), but such omnipotence was as rare among folklore males as it was among folklore mounts. For every Widow-Maker

than the exhausted land of New England. They were pioneers, but they were also vagabonds and exiles:

O Mollie, O Mollie, it is for your sake alone,
That I leave my old parents, my house and my home,
That I leave my old parents, you've caused me to roam –
I am a rabble soldier and Dixie is my home.

The West was a place of escape. For some, like John Murray, who left his home "to dodge the ball and chain," it was a matter of necessity. For others, like "The Good Old

Rebel," it was more or less a matter of personal choice:

I won't be reconstructed! I'm better now than then;
And for a carpet-bagger, I don't give a damn.
So I'm off for the frontier, as soon as I can go,
I'll prepare me a weapon and start for Mexico.
For I'm a good old rebel, that's what I am
And for the Constitution, I don't give a damn.

But generally they were simply "rambling boys" chasing romance and the American dream. Their lore reported, sometimes with

Before I turned, the spirit had left him
And gone to the Giver – the cowboy was dead.
We beat the drum slowly and played the fife lowly,
And bitterly wept as we bore him along;
For we all loved our comrade, so brave,
We all loved our comrade although he'd done wrong.

Mostly it was much less dramatic. Mostly it was the way it was with that anonymous owner of the "ten-dollar horse and forty-dollar saddle" who helped take the 2-U herd up the "Old Chisholm Trail." At the end of this ordeal of storm and stampede, bad food and worse weather, the cowboy reports:

sentiment, sometimes with humor, what they found, as in this song, the most beautiful in America, named "The Streets of Laredo:"

It was once in the saddle I used to go dashing,
It was once in the saddle I used to go gay;
First to the dram-house, and then to the card-house;
Got shot in the breast, I am dying today.
Go bring me a cup, a cup of cold water,
To cool my parched lips, the cowboy said;

I went to my boss to draw my roll.
He had me figured out nine dollars in the hole.
I'll sell my outfit just as soon as I can.
I won't punch cattle for any damn man.

But there's a final, epilogue verse:
With my knees in the saddle and my seat in the sky,
I'll quit punching cows in the sweet by and by
Coma ti yi yippy yippy ya, yippy ya
Coma ti yi yippy yippy ya.

And that pretty much sums up the way it must have been.

Charlie Siringo was one tough cowpoke who never flinched at the hardships the West presented him. And yet, when he lost the red silk sash he wore around his waist, and had to slap on suspenders for the first time in his life, he was heard to confess, "It almost broke my heart."

Proper garb: Charlie's complaint demonstrates the importance of proper garb to the men who rode the West. Clothes may or may not make the man, but in the days of the cattle kingdom they assuredly made the cowboy. Why, without his broad-brimmed hat and narrow-toed boots, a cowboy might easily be confused with a sheepherder or farmer or some other lesser form of life.

Proudly clad in such items, though, the cowboy approached the status of a legend. Small wonder that as soon as he hit town after a few months driving cattle, one of his first stops was to an emporium like Jacob Karatofsky's Great Western Store in Abilene, or Meyer Goldsoll's Old Reliable House in Ellsworth, Kansas, to outfit himself with a set of handsome new duds.

Like the cowboy himself, cowboy clothing had its roots in New Spain: early cowboys wore the sombreros, cotton pants and shirt and short jacket akin to those worn by the *vaqueros* of Spanish California and Texas. But just as the *vaquero* was Americanized into the "buckaroo," so too was the cowboy's clothing on the plains of Texas or the Dakotas. Take that sombrero, for example: cowboys driving cattle long distances across the prairie found that they needed a headpiece that could better shelter them from the blazing western sun. So the cowboy hat developed, with its broader brim (3 to 5 inches was usual) and higher crown.

Although many westerners made cowboy hats, its true godfather was an eastern hatmaker named John Batterson Stetson. Legend has it that Stetson visited Colorado in 1865 and, as he sat around a campfire with some friends, produced a hat from beaver and rabbit felt. A passing cowboy saw the

product and was so impressed with it that he offered Stetson $5 on the spot. Sensing potential success, Stetson returned to Philadelphia and began manufacturing his new hats, then hurriedly shipped them back west. He met with almost immediate success.

One Stetson model, "The Boss of the Plains," fully lived up to its grandiloquent title, becoming the most popular cowboy hat in the cattle kingdom; his mammoth "Carlsbad" model (the lofty topper Hoss Cartwright wore on the *Bonanza* television

series) was nearly as popular. By the turn of the century, the Stetson company employed some 3,500 workers and produced 2 million hats a year.

The cowboy hat's popularity was deserved, for here was a chapeau with a multitude of uses. Its wide brim shaded the face, its high crown kept the head relatively cool. Hats that were made from best quality beaver felt could even hold water, their headbands letting them retain their shape when wet. That headband, too, had its uses: if made from rattlesnake skin it was said to work wonders against headaches.

No less important than the hat was the

Left, cowgirl in fancy duds. **Right,** Josephine "Chicago Joe" Hensley, madam of a Montana brothel, in respectable Victorian dress.

cowboy boot. Among the most famous bootsmiths was H.J. Justin, who worked at a barbershop in Spanish Fort, Texas. Justin began repairing boots for the cowboys coming off the trail to get haircuts; soon he was making them new boots, too. He did the job so well that he was able to start his own business, and for much of the 19th century the word "Justin" was almost synonymous with "boot" on the southern plains.

As anyone who has strolled long distances in them knows, cowboy boots were not made for walking – try it, and they'll seem a painful piece of shoe engineering indeed. But they were extremely well-designed for life on horseback. The high leather

example, the bandanna, or wild rag, which could be used to soak up sweat, block dust and keep the cowboy's face warm at night. As for pants, in 1853 a man named Levi Strauss stitched his first pair of trousers for miners in the California goldfields; it took a few years before he started riveting the denim and dying the material blue, and a few more years for the product to take on the name "blue jeans."

It's in the jeans: Those Levis eventually set the standard for what cowboys wanted in a pair of pants. They were tight, to obviate the need for the suspenders that Charlie Siringo hated, and they had pockets placed in front, so objects wouldn't slide out when the

tops shielded the wearer from brush and rocks, the boots' sharp heels steadied him during roping.

Pointed toes helped the cowboy slip easily into the stirrup, and the high heels prevented his feet from slipping forward once there. Simple and plain at first, the cowboy boot soon acquired some decorative edges, as Justin and other boot makers began stitching Lone Stars, longhorns and other designs into the leather. Plain or decorative, a first-quality cowboy boot came at a considerable price: $25 or so in the 1880s, almost a month's pay for a working cowboy.

There were other cowboy essentials – for

cowboy hunkered down around the roaring campfire. But sometimes the pants did not go out alone: instead, over them, the cowboy would wear tidy leather chaps – from the Spanish *chaparrejos* – britches that protected his legs from thorns and brush.

Although we think of cowboy garb as classic and immutable, over the years hats and boots and other staples have changed with the cowboy's preferences. As cowboy and author W.S. James conceded, "the cowboy has his flights of fancy as clearly defined as the most fashionable French belle." Pants were first tucked into boots, then left outside. The colder weather of the northern plains required heavier clothing than did Texas, so Montana cowboys favored wool rather than cotton shirts and pants and vests, and an oilskin slicker to ward off the snow and rain. Even the Montana hat was different: cowboys found that they had a harder time keeping their hats on their heads in the stronger northern winds, so Montana cowboys took to favoring hats with a more narrow brim.

Show biz: And eventually, show business – Wild West shows and rodeos and personal appearances and motion pictures – had an influence on what was worn on the open range. Cowboys began tentatively experimenting with more gaudily stitched shirts,

maker Cosimo Lucchese is supposed to have sighed: "We used to make boots to fit a stirrup. Now we make them to fit the gas pedal of a Cadillac." Ah, well. Real cowboys still wear the stuff, too. And all across the West craftsmen continue to make customized hats and boots more or less as they were made a hundred years ago.

What do you look for in a cowboy hat or boot? The gold standard for the cowboy hat remains the beaver fur felt model, which is rated by Xs: a 30X beaver hat contains a higher proportion of dense, high-quality beaver fur felt than does a 10X beaver hat, and costs correspondingly more – about $450 compared to $250.

with nickel-studded chaps and hats that approached the mountainous, like the famed ten-gallon hat popularized by western movie star Tom Mix.

Today, western wear is a nearly $10-billion-dollar business, and as any devotee of Ralph Lauren or Calvin Klein can tell you, cowboy style is *a la mode* from Paris, Texas, to Paris, France. Indeed, western wear sometimes seems to become too popular for its own good. A few years ago, cowboy boot

Left, chaps protect the legs from brush and thorns. Above, Levi Strauss stitched his first pair of pants for California miners in 1853.

As for boots, the best ones have outsoles, insoles, heels and lining made entirely from leather; some boot makers have branched from cowhide to more exotic materials like elephant. The finest quality store-bought boots run up to $500; a customized boot made by one of the West's bespoke boot makers can cost twice as much. Old West authenticity doesn't come cheap. But then, it never did, even in the days of the open range.

As W.S. James wrote, "The cow-boy's outfit, as a rule, is of the very best from hat to boots. He may not have a dollar in the world, but he will wear good, substantial clothing, even if he has to buy it on a credit."

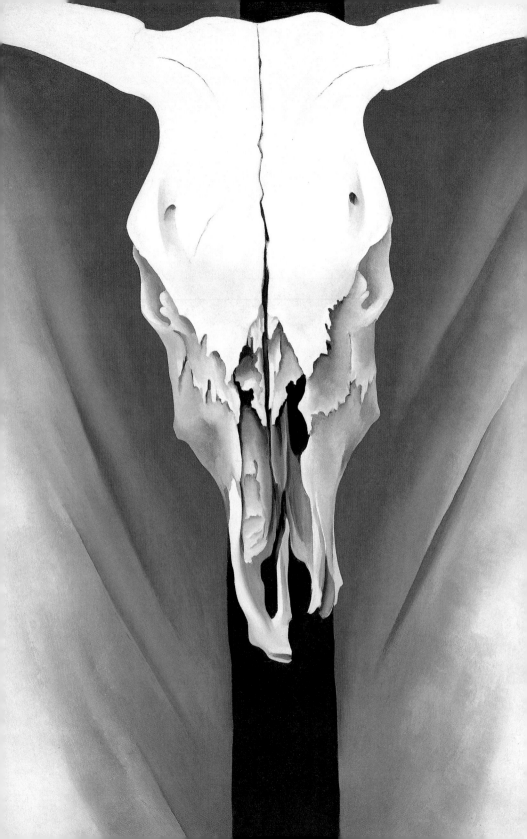

Too marvelous for words? It might be the theme song for the West, whose majestic vistas and great open spaces seem to defy mere language. Even Walt Whitman was constrained. Awestruck by the vastness of the Kansas prairie, the poet could write only of a "great something, stretching out into its own unbounded scale."

Happily for us, many artists have been drawn to the West to depict what words alone were unable to convey fully. They were people like George Catlin, a young lawyer and artist from Pennsylvania who set out in 1832 to chronicle the wild country west of the Mississippi River. For him the West was America in its virgin state, a wilderness known only by the Indians, a fresh new canvas on which a young, self-taught painter could make his mark.

Untamed country: Just as the wilderness was disappearing under the tread of a westering nation, so too, Catlin feared, was the Indian way of life. During an 1,800-mile (2,900 km) steamboat journey up the Missouri River, he tried to capture a glimpse of the still "untamed" life of the Mandan, Sioux, Crow and Blackfoot. Later he toured the Great Lakes region and the southern plains in an effort to document all the "wild" tribes he could find of the United States.

Catlin assembled an "Indian Gallery" of more than 500 paintings that he hoped would preserve "for the benefit of posterity... the living monuments of a noble race." Catlin's portrayals were impressively authentic. He captured a myriad of details about Indian life and customs that would have escaped a lesser artist. Still, there is an unmistakable element of nostalgia in his work. His "noble" Indians are symbolic of a primitive West unsullied by "civilization." In fact, he often deleted subject matter that suggested the mere influence of European culture. His Indians are stoic, timeless, unchanging inhabitants of a wild and pristine wilderness.

Catlin's contemporary, Alfred Jacob Miller, brought a similar vision to his portrayal of the western trapper. In 1837 Miller was invited to accompany William Drummond Stewart, a Scottish nobleman, on a western adventure that led them to a fur-trappers' rendezvous.

Set in the shadow of Wyoming's Wind River Mountains, Miller's field drawings picture mountain men setting beaver traps in icy streams, telling campfire tales, bartering for Indian brides, and generally whooping it up at their annual rendezvous. Like Catlin's Indians, Miller's mountain men roam freely

through an idealized West, often in the light of a glowing sunset.

Miller was the first artist to provide Easterners with a visual experience of the Rocky Mountains and the only painter to portray the life of the western trapper. Although he didn't realize it, he was depicting a way of life that would soon vanish. The fur trade reached its climax in the 1830s and quickly faltered as both the demand for furs and the supply of beavers dwindled. The last rendezvous, a much more subdued affair than the boisterous gathering Miller had attended, was held in 1843.

Nevertheless, Miller had created an icon.

Left, *Cow's Skull: Red, White, and Blue*, by Georgia O'Keeffe, 1931. **Right**, cowboy artist in Terlingua, Texas.

His patrons wanted images of a simpler, wilder period, and that's exactly what he gave them. Although he never again set eyes on the Rocky Mountains, he used his sketches and his imagination to create scenes that still resonate in the American imagination.

If Miller's paintings evoked the romance of an era, Karl Bodmer's work captured the details of the land and people. Like Miller, Bodmer came west under the sponsorship of a wealthy adventurer, Prince Maximillian of Germany. And like Catlin, he was intrigued by the Indians he encountered during his travels up the Missouri River in 1833–34.

Trained as an engraver, Bodmer had learned to make precise renderings of plants, ani-

Into the setting sun: Back in America, the lure of gold and silver and open farmland began to attract increasing numbers of newcomers across the Great Plains. In 1859, a young artist from Massachusetts joined a group of pioneers looking for a wagon route through the Rocky Mountains. Born in Dusseldorf, Germany, Albert Bierstadt had been schooled in the tradition of Europe's romantic artists. From his point of view, reality was just a starting point. To convey the emotion of a scene, exaggeration often took precedence over accuracy.

In Bierstadt's portrayals of the Oregon Trail, for example, tepees and covered wagons are washed in rich golden light. Indians

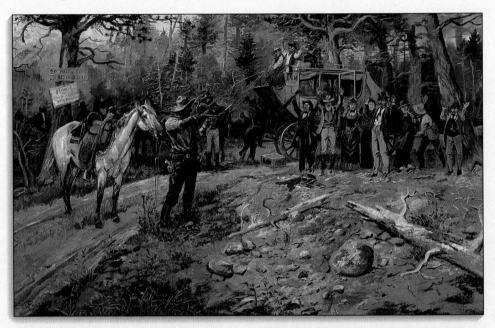

mals and landscapes. His skill as a draftsman enabled him to capture nuances of line, color and light that had escaped Catlin, Miller and other early artists.

Despite the hardships of traveling in the West, including Indian attacks and below-zero temperatures, Bodmer tended to paint wonderful landscapes that offered a more vivid reflection of western spaces and landforms. His detailed renderings of exotic places like the *Mauvaises Terres* (known today as the Dakota Badlands) dazzled viewers at the Paris Exhibition of 1836, providing the most reliable evidence to date of a land unlike anything in Europe.

are friendly. Water is plentiful. Livestock graze on fertile grasslands. The mountains and grasslands are dramatic yet inviting. This is the West as the promised land, where Americans needing a place to invest their hopes and dreams could look toward the glow of a distant horizon.

Bierstadt himself followed what poet Joaquin Miller described as "the path of the setting sun," heading west to landscapes of ever increasing grandeur. In Bierstadt's West, clouds swirled across massive peaks that seemed to pierce the sky. His use of striking colors and huge canvases caught the eye of the American public.

One of Bierstadt's admirers was George Armstrong Custer. As Custer traveled through the Wichita Mountains, he described the scenery as being worthy of Bierstadt's brush, "the structure of the mountains reminding one of the paintings of the Yosemite Valley, in the blending of colors – sombre purple, deep blue, to rich crimson tinged with gold."

But not everyone was fond of Bierstadt's romantic renditions of the Yosemite. "Portraits should be accurate," wrote Mark Twain. "We do not want this glorified atmosphere smuggled into a part of Yosemite where it surely does not belong. I may be wrong, but still I believe that this atmosphere of Mr Bierstadt's is altogether too gorgeous."

was quick to respond: "I did not wish to realize the scene literally… [but] to preserve and convey its true impression."

As with Bierstadt's work, humans, if they appeared at all, were dwarfed by the immensity of the surrounding terrain. Beyond the canvas, however, wagon trains and railroads were rapidly transforming the West, causing some Americans to push for the preservation of the most glorious of western landscapes. To this end, Moran's paintings helped persuade Congress to create Yellowstone, the world's first national park.

Cowboy artists: For artists of the 1880s like Frederic Remington, the western story was less about the landscape and more about the

The same critique could have been made of Thomas Moran. Moran, who went west with the Hayden Survey in 1871, was the first artist to celebrate the grandeur of Yellowstone and later the Grand Canyon on a scale that rivaled Bierstadt's mountain scenes. Moran didn't intend to make an exact rendering but to imbue his work with the emotional power of the western landscape, often working on enormous canvases to convey the sheer vastness of the scene. To those critics demanding accuracy, Moran

<u>Left</u>, *The Hold Up*, by Charles Russell, 1899.
<u>Above</u>, Catlin's *Grand Pawnee Chief, Keokuk*.

people who were changing it. Cowboys and cavalrymen dominated Remington's canvases. Here were "men with the bark on" who demonstrated their grit every day as they met the challenges of a harsh land and its native inhabitants.

As a young man, Remington sought adventure in the West. He rode with the cavalry and worked briefly as a rancher in Kansas. Always a keen observer, he incorporated details of his western adventures into paintings and sculpture that depicted what he regarded as the winning of the West. In his early work, the land was little more than a backdrop for a great human drama played out by cowboys, cavalrymen, Indians, mountain men and other real-life Westerners.

Meanwhile, another young man dreaming of adventure in the West left a comfortable middle-class upbringing in St Louis to ride the range. Sixteen-year-old Charles Russell fell in love with Montana. After spending several years working with a trapper in the Judith Basin, Russell was hired as a horse wrangler. For 11 years, he worked at the spring and fall roundups, teaching himself to draw and paint during slack time.

It was in 1887 that one of Russell's watercolors first caught the public's attention. His portrait of a starving cow surrounded by coyotes became a poignant sym-

bol of the blizzards that had devastated ranchers. As it happened, the winter of 1887 marked the beginning of the end for the big cattle operations and the open range that Russell loved so well.

For Remington, the West was a proving ground. For Russell, it was a celebration of freedom. But as the 19th century drew to a close, the West of their youth was quickly fading. In the fall of 1900, Remington visited Colorado and New Mexico only to find that the rugged frontier had given way to "brick buildings and derby hats... It spoils all my early illusions, and they are my capital."

"The West is dead," said Russell. "You may lose a sweetheart, but you won't forget her." Between them, the "cowboy artists" stored up plenty of memories and created thousands of pictures. Their images of cowboys, cavalrymen and Indians continue to evoke the spirit of what Russell called "the West that had passed."

New sensibility: Indeed, the Old West may have been and gone, but a new sensibility was already taking shape. Newcomers like Ernest Blumenschein *(see page 26)* and Bert Phillips, co-founders of the Taos Society of Artists, were drawing fresh inspiration from western people and landscapes, and Indian artists like pueblo potter Maria Martinez were beginning to emerge as major figures in the art of the West. In fact, by the 1960s, Indian art was undergoing a full-fledged renaissance as young artists like Alan Houser, Fred Kabotie, Fritz Scholder and R.C. Gorman brought together elements from both Native American and western traditions.

The most famous of this new generation of western artists is undoubtedly Georgia O'Keeffe, who came to Taos, New Mexico, in 1917 and instantly fell in love with the place. In a letter to photographer Alfred Stieglitz, she described the New Mexican landscape as "a perfectly mad looking country – hills and cliffs and washes too crazy to imagine all thrown up into the air by God and let tumble where they would."

O'Keeffe, who lived from 1887 to 1986, portrayed a land that existed beyond human history in the realm of geologic time. What seemed to matter most in her world of clay hills and sandstone walls were the aesthetics of earth and sky. At the same time, her personal history became entwined with the landscape. Objects such as bones and skulls and luscious blooming flowers became a sort of personal winter count, marking her passage through a landscape filled with extraordinary shape, color and sensuality.

Like so many western artists, O'Keeffe embraced the West that writer A.B. Guthrie described as an "adventure of the spirit... more than journey's end, it is the journey that enchants us." And as in any journey, it is helpful to remember, with the help of a few pictures, where we've been.

<u>Left</u>, N.C. Wyeth's *Hahn Pulled His Gun and Shot Him Through the Middle*, 1906. <u>Right</u>, John Mix Stanley's *The Smoke Signal*, 1868.

The setting may be a dusty county fairground, and when the announcer recites the Cowboy's Prayer – the standard invocation at these occasions – his crackling voice floats over the cottonwoods like a memory. Or maybe it's the National Finals in Las Vegas where the wild and woolly West gets a sequined infusion of casino glitz.

Riding for fortune: Either way, the drama will probably lift you up out of the bleachers. There's the bronco – snorting, fiery-eyed. There's the cowboy – and you can barely begin to imagine what he's feeling. The chute opens. The horse lunges out and, hanging atop him, bareback, the cowboy waves one hand in the air as if he were the happiest hombre in the world, while his other hand clutches leather with a grip that could bend steel. Eight seconds – that's all the time he has to maintain his position on that horse. But when you're riding for your fortune and your life, those eight seconds can stretch into an eternity.

This is rodeo. No other sport offers quite the same high-velocity, primal excitement. And no other sport has deeper roots in the West. Today professional rodeo is big business indeed: the Professional Rodeo Cowboy Association (PRCA), headquartered in Colorado Springs, Colorado, sanctions about 800 rodeos a year in the United States and Canada that together award prize money totaling $21 million.

Top rodeo riders acquire at least some of the perquisites of major athletes: a goodly income from prize money, plus more from product endorsements for boots and blue jeans and snuff. But despite all the big-money trappings, rodeo is still the West's own down-home test of cowboy skill.

Most rodeo events are clear descendants of chores that cowboys performed on ranch or range. After a long week's work, it was natural enough that they might compete to see who was the fastest at roping a calf, or who could ride the toughest horse.

These informal competitions grew into community events and then into rodeo. Numerous western towns have claimed that they were the first to hold an official rodeo, but most historians award the prize to Prescott, Arizona, and the rodeo that was held there on July 4, 1866.

(Both location and date must have been fortuitous. The Prescott rodeo is still going strong 150 years later. And although the professional rodeo season now stretches through most of the year, the Fourth of July remains a preferred date: across the West the

calendar is filled with so many rodeos that riders call it "cowboy Christmas.")

By the turn of the century rodeo had been taken up by showmen like Buffalo Bill Cody, who added rodeo events to his Wild West show, then it took off on its own: in the 1920s rodeos regularly filled New York's Madison Square Garden. Along the way rodeo nurtured a number of larger-than-life characters who rode hard and played harder.

One of the most fascinating was Bill Pickett (*see illustration on page 62*). A black cowboy from Texas, Pickett starred in the 101 Ranch Wild West Show, where he developed his unique method of steer wrestling. Riding his

Left, a Navajo cowboy bows his head during the playing of the national anthem at the beginning of a rodeo. **Right**, boots and hoofs.

horse, Spradley, Pickett would chase down a longhorn, then slide down his horse's side to come within a whisper of the galloping steer. He'd grab the bovine's head, twist it towards him, then render the steer helpless by biting it on the lip. Pickett called this technique bulldogging, because it was akin to the way cattle dogs controlled steers, and it made him a legend.

Equally legendary was New Mexican Bob "Wild Horse" Crosby, known as King of the Cowboys. A champion steer roper, Wild Horse was so feverishly dedicated to the cause that even severe rodeo-inflicted injuries – including a gouged-out eye and a gangrenous leg – didn't prevent him from

or to their own, non-PRCA, but well attended all-women rodeos.

PRCA rodeo events are divided into two categories. In timed events, cowboys compete against both the animal and the clock. Team roping – the only team event in rodeo – draws on techniques cowboys employed when they had to catch an especially large steer for branding. Two cowboys urge their quarter horses after the steer.

One of the riders – the header – ropes the steer around the horns, then rides to the left, turning the steer around so that his partner – the heeler – can rope the steer's hind feet. It's a unique division of labor: not only do many cowboys specialize in working as header or

competing with all his remaining faculties.

Nor, in those days, were women excluded from the excitement. The daughter of a Wyoming rancher, Prairie Rose Henderson was the first woman to enter a rodeo competition, competing in bronc riding at the Cheyenne Frontier Days Celebration in 1901. The judges first balked but could find no rules excluding women.

All-women rodeos: Prairie Rose performed so well that "cowgirls bronc riding" became a regular part in many rodeos. Today, however, the ranks of professional rodeo riders allow only men to compete: women are relegated to just one event – barrel-racing –

heeler, their horses specialize, too, with the header horse being generally taller and heavier, the heeler horse being smaller and more agile.

Ropin' and ridin': Solo calf roping is a contest of accuracy and speed. Here a single cowboy rides after a calf, then tosses his lasso around the calf's shoulders. As soon as the calf is caught the cowboy's horse halts and the cowboy dismounts.

He runs toward the calf, throws it to the ground, then ties three of its four legs together. Throughout this process his trusty (and well-trained) horse stands at the other end of the rope, taking up the slack while making sure the rope isn't tight enough to drag the calf.

Steer wrestling: In the last timed event, steer wrestling, a cowboy rides behind a steer on his quarter horse, then slides down and attempts to wrestle the steer to the ground. The method is similar to that devised by Bill Pickett, except that the cowboys, while still often called bulldoggers, don't subdue the calf with their teeth, as Pickett did.

Roughstock events are the second category of rodeo events. Each of them requires that the cowboy hang onto an animal (horse or bull) for a minimum of eight seconds: the judges will award him extra points if he hangs on with skill and style. Of these events,

one that makes the most spectators think that rodeo cowboys are out of their minds. What would possess a person to climb onto a 2,000-pound bull, wrap a rope around his hand, and then hang on as the bull spins, jumps, plunges, lunges and otherwise attempts to violently divest itself of its human cargo? That's what bull riders do, and they claim to love it. Anybody who would make such a claim is probably an unusual sort of person, and certainly the rodeo subculture is one of the most distinctive in America.

The PRCA estimates that there are 400 cowboys who do rodeo full-time and about another 8,000 who go at it part-time. Most aspiring rodeo cowboys get started early –

bareback riding is often considered the most physically demanding. Seated saddle-less on a bucking horse, the cowboy must use one hand (and one hand only) to hang on; if he touches the animal (or himself) with the other, he'll be immediately disqualified. Saddle bronc riding is sometimes considered rodeo's classic event: when you see a skilled saddle bronc rider, fluid, elegant, spurring his horse in synchronized time with its bucking, you'll see why it's earned that title.

The last roughstock event is probably the

Left, a calf roper speeds across an arena. **Above**, waiting for the show.

five-time all-around rodeo champion Ty Murray said he knew he wanted to be a rodeo star at age five – and hone their skills at 4-H and college rodeos. They may move on to county fair competitions, where a first prize could garner them $400 or so, and then into the ranks of the PRCA.

It's not an easy life. If you count only the time he spends atop a horse or wrestling a steer, you could argue that many professional rodeo cowboys work only 60 seconds a year. But you could also argue that it's a 100-hour-a-week job, if you include the time spent driving from rodeo to rodeo, traveling with four or five other cowboys to economize, all of them crowded in one of those big old broken-down sedans that go by the name "cowboy Cadillac."

One championship rider said that aspiring rodeo stars not only had to learn how to rope and ride but how to put up with having to share a motel room with 10 other cowboys where the bathtub was the only available place to sleep.

If they're skilled and lucky, these rodeo cowboys might win enough to get themselves up out of that bathtub – or at least enough to pay their entry fees for the next rodeo. If they're skilled and luckier, they'll start competing in the big events – the Houston Livestock Show and Rodeo, Cheyenne

Frontier Days, Denver's National Western Stock Show. And if they're champion-caliber cowboys, they could find themselves on their way to the National Finals Rodeo, held each December in Las Vegas. Here the fifteen top money makers in each of the rodeo events vie to win the biggest prizes in rodeo.

Rodeo is, however, more than just cowboys. In bull riding, the rodeo clown, whose title is now often upgraded to bullfighter, has the essential and potentially fatal job of distracting the maddened bull once it has bucked off its cowboy, giving the cowboy time to escape goring. Another figure lending authority and continuity to the event is the

rodeo announcer, many of whom have been in the business for decades and boast their own fame and following.

As for the animals involved in rodeo, they're as essential as the cowboy. Events like team roping and solo roping depend on well-trained horses. In bronc riding and bull riding, the animal's mettle is judged right along with the cowboy's: the judges will award the rider more points if he rides an aggressive bronco than a more docile steed. Indeed, some of the greatest bucking horses, like Midnight and Five Minutes to Midnight, have passed into rodeo legend.

It is rodeo's treatment of those animals, though, that has made the sport controversial. Throughout the last two decades, animal-rights groups have been vociferous in their attacks on the sport. They see it as institutionalized mistreatment of rodeo animals, objecting particularly to the flank strap used on bucking broncs and bulls. Defenders argue just as strongly that rodeo cowboys and stockmen have a substantial economic incentive to make sure the animals stay healthy. As champion Larry Mahon said, "A cowboy looks at a great bucking animal the way he would a great athlete . . . A lot more cowboys get hurt than animals."

And despite the controversy, rodeo seems here to stay. It's a rawhide link between the Old West and the New, it provides a brand of excitement both wholesome and intense. The rodeo cowboy remains a symbol of toughness and independence. And where else but at a rodeo would you hear that Cowboy's Prayer? Written a few decades ago by rodeo announcer Clem McSpadden, and still recited at the start of countless contests across the West, it ends with this invocation:

Help us compete in life as honest as the horse we ride and in a manner as clean and pure as the wind that blows across this western country.

So, when we make that last ride, that we know is inevitable, to the country up there – where the grass is green and lush and stirrup high and the water runs crystal clear and deep, You will tell us, as we enter that Arena, our entry fees are paid.

Left and right, romance of the rodeo. The first was held on July 4th, 1866. Now there are so many rodeos held on July 4th riders call the date "cowboy Crhistmas."

Speeding across the highways of the northern plains, it's possible to encounter colorful place names that call up images of the old West: names like Cheyenne, Wolf Point, Medicine Bow, Absaroka. These names are imprints left by ancient people. Even the highways – many of them built on prehistoric trails – recall an earlier time when the plains were trampled by hundreds of thousands of bison hunted by Arapaho, Cheyenne, Sioux, Blackfeet, Gros Ventre, Shoshone and others. All were patriot warriors who fought a valiant but losing struggle against the white invaders.

Celebration of life: As recently as a century ago, it was commonly believed that Indian people would disappear. But the myth of the "Vanishing Red Man" proved untrue. In spite of their tragic history after the arrival of white people, there are still more than 300 distinct Indian tribes in the United States, with a population exceeding 1½ million – a far cry from the 250,000 survivors at the turn of the century.

Today, a cultural renaissance is blooming across Indian Country. It has been gathering force for the past 20 years. Indian people are rediscovering traditions that were nearly lost during the years of war and hardship. Indian pride is being reasserted in schools, businesses and tribal governments, atop the buttes where vision quests are held, on the prairies where sun dance lodges are erected. And, perhaps most important for the traveler seeking a firsthand experience of Indian culture, at the celebration of life and culture known as powwow.

Said to be a Narraganset word meaning "medicine man," powwow now refers to a celebratory gathering of dancers, singers, craftsmen, culinary experts, families, friends and local communities. In short, a celebration of Indian life and tradition. Powwows occur in many Indian communities at least once a year, sometimes more. A point of pride, the events are well attended by local Indian people as well as by Native American visitors from every corner of the United

States and Canada. In cities, powwows take place in huge gymnasiums or in grassy parks. But in Indian Country they are usually held outdoors, either at prepared powwow grounds or on the open prairie.

Powwow camp: The first sight of a powwow camp is always stirring – a bustling nest of activity framed by a halo of dust. Most of these camps are formed in a circle that has a permanent arbor at the center. Shelters radiate from all directions, crisscrossed with meandering automobile paths and alive with

the sounds of playing children, whinnying horses, radios and the talk of old friends. The camp is in constant motion as cars come in and out of access roads, and visitors set up their temporary residences. In addition to the fancy motor homes and simple green pup tents, there are often a number of traditional painted tepees. The arbor is the nucleus of the gathering. It is usually circular or rectangular, open at the center, with seating around the edge shaded by a roof of pine boughs thrown over the frame.

Circling the arbor is a dirt midway about 25 feet (7.6 meters) wide. Along the walkway are booths and stands of various types selling Indian tacos, fry bread, hamburgers, tanned deerskins, newly made beadwork, jewelry and a thousand other handcrafted or homemade treasures.

Shaking the earth: Everything is ready for the main event. It all starts with the grand entry, the most colorful and moving part of the entire powwow. This is not to be missed, for it is here that the various categories of dancers enter the arena attired in traditional finery, dancing in time to Indian songs that may be hundreds of years old. The first drum sounds and from that moment forward the camp moves to the steady pulse and cascading melodies of Plains Indian music, much of it sung by men in powerful, piercing falsettos.

The grand entry is a key to understanding the various dance styles you're likely to see at a powwow, and the order in which participants enter is a useful way of judging their relative importance. Leading everyone into the arena is the honor guard, usually bearing two flags: the Feathered Staff represents traditional Indian values, and the Stars and Stripes represents the United States. The flags are carried only by veterans. As patriots who have always fought to protect their country, Indians consider it a high honor to bear the banners.

After the flags come the honored guests. These are tribal or national leaders, Indian or non-Indian politicians and other prominent people. Among this group are the "royalty," young ladies chosen to represent their communities at powwows and other social events throughout Indian Country. The "princess" titles – "Miss Northern Cheyenne Powwow," for example – are a recent addition to the powwow scene, but they offer exceptional and talented young women an opportunity to learn and travel.

Next in line are the dancers, with the traditionals first. These dancers are closer to the old ways than most, as demonstrated by their dignified attire and maturity. Black-tipped golden eagle feathers form the foundation of their outfits, and the stately dancers prefer conservative, time-honored steps.

Grass dancers: Following the traditionals are the grass dancers – relative newcomers, although they descend from the earlier Northern Plains grass dancers. They are readily distinguished by the absence of a feathered bustle and by the long, brilliantly-colored yarn fringes on their outfits. Even their dancing is different; their movements are smoother and use the shoulders more than the other styles.

The fancy dancers are next, bedecked in vividly colored, chicken-hackle feathers that form bustles worn between the shoulders and below the small of the back. They are the most energetic and creative of the male dancers, leaping into the air, sending their bodies into wild spins.

Next to enter the arena, keeping in perfect time with the singing, are the traditional female dancers. They are recognized as the strength and foundation of the Indian people. Strong and dignified, they have passed on the Indian system of values and customs over the years, even through tough times. Today, they usually wear beaded wool or deerskin dresses and moccasins and carry a beaded bag and, in some tribes, an eagle-wing fan. A quilled wheel or colored feather may decorate their hair.

Still dancing to the same driving entry song, the female jingle-dress dancers usually follow. This style, too, is a new arrival on the plains. Said to have originated in the dream of a Chippewa holy man more than 70 years ago, the form-fitting dresses are made of cloth and decorated with tin cones shaped from the tops of chewing-tobacco containers, similar in style to earlier elk tooth and cowrie shell dresses. The dress's shape causes the dancer to move differently, with a more up-and-down step, and best of all, the cones make a noise – a clacking sound much like native dewclaw hoof "bells." So, with a feather fan in one hand and a scarf or bag in the other, and crested with a French braid and white plume, these beautiful dancers enter the arena.

The girl fancy dancers are next in line. They are the counterpart to the males, and they wear equally brilliant colors. The girls' oufits seem to be more creative; a greater variety of colors and materials make up their attire, and the yokes of their dresses are usually decorated with designs of beads and

Honor dance: But there is more to pow-wows than singing and dancing. Powwows are a time for tribes from all over the country to gather as a distinct people, to gain strength from their cultural diversity and reaffirm their commitment to common values. Pow-wows give Indian people a place that is rich with tradition and bright with hope for the future, a place where they are no longer a minority in their own land. Powwows also give them an opportunity to look back on the events of the preceding year, to recognize achievements, acknowledge milestones and reflect on personal losses.

"Honor dances" are often held for exceptional members of the community, a returning

sequins. Shawls are draped about their shoulders and held outstretched like wings. Soaring, gliding and banking, barely touching the earth, the graceful birds descend.

Finally, the future of the Indian people enters the arena, dressed in their finest. Divided by age and dance style, the youngsters are miniatures of the adults they imitate, some wearing traditional outfits while others exhibit the attire of other categories. Now everyone is in the arena together – dancing hard, all at once, and shaking the earth.

Left, gazing through gold-rimmed glasses. **Above**, the powwow grounds at Crow Fair in Wyoming.

veteran, perhaps, or a tribal leader. "Giveaways" are held, too, in which a family gives blankets, shawls, bustles, headdresses and other gifts in honor of their child receiving an Indian name, having a person "dance Indian" for the first time, acknowledging the end of a year's mourning for the passing of a relative, and, more recently, to honor a family member for receiving a college degree.

Traditional dancers love to powwow and to take part in the incomparable energy of the grand entry. Outfitted from head to foot with headdress, breastplate, feather bustle, quilled arm bands, blue wool leggings and beaded moccasins, all highlighted by ringing brass bells, they come to dance. Most don't compete in the contests but come to enjoy themselves and to be with friends, relatives and familiar customs.

When the master of ceremonies announces that a grand entry will soon take place, the dancers begin to gather at the entrance. With much bustle, bells, laughter, apparent confusion and beauty, the lead singer of the host drum starts the song and the grand entry begins. As the drum establishes the strong pulsating rhythm, the honor guard leads the proud procession holding their banners high.

The traditional dancers enter, excited and proud. Positioning the head, body and arms at a cocky angle, the dancers appear, one

after another, strutting, twisting, leaning, perhaps mimicking a prairie bird or reliving the old warrior ways, but always following the heavy, persistent beat as their beaded moccasins pound the earth.

For the participants, this is a time of warriors, of Indians, of pride in their people. They are there dancing in the middle of the prairie. They are dressed like the old ones, moving together in the grand entry, united by the cadence, becoming one in celebration of Indian traditions. They see friends and relatives as they dance, shaking their hands as they pass each other – looking good.

As the tempo quickens, they dance harder.

The sweat begins to trickle and they feel it purging their bodies. The voices and unifying rhythm are overwhelming. It's an experience, the dancers say, of incomparable joy.

The powwow road: Although powwows were originally a Plains Indian phenomenon, they are now held throughout the country, from the California to the Atlantic Coast (*see Travel Tips*). Some dancers spend much of their summers traveling from one powwow to another. The general schedule is usually as follows: during the preceding week, people begin to arrive and set up camp; by Friday the grounds are full, and at about 7pm the first grand entry begins.

The dancing lasts until the early morning, and the camp sleeps late the next day. Just before noon things are astir again, and the next grand entry usually happens in the early afternoon. These first entries are for children, who dress and compete in the same manner as adults. The biggest grand entry is on Saturday about 7pm. By now those participants who work during the week have arrived, and the powwow has attained its maximum size. Most celebrations have other grand entries at about 1pm and 7pm on Sunday. Sometime during the night, the winners of the various contests are determined, announced and awarded cash prizes.

In general, powwows are open to outsiders, and there are often dances that spectators are invited to join. It's a great opportunity to experience Native American culture firsthand, but as always, there are a few rules that should be kept in mind.

First, unless otherwise indicated, alcohol is strictly forbidden on the powwow grounds. Second, Indian people tend to be conservative when it comes to dress, so think twice about wearing shorts or a halter top, even if it's hot. Third, some photography is usually allowed, but there may be restrictions or an additional fee.

In either case, you must ask permission of the powwow organizers and of anyone whom you plan to photograph. Fourth, participate in dancing only if you have made prior arrangements or are invited by the master of ceremonies. And finally, as with all Indian events, approach powwows with a good heart. Respect the dancers, singers and other spectators, and they will respect you.

Left, making camp. Right, powwow princess.

Give us your tired, your upper middle-class, your city slickers with caffeine nerves and commuter jitters, and we'll turn them into ridin' and ropin' Westerners. That was, and is, the promise of the dude ranch, as unique an institution as ever set up housekeeping in the American West. What other vacation spot would ask guests to help water the horses and round up the heifers – and then ask them to pay for the privilege? But so strong is the American admiration of the cowboy lifestyle that people have spent a century's worth of summers at these homes away from home on the range.

Dude ranches began as a mix of romantic escapism and economic necessity. In the late 19th century, cattle ranchers in the newly opened frontiers of Wyoming, Colorado and the Dakotas found eastern friends and family – and sometimes perfect strangers – arriving at their doorsteps in droves. The visitors needed a base while they hunted buffalo and explored the scenic wonders. Such was the code of hospitality that the ranchers felt obliged to board and bed these guests for free and soon found that they were being eaten out of house and home. Dakota rancher Howard Eaton, for example, tallied up the number of free meals he served over the course of a year – and came up with 2,200.

Singalongs and cigarettes: Eaton hated charging visitors for staying at his ranch. But he hated going broke even worse. And so, in 1882, the Eaton Ranch became the first dude ranch in the United States to accept paying guests, charging them $10 a week. Ironically, it was those guests that soon saved Eaton from economic disaster. The blizzards of 1886–87 and the economic panic of 1893 sent many cattle ranches into bankruptcy. Eaton managed to hang on, however, thanks to the profits he garnered from his guests. Later, he would concentrate on pleasing guests over raising cattle as he moved his operation to the Big Horn Mountains of Wyoming, more convenient for leading pack trips into Yellowstone National Park.

Gregarious, charming, savvy about every

aspect of western plants and animals, cowboys and Indians, Eaton was the best possible advertisement for the pleasures of a dude-ranch vacation. But he quickly had lots of company, as dude ranches began opening from Montana south to Colorado. Meanwhile, the railroads had discovered that a dude-ranch vacation could serve as a lure to draw paying passengers on westbound trains and so began promoting dude ranches in their tourist brochures. Popular magazines like the *Ladies Home Journal* and the *Satur-*

day Evening Post published paeans to the ranch vacation. Women, especially, were seen to benefit. Back East they might be condemned to enduring social chitchat on the porch of a resort hotel. Out on the ranch they could ride and hike and fish just like men. Eventually, Hollywood got into the act. Studio publicists planted magazine stories that had their stars relaxing glamorously at western dude ranches. In Montana, actor Gary Cooper's father, Judge Charles Cooper, even attempted to launch a chain of dude ranches that would capitalize on his son's Hollywood stardom.

The Cooper Ranch, alas, never materialized. But by World War II dude ranches had blossomed throughout the West, with particular concentrations around Cody and Jackson Hole, Wyoming, in Gallatin County, Montana, and around Tucson, Arizona. Most of the ranches offered the basics: lots of horseback riding, including lessons and guided pack trips into the backcountry, wholesome entertainment like rodeos and gymkhanas and campfire singalongs, comfortably rustic surroundings and great quantities of hearty food. But there were some regional variations. Montana and Wyoming ranches tended toward the comfortably spartan, but Arizona dude ranches soon acquired the trappings of luxury resorts, including swimming

hinted at one difficulty. Was being a dude a matter of pride or shame? To many, the term carried definite connotations of eastern effeteness, like the pair of ranch visitors described this way by a grizzled wrangler: "One wore lavender angora chaps, the other bright orange, and each sported a tremendous beaver sombrero and wore a gaudy scarf knotted jauntily about his throat."

But, fearful that the paying guests might take offense, ranch owners took pains to say that "dude" was not an insult but simply a description of anybody who was not a native of the Rocky Mountains. Many dudes, they maintained, could outride westerners – and that went for women and children, too.

pools and golf courses. Nevada dude ranchers lassoed a particularly lucrative specialty. In an era when divorces were impossible to come by in much of the country, the state of Nevada permitted them to anyone who had established a six-week residency. That inspired the brainstorm of socially well-connected ranch owner Cornelius Vanderbilt, Jr, who operated two ranches near Reno. He designed a dude-ranch divorce: six weeks for $795, including a pack of cigarettes a day and a bottle of liquor a week.

Naturally, there were a few bumps along the trail as Easterners got a crash course in western ways. The very name "dude ranch"

Westerners had to make some adjustments, too. Ranchers had to learn how to manage herds of tourists instead of herds of cattle, and ranch wives had to cook for more demanding eastern palates. Even the horse underwent some changes. A good dude horse possessed a capable trot and gallop, and, most important of all, a good disposition: some dude ranches began to breed their own horses to promote those traits.

Probably the biggest adjustments were made by the ranch wranglers. In some ways, a dude ranch was a boon to the working cowboy: as working cattle ranches became fewer and farther between, the dude ranch provided a place where cowboys could still be paid for their skills. But other skills were required, too, along with some social graces. As one ranch manager said, "There is a real future here for a cowhand who can ride, play the guitar, and still smell nice." A good dude-ranch wrangler was gallant to the ladies, pals with the men and a hero to the children. The duties could be arduous indeed, as one cowboy song lamented:

I'm a tough, hard-boiled old cow-hand with
* a weather-beaten hide,*
But herdin' cows is nuthin' to teachin' dudes
* to ride.*
I can stand their hitoned langwidge and their
* hifalutin' foods –*

owners or to the very wealthy became accessible to millions of middle-class Americans.

That's still true today. Dude ranches may have more competition for vacation time and money than they once did; few people take more than a week or two at a time for vacation. But the dude ranch has learned to change with the times. Organizations like the Dude Ranchers Association and the Colorado Dude and Guest Ranch Association number hundreds of members.

Today's dude ranches are a sight more plush than the ranches of yore. Some have added healthful spa cuisine entrees to the old standards of steak and biscuits and beans; others entertain guests with swimming pools

But you bet your bottom dollar I am fed up on
* wranglin' dudes.*

Still, despite a few burrs under the saddle, dudes and wranglers and ranchers all generally got along fine. Many families returned to the same dude ranch summer after summer, generation after generation. Teenagers who had honed their horsemanship skills as children came back to work as wranglers on summers off from college. And an experience – seeing the West from the back of a horse – that had once been limited to ranch

and even dinner theater. Yet many others stick to their roots, focusing on horseback riding, pack trips and riding lessons. A few ranches even let guests join a cattle drive.

Life on the ranch isn't cheap; rates can easily run to $200 a day. Be sure to investigate several options before making a decision; ideally you should talk to other people who have stayed at the ranch that interests you. Once you've made your selection, pack up those cowboy boots and get ready to enact every Wild West fantasy you've ever had.

Left, wrangler at work. **Above**, a home away from home on the range.

● *More information on dude ranches can be found in the Travel Tips section.*

The frontier may be long gone, but its legacy is alive and well. You'll find it in the tumbledown shacks of ghost towns and the dusty parade grounds of frontier forts, in wagon ruts on the Oregon Trail and in the thick-walled chapels of old Spanish missions.

There are stories in these places, tales of struggle and determination, big dreams and dashed hopes, and the uneasy – sometimes violent – confrontation between native and invading cultures. There are also telling, often heartbreaking details. A child's crutch leans against the wall of an ancient Anasazi pueblo; tobacco offerings sway in the wind at the Wounded Knee monument; gravestones at the Little Bighorn Battlefield are inscribed with the same anonymous epitaph: "US Soldier, 7th Cavalry, Fell Here, June 25, 1876."

Travelers can visit legendary places like Tombstone, Arizona, where Wyatt Earp and John "Doc" Holliday faced off with the Clantons and McLaurys; the courthouse in Lincoln, New Mexico, where Billy the Kid made his most daring jailbreak; or the #10 Saloon in Deadwood, South Dakota, where Wild Bill Hickok was shot and killed while holding black aces and eights – known forever after as the "Deadman's Hand."

But there are more than old ghosts in the Wild West. There's a living connection between past and present. Hopi and Zuni Indians are descendants of Anasazi cliff dwellers. Modern cowboys are the cultural heirs of Spanish *vaqueros*. Present-day Mormons are the sons and daughters of pioneers who pulled hand carts across the Great Plains to start a new life in a latter-day Zion.

Want to do more than merely see the sights? There are plenty of opportunities to join in, too. How about catching a ride on a narrow-gauge railroad in Colorado's stunning San Juan Mountains? A horseback ride through the North Dakota Badlands, site of Teddy Roosevelt's short-lived Elkhorn Ranch? A float trip on the Colorado River tracing John Wesley Powell's journey through the Grand Canyon? A week or two at a dude ranch learning to ride, rope and round up cattle?

Above all, the Wild West is embodied in the land itself. Here are the sweeping panoramas captured by frontier painters like Thomas Moran and Albert Bierstadt and photographed by Timothy O'Sullivan, John Hillers and, later, Ansel Adams. The Grand Canyon. Death Valley. Monument Valley. Yosemite. They have been imprinted on the American psyche by countless movies and advertisements but have lost none of their power to inspire.

These wide open spaces say more about the West than any book or person ever could. Although crisscrossed by highways and increasingly hemmed in by suburban sprawl, the West still appeals to pioneering souls with the promise of adventure, freedom and a fresh new start.

Preceding pages: Mather Point, Grand Canyon National Park; daybreak on the Teton Range, Wyoming; Great Sand Dunes, Colorado; cowboy and cactus, Arizona. **Left**, Nevada ranch at the foot of Ruby Mountains.

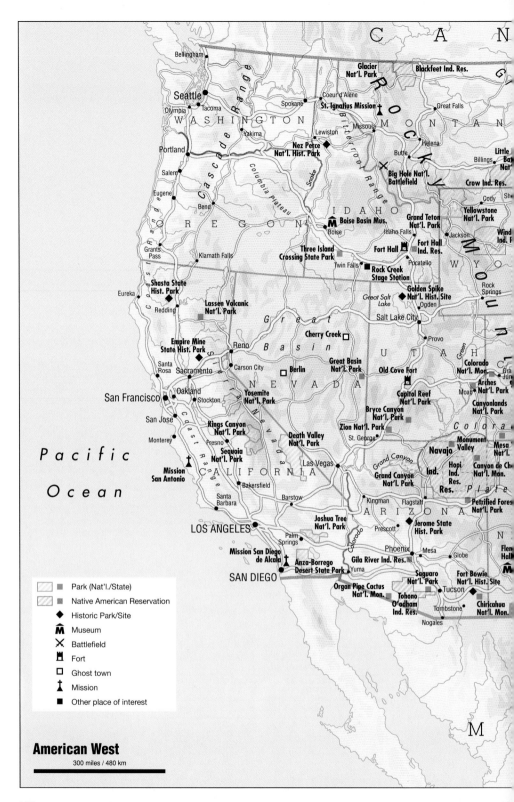

American West

300 miles / 480 km

Park (Nat'l./State)

Native American Reservation

Historic Park/Site

Museum

Battlefield

Fort

Ghost town

Mission

Other place of interest

152

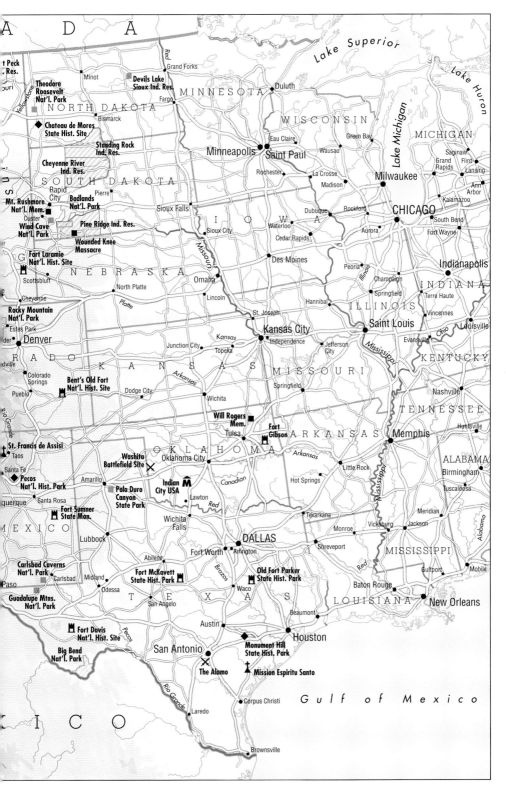

ADA

Lake Superior

t Peck
. Res.
ouri

Theodore
Roosevelt
Nat'l. Park

Minot

Devils Lake
Sioux Ind. Res.

Grand Forks

MINNESOTA

Red

Duluth

Yellowstone

NORTH DAKOTA

Bismarck

Chateau de Mores
State Hist. Site

Fargo

WISCONSIN

Lake Huron

Standing Rock
Ind. Res.

Eau Claire

Green Bay

MICHIGAN

Saginaw
Grand
Rapids

Flint
Lansing

Cheyenne River
Ind. Res.

SOUTH DAKOTA

Minneapolis

Saint Paul

Wausau

Lake Michigan

Ann
Arbor

Rapid
City

Mt. Rushmore
Nat'l. Mem.

Custer

Badlands
Nat'l. Park

Pierre

Rochester

La Crosse

Madison

Milwaukee

Kalamazoo

Wind Cave
Nat'l. Park

Pine Ridge Ind. Res.

Sioux Falls

Dubuque

Rockford

CHICAGO

South Bend

Wounded Knee
Massacre

Sioux City

IOWA

Waterloo

Aurora

Fort Wayne

Fort Laramie
Nat'l. Hist. Site

Scottsbluff

NEBRASKA

Cedar Rapids

Des Moines

Peoria

Indianapolis

Omaha

Illinois

Champaign

INDIANA

Cheyenne

North Platte

Lincoln

Springfield

Terre Haute

Rocky Mountain
Nat'l. Park

Platte

ILLINOIS

Vincennes

der

Estes Park

Denver

St. Joseph

Hannibal

Ohio

Louisville

RADO

Junction City

Kansas

Kansas City

St. Louis

Evansville

KENTUCKY

dville

Colorado
Springs

Topeka

Independence

Jefferson
City

Mississippi

Pueblo

Bent's Old Fort
Nat'l. Hist. Site

KANSAS

Dodge City

Arkansas

MISSOURI

Springfield

Nashville

io Grande

Wichita

TENNESSEE

St. Francis de Assisi

Taos

Will Rogers
Mem.

Fort
Gibson

ARKANSAS

Memphis

Huntsville

Santa Fe

Pecos
Nat'l. Hist. Park

Washita
Battlefield Site

Tulsa

OKLAHOMA

Arkansas

ALABAMA

querque

Amarillo

Oklahoma City

Little Rock

Birmingham

Santa Rosa

Indian
City USA

Canadian

Hot Springs

Tuscaloosa

Palo Duro
Canyon
State Park

Lawton

Fort Sumner
State Mon.

Red

MEXICO

Lubbock

Wichita
Falls

Texarkana

Meridian

Monroe

Vicksburg

Jackson

Alabama

Carlsbad Caverns
Nat'l. Park

Abilene

Fort McKavett
State Hist. Park

Brazos

DALLAS

Old Fort Parker
State Hist. Park

Shreveport

MISSISSIPPI

Carlsbad

Midland

Fort Worth

Arlington

Paso

Odessa

Waco

Red

Baton Rouge

Gulfport

Mobile

Guadalupe Mtns.
Nat'l. Park

TEXAS

San Angelo

Beaumont

LOUISIANA

New Orleans

Fort Davis
Nat'l. Hist. Site

Pecos

Austin

Houston

Big Bend
Nat'l. Park

San Antonio

Monument Hill
State Hist. Park

The Alamo

Mission Espiritu Santo

ICO

Rio Grande

Corpus Christi

Laredo

Gulf of Mexico

Brownsville

153

EAST TEXAS

A Wild West tour of East Texas should begin in San Antonio, heart of the old Spanish frontier, site of the great events of the Texas Revolution, and jumping-off point for the Chisholm Trail.

From 1690 through 1792, more than two dozen Franciscan missions were established throughout Texas, as the Spanish attempted to convert the Indians to Catholicism and transform them into *gente de razon* (people of reason) – and productive taxpayers. But Comanches, Kiowas and other Indians often raided the outposts, and the mission presidios became scenes of conflict. The most famous is **Mission San Antonio de Valero**, established in 1718 and better known as the **Alamo**, scene of the fierce confrontation during the Texas Revolution between Mexican General Antonio López de Santa Anna and a group of frontiersmen that included Jim Bowie, William B. Travis and Davy Crockett.

After being run out of Texas in 1835, Mexican troops returned to San Antonio to crush the rebellion. They were met at the Alamo by fewer than 190 Texans. The conflict came to a bloody climax on March 6, 1836. And although the Texans were killed to a man, their heroic defense inflicted major casualties on Santa Anna's army and made "Remember the Alamo" the rallying cry of the revolution. The chapel and long barracks still stand at the site, and portions of the outer wall have been unearthed.

Alamo City: The city of **San Antonio** was founded near Mission San Antonio de Valero in 1718, and in 1772 the "Alamo City" became the seat of government in Texas. The **Spanish Governor's Palace** was a 10-room, L-shaped adobe on the **Military Plaza**, and a furnished restoration may be visited today. A block away is **San Fernando Cathedral**, one of San Antonio's most historic structures, dating from 1738.

A few miles south of the Alamo, **Mission San Jose** was founded in 1720 and became the "Queen of Missions." The ornate chapel is distinguished by the beautifully-sculptured "Rosa's window"; the flour mill, built in 1790, was the first in Texas. In 1731 three other missions were established: **Mission Concepcion**, between the Alamo and San Jose; and, south of San Jose, **Mission San Juan Capistrano** and **Mission San Francisco de la Espada**. Near the latter two missions are remains of an extensive irrigation system, including an arched aqueduct and a dam on the **San Antonio River**.

A short walk from the Alamo, the **General Cos House** is where Mexican forces surrendered San Antonio on December 9, 1835. The **Institute of Texan Cultures** celebrates more than two dozen ethnic groups who settled Texas. The **Buckhorn Hall of Horns**, long displayed in the celebrated Buckhorn Saloon, today may be visited at the **Lone Star Brewery**, along with a **Hall of Texas History Wax Museum**. Facing the Alamo Plaza is the **Menger Hotel**: the oldest section was built in 1859; the **King Ranch Suite**, where

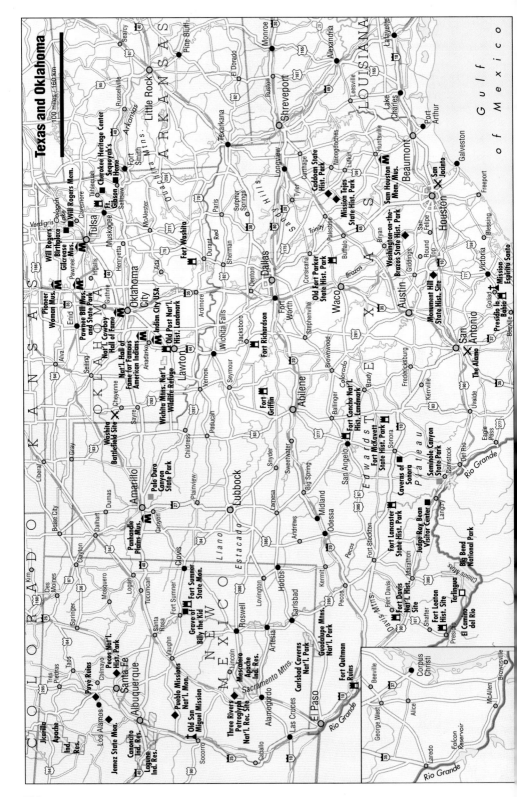

Texas and Oklahoma

100 miles/160 km

Searcy · Pine Bluff · Little Rock · Russellville · El Dorado · Monroe · Alexandria · Lafayette · Lake Charles · Port Arthur · Galveston · Freeport · Blessing

LOUISIANA

Gulf of Mexico

Tahlequah · Cherokee Heritage Center · Sequoyah's Home · Will Rogers Mem. · Fort Smith · Shreveport · Texarkana · Longview · Carthage · Nacogdoches · Lufkin · Huntsville · Beaumont · Houston · San Jacinto

Will Rogers Birthplace · Pioneer Woman Mus. · Gilcrease Mus. · Tulsa · Muskogee · Ft. Gibson · Claremore · Oologah Lake · Verdigris · Pawnee · Henryetta · McAlester · Durant · Paris · Sulphur Springs · Trinity · Palestine · Buffalo · Bryan · Round Top · Giddings · San Felipe · Blessing · Victoria · Goliad · Beeville

ARKANSAS

Ouachita Mtns. · Kiamichi Mtns. · D'Arbonne Hills

Caddoan State Hist. Park · Mission Tejas State Hist. Park · Sam Houston Nat'l. Mem. Mus. · Washington-on-the-Brazos State Hist. Park · Monument Hill State Hist. Site · Presidio la Bahia · Mission Espiritu Santo

Pawnee Bill Mus. and State Park · Nat'l. Cowboy Hall of Fame · Oklahoma City · Indian City USA · Old Post Nat'l. Hist. Landmark · Enid · Guthrie · Ada · Ardmore · Sherman · Denton · Fort Worth · Dallas · Waco · Corsicana · Austin · San Antonio · The Alamo

OKLAHOMA

Nat'l. Hall of Fame for Famous American Indians · Anadarko · Lawton · Wichita Mtns. Nat'l. Wildlife Refuge · Wichita Falls · Jacksboro · Fort Richardson · Seymour · Stephenville · Brownwood · Kerrville · Fredericksburg · Uvalde · Eagle Pass

Cheyenne · Washita Battlefield Site · Sayre · Childress · Paducah · Vernon · Abilene · Ballinger · Brady · Sonora

Setling · Selling · Alva · Liberal · Gray · Boise City · Dumas · Plainview · Snyder · Sweetwater · Big Spring · San Angelo · Fort Concho Nat'l. Hist. Landmark · Fort McKavett State Hist. Park · Caverns of Sonora · Seminole Canyon State Park · Del Rio

Fort Griffin · Colorado

KANSAS

COLORADO · Kim · Springer · Des Moines · Tres Piedras · Taos · Chimayo · Santa Fe · Puye Ruins · Jicarilla Apache Ind. Res. · Los Alamos · Jemez State Mon. · Canoncito Ind. Res. · Albuquerque · Laguna Ind. Res. · Pueblo Missions Nat'l. Mon. · Old San Miguel Mission · Socorro · Caballo

NEW MEXICO · Clayton · Mosquero · Logan · Tucumcari · Santa Rosa · Vaughn · Fort Sumner · Grave of Billy the Kid · Fort Sumner State Mon. · Clovis · Roswell · Lincoln · Mescalero Apache Ind. Res. · Three Rivers Petroglyph Nat'l. Rec. Site · Alamogordo · Sacramento Mtns. · Artesia · Carlsbad · Las Cruces · El Paso

Amarillo · Palo Duro Canyon State Park · Canyon · Panhandle Plains Mus. · Dalhart · Plainview · Lubbock · Lamesa · Andrews · Midland · Odessa · Kermit · Hobbs · Lovington

Llano Estacado

Pecos · Fort Stockton · Marathon · Big Bend National Park · Chisos Mtns. · Terlingua · Presidio · El Camino del Rio · Shafter

Fort Davis Nat'l. Hist. Site · Fort Davis · Fort Leaton State Hist. Site · Davis Mtns.

Guadalupe Mtns. Nat'l. Park · Carlsbad Caverns Nat'l. Park · Fort Quitman Ruins

Fort Lancaster State Hist. Park · Judge Roy Bean Visitor Center · Langtry

TEXAS

Edwards Plateau

Pecos Nat'l. Hist. Park · Pueblo Missions Nat'l. Mon. · Brazos State Hist. Park · Old Fort Parker State Hist. Park

Beeville · Corpus Christi · George West · Alice · McAllen · Falcon Reservoir · Laredo · Brownsville · Rio Grande

156

Richard King died of stomach cancer in 1885, may be toured; and a visit to the **Teddy Roosevelt Bar** is a must – Roosevelt's colorful Rough Riders trained in San Antonio during the Spanish–American War, and the future president and his officers made the Menger their headquarters.

Presidents and Kings: About 70 miles (110 km) north of San Antonio (via Highways 281 and 290) is the **Lyndon B. Johnson National Historical Site**, a 1,570-acre (635-hectare) site that encompasses the birthplace, ranch and family cemetery of the 36th President. In addition to Johnson's homes and memorabilia are several other restored or reconstructed buildings and a working farm reflecting life in the Hill Country in the early 20th century.

Perhaps the West's oldest and certainly the most famous large cattle operation is the **King Ranch**, about two hours southeast of San Antonio off Route 141 just west of **Kingsville**. Richard King, who came to South Texas as a steamboat captain during the Mexican War, acquired a 75,000-acre (30,400-hectare) Spanish land grant along Santa Gertrudis Creek in 1852. As he stocked his rapidly-growing ranch with cattle from Mexico, he also stocked it with Kinenos, loyal *vaqueros* and their families who, generation after generation, made the spread their home. The big frame house built by King burned down in 1912 and was replaced by a 25-room mansion that still commands the site.

The King Ranch ultimately stretched over 1.1 million acres (445,000 hectares), in addition to millions of acres abroad. The ranch developed the first American breed of cattle, the Santa Gertrudis, as well as the Quarter Horse, and its stables have won every title in thoroughbred racing, including the Triple Crown. Today the King Ranch still encompasses more than 800,000 acres (324,000 hectares), and at the **ranch museum** near Kingsville a bus tour is available for one of the West's most legendary spreads.

About a 90-minute drive to the north is **Goliad**, where **Mission Espiritu Santo**, founded in 1749, once housed a large Indian population and 10,000 head of cattle. Nearby, the **Presidio La Bahia** grew into one of the strongest forts on the Spanish frontier and is today the best example of a Spanish presidio in Texas. During the Texas Revolution, Colonel James Fannin and 400 men abandoned the presidio in the face of superior forces, but they were pursued and forced to surrender east of Goliad after a brief battle. Incarcerated in the presidio, Fannin and most of his men were massacred on Palm Sunday in 1836.

Just over an hour east of Goliad is the site of the vast ranch carved out by legendary cattleman Shanghai Pierce. The ranch office is part of the public library at tiny **Blessing** at the intersection of Routes 616 and 71. Across the square is the **Hotel Blessing**, built in 1906 by Shanghai's brother Jonathan Pierce. A stay in the Hotel Blessing is an experience from the past, with inexpensive rooms out of a Western movie and bountiful home-cooked meals in the dining room. The colorful Shanghai built a towering statue of himself at a cemetery near the ranch headquarters east of

Bluebonnets in the hill country of San Antonio.

Blessing, and in 1900 he was buried there in a grave that is easy to find.

Victory and independence: The climax of the Texas Revolution occurred on April 21, 1836, at what is now the **San Jacinto Battlefield State Historical Park** east of present-day **Houston** (between Interstate 10 and Highway 225). After the massacres at the Alamo and Goliad, General Sam Houston conducted a strategic retreat with the remaining Texas soldiers. Santa Anna, now as Mexico's president, pursued with superior forces, but Houston turned and launched a desperate attack at San Jacinto. Santa Anna's command was routed, and after *el presidente* was captured, he signed a treaty ordering all Mexican forces out of Texas and recognizing the Rio Grande – not the Nueces River – as the boundary of the new republic. Thus Texas was prodigiously expanded, and the stage was set for war between the United States and Mexico. The site of this enormously consequential battle is well-marked. There is an excellent museum at the base of the 570-foot (170-meter) **San Jacinto Monument**.

The first American pioneers to settle Texas were members of the "Old Three Hundred." Beginning in 1821, Stephen F. Austin, the "Father of Texas," arranged to bring in the first of 300 pioneer families he had agreed to import as an impresario of the government of Mexico. This initial Anglo–American colony in Texas centered on **San Felipe de Austin**, located on the **Brazos River** 30 minutes west of present-day Houston via Interstate 90. San Felipe was a village of log cabins from which Austin, who was granted complete political and judicial powers, ruled the growing colony. Originating here were Texas' first English-speaking newspaper, the Texas Rangers, and the independence movement – through the Conventions of 1832 and 1833 and the Consultation of 1835.

During the Texas Revolution, the town was burned, however, and the "Birthplace of Anglo–American Settlement in Texas" never recovered. Much of the

Historic farmstead at LBJ State Historic Park.

old site is preserved within **Stephen F. Austin State Historical Park** which, in addition to several monuments and markers and a statue of Austin himself, includes an excellent reconstruction of Austin's dogtrot log cabin.

A short distance to the northwest (at Routes 1457 and 237) is **Round Top**, established in 1836 and today clustered around picturesque **Henkel Square**. The square offers visitors commercial buildings and dwellings of the early- to mid-19th century, as well as a split-rail fence and nearby Lutheran church built of stone in 1866. Also nearby is **Moore's Fort**, erected by Indian fighter John Moore in 1828, and the **Winedale Historical Center**, a 19th-century farmstead with restored log cabins, a smokehouse and barns, a two-story plantation house, and a stagecoach inn with the strong German architectural influence of the area.

A little farther north is **Independence**, founded in 1824 as Coles Settlement by John P. Coles, one of Stephen F. Austin's Old Three Hundred. In 1836 the town's name was changed to commemorate the independence of Texas from Mexico. The original home of John Coles may be toured, along with the ruins of old **Baylor University** and other pioneer structures. A few miles to the east is **Washington-on-the-Brazos State Historical Park**, where the Texas Declaration of Independence was signed on March 2, 1836.

The park contains a reconstruction of **Independence Hall**, where the Declaration was written and signed; **Barrington**, the plantation home of Dr Anson B. Jones, the last president of the Republic of Texas; and the superb **Star of the Republic Museum**, which depicts all aspects of life in the republic.

Hero's home: About an hour to the northeast is **Huntsville**, where the hero of San Jacinto eventually made his home. As a young officer, Houston performed valorously with Andrew Jackson during the Creek War of 1813–14, later was governor of Tennessee, lived among the Cherokees, was twice elected president of the Republic of Texas, and then served

Mission San Antonio de Valero, better known as the Alamo.

the Lone Star State as governor and senator. Houston built a large dogtrot house for his growing family and practiced law from a nearby log cabin. When he was elected governor, he sold the house, and when he returned to Huntsville he rented the architecturally unique **Steamboat House**, where he died in 1863. These structures may be visited at the **Sam Houston Memorial Museum Complex** adjacent to **Sam Houston State University**; the larger-than-life frontier hero is buried in Huntsville's **Oakwood Cemetery**.

Just over 100 miles (160 km) to the northeast via Routes 190 and 59 is **Nacogdoches**, which claims to be the oldest town in Texas. The **Old Stone Fort**, built as a Spanish trading post in 1779, today is a museum on the campus of **Stephen F. Austin State University**. A mile away is **Millard's Crossing**, a collection of restored 19th-century buildings furnished with pioneer memorabilia.

Half an hour west of Nacogdoches on Route 21 is the **Caddoan State His-**

toric Site. Here visitors will find two impressive ceremonial mounds of about 300 by 350 feet (91 by 107 meters) each, a full-size replica of a Caddoan "bee-hive" house, and exhibits on the Caddo way of life. It was the Caddo Indians who gave Texas its name. The location of the first Spanish mission in Texas is commemorated just a few miles down the road at the **Mission Tejas State Historical Park**.

Two hours to the west and 4 miles (6.5 km) north of **Groesbeck** is **Fort Parker**. This stockaded settlement was erected by the Parker clan in 1834. The tall stockade was reinforced with sturdy blockhouses, a recessed double gate and firing platforms with loopholes. These elaborate precautions went for naught, however. When a large Comanche war party showed up in 1836, the front gates were wide open and many of the men were working outside the walls. The warriors galloped inside the gate, killed seven settlers, wounded others and raced away with five captives. The most famous captive was 9-year-old Cynthia Ann Parker, who later became the wife of Chief Peta Nocona and bore three children, including the last great Comanche chief, Quanah Parker. Beautifully reconstructed, Fort Parker today is a state historical site.

Forty-five miles (72 km) west of Fort Parker is **Waco**, known as "Six-Shooter Junction" during its heyday as a stop-over on the Chisholm Trail. In 1870 a toll bridge was built across the Brazos River to accommodate cattle herds and other traffic. Constructed by the Roebling Company of New York City, the 475-foot (145-meter) span was the longest suspension bridge in the world – until the Roeblings built the Brooklyn Bridge a few years later.

The **Texas Ranger Hall of Fame** at **Fort Fisher** near the **Baylor University** campus boasts a superb gun collection, eye-catching displays, an excellent library, and a film that depicts the story of the Rangers from their formation in 1835. This tribute to the world's most famous law-enforcement body is a fitting conclusion to a frontier journey through East Texas.

Left, Mexican-style cowboy hat, often seen in Texas. **Right,** a mural honors Mexico, Texas's neighbor to the south.

Few places are as rich in frontier history as West Texas. Settled in the glory days of the Old West, the region is home to sprawling ranches, broken-down ghost towns, handsome landscapes, and modern cities that have grown up around old-time cow towns.

A fruitful trip starts in **Fort Worth**, billed as the town "where the West begins." The **Stockyards National Historic District** features a museum in the old **Livestock Exchange Building**, a working antique railroad and western-style stores and restaurants along traditional boardwalks. A short drive away, across the **Trinity River** just north of downtown Fort Worth on Central Avenue, is one of the West's most historic graveyards. **Oakwood Cemetery**, the "Westminster Abbey of Fort Worth," is the final resting place of numerous frontier notables.

No other cemetery has three gunfighters of this caliber: gambler Luke Short, who killed former city marshal Longhair Jim Courtright (at a Main Street site designated by a marker), and Killin' Jim Miller, the West's premier assassin. Impressive mausoleums house the remains of cattle barons such as Burk Burnett and W. D. Waggoner.

Downtown at **Fire Station No. 1**, dioramas and displays present the colorful history of Fort Worth from its years as a military post and cow town, while the **Cattle Raisers Museum** portrays the past of the Texas cattle ranching industry. Seven rustic structures from the 1850s constitute the **Log Cabin Village**, and a tour of **Thistle Hill**, built in 1903 by W. D. Waggoner's free-spending daughter, Electra, offers a visit to the last surviving mansion of the cattle-baron era. Matchless collections of the paintings and sculptures of Charles Russell, Frederic Remington and other western artists are displayed at the **Amon G. Carter Museum of Western Art** and the **Sid Richardson Collection of Western Art**.

After an immersion in western history and culture in Fort Worth, drive about an hour to the northwest and tour old **Fort Richardson** on the outskirts of **Jacksboro**. The most impressive buildings surrounding the parade ground are the two-story hospital and the ten-room commanding officer's quarters, which once housed the Army's best Indian fighter, Colonel Ranald Mackenzie of the Fourth Cavalry. The bachelor officers' quarters contain a museum, while across the parade ground a company barracks is furnished.

The Panhandle: Pick up the trail again far to the west in the Texas Panhandle just south of **Amarillo**. Here on the campus of **West Texas A & M University** in **Canyon**, the **Panhandle-Plains Museum** beckons with its Old West exhibits, gun collection, Indian artifacts and T-Anchor ranch buildings.

Canyon is the gateway to **Palo Duro Canyon State Park**, where multicolored walls plunge a thousand feet from the tabletop of the high plains to the canyon floor. Discovered by the expedition of Francisco Vásquez de Coronado in 1540,

Palo Duro Canyon was for centuries the winter haven of Comanche Indians. In 1874 the Comanches were routed from their longtime refuge by Colonel Ranald Mackenzie in the last large-scale battle of Texas's Indian wars. Legendary cattleman Charles Goodnight soon established his famous **JA Ranch** in the canyon, and a dugout there was built for JA line riders.

Visitors may hike and camp, take the **Sad Monkey Train** through some of the most spectacular vistas of Palo Duro, and ride horseback where Comanche warriors, Comanchero traders, US cavalrymen and JA cowboys once rode. The highlight of a summer visit to Palo Duro Canyon is an evening in the outdoor amphitheater viewing the spectacular musical drama *Texas*, which runs from mid-June through August.

About 100 miles (160 km) south in **Lubbock** is the internationally-famous **Ranch Heritage Museum**, where more than 30 authentic structures, including ranch houses, barns, dugouts, bunkhouses and windmills, have been moved to a 14-acre (6-hectare) site near **Texas Tech University**. There are excellent displays in the museum building, but the vintage structures from the XIT, 6666, Matador and other frontier spreads provide a living history of ranching unmatched anywhere in the West.

It's about another 110 miles (180 km) on Highway 385 and Interstate 20 to **Pecos**, where the **Orient Saloon and Hotel** is a celebration of the late 19th century. The barroom sports bullet holes from an 1896 shootout in which gunfighter Barney Riggs killed two adversaries. Nearby is the grave of gunman Clay Allison, resting in the shadow of an exact replica of Judge Roy Bean's saloon. In 1883 Pecos was the scene of cowboy contests, and the annual **Fourth of July West of the Pecos Rodeo** is touted as the "World's First Rodeo," one of many to make the claim.

Old ghosts: About a 90-minute drive to the south on Route 17 is **Fort Davis National Historic Site**, nestled in the beautiful **Davis Mountains** beside **Limpia Creek**. Established in 1854 to

Fort Worth parade honors the stagecoach.

protect the Overland Trail from San Antonio to El Paso, Fort Davis was abandoned at the outbreak of the Civil War. When the Army returned in 1867, the original log and picket structures were in ruins, but Fort Davis was expanded with substantial adobe and stone construction into a regimental headquarters. Fort Davis was the long-time home of Colonel Benjamin Grierson's Tenth Cavalry. Known as "buffalo soldiers," his black troopers were heavily engaged against hostile Indians, last seeing action against Victorio's Apaches in the early 1880s.

Today Fort Davis is matched in size and quality of restoration only by Fort Laramie, Wyoming. Attired in 19th-century uniforms, guides conduct military demonstrations during the day, and periodically a loudspeaker emits martial music from the band manuals of 1875. The barracks, the commanding officer's quarters and the sutler's store, each furnished in period detail, are not to be missed, and a look across the parade ground at officers' row offers a haunting glimpse into the 19th century.

While visiting the sprawling fort, consider staying at the **Hotel Limpia**, an atmospheric turn-of-the-century hostelry on the historic **town square** of Fort Davis, which began as a "hog ranch" just south of the outpost that gave the community its name. The courthouse, built in 1910, was equipped with a dungeon cell for lawbreakers, and venerable mercantile structures and churches are tangible reminders of the old frontier town.

The drive south from Fort Davis on Routes 17 and 67 passes through the rock and adobe ruins of **Shafter**, a 19th-century silver mining town. Just past the border town of **Presidio**, you'll come to **Fort Leaton State Historical Park**. In 1848, at the close of the Mexican War, frontiersman Ben Leaton constructed a massive adobe trading post beside the **Rio Grande** and astride the Chihuahua-to-San Antonio Trail. More than 40 flat-roofed rooms were arranged around a large patio, with a high-walled adobe corral along the east side. Leaton traded

Below, historic ranch. Right, Officers' Row, Fort Davis National Historic Site.

with local Indians and supplied Army patrols. On one occasion, he lured Indians inside his patio with liquor, then had them gunned down from the surrounding rooftops so that he could sell their scalps for bounty in Mexico. The site has been extensively restored, and in addition to museum displays there is a big wooden-wheeled Mexican freight cart of the type involved in the explosive El Paso Salt War of 1877.

From Fort Leaton, it's a curvy drive to the ghost town of **Terlingua** along glorious **El Camino del Rio** (Route 170), which leads over mountains, through canyons and past breathtaking geologic formations overlooking the river. Mercury was mined at Terlingua until the 1940s; in its heyday, some 2,000 souls lived there. Although the imposing upper works are gone now, collapsed tunnels and open shafts are dangerous reminders of the old days. The most impressive ruin is the two-story adobe hotel perched atop the highest hill. The building served as an office and residence for the Anglo-American owners;

the open second-story area beneath a tile roof provided a breezy area for dining and dancing. The adobe company store still serves tourists, while the old school and Catholic church are decaying gracefully. There are scores of abandoned stone dwellings, and the old *cemeterio* on the outskirts of town serves as a quiet remembrance of the many Mexican families who once lived here.

Unforgiving country: A few miles away is the west entrance to **Big Bend National Park**, more than 800,000 acres (324,000 hectares) of volcanic desert, soaring mountains and precipitous canyons. Ranchers in the Big Bend region had to utilize at least 100 acres (40 hectares) per cow, and Texas Rangers in need of arrests could sweep the isolated canyons that served as outlaw hideouts. The land is unforgiving (as the saying goes, "everything in Big Bend sticks, stings or bites") but richly rewarding. Big Bend abounds in desert wildlife, with more than 430 species of birds and 1,100 types of plants.

The most spectacular attractions are Santa Elena Canyon, the **Chisos Moun-**

Room and board.

tains and **Boquillas Canyon**, but abandoned ranches and the deserted **Hot Springs** resort are among the numerous smaller treasures. River-rafting is popular; daily horseback rides are available; and hundreds of miles of nature trails and primitive paths offer endless possibilities to hikers and campers.

After leaving the park, it is only an hour's drive north on Highway 385 to tiny **Marathon**, established in 1882 as a railroad town. About 4 miles (6 km) below the townsite, **Camp Pena Colorado**, a 19th-century military outpost built beside a big natural spring, is now a county park. During the 1920s, Alfred Gage, a San Antonio banker who owned a 500,000-acre (202,000-hectare) cattle ranch near Marathon, built a two-story lodge for his friends and family. Gage died soon after, and new owners converted the lodge into the **Gage Hotel**, the town's only hostelry. It offers superb meals and rooms with ranch-style furnishings. There is no more picturesque accommodation in West Texas.

From Gage, it's about 125 miles (200 km) east on Highway 90 across an empty stretch of brush country to the **Judge Roy Bean Visitor Center** at the dusty little town of **Langtry**. Bean was a frontier drifter who ended up in California for a time during the Gold Rush era, then operated a saloon in San Antonio for 20 years before shifting his business west of the Pecos River to Vinegaroon.

After becoming a justice of the peace, he held court in his one-room bar (a billiard room was added later – Bean died on the ornate pool table there in 1903). Bean worshiped British actress Lily Langtry, whom he never met, and renamed Vinegaroon "Langtry" in her honor, then dubbed his saloon the "Jersey Lilly." He became renowned for eccentric legal decisions (when a man was killed in a shootout in his saloon, Bean noted that he was armed and carried two $20 gold pieces, so he fined the corpse $40 for "carrying a concealed weapon"). And when an 1896 championship boxing match in El Paso was blocked by do-gooders, Judge Bean hastily constructed a ring on the Mexi-

Judge Roy Bean's Jersey Lilly Saloon, named after Lily Langtry.

can side of the Rio Grande just south of town. After a special train carrying sportsmen, gamblers, journalists, the heavyweight champ Peter Maher and the challenger Bob Fitzsimmons arrived in Langtry, everyone had an overpriced beer at the Jersey Lilly, then walked down to the river to watch Fitzsimmons knock out the champ in the first round. Today travelers may go to the south edge of Langtry and peer down at the prizefight site, then return to town and photograph Bean's house, across the street from his saloon. He optimistically labeled his little home an "Opera House" where Lily Langtry might perform, but she didn't visit until 10 months after Bean's death. The judge's weathered old saloon is part of the visitor center, as is an extensive cactus garden.

The girl I left behind: Eighteen miles (29 km) to the east is a scenic turnout with a stunning overlook of the confluence of the Pecos River and the Rio Grande. About a mile away, **Seminole Canyon State Park** offers hikes into yawning crevices where you get a look

at 4,000-year-old Indian cave art. Turn north on Highway 277 at **Del Rio** (where Roy Bean is buried near the stone trading post that today is the **Whitehead Memorial Museum**) and then head east on Highway 190 to the turnoff for **Fort McKavett State Historical Park**. Established in 1852 and abandoned in 1883, the post has eight company barracks, a large hospital, a stone schoolhouse and twelve officers' quarters, including a building once occupied by Colonel Ranald Mackenzie. There is an excellent museum, and visitors may arrange to sleep overnight in the old barracks.

Fifteen miles to the east are the ruins of **Mission San Saba**, twice attacked by Comanches in the 1750s. Although the mission was abandoned after the second assault, rumors of a lost Spanish silver mine brought Jim Bowie, whose party did not find the mine but engaged in an epic battle against a large Comanche war party.

Double back to Highway 277 and continue north to **Fort Concho National Historic Landmark** in **San Angelo**. No territory experienced as many confrontations between settlers and Indians over as long a period as Texas, and consequently more forts – more than 30 – were built here than anywhere else. Fort Concho was established near the **North Concho River** in 1867; its impressive stone structures were erected by skilled German immigrants from Fredericksburg. Both white and black soldiers operated out of Fort Concho, which was commanded at different times by Colonel Ranald Mackenzie, Colonel Benjamin Grierson and Colonel William R. Shafter.

When the military moved out, civilians moved into officers' row, which offered the best dwellings for the growing community of San Angelo. These buildings still stand, along with the chapel, barracks, a sun-dial and the two-story headquarters, which houses a museum. Another nearby museum is **Miss Hattie's**, a one-time bordello where soldiers and cowboys roistered for decades. Little wonder that when the troops marched out in 1889 they sang, "The Girl I Left Behind Me."

Left, pumping oil. Right, silhouette at sunset.

170

OKLAHOMA

First there was Indian Territory. In 1830, President Andrew Jackson expelled the Cherokees from their homeland in Georgia and forced them on the Trail of Tears to Indian Territory, now eastern Oklahoma. They were soon joined by other exiled tribes – Creeks, Seminoles, Southern Cheyennes, Apaches and more. For some, Indian Territory was a prison, for others a last-chance refuge.

Neither prison nor refuge was destined to last. Homesteaders started pouring into the territory in the 1870s, and in 1889 the first great land run threw open more than 2 million acres (809,000 hectares) of prime prairie land. Indian Territory was dismantled piece by piece until, in 1907, the state of Oklahoma was admitted to the Union.

Oklahoma is still very much in touch with its cowboy-and-Indian heritage. Historic sites and museums recall the heady days when "sooners" raced each other for prime homesteads, and with more than 35 tribes, the state is a major center of Native American cultures.

Cowboys and Indians: There is no better way to start a trip in Oklahoma than to visit the **National Cowboy Hall of Fame** and **Western Heritage Center** in **Oklahoma City**. The cowboy has long ranked as the country's premier folk hero, and the Hall of Fame is a magnificent tribute to the cowboy tradition. From chuck wagons and cowboy gear to western art, visitors can revel in the lore and history of the West's favorite sons.

While in Oklahoma City, Old West buffs should also tour the **State Museum of History** and the **Harn Homestead and 1889er Museum**, where a farmhouse, massive barn and one-room schoolhouse stand on a 10-acre (4-hectare) site homesteaded in 1889. If you're more interested in shopping, you may want to stop at **Stockyards City**, where shops in the historic cattle-trading district offer a huge selection of cowboy hats, boots, saddles and other authentic western gear; cattle auctions are held Monday through Wednesday.

You can get a taste of the state's Indian heritage about 50 miles (80 km) southwest of Oklahoma City in the town of **Anadarko**. Each August, thousands of Indian and non-Indian visitors come here for the **American Indian Exposition**, one of the largest gatherings of its kind in the country. The exposition is a week-long celebration of Native American cultures featuring traditional musicians, dancers and artists from the United States and Canada.

Indian City, USA: There are several interesting attractions that operate year-round, too. **Indian City, USA**, is a walk-through recreation of Indian villages representing several tribes, all explained by knowledgeable Indian guides. There is a museum and gift shop here, too, and a series of dance and music exhibitions, art shows and lectures. For a calendar of events, consult Indian City directly.

Across the highway, the **National Hall of Fame for Famous American Indians** pays tribute to exceptional figures in Native American history – some well known, others fairly obscure. The **Southern Plains Indian Museum** is also in town and, in addition to its fine collection of artifacts, provides an excellent outlet for contemporary Plains Indian arts and crafts. The **Anadarko Philomathic Museum** exhibits pioneer and military relics, paintings, photographs and an Indian doll collection.

Fort Sill Military Reservation is about 35 miles (56 km) south of Anadarko. Although now a modern military facility, the fort's **Old Post National Historic Landmark** preserves a number of historic structures, including the old post headquarters, 1875 chapel and the guardhouse that once held Geronimo and other Chiricahua Apache prisoners.

Although many Apaches were later shipped to a reservation in New Mexico, some chose to stay in western Oklahoma. Their descendants still live in the area. Geronimo was never released from exile. He died and was buried at Fort Sill in 1909, already enshrined in Wild West mythology. **Geronimo's gravesite** and the graves of other Indian leaders – including Comanche chief Quanah Parker and Kiowa chiefs Satank and

Satanta – are on Chiefs Knoll in the **Fort Sill Cemetery**. Ask the staff at the **Fort Sill Museum** for directions. In nearby Lawton is the **Museum of the Great Plains**, with indoor and outdoor displays depicting the fur trade, Indian life, cattle ranching and pioneer farming.

While you're in the area, consider a side trip to the **Wichita Mountains National Wildlife Refuge**, where a herd of bison once again roam the grasslands of the southern plains. These burly, seemingly placid animals were the very lifeblood of the Plains Indians and figured prominently in their spiritual life. Seeing the prairie littered with carcasses left to rot by professional hide-hunters, Satanta, the war chief of the Kiowas, asked a delegation of military men, "Has the white man become a child that he should recklessly kill and not eat? When the red men slay game, they do so that they may live and not starve."

The tragedy of the Southern Plains is recalled at the **Washita Battleground Historic Site**, about 120 miles (200 km) west of Oklahoma City near **Cheyenne**.

It was here that, in 1868, a young glory-seeking officer named George Armstrong Custer rode down upon a sleeping Cheyenne village headed by Chief Black Kettle. Only three years earlier, Black Kettle had survived the Sand Creek Massacre in Colorado and had worked hard since then to maintain peace between his people and the whites. His efforts came to nothing on that cold winter dawn as Custer's troops swept into camp cutting down just about anything that moved.

More than 100 Cheyennes were killed that day, including Black Kettle and his wife. Only 11 of the dead were warriors. Upon his return, Custer was publicly congratulated by his commanding officer for "efficient and gallant services."

Badmen and boomers: Return to Oklahoma City and head north on Interstate 35 about 25 miles (40 km) to **Guthrie**, created almost overnight during the land rush of 1889. Guthrie served as Oklahoma's seat of government from 1890 until 1910; the **Oklahoma Territorial Museum** chronicles life in the old In-

Left, *End of the Trail* at the Cowboy Hall of Fame. Below, Will Rogers' Birthplace.

dian Territory. The last territorial governor and the first state governor were inaugurated next door, at the **Carnegie Library**. The old opera house, the Guthrie railroad hotel and several commercial buildings are among the city's splendid Victorian structures.

Continue north on Interstate 35 and then east on Route 51. About 9 miles (15 km) outside of **Stillwater**, you will see a sign and an unpaved road leading to the ghost town of **Ingalls**, site of a classic western shoot-out. Indian Territory was always a favorite haunt of fugitives, keeping lawmen busy with countless holdups, manhunts and shootings. One of the most explosive episodes took place here on September 1, 1893, when a gang of notorious desperadoes known as the "Oklahombres" tried to shoot their way past a local posse sent to round them up. By the time the smoke cleared, one bystander lay dead, another was shot in the chest, and three officers were fatally wounded. All but two of the outlaws escaped.

It's a short drive north to **Pawnee**, home of the **Pawnee Bill Museum and State Park**. Gordon W. Lillie, better known as Pawnee Bill, led a group of "boomers" into the territory in 1889, taught at the Pawnee Indian Agency, and then organized a popular Wild West show. For several years he worked in partnership with Buffalo Bill Cody, but eventually Lillie returned to his 2,000-acre (810-hectare) ranch. The 14-room stone house, built in 1910, is maintained for tourists, along with other ranch buildings and an outstanding museum.

"The Cherokee Kid": Pick up the trail again at the **Gilcrease Museum** in **Tulsa** which houses one of the premier collections of western art and artifacts in the country, including major works by Thomas Moran, Frederic Remington, Charles M. Russell and George Catlin.

About 3 miles (5 km) northeast of Tulsa is the little railroad town of **Oologah**, site of the **Will Rogers Birthplace**. In 1856 Clem Rogers, who was part Cherokee, began ranching on land held in common by the Cherokee Nation for use by any of its citizens, free of

Pawnee Bill Museum and Ranch.

rent or taxes. Twelve years later he moved his operation east to superb rangeland in the **Verdigris Valley** and was soon running cattle with his CV brand on 60,000 acres (24,000 hectares). By 1875 Clem and his wife Mary, also part Cherokee, completed a two-story log house with seven large rooms. The hewn logs were covered with weatherboarding, which was painted white, and the imposing dwelling became a focal point for the entire area.

On November 4, 1879, their eighth and final child was born – William Penn Adair Rogers, who as humorist and homespun philosopher became one of America's most popular entertainers. At the turn of the century, when Will ranched the old home place, he used a Dog Iron brand, and today it is called the **Dog Iron Ranch**. In 1959 Will's descendants donated the house to Oklahoma, because the Verdigris Valley was about to be flooded by the new Oologah Dam and Reservoir. The house was moved to high ground about a mile from its original location, and a barn was

built by Amish workers in the fashion of the original. A memorial to Rogers stands in nearby **Claremore**.

To the southeast of the Rogers home is **Tahlequah**, capital of the Cherokee Nation since 1839. The brick **Cherokee National Capitol** was built in 1869 and eventually became the county courthouse. A few miles south of town is the **Cherokee Heritage Center**, featuring a museum with Indian artifacts and a reconstruction of Cherokee villages from the 17th to 19th centuries.

A brief drive west brings you to **Fort Gibson**, established in 1824 as the westernmost outpost of the US Army. Sam Houston stayed here in 1829 and married a Cherokee woman. Among the famous military figures who served at the fort were future president Zachary Taylor, Confederate officers Robert E. Lee and J.E.B. Stuart, and Confederate President Jefferson Davis, who was court-martialed for being "highly disrespectful, insubordinate, and contemptuous." During the Civil War, more than 6,000 Union troops manned Fort Gibson to safeguard the "District of the Frontier" from Confederates.

The site encompasses a reconstructed stockade with blockhouses, barracks, stables, a guardhouse, stone magazine and a two-story officers' quarters. Rumor had it that the stockade was intended to keep the soldiers in the fort as much as to keep the Indians out, because nearby "hog ranches" – actually gambling halls and bordellos – were reputed to be vile.

About an hour to the southeast, outside the town of **Sallishaw**, is **Sequoyah's Home**, a log cabin built in the late 1820s. Born about 1760, Sikwayi (corrupted by English usage to "Sequoyah") developed the Cherokee system of writing, the first written Indian language north of Mexico. "I thought that would be like catching a wild animal and taming it," he later said. Within months, tribal members learned to read and write their own language and began publishing their own newspaper, the *Cherokee Phoenix*. Sikwayi later became an influential leader among the Cherokees and was sent to Washington, DC, to represent the tribe.

A hat for all seasons.

OUTHOUSES

Bob Ross, a native Montanan, is a former conservationist with the Department of Agriculture. For 28 years he crisscrossed the nation's fourth largest state, meeting with ranchers and inspecting their soil. He retired, or so he thought, in 1977. These days, his business card identifies him as a cowboy poet-humorist-entertainer. Noticeably missing is the O word, the source of Ross's retirement nest egg. Bob Ross, you see, is into outhouses.

Outhouses were a fixture on the frontier horizon for years, stretching like sentinels across the West from Oklahoma to California to Montana. Ross grew up in Musselshell, Montana. Population: 50 people on a Saturday night, he says. The family home was of logs with a sod roof. Out back stood an outhouse – a three-holer.

Ross didn't give it much thought until many years later, when his job took him back and forth across the state, the horizon as distant and unpeopled as anywhere in America. It was hard *not* to see the old privies, some of them tumbling down or leaning away from the prevailing winds. Ross was a great reader of western history. He realized these outhouses represented a part of that history; also that year by year many were dying of benign neglect. He'd seen a book on outhouses, a picture and caption affair, called *Sittin' and a-Thinkin'*, and he got to thinking about a writing book himself – something to pass out to family and friends. *Muddled Meanderings in an Outhouse*, he titled it.

"The printer called to tell me the first 1,000 books would cost me $1,650, but he could give me 2,000 for only $250 more. I figured I'd really have to hustle to give away 1,000," says Ross.

But still, a bargain was a bargain. "The printer suggested I take some downtown to the local bookstore and sell them there. It had never entered my mind to sell the book. I put a price of $2 on them, dropped off about a dozen copies. In three weeks' time, those babies had vanished."

Long about then, his phone started ringing and the letters started coming. The book had made it to Ohio and Pennsylvania. Somebody in California had heard of it and wanted some copies. Ross started keeping books in his car and dropped off copies in bookstores, drug stores, gift shops, even restaurants. When it came time for a second printing, Ross took a deep breath and ordered 10,000 copies. He need not have worried. Today, some 20 years after first publication, *Muddled Meanderings* is in its 18th printing.

Biffie, donnicker, backhouse, Mrs Jones, Johnnie, comfort station, latrine, Bob Ross has heard them all. He's seen outhouses made of wood, canvas, stone, tin, and yes, brick. He's seen them with porches, topped with TV antennas, painted with peace signs. He knows of one-holers, two-holers, four-holers, even a 14-holer constructed back in the 1930s by the Civilian Conservation Corps. He's witnessed gabled roofs, Victorian gingerbread, A-frames, not to mention plenty of two-story outhouses, the elevated "plumbing" necessarily offset.

No, Bob Ross hardly knew what a fertile subject he'd stumble upon when, years ago, he decided to make outhouses his hobby. Nowadays, he's quick to acknowledge his good fortune. "Outhouses have been good to us," he says. ∎

d-fashioned
ivy.

NORTHERN NEW MEXICO

"I loved it immediately," artist Georgia O'Keeffe wrote of her first visit to northern New Mexico. "From then on, I was always on my way back."

Like so many travelers before her, O'Keeffe was enchanted by the landscape – the multicolored earth, sun-washed mesas and rolling hills of piñon and juniper – as well as by the unique blend of Indian, Hispanic and Anglo cultures. One feels a deep sense of history here. Pueblo Indians can point to the ruins of ancient villages and say, "This is where our ancestors came from." Hispanics can point to the old missions built by early Spanish settlers. And Anglos, the newcomers, can trace their forefathers' arrival in the wagon ruts of the old Santa Fe Trail.

Capital city: The very heart of northern New Mexico is **Santa Fe**, and the historic **Plaza** is the heart of Santa Fe. Established in 1609, Santa Fe served as the capital of the Spaniards' northern colony for some 200 years, interrupted only by the Pueblo Revolt of 1680 when they were ousted by rebellious Indians. In the 1820s, during a brief period of Mexican rule, the first American traders arrived in the Plaza after an arduous journey on the Santa Fe Trail.

And in 1846, American troops under the command of General Stephen W. Kearny marched into the Plaza virtually unopposed and laid claim to New Mexico for the United States government. The Plaza is still the center of activity in Santa Fe, although it's now clearly dominated by the tourist trade. Some of the town's most important events are held here, including the **Indian Market** in August and the **Spanish Market** in July.

The oldest building on the Plaza is the **Palace of the Governors**. Here Indians sit under the *portal* selling jewelry, pottery and other crafts much as they have for centuries. Built by the Spanish in 1610, the palace is the oldest public building in the country and has been occupied by virtually every invader who

rolled into New Mexico, including a small force of Texas Confederates who held it for a few weeks during the Civil War. Today, the palace serves as a museum, with exhibits focusing on the Mexican and early American periods and on the history of the building itself.

About a block away, on the northwest corner of the Plaza, is the **Museum of Fine Arts**, housed in a handsome Pueblo Revival building built in 1917. The museum's permanent collection features works by some of the best-known artists associated with northern New Mexico, including Ernest L. Blumenschein and Bert Geer Philips, who founded the Taos art colony around the turn of the century, and Georgia O'Keeffe, whose paintings are exhibited in an intimate upstairs gallery.

Just east of the Plaza, at the end of San Francisco Street, is the **Cathedral of Saint Francis**, built in the late 1800s by Archbishop Jean-Baptiste Lamy, the model for Willa Cather's novel, *Death Comes for the Archbishop*. Romanesque in style, the cathedral is home to a little *santo* known as *La Conquistadora*. It was carried by Don Diego de Vargas in 1692 when, after a 12-year hiatus following the Pueblo Revolt, he reclaimed New Mexico for the Spanish crown. De Vargas promised to honor Our Lady if she granted him victory, and she is still celebrated at the **Santa Fe Fiesta**, held on the first weekend after Labor Day. Across from the cathedral, the **Institute of American Indian Arts Museum** displays contemporary Native American art in all media.

Historic byways: Maneuvering through Santa Fe's ancient, narrow streets is complicated by the monochromatic, ground-hugging architecture. Will Rogers quipped that Santa Fe must have been laid out by someone "riding a jackass backwards." Fortunately there is plenty of history within easy walking distance of the Plaza.

To the south of the Plaza on the Old Santa Fe Trail near Water Street is another Romanesque structure, **Loretto Chapel**, completed in the 1870s and famous for its "miraculous" spiral staircase. The staircase was built without

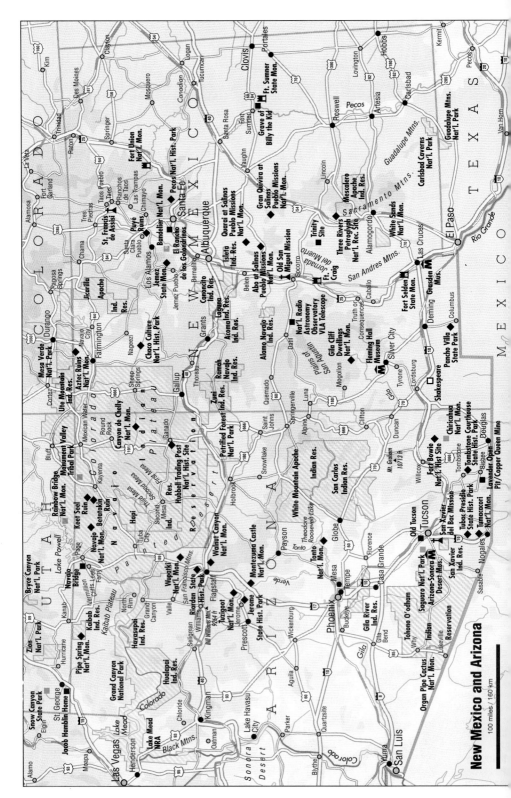

New Mexico and Arizona

100 miles / 160 km

nails by a mysterious carpenter who is said to have been St Joseph himself.

A bit farther afield, on Guadalupe Street at Agua Fria, is the **Santuario de Guadalupe**, a 200-year-old adobe mission that stood at the end of El Camino Real – the road from Mexico City. It now serves as an arts center.

You'll find several historic houses a short walk south of the Plaza in a neighborhood known as **Barrio de Analco** (East DeVargas Street around the Old Santa Fe Trail), occupied in the early 17th century by Indian servants. The most impressive structure here is the adobe **San Miguel Mission**, perhaps the oldest continuously used church in the United States. It was built in 1636 by Tlaxcalan Indians from Mexico and was badly damaged during the Pueblo Revolt of 1680. Nearby, **The Oldest House** is indeed an old dwelling, although its claim of being the oldest in America is doubtful. In any case, it's now more of a gift shop than a home.

For a glimpse of a decidedly upscale side of Santa Fe, consider a stroll along **Canyon Road**, where you'll find some of the town's most fashionable galleries, shops and homes. Here the ancient **Acequia Madre** (literally, "mother ditch") irrigated Spanish fields for centuries. Water still flows in the Acequia during spring and summer, but the fields of corn, chile and alfalfa are a memory. Canyon Road's old adobe homes and hidden courtyards were the center of Santa Fe's art colony in the 1920s and '30s; today, only the most successful artists can afford them. The imposing **Cristo Rey Church**, at Upper Canyon Road and Cristo Rey Street, is the largest adobe structure in the United States. It was built in 1940 to commemorate the 400th anniversary of Coronado's journey into the Southwest.

From Canyon Road, it's a short drive to **Camino Lejo**, where you'll find three of Santa Fe's finest museums. The **Museum of Indian Arts and Culture** (and the associated Laboratory of Anthropology) is dedicated to chronicling the history of Indian pottery, jewelry, weaving and other arts from ancient cultures to the present. Next door, the

Museum of International Folk Art is often voted "Santa Fe's favorite" by residents; it features an enchanting collection from around the world, although it's particularly strong on Spanish Colonial art. Modeled loosely on a Navajo hogan, the **Wheelwright Museum of the American Indian** features the art and artifacts of American Indians, with a special emphasis on Southwest natives. The museum store is set up like a trading post and is well worth a visit.

Life on the trail: The area outside Santa Fe is equally rich in history and culture. A half-day trip to **El Rancho de los Golondrinas**, about 15 miles (24 km) south of town, gives a sense of the grit and gumption required of early Spanish settlers. Golondrinas is a 200-acre (80-hectare) reconstruction of a Spanish rancho complete with an 18th-century chapel, farm buildings, traditional *horno* ovens and a herd of odd-looking *churro* sheep. The site is open from April through October. The first weekends of June and October are given over to the planting festival and harvest festival

Museum of Fine Arts, Santa Fe.

respectively, when the rancho hums with living-history demonstrations.

About 28 miles (45 km) east of Santa Fe, **Pecos National Historical Park** preserves the ruins of the once-imposing Pecos Pueblo, established in about 1300 and colonized by the Spanish in the early 17th century. The village served as a vital trading center between Pueblo and Plains Indians before its decline in the late 1700s. It was abandoned in 1838 when the last 17 residents moved to Jemez Pueblo.

While you're at the park, ask rangers for directions to the nearby Civil War battlefield at **Glorieta Pass**, known (with more than a little exaggeration) as the "Gettysburg of the West." Here in 1862 Union troops stopped the advance of ambitious but ill-prepared Confederates intent on conquering New Mexico and marching onwards into the gold fields of Colorado.

From Glorieta, Interstate 25 follows the old Santa Fe Trail north for about 85 miles (137 km) to **Fort Union National Monument**. The fort was established in 1851 to protect travelers from Indians and served as an important way station on the Santa Fe Trail. Rebuilt several times and now in ruins, the ghostly adobe walls speak volumes about the loneliness and hardships of frontier life.

Ask a park ranger where to find the wagon ruts of the **Santa Fe Trail**. Trade on the trail was started in 1822 by a bankrupt merchant from Franklin, Missouri, named William Becknell. Figuring that Mexico, close to independence from Spain, was about to open its border with the United States, the irrepressible Becknell was determined to be the first man across and to make a tidy profit in the bargain. He and his comrades arrived in Santa Fe after a six-week journey on November 6, 1822, and quickly sold their load of calico, rifles, nails and tools. When they left for home – their pockets heavy – they were already planning next year's trip.

For 60 years, the 900-mile (1,450-km) trail from Franklin to Santa Fe was a road to riches. Lured by handsome profits, merchants sometimes led caravans of as many as a hundred wagons. Although the journey was long and trying, many stayed "in the trade" for years, intoxicated by the excitement of trail life and by the fandangos and round-the-clock gambling in Santa Fe. As Susan Magoffin, wife of an early trader, wrote: "Oh, this is a life I would not exchange… I breathe free without that oppression and uneasiness felt in the gossiping circles of a settled home."

The high road: To the north of Santa Fe, consider a drive through the breathtaking **Sangre de Cristo Mountains** on Route 76, also known as the high road to Taos. Along the way, you'll pass through quiet 18th-century Hispanic villages where traditional artists and craftsmen sell their work from galleries and informal studios.

You can pick up the high road at the village of **Chimayó** about 30 miles (50 km) north of Santa Fe on Highway 84/285. The village was established around 1740 and is famous for its weavers. Particularly well-known are the Ortega and Trujillo families, both of whom produce and sell high-quality work.

Santa Fe style on fashionable Canyon Road.

The other big attraction here is the Santuario del Señor de Esquipulas, which is better known as the **Santuario de Chimayó**. Built as a private chapel in 1814, the santuario has been called "the Lourdes of America" because of the healing power attributed to the earth contained in a hole (*el posito*) in the chapel floor. An adjacent room is filled with carved *santos*, including the patron of the village, Santo Niño de Atocha, along with offerings left by thousands of penitents, including canes, crutches, photographs, rosary beads and heart-breaking letters.

About seven miles (11 km) east on Route 76 is the tiny village of **Cordova**, known for its traditional wood carvers. The specialties here are saints and *animalitos* (little animals) painstakingly carved in aspen or cottonwood. Traditionally, details are carefully incised into the wood, although nowadays a few carvers may paint their creations (especially the popular *truchas*, or trout) to please tourists. The studio of the Lopez-Ortiz family is marked by signs on the main village road. Museums around the world have collected the family's work for generations.

Beyond Cordova, the high road rolls through Truchas, Ojo Sarco, Las Trampas and Chamisal. To get a feeling for village life, linger a while at one of the old-fashioned general stores for a cold drink and a chat. Every community has a *camposanto* (graveyard) and at least one church, often dating to the 1700s. The massive adobe church of **San Jose de Gracia** (1776) in **Las Trampas** is particularly impressive. It is open daily in summer but closed to visitors the rest of the year except during Sunday Mass and other religious occasions.

Three villages: Continuing north on Route 518, the road descends onto the high plateau of the "three Taoses": Ranchos de Taos, the town of Taos, and Taos Pueblo.

Ranchos de Taos, a Spanish settlement now swallowed up by Taos proper, is the site of the **Church of San Francisco de Asis**, built about 1776 by

Santuario de Chimayo, the "Lourdes of America."

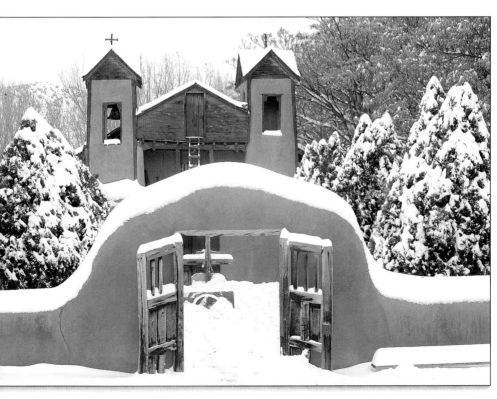

Franciscan missionaries. Massive but graceful, the adobe structure has attracted thousands of photographers and painters, including Georgia O'Keeffe, who completed well-known paintings of the church.

Just up the road, three of New Mexico's cultures converge at the historic village of **Taos**. Established by Spanish missionaries in the early 17th century, Taos became an important rendezvous and trading center for American mountain men, including Kit Carson, who later settled in the town. After the turn of the century, Taos became the heart of a thriving art colony, thanks largely to the efforts of New York painters Bert Geer Phillips and Ernest Blumenschein who were forced to stop in Taos in 1898 when their wagon wheel broke during a cross-country trip. Captivated by the sleepy Hispanic town and neighboring Taos Pueblo, the artists stayed and, together with Joseph Henry Sharp and others, organized the Taos Society of Artists in 1912.

The village's reputation was boosted

yet again with the arrival of Mabel Dodge, the New York socialite and patron of the arts who entertained D.H. Lawrence, Georgia O'Keeffe and other illustrious guests. Dodge later divorced her husband and married a Taos Indian, Tony Luhan. Their beautiful home is now an inn with rooms named after their most famous guests.

Today, Taos caters to travelers who come for the glorious mountain scenery, unique cultural mix and first-rate skiing. The old **Plaza**, with its many shops and galleries, is still the center of the town's activities, and there are plenty of well-maintained historic sites nearby.

Just a short walk to the east, for example, the **Kit Carson Home and Museum** pays homage to that legendary scout and mountain man. Carson bought this 12-room hacienda in 1843 as a wedding gift for his bride, Josefa Jaramillo, daughter of an influential Mexican family. The museum features period rooms and exhibits on early Taos history, Indian archaeology and the wild days of French and American trappers. Carson is considered a hero for his many military exploits, including the defense of Taos during the Civil War. But he was no angel. During his long career as an Indian fighter, he rounded up thousands of Navajo (massacring a fair number in the effort) and forced them on the "Long Walk" to an internment camp in eastern New Mexico. He is interrred in Taos at **Kit Carson Memorial State Park**.

To the north of the Plaza on Bent Street, the **Governor Bent Museum** was the home of Charles Bent, an Indian trader and mountain man who became the first American governor of New Mexico Territory. Bent was killed here in 1847 during a rebellion against American rule that culminated in a bloody siege at Taos Pueblo. The house is still furnished with the family's belongings.

A driving tour outside of town might include stops at the **Millicent Rogers Museum**, home to an impressive collection of Indian and Hispanic art; the dramatic, 660-foot (200-meter) chasm of the **Rio Grande Gorge**; and the **D.H. Lawrence Ranch and Shrine**, where

Anasazi ruins at Bandelier National Monument.

the novelist lived and worked for many months between 1922 and 1925; his ashes are buried in a chapel at the ranch.

Sacred dance: Looming over the entire area is **Taos Mountain**, the sacred peak of the Tiwa-speaking Taos Indians whose terraced adobe homes are perhaps the most picturesque Indian pueblo in New Mexico. Only a few miles from the modern town of Taos, **Taos Pueblo** has nonetheless remained culturally intact. Typical of many northern pueblos, the village is divided into two social groups, the North House and South House, on either side of the Taos River. The two halves alternate civic and religious obligations and compete in footraces during the pueblo's well-known **Feast of San Geronimo** in late September, a good time to visit.

In 1847, New Mexican rebels instigated an uprising against the new American government. After murdering Governor Bent, a mob fled to the church at Taos Pueblo, only to be blasted out by US soldiers, who killed about 150 people. The remains of the church still stand outside the pueblo and may be visited on the self-guiding tour.

At Taos Pueblo, as at other Indian villages, it's essential to abide by tribal regulations. Some places such as *kivas* (ceremonial chambers) and churches may be strictly off-limits. Photography may also be restricted, especially on ceremonial occasions. Do not attempt to take pictures without permission from tribal authorities and your subjects.

Visiting the pueblos can be a magical experience, particularly during feast days when the villages celebrate with traditional music, dance, dress and food. Ceremonial dances, such as the deer, buffalo and corn dance, are equally inspiring, although it may be difficult to find out exactly when they're held (information is sometimes available from the Eight Northern Pueblos, Indian Pueblo Cultural Center or tribal offices). Keep in mind that dances are strictly religious events and should be accorded the proper respect.

There are several pueblos within an hour's drive of Santa Fe. The most re-

Abiquiu landscape near Georgia O'Keeffe's home.

warding for tourists are probably **Santa Clara** and **San Ildefonso**, set on the Rio Grande north of town. Both are traditional, well-maintained villages that have carved a lucrative niche for themselves in the pottery market. The black-on-black style revived by world-famous potters Maria and Julian Martinez in the early 1900s has spawned a lively trade in Indian pottery of all types. Both villages have good pottery shops and are used to visitors during feast days and dances. Santa Clara also owns the Anasazi ruins at **Puye Cliff Dwellings**. The ancestral home of Santa Clara and other Tewa-speaking pueblos, the ruins are cut directly into the soft volcanic tuff of the **Pajarito Plateau** and require some precarious ladder-climbing to visit.

The same is true of **Bandelier National Monument**, a short drive to the south. The park preserves some 32,000 acres (13,000 hectares) of **Frijoles Canyon** and the surrounding area settled by the Anasazi in the 12th century. The mile-long Ruins Trail leads visitors to some of the most dramatic sites.

The "New West" is represented here, too. Just outside the park is **Los Alamos**, where the scientists of the top-secret Manhattan Project developed the world's first atomic bombs during World War II. The history of the project and the evolution of nuclear technology are presented at the **Los Alamos County Historical Museum** and the **Bradbury Science Museum**.

To the west of Los Alamos, Route 4 leads through the **Valle Grande**, a caldera formed by a volcanic eruption more than a million years ago. The road curves sharply south at the village of La Cueva and then passes **Jemez State Monument**, where the ruins of a 12th-century pueblo and 17th-century Spanish mission stand at the foot of the **Jemez Mountains**. The church was destroyed during the Pueblo Revolt of 1680. The Indians abandoned the site soon after, eventually settling at **Jemez Pueblo** about 12 miles (19 km) south.

Ancient cities: From Jemez it's about an hour's drive to **Albuquerque**, founded in the early 18th century and now New Mexico's largest city. You can still get a feeling for the original Spanish village at the **Old Town** plaza, where the handsome **Church of San Felipe de Neri**, built in 1793, stands next to gift shops and restaurants.

Several museums are worth a visit, too. The **Albuquerque Museum** records local history; the **Maxwell Museum of Anthropology** features exhibits on Indian cultures from prehistoric times to the present; and the **Indian Pueblo Cultural Center** offers a lively schedule of Indian dances, demonstrations and other special events.

If time allows, consider exploring the more remote western pueblos. About 65 miles (105 km) west of Albuquerque off Interstate 40, **Acoma Pueblo** may be the most dramatic in the state. One of the oldest continuously inhabited villages in the country, the village of Acoma, now called **Sky City**, is perched atop a 365-foot (111-meter) mesa. Although most people now live in outlying towns, the old pueblo is still occupied by about a dozen families and is kept in excellent repair for a variety of ceremonial events.

Traditional dress at the Santa Fe Indian Market.

The guided tour of Acoma includes a stop at **San Esteban del Rey Mission**, a monumental adobe church built in the 17th century. All the materials used in the church were carried to the top of the mesa by Acoma laborers, including the massive ceiling beams, which came from Mount Taylor nearly 50 miles (80 km) away. Legend has it that the giant logs never once touched the ground.

Across the highway, **Laguna Pueblo** has none of the drama of Acoma, although the **San Jose Mission** in Old Laguna is one of the prettiest in New Mexico. Farther west, **Zuni Pueblo**, the state's largest, is well-known for silversmithing. Shops near the old village are filled with exquisite jewelry. About 33 miles (53 km) east of Zuni on Route 53, the ruins of a 13th-century pueblo stand atop a towering mesa at **El Morro National Monument**.

The scores of inscriptions at the base of the mesa range from Anasazi petroglyphs to the signatures of early Spanish and American explorers, including Juan de Oñate, who passed by in 1605,

and Diego de Vargas, who came in 1692.

About 65 miles (105 km) north of Interstate 40 in a remote canyon reached only by an unpaved road (impassable in bad weather; call for conditions) is **Chaco Culture National Historical Park**, the single most important archaeological site in New Mexico. Chaco served as the hub of Anasazi culture between the years 900 and 1115. Among the nine "great houses" at this site, the largest and most complex is **Pueblo Bonito**, a five-story, three-acre, D-shaped masonry structure built over several generations.

The many kivas at Pueblo Bonito indicate the importance Chacoans placed on religious observance, as does the nearby **Casa Rinconada**; at 63 feet (19 meters) across, it is one of the largest *kivas* in the region.

The presence of roads radiating from Chaco to other Anasazi sites suggests that it may have served as a ceremonial and trading center for the entire region. Whatever its true nature, few places speak as powerfully of the beauty and complexity of Anasazi culture.

Feast day at San Juan Pueblo.

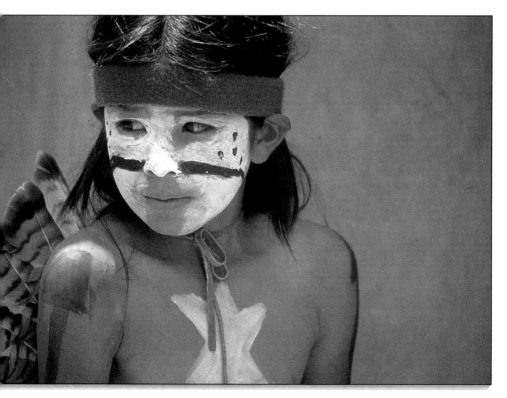

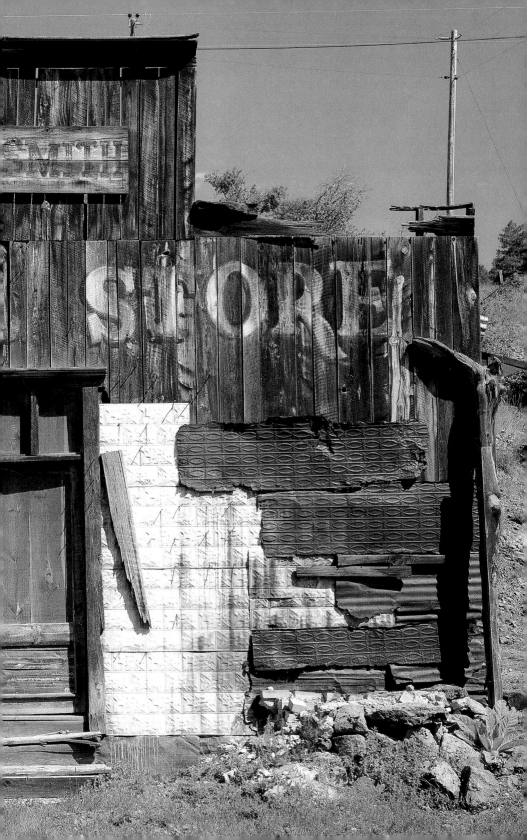

SOUTHERN NEW MEXICO

When the first Spanish settlers arrived in the late 1700s, southern New Mexico was dominated by the Apache Indians. They were a rugged people, well-adapted to a life of hunting and gathering on the region's dry plateaus and torrid flats. They were also expert fighters. Apache attacks held back the Spanish frontier for more than a century, allowing only a few scattered settlements along the Rio Grande to survive.

Things changed when the United States took possession of the territory in 1848. After a spate of Apache raids on American camps and wagon trains, the government dispatched the army, under the command of General James H. Carleton and Kit Carson, to eliminate the "Indian problem." Within a year, the Mescalero Apaches were rounded up and marched off to an internment camp at Fort Sumner.

By the late 1800s, southern New Mexico was swarming with a ragged band of prospectors, merchants, cowboys and drifters, one of whom – a scruffy, buck-toothed, affable young man named William Bonney – was destined to become one of the legendary killers of the Old West: Billy the Kid.

Talking to heaven: Start your tour at **Salinas Pueblo Missions National Monument** 85 miles (140 km) south of **Albuquerque** off Highway 60. The monument preserves the remains of three separate Indian pueblos – Quarai, Abo and Gran Quivara – that were colonized by the Spanish in the 17th century. Trails at each site lead to the ruins of the old mission churches and to the Indian *kivas* and dwellings. Oppressed by the Spanish and harassed by Apache and Comanche raiders, the Indians abandoned the site in the 1670s.

Socorro, farther south on Interstate 25, was also the site of an early Spanish mission. It was destroyed during the Pueblo Revolt of 1680 when the Pueblo Indians rose up against the Spanish, slaughtered priests and administrators and sent the survivors packing to El Paso. A second church, the **Mission of San Miguel**, was built in 1819–21 on the "royal road" between Santa Fe and Mexico City.

The Americans solidified their hold on the region in 1854 with the construction of **Fort Craig**, about 32 miles (52 km) south of Socorro outside the little town of **San Marcial**. The fort saw action during the Civil War when an army of Texas Confederates defeated Union troops nearby at the Battle of Valverde in 1862.

It wasn't until the silver boom of the 1880s, however, that Socorro made it big, becoming one of the largest and wildest towns in New Mexico. Things have quieted down considerably since then, but several fine 19th-century buildings still stand around the old town plaza, witness to the town's wealth.

To the west of Socorro is a vast, sparsely populated region of rugged canyons and island-like mountains peppered with the ruins of old mining towns. There are surprises out here, too. Just outside the little town of **Datil**, for ex-

Preceding pages: general store at Mogollon ghost town in the Gila Mountains. Left, Land of Enchantment. Right, keeper of the jailhouse keys.

ample, is the very modern, very impressive **Very Large Array**, the world's largest radio telescope with more than 25 enormous antennas mounted on miles of railroad tracks. What better place to talk to the heavens than this remote valley ringed with mountains known as the **Plains of St Agustin**?

Much of the activity in this region is centered around **Silver City**, the boyhood home of Billy the Kid, who was known then by his given name, William Bonney. The town was the site of the Kid's first crime as well as his first jailbreak: After pilfering a batch of clothes from a Chinese laundry, he managed to escape from the local calaboose by squeezing up the chimney.

Silver City is fairly old by western standards. Spanish miners settled here in 1800 after Indians told them about veins of copper in the nearby Santa Rita Basin. And mining is still big business. The **Santa Rita Mine**, about 15 miles (24 km) east of town on Route 152, is the biggest open-pit copper mine in the world. Another copper mine lies south of Silver City near the town of **Tyrone**, established by the Phelps-Dodge Company in 1915.

Hard luck: Other towns in the area weren't so lucky. To the south of Silver City, about 4 miles (6.5 km) outside of Lordsburg, is **Shakespeare**, founded during the silver boom of the 1870s and now a privately owned ghost town with a cluster of well-kept buildings that include an old saloon, general store and the **Stratford Hotel**, where Billy the Kid may have worked as a dishwasher. To the north of Silver City is **Pinos Altos**, a former gold-rush village with a small museum, an old opera house and at least one good saloon. Farther afield (about 75 miles/120 km north of Silver City via Highway 180 and Route 159) is **Mogollon**, where restored buildings and shops bear witness to the old mining town's rough-and-ready past.

You'll find a ghost town of a different sort at **Gila Cliff Dwellings National Monument**, the 700-year-old home of the Mogollon culture. Like so many ancient southwesterners, the Mogollon **Bathing beauty.**

196

chose a breathtaking site for their homes. Situated about 45 miles (70 km) north of Silver City in the rugged canyons of the upper Gila River, the Mogollon built their stone houses 180 feet (55 meters) above the canyon floor. A mile-long trail leads up the canyon and into the dwellings. To learn more about the Mogollon, pay a visit to the **Fleming Hall Museum** on the campus of **Western New Mexico University** in Silver City, where you'll find a large exhibit of Mimbres pottery produced by the Mogollon from 900 to 1100. Local history is also featured at the **Silver City Museum** on West Broadway.

While you're in the area, consider stopping at three other historic sites. Located on the Mexican border just outside the tiny town of Columbus, **Pancho Villa State Park** stands on the site of old Camp Furlong where, in 1916, Mexican revolutionary Pancho Villa swept across the border with a small army and killed 18 Americans. The US Army dispatched the World War I hero General John "Black Jack"

The Pecos River winds lazily across the plains.

Pershing and 6,000 soldiers to punish Villa, but gave up the chase after 11 fruitless months of searching.

To the northeast, just outside of **Las Cruces**, is the old village of **Mesilla**, a stop along El Camino Reale and, centuries later, the Butterfield Stage Line. Several fine old buildings remain, including the **Mesilla Courthouse** (which is now a gift shop) where Billy the Kid was tried and convicted for the Lincoln County murders in 1881 and then shipped to Lincoln for hanging (he promptly escaped). The **Gasden Museum** focuses on the area's Indian and Spanish legacy.

About 16 miles (26 km) north, just off Interstate 25, is **Fort Selden State Monument**. The fort was built in 1865 to protect wagon trains and fight Indians. Exhibits are occasionally enlivened by rangers and living-history volunteers in period uniforms.

White Sands: From Las Cruces, it's a 50-mile (80-km) drive across the dark volcanic plain of the Tularosa Valley to **White Sands National Monument**,

where grains of gypsum blown off the nearby San Andres and Sacramento mountains have formed brilliant white dunes that slowly migrate across the desert floor. To the north, in a desolate, lava-strewn area known as **Jornada del Muerto**, the world's first atomic bomb was tested at the Trinity Site in 1945.

North of White Sands, about 5 miles (8 km) off Highway 54, is **Three Rivers Petroglyph National Recreation Site**, one of the finest ancient rock-art sites in the Southwest. A variety of animals, people and mysterious symbols are among the hundreds of images that were carved into the dark boulders by the Mogollon between 900 and 1400.

To the east, the **Mescalero Indian Reservation** is draped across the forested slopes of the **Sacramento Mountains**. The reservation was created in 1872 after the Mescaleros escaped from the internment camp at Fort Sumner. Forty years later, a band of Chiricahua Apache who had been imprisoned with Geronimo in Oklahoma were allowed to join their Mescalero cousins. Today, the Mescaleros operate a ski resort and luxury lodge and have interests in ranching and timber.

Their biggest festival is held during the Fourth of July weekend. The central event is the Sunrise Ceremony, a girls' coming-of-age ritual at which masked mountain spirits with crested head-dresses come to dance. Many events, including a powwow, rodeo and craft sale, are open to the public.

Lincoln County War: The legend of Billy the Kid was born in 1878 in the dusty little town of **Lincoln**, north of the Mescalero Reservation on Highway 380. Originally a Spanish settlement called Las Placitas, Lincoln was renamed in 1869 after the United States Army established nearby Fort Stanton and American ranchers and farmers moved into the area.

Among the most prominent were a couple of businessmen and ranchers named Lawrence Murphy and James J. Dolan who, with the help of key officials, including the local sheriff, William Brady, were making a fortune by selling **RIP, Billy.**

beef and other supplies to the Army and Indian traders.

In 1877, a young, upper-class Englishman named John Tunstall arrived in Lincoln and opened a general store with a local partner named Alexander McSween. Tunstall also bought a cattle ranch and hired a few ranch hands, including a young man named William Bonney, who was often called "the Kid" because of his age and slight build.

The rivalry between the Tunstall and Murphy factions quickly took a nasty turn. On February 18, 1878, gunmen sent by Sheriff Murphy killed Tunstall in cold blood, setting off a series of shootouts and murders that came to be known as the Lincoln County War.

Tunstall's ranch hands found his body and promptly took justice into their own hands. Together with a gang calling themselves the Regulators, the Kid hunted down and killed two of Tunstall's murderers and later ambushed Sheriff Murphy on Lincoln's main street. The war ended after Tunstall's partner, Alexander McSween, was killed during a

five-day siege of his home in Lincoln. Billy the Kid escaped the burning house and, after several months evading the law, gave himself up in exchange for amnesty. The deal fell through and the Kid made another of his miraculous escapes – this time he simply slipped the handcuffs over his skinny hands and walked out of the jailhouse.

The Kid was captured again in 1881 and promptly convicted of murder. But, once again, he busted out of jail, killing two guards in the process. The Kid remained at large for another few months until Sheriff Pat Garrett tracked him down and shot him dead at Fort Sumner.

The story of the Lincoln County War and the violent exploits of Billy the Kid are well-documented in Lincoln. Known as "the town that time forgot," it is an exceptionally well-preserved village, with historic sites administered by the Lincoln State Monument and Lincoln County Historic Trust. Visitors can stroll through historic buildings, including **Tunstall's Store** (complete with original inventory) and the **Lincoln County**

<u>Below</u>, gifts for the Kid. <u>Right</u>, the Tunstall Store looks much as it did at the time of the Lincoln County War.

Courthouse, where the Kid pulled off his most daring escape. On the first weekend in August, the town celebrates the **Last Escape of Billy the Kid Pageant**, which features a parade, a fiddler's contest and a reenactment of the Kid's bullet-flying deliverance.

Billy the Kid is buried about 150 miles (240 km) away at **Fort Sumner**. This is the same area, incidentally, where the Mescalero Apaches were confined by the US Army in 1863. Months later, the Mescaleros were joined by some 8,500 Navajos who had been ruthlessly rounded up by Kit Carson and forced to march 300 miles (480 km) to Bosque Redondo, an event the Navajo remember bitterly as the Long Walk.

Confinement was disastrous for the Navajo. Thousands died of disease and starvation before they were finally granted a reservation in 1868. A visitor center chronicles the history of the fort and the Army's disastrous policy of Indian removal.

Last stop on this tour is **Carlsbad Caverns National Park**, set near the Texas border about 16 miles (26 km) south of the town of Carlsbad. Honeycombed beneath the **Guadalupe Mountains**, the cave's vast underground chambers were carved out of an ancient bed of limestone by groundwater made slightly acidic by soil and air. The seepage of calcite-laden water into the caverns has resulted in bizarre geologic formations: stalactites hanging from the ceiling like clusters of icicles, thick stalagmites reaching up from the floor, delicate antler-like helictites, smooth sheets of flowstone, calcite "lily pads" floating on the surface of subterranean pools, long, thin "soda straws," fragile growths of aragonite, and a variety of other formations such as curtains, "cave pearls," dams and popcorn.

Pictographs at the mouth of the cavern suggest that Indians may have visited the interior as much as 12,000 years ago. It wasn't until the turn of the century, however, that it was systematically explored. A cowboy called Jim White stumbled across the entrance, where he discovered deep deposits of bat dung, or guano, a valuable fertilizer. It wasn't long before White began exploring the interior and promoting the cave as a natural wonder, using guano buckets to lower tourists into the dimly lighted chambers. The cave was designated a national monument in 1923, and White was named chief ranger.

These days, the park welcomes about 800,000 visitors each year (no guano buckets required) who come to see the caverns' otherworldly "decorations," explore the rugged Guadalupe Mountains, and watch thousands of bats spiral from the entrance of **Bat Cave** on summer evenings.

There are at least 80 caves in the park, and many remain unexplored. Visitors may join one of several walking tours or take an elevator that drops some 750 feet into the spectacular **Big Room**. Amateur spelunkers can make reservations for a ranger-led tour of undeveloped **New Cave** in **Slaughter Canyon**. A scenic drive, nature trail and backcountry camping are available for those who want to remain above ground and explore the surrounding area.

Left, mission churches are found throughout New Mexico. Right, tarantula on limestone, Carlsbad Caverns.

NORTHERN ARIZONA

This is the quintessential Southwest. Perched on the edge of the Colorado Plateau, northern Arizona is a land of unending sagebrush flats, ponderosa-pine forests and such archetypal western landscapes as Monument Valley and the Grand Canyon. Mesas stairstep on the horizon, slickrock canyons crease the earth, and solitary blue mountains float far in the distance.

Native people have made a living in this arid land for thousands of years, and many still grow corn and herd sheep in the traditional ways of their ancestors. More recent traditions are still alive, too – those of cowboys and miners and early Mormon settlers who once occupied the many ghost towns and frontier forts that are scattered throughout this lonesome country.

Apache raid: Begin your journey in the western corner of the state at **Oatman**, a former gold-mining town on old Route 66 where you'll be greeted by droopy-eyed burros standing in the middle of the street, happy to take handouts from tourists. The town is named after the Oatman family, a pioneer clan attacked by Apaches in 1851. The parents were killed and their two daughters, Olive and Mary Ann, were held captive at a spring a half-mile north of town. Though Mary Ann died, Olive was finally released five years later. Today, the town's single dusty street is lined with classic wood-front shops and hotels with cool lobbies and dark saloons.

Old mine shafts in the surrounding **Black Mountains** are evidence of Oatman's once-thriving industry. You may still encounter a few hard-rock prospectors, although they're more likely to be riding in Jeeps than on burros.

From Oatman, it's about 25 miles (40 km) through spectacular desert and mountain scenery to **Kingman** and then another 20 miles (32 km) north on Highway 93 to **Chloride**, one of the oldest mining camps in the area. Chloride boomed in the 1860s, when gold and silver were mined in the **Cerbat Moun-**

tains. The town's population swelled to 5,000 at one point, but by 1949 it was a ghost town.

A handful of folks still live in Chloride; they seem to enjoy the peace and quiet. But at the end of June each year, their solitude is broken by the town's biggest fete, **Old Miners Day**. There's a big swap meet, a parade at high noon, burro rides, arts and crafts, a display of old mining equipment at the **Jim Fritz Historical Museum**, and a melodrama at the **Silver Belle Playhouse**. You can poke around in some of the abandoned mining buildings while you're at it.

It's a long lonesome drive on Interstate 40 and Route 89 into the cool pine forests around **Prescott**, a lovely town set in the mountains at an elevation of about 5,300 feet (1,600 meters). Like so many towns in this region, Prescott was born (in 1863) when gold was first discovered in the nearby **Bradshaw Mountains**; it served twice as the territorial capital between 1863 and 1889. Visitors can still stroll along **Whiskey Row**, where miners and cowboys once

came to slake their thirst or get flat-out drunk. Across the plaza, the **Yavapai County Courthouse** (1917) lends a dignified air to the town square, as do the palatial Victorian homes that still grace the historic district.

While you're in downtown Prescott, consider stopping at the **Sharlot Hall Museum** on West Gurley Street, a collection of historic buildings that include the log **Governor's Mansion** (the territory's first capitol) and an 1875 house once occupied by famed explorer and territorial governor John C. Fremont before he was kicked out of office for neglecting his duties. A few miles north of town on Route 89, the **Phippen Museum of Western Art** has a good collection of paintings and bronzes. If you're visiting in summer, you may want to stick around for the **Frontier Days Rodeo** held on the Fourth of July. Founded in 1888, it claims to be the oldest rodeo in the world.

For a somewhat more cerebral experience, consider the popular **Cowboy Poetry Gathering** in August.

Slippery slope: From Prescott, it's about 28 miles (45 km) on Highway 89A to **Jerome**, a once-bustling mining town built on the steep slopes of Cleopatra Hill. Jerome has seen its share of booms and busts – first with the discovery of silver in the early 1880s and then with copper in 1914. After the Crash of 1929, the town went downhill fast – in both senses of the phrase. Underground blasting caused many buildings to slide down the mountainsides. Most were destroyed, but a few like the Sliding Jail stand several hundred feet from where they were built. You can learn more about Jerome just outside of town at **Jerome State Historic Park**, site of the 1916 mansion of colorful mine owner Jimmy "Rawhide" Douglas.

While you're in the area, stop at nearby **Tuzigoot National Monument**, an ancient pueblo perched on an open ridge, with rooms spilling randomly down the hillside. The settlement was built by the Sinagua, a village-dwelling people who farmed the **Verde River** floodplain some 600 years ago. At its peak, the pueblo was home to perhaps 225 souls. It was abandoned by the Sinagua in around 1425 for reasons that are still unclear.

Highway 89A continues north to the classy, boutique-filled town of **Sedona** and then climbs through stunning **Oak Creek Canyon** to **Flagstaff**, the commercial center of northern Arizona. The Atlantic & Pacific Railroad rolled into Flagstaff in 1882, and it still has the air of a railroad town. The Arizona Lumber Company arrived a few years later and made a killing on the ponderosa forest that fringes town. The owners, Michael and Timothy Riordan, sank much of their fortune into a cavernous log mansion. Built in 1904 and now preserved at **Riordan State Historic Park**, it's one of the finest buildings of its kind.

One of Flagstaff's longest-lived institutions is the gracious **Museum of Northern Arizona**, just outside town on Highway 180. The museum focuses on the natural and cultural history of the Colorado Plateau, with a special emphasis on the region's geology and Native American cultures. A series of exhibits each summer showcases the fine

Graffiti expresses anger over Navajo–Hopi land dispute.

work of Hopi, Navajo and Zuni artists.

Another short side trip leads to two other ancient pueblo sites. Tucked into the terraced limestone cliffs just east of Flagstaff are the small Sinagua dwellings of **Walnut Canyon National Monument**.

Between 1125 and 1250, the Sinagua grew corn, beans and squash on the canyon rim and took advantage of the diverse plant life – walnut trees and grapes along the stream, cacti and wolfberry on the rocky hillsides, and pinyon pine and juniper on the mesa tops. The short **Island Trail** leads part of the way into Walnut Canyon and provides views of many of the rooms.

About 30 miles (50 km) to the north, the Sinagua pueblos of **Wupatki National Monument** are set beneath the magnificent **San Francisco Peaks**, the highest mountains in Arizona. Several distinct sites, including **Wupatki**, **Lomaki** and **Wukoki** ruins, may be reached on self-guiding trails. Pay particular attention to the extraordinary skill with which these structures were made.

More than 700 years old, they still withstand the elements.

From downtown Flagstaff, it's about a 45-minute drive west on Interstate 40 to the small town of **Williams**, named for the crusty mountain man Old Bill Williams. The town honors its heritage on Memorial Day weekend at the **Buckskinner Rendezvous**, a rather tame re-creation of a mountain-man gathering. At this modern-day version, men, women and children gather just south of town in **Buckskinner Park** under the green shoulders of **Bill Williams Mountain**. They set up tepees, stitch hide clothing, shoot blackpowder rifles and sell handmade knives on Traders Row. It's a friendly, mellow scene, and all are welcome to join.

The Grand Canyon: Williams is also home to the **Grand Canyon Railway**. All year long, a vintage steam train, circa 1901, chuffs up to the **South Rim** of the **Grand Canyon**. At the sound of the whistle, the *Williams Flyer* departs northbound each morning for the 2¼-hour, 65-mile (105-km) trip. Travelers

A Navajo boy tends the family herd.

ride in restored Harriman coach cars and are entertained by roving musicians and would-be train robbers.

Theodore Roosevelt called the Grand Canyon "the one great sight that every American should see" and declared it a national monument in 1908; it was expanded and redesignated a national park in 1919. The *Flyer* makes a three-hour layover at **Grand Canyon Village**, plenty of time for lunch and a leisurely view of the wondrous gorge from the porch of the famous **El Tovar Hotel**, a rustic gem built of rough-hewn logs and limestone in 1905. If you want to see more of the canyon, hop on a tour bus or stroll the rim trails. The **Bright Angel Lodge**, **Kolb Brothers Studio**, pueblo-syle **Hopi House** and other historic buildings are within walking distance.

Navajo Country: Grand Canyon National Park is bordered on the east by the 17 million-acre (7 million-hectare) **Navajo Nation**, the largest Indian reservation in the country. More than 200,000 Navajos make their home here, many of whom still follow traditional ways de-spite the decidedly modern look of most reservation towns. It's not uncommon to come across round earth-and-timber hogans or to see Navajo kids tending sheep much as their grandparents did. From the salmon-colored sands of Monument Valley to the pastel rocks of the Painted Desert, Navajos have adapted to this harsh but beautiful land with both reverence and tenacity.

Perhaps the best place to start a tour of Navajo Country is the **Hubbell Trading Post National Historic Site** on Highway 264 at **Ganado**. The post was opened by John Lorenzo Hubbell in 1876 and has been in business ever since – the oldest continuously operated trading post in the Navajo Nation. Today, the post looks and feels much as it did in the old days, and Navajos still travel for miles to do business here. The low stone building, constructed by Hubbell in 1883, is crammed with groceries, tobacco and other supplies for customers, along with exquisite Navajo blankets, jewelry, sand paintings and pottery for collectors and tourists. If **Hand-woven blankets.**

time allows, you can tour the Hubbell home and farm, and watch Navajo weavers working at their looms. The setting, amid giant cottonwood trees along Pueblo Colorado Wash, is beautiful.

It's about a 45-minute drive north on Highway 191 to **Canyon de Chelly National Monument**, where the ancient Anasazi built stone dwellings in the alcoves of soaring sandstone cliffs between 350 and 1300. Navajo farmers still live in the canyon in summer and on the rims in winter, and they control access into the canyon. Tours may be arranged with Navajo guides in Jeeps, in trucks known locally as "shake-and-bakes" or on horseback. Otherwise, the only way to see the canyons is from **North** and **South Rim roads** and on a steep, ¾-mile hiking trail to **White House Ruin**.

Salmon-colored sands of Monument Valley.

Equally spectacular are the Anasazi ruins at **Navajo National Monument**, set on the edge of Tsegi Canyon just outside **Kayenta** in the northern part of the reservation. From the visitor center, it's a short walk on the Sandal Trail to an overlook of **Betatakin**, a dramatic cliff dwelling built under a sweeping alcove some 800 years ago. For a closer look, join one of the ranger-led tours in summer. Navajo National Monument also contains the largest ruin in Arizona, **Keet Seel**, a 180-room pueblo dating to the late 13th century. For travelers with a taste for adventure, Navajo guides lead an 8-mile (13-km) horseback-riding trip to Keet Seel.

Monument Valley: Kayenta is also the gateway to **Monument Valley Tribal Park**, about 22 miles (35 km) north on Highway 163. Immortalized in countless films – most memorably by John Ford, who shot *Stagecoach* here in 1938 – the region's solitary mesas and sparkling dunes sprawl across miles of open country, only a small portion of which falls within the park. A 17-mile (27-km) dirt road loops through the park, passing sandstone formations such as the Mittens, John Ford's Point and Rain God Mesa, sculpted over thousands of years by water and wind. Tours of the park, including horseback riding trips,

can be arranged at the tribal visitor center, which is open all year.

Hopi homeland: Although neighbors for centuries, the Navajos and Hopis are worlds apart culturally. Completely surrounded by the Navajo Nation, the **Hopi Reservation** is centered on three narrow mesas where the village-dwelling Hopi have lived for more than a thousand years. The best place to start is at the **Hopi Cultural Center** on **Second Mesa**, where you can pick up information about Hopi life and culture, have a taste of traditional blue corn and piki bread at the restaurant, and ask about touring one of the Hopi villages.

There are a dozen autonomous villages, each known for a particular art or craft – one for pottery, another for kachina carvings, another for finely woven baskets. The Hopi observe an annual round of ceremonies, all inviting rain for their crops. Outsiders are welcome at some dances, but only with permission from the villagers. Photography, drawing and audio recordings are strictly prohibited.

The Arizona Strip: Far to the northwest of Hopi, just over the border of the Navajo Nation, is **Page**, a modern town built in the 1960s during construction of the **Glen Canyon Dam**. The **John Wesley Powell Memorial Museum** (Powell Boulevard and North Navajo streets) features photographic exhibits on the famed one-armed explorer and geologist who in 1869 was the first person to run the Colorado River through Grand Canyon. You can even see Major Powell's old iron bedstead. The museum also contains photographs of other pioneer river runners as well as the building of Glen Canyon Dam, which backs up **Lake Powell** on the **Colorado River**. The towering dam is one of the most stunning engineering feats in the country. Its effects on the downstream environment, however, have been enormous – and controversial

From Page, it's about 40 miles (65 km) to **Lees Ferry**, a historic ferry crossing of the Colorado River and the only put-in on the river for nearly 300 miles (480 km). These days, travelers cross

Murals decorate the interior of the Watchtower, built in 1933 on the Grand Canyon's south rim.

the river on the new **Navajo Bridge**, 467 feet (142 meters) above the green thread of the river.

From Lees Ferry, continue west on Highway 89A, a long, lonely drive that follows the base of the **Vermillion Cliffs**. It also traces the route taken by Fathers Domínguez and Escalante, Spanish priests who set out on an aborted trek from Santa Fe to California in 1776. In October, as winter was setting in, the expedition was out of food and had to eat one of their horses. They were saved by Paiute Indians, who gave them seeds and nuts and told them where water could be found. A historical marker in **House Rock Valley** marks one of their camping places, which the priests named San Bartolome.

In front of you swells the long, forested **Kaibab Plateau**. Its edge is the North Rim of the Grand Canyon. The highway winds up into the cool conifer forests of the Kaibab and then drops back down to the small town of **Fredonia**.

From Fredonia, take Highway 389 west 14 miles (23 km) to **Pipe Spring**

National Monument. Here the faint but welcome sound of trickling water attracted Native Americans, government surveyors and Mormon ranchers to the dry, empty country known as the Arizona Strip. The first Anglo settler at Pipe Spring was "Doctor" James Whitmore, a Mormon rancher searching for good grazing land. Whitmore liked the looks of this spot at the base of the Hurricane Cliffs. In 1863, he built a crude dugout just down the hill from the spring and started ranching.

After Whitmore was killed in 1865, Mormons erected a fort at Pipe Spring as protection from Indians. The two-story stone fort soon served as a ranch, where Mormons maintained a herd of cattle tithed to the church.

The big rock ranch house is fully restored to its 1870 appearance. In an upstairs bedroom, visitors can see Arizona's first telegraph station. To the west is a rock cabin where Major John Wesley Powell's survey crew stayed in 1871. Gardens, trees, and a blacksmith shop surround the ranch grounds.

The Colorado River flows through Horse Shoe Bend near Page, Arizona.

SOUTHERN ARIZONA

Away from the modern skyscrapers of downtown Phoenix and Tucson, southern Arizona looks just as you've always imagined. Coyotes howl at twilight, many-armed saguaro cactus stand silhouetted against an orange-red sunset, and craggy mountains are like sky islands floating in pale desert haze. The old ways endure. Cowboys round up cattle on the range, modern Indian tribes live alongside the remnants of ancient civilizations, Spanish and Mexican influences permeate everything from food to music, descendants of homesteaders live in log cabins and work the land, and larger-than-life characters in battered Stetsons, jeans and worn-down cowboy boots are as plentiful as the hopes that brought them here.

This tour begins southeast of **Flagstaff**, on Highway 87, in the Old West town of **Payson**. Like many of Arizona's small towns, Payson began as a gold-mining camp in 1881, but it is now more popular as a local shopping center, a getaway destination and a base for touring the 2,000-feet (610-meter) cliffs of the **Mogollon Rim**, which tower above the town. Zane Grey, the prolific western author and outdoorsman, fell in love with the area in the early 1900s and made many hunting expeditions and research trips here.

"For wild, rugged beauty, I had not seen its equal," he wrote. More than half of Grey's novels and short stories were set in the **Tonto Basin**. *To the Last Man*, a fictionalized account of the local Pleasant Valley range war, was filmed just south of Payson.

Grey built a hunting lodge on land he bought from his friends, the Haughts, a ranching family, but unfortunately the building burned down in the huge Dude Fire of June 1990, which cost six firefighters their lives. Those of Grey's things that did survive – including the author's tooled leather saddlebags, first editions of several of his books and an embroidered waistcoat – are on display at the **Museum of the Forest**, run by the

Gila County Historical Society, on Main Street in Payson. A small **Zane Grey Museum** (also on Main Street) is run by cowboy artist Mel Counseller and his wife Beth, using their own large collection of Zane Grey memorabilia.

House of metal: The tour continues south on Highway 87, then turns southeast on Highway 188 to **Theodore Roosevelt Lake and Dam**, part of the historic Salt River Water Project, which has helped spur Phoenix's boom. The dam, built in 1911 and dedicated by Roosevelt, is still the largest masonry dam in existence. A new concrete dam has been built over the old one for stabilization purposes; motorists cross on a new suspension bridge.

Before damming, this basin was home to the Salado people, an offshoot of the Hohokam culture to the west, who grew cotton and farmed along the Salt River in 1150. The Salado hunted game and harvested cactus fruits in the foothills surrounding the basin, and eventually some groups moved into the cliffs, building two large adobe pueblos around

1300 that were abandoned about 150 years later for reasons that are still unclear. One of the ruins, a 16-room complex with a 12-room annex, may be visited at **Tonto National Monument**. Examples of the Salados' beautiful cotton clothing and pottery, which were used for trade, are on display.

Just to the south, in the town of **Globe**, is another, larger Salado ruin known by the Apache name of **Besh-Ba-Gowah** (House of Metal – a reference to the abundant precious metals that attracted newcomers to the area in the late 1800s). Besh-Ba-Gowah was begun in 1225 and abandoned around 1400.

The 200-room pueblo was first excavated in the 1930s, but excavation has been sporadic ever since. Now partially stabilized, the ruin is still revealing its secrets. Large quantities of pottery have been uncovered at the site and are on display in the small museum.

Globe is better known as the site of enormous silver and copper deposits, which led to boom growth between 1870 and 1920 and the success of the Old Dominion Copper Company, one of the largest operations in the world. You won't miss the enormous man-made terraces on the north side of town – they look almost extraterrestrial. Globe's name actually came from the extraction of a large piece of globe-shaped silver with the rough outlines of the continents upon it. Downtown Globe retains a turn-of-the-century feel, and you can take a historic walking tour of 25 buildings ranging from the 1906 **Gila County Courthouse** (now the **Cobre Valley Center for the Arts**) and the "Oldest Woolworth's in the West" (1916). Sleepy Globe was one of writer Edward Abbey's favorite towns.

Apache country: Heading east on Highway 60, you cross the **San Carlos Apache Reservation**. Globe was originally part of the reservation, but when silver was found there in 1870, the boundaries were redrawn, causing prolonged bitterness with the San Carlos Apache, who allied with Geronimo and other warring Apache leaders to fight encroaching white settlement. Peace came when Geronimo surrendered in 1886, and the Apache now hold the popular **Apache Days** in Globe in October and a rodeo in November in **San Carlos**. Continue south through the cotton country of Safford to **Willcox**, interesting only for its apple cider and for being the location of the **Rex Allen Cowboy Museum** (Railroad Avenue), commemorating the veteran cowboy actor who grew up here.

Take Highway 186 from Willcox to **Chiricahua National Monument** and you won't be disappointed. These mountains act as a protected corridor for Mexican wildlife such as Apache fox squirrels, and Chihuahua and Apache pines, which live alongside more usual Sonoran Desert wildlife. The monument was actually set aside to protect a number of strangely eroded rhyolite rocks that were formed here when nearby Turkey Caldera exploded 25 million years ago. Later, erosion from rainfall carved totem poles, balanced rocks and other strange shapes. The Chiricahuas are often soaked with rain, making this seem more like a rain forest than desert

Bobcats roam the West.

mountains, with dripping surfaces of deep-green vegetation. It is a magical place – well worth exploring. For centuries, these mountains were home to the Chiricahua Apaches, who, led by Geronimo and Victorio, successfully kept Anglo settlers at bay in the mid-1800s. They knew every nook and cranny and outwitted would-be capturers for years. When the Apache were eventually overcome, the Chiricahua Mountains became home to the Erickson family, whose turn-of-the-century **Faraway Ranch** may be visited close to the park visitor center.

For more about the Apache, visit **Fort Bowie National Historic Site**, which preserves the ruins of an Army outpost built alongside a Butterfield Stage stop as a base for fighting the Apache.

From the Chiricahuas, drop south on Highway 666 to **Bisbee** in the **Mule Mountains**. Like Globe, Bisbee is a historic copper-mining town which grew from a rowdy, cosmopolitan mining camp in 1877 to a sophisticated, wealthy town with many fine Victorian brick

An O'odham boy at an Indian festival.

buildings erected in **Mule Pass Gulch** in the early 1900s. Claims were won and lost in the early, hard-drinking, gambling days, but the first major mining operation began when the Copper Queen Mine was bought by Judge Dewitt Bisbee and other San Franciscan businessmen in 1880. Later, competition from Phelps Dodge, which bought land adjoining the Copper Queen and built a railroad to ship ore, led to a merger of the two companies.

The town's colorful history, which included lynchings and murders in the early days, a teeming population of miners, working girls and hopeful immigrants, is showcased to wonderful effect at the **Bisbee Mining Museum** housed in the 1897 **Phelps Dodge General Office Building**. Especially poignant is an exhibit on the Bisbee Deportation of 1917, when 1,000 striking miners were loaded at gunpoint into boxcars and expelled from the state. Visitors can take an underground tour of the **Copper Queen Mine** or simply view the enormous **Lavender Open Pit**. You can

also follow an enjoyable, self-guided historic walking tour of downtown Bisbee and view the fine buildings, many of which were rescued by artists in the 1970s and today house restaurants, art galleries, gift shops and the famous **One Book Bookstore**, opened by the late Walter Swann to sell his memoirs. Bisbee's most famous building is the **Copper Queen Hotel**, a beautiful *grande dame* of a place, built in 1902 and bustling ever since. John Wayne's room is still the most popular.

A town called Tombstone: Just a few miles north on Highway 80 is Arizona's most infamous town, **Tombstone**, the location of the O.K. Corral gunfight in 1881. Known as "the town too tough to die," Tombstone is still a rowdy place – but the victims are now the visitors, trailing from tourist trap to tourist trap in search of the town's authentic past, which was long ago sold down the river of commerce. There's plenty of entertainment: You can watch a staged gunfight at the **O.K. Corral**; stand and listen to the bored, monotonous commentary of the "floozie" in the old **Bird Cage Theater**, where working girls plied their trade and dodged bullets; or take a carriage ride around town, driven by yet another costumed cowboy. Most important of all, don't leave town without a visit to **Boothill Cemetery**, where the three Clanton brothers and other young victims of violent deaths are buried beneath what look like fake tombstones. The epitaphs range from amusing to sobering, although you may find the piped-in Willie Nelson songs and other forms of commercialism a bit tacky in what should be a place of rest.

For the best perspective, head over to the elegant 1882 Victorian red-brick **Tombstone Courthouse State Historic Park** on Third and Toughnut streets, where the original courthouse setup may be viewed, as well as exhibits discussing the numerous lynchings that took place in the town as vigilantes exacted their own justice. Here are exhibits about the Gunfight at the O.K Corral, which pitted US Marshal Wyatt Earp, his brothers Morgan and Virgil, and "Doc"

Old-style signs at Tucson (**left**) and Tombstone.

Holliday against the Clanton and the McLaury boys, ranchers whose extra-curricular activities included cattle rustling and harboring stagecoach robbers. Two favorite theories are offered about what actually happened during the 30-second gunfight, in which three members of the Clanton gang were killed and Virgil and Morgan were wounded; you can make up your own mind.

An unusual lunch spot is the **Nellie Cashman Restaurant and Pie Salon**, which was once a hospital run by an Irish mining camp follower known as the "Angel of Tombstone." The food is so-so western fare, but then most people come for atmosphere, not *haute cuisine*.

Dove of the desert: After all the ballyhoo, it's a relief to head through gorgeous golden grasslands and nature refuges along the United States–Mexico border, where Hispanic influence is strong. Just past the border town of **Nogales**, head north on Interstate 19 to **Tumacacori National Monument**, which preserves three Spanish missions, of which Tumacacori is the only one open to the public. **San Jose de Tumacacori** includes an intact, white-domed sanctuary, the remains of the nave and altar, a brick belltower, an unusual circular mortuary chapel and adjoining cemetery, and a *convento*, or monks' quarters.

Tumacacori and Guevavi (near Nogales) were founded in 1691 by Father Eusebio Kino, an Italian Jesuit from Spain who brought Christianity to the Pima Indians (now known as Tohono O'odham). The present adobe mission was begun in 1800 by the Franciscans, who replaced the Jesuits following the Pima Indian Revolt of 1756. It was completed by 1820, but Mexican independence from Spain led to the mission's decline and, following severe Apache raiding, the residents moved in 1848 to the **Mission of San Xavier del Bac** (known as the "White Dove of the Desert"), just south of Tucson.

The shimmering, white-washed San Xavier del Bac was founded by Father Kino in 1700, but the present church dates from 1778. It is perhaps the best

Storefront in Tombstone, "the town too tough to die."

example of Spanish mission architecture in the United States. While visiting Tumacacori, stop by the tiny town of **Tubac**, the oldest European town in Arizona. Tubac, now known for its art galleries, housed the first Spanish garrison, or *presidio*, which was built there following the first of a series of Pima Indian revolts in 1752. A state historic park now preserves the site.

Old Pueblo: In 1776, the Spanish moved the presidio from Tubac to **Tucson**, nicknamed "the Old Pueblo." Spanish and Mexican influences remain strong in the thick-walled adobe buildings and easy life-style of this lovely city surrounded by mountains. The best way to see the old town is to park your car at the **Tucson Museum of Art** off Alameda Street and take a historic walking tour. Across the street is the 10-acre (4-hectare) **Presidio Park**, site of the original walled presidio and the attractive, 1928, tile-domed **Pima County Courthouse**. Next to the art museum are five of the oldest houses in Tucson: the **Edward Nye Fish House** (1868), the **Stevens**

House (1856) and the **Sam Hughes House** (1858), all built by Anglo businessmen who moved here when the United States acquired the region in 1854. **La Casa Cordova**, built in 1848 during Mexican rule, is one of the oldest houses in the area. In 1900, a French stonemason named Jules le Flein constructed what is now **El Charro Restaurant** on North Court Street from volcanic stone (the food is delicious). Along the way, you'll walk by two sites – **Governor's Corner** and the **Fremont House Museum** – which date from Tucson's 10-year stint as the territorial capital before it was moved to Prescott in 1877.

If you have time, head over to the **University of Arizona**, a mile east of downtown, founded in 1891 and originally housed in a building known as Old Main. There's a lot to see on campus, including museums and galleries.

Your last taste of the Old West can be had by driving 12 miles (19 km) west on Speedway Boulevard to the outskirts of Tucson. Here, you can watch stuntmen and gun battles, and tour the soundstage of **Old Tucson Studios**, a movie set used since 1939 to film *Rio Lobo* and other Western movies as well as TV shows like *Little House on the Prairie, Bonanza* and *Gunsmoke*. Reconstruction is underway after a recent fire, so call ahead to make sure it is open.

The Sonoran Desert is spectacular out here. If you want to learn more about its nocturnal wildlife, continue north on Kinney to the **Arizona Sonora Desert Museum**, a living museum where special exhibits allow you to see the shy animals and unusual plants of this most luxuriant of all American deserts. From here, pay a visit to the western unit of **Saguaro National Park**, which preserves stands of young saguaro cactus, Arizona's world-famous symbol.

These cacti sport record-breaking statistics: 200-year life spans, weights that reach several tons, ability to go without water for a year, and many other adaptations to this hot, dry habitat. Another area sits east of Tucson and includes stands of older saguaro as well as a mountain drive. This is Arizona in the wild – an experience you'll remember.

Left, shrine near the old mining town of Bisbee. Right, the 18th-century Mission San Xavier del Bac is known as the "White Dove of the Desert."

EASTERN COLORADO

We can only imagine what early pioneers thought when they first saw the Rocky Mountains jutting into the heavens. After weeks of trekking across the prairie, they must have been stopped in their tracks by the sight.

Wrenched from the earth some 50 million years ago and chiseled by great waves of glacial ice, the Rockies march through the heart of Colorado with more than 100 peaks exceeding 11,000 feet (3,400 meters). If ever there was a place where geography determined the course of human events, this is it.

The first American to explore Colorado was Zebulon Pike, sent by President Thomas Jefferson in 1806 to explore the western frontier of the Louisiana Purchase. Pike was captured and imprisoned by the Spanish but not before reaching the present-day site of Pueblo about 50 miles (80 km) south of the landmark that now bears his name: Pikes Peak.

By the 1830s, buckskin-clad mountain men were trapping beaver on Colorado's streams and rivers and trading at an adobe fort on the Santa Fe Trail built by William and Charles Bent and their partner, Ceran St Vrain. The tepees of the most powerful tribes of the southern plains – the Arapaho, Cheyenne, Kiowa and Comanche – were a common sight outside its earthen walls.

But peace with the Indians didn't last. Gold was discovered on the South Platte River in 1858, and a boom town named Denver City sprang up overnight. The Indians' fate was sealed. The newly formed *Rocky Mountain News* called for "extermination against the red devils," and, for all practical purposes, that's exactly what they got. The violence climaxed in 1864 when US soldiers swept into a peaceful Cheyenne camp at Sand Creek about 40 miles (65 km) northeast of Fort Lyon and massacred more than 200 Indians, many of them women and children.

Denver and environs: Today, the site of that first big gold strike and of the ram-shackle camp that was hurriedly thrown up around it are buried under modern roads and skyscrapers. Still, evidence of Denver's Wild West roots aren't too hard to find if you know where to look. In the **Larimer Square Historic District**, for example, there are more than a dozen buildings that date to the 1870s and '80s when the scruffy town of shacks and cabins began to take on a more respectable appearance; most of the old Victorian buildings now house shops and restaurants.

Although the silver crash of 1893 put a crimp in Denver's big-spending ways, there were enough minerals in "them thar' hills" to tide the city over. Stately new buildings like the **Brown Palace Hotel**, **Denver Union Station**, **Colorado State Capitol** and the lavish mansions of the **Capitol Hill** neighborhod were built just as quickly as the money poured in from the mines. For an inside look at high Victorian style, visit the **Molly Brown House Museum** (1340 Pennsylvania St), home of the "unsinkable" lady who became a celebrity for

Preceding pages: Concho belt and Navajo rug. Left, snow-dusted peaks of Maroon Bells. Right, a sensitive soul.

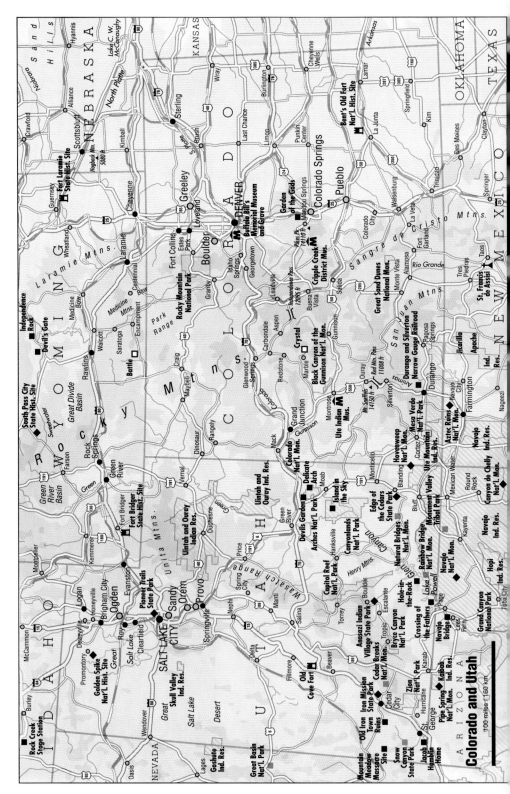

Colorado and Utah

100 miles / 160 km

surviving the disaster of the *Titanic*.

Denver also has several fine museums, most of which are within walking distance of historic areas. At the **Denver Art Museum**, for example, you'll find an excellent collection of American Indian and Hispanic art as well as classic works from Europe and Asia. A few steps away, the **Colorado History Museum** chronicles the state's colorful past in the old **Byers-Evans House**, built in 1880 and home to two of the city's most influential families. Also nearby, the **US Mint** offers a tour of the minting process and a display of nearly $1 million in gold ingots.

Housed in a handsome old building that once served as a high-class bordello, the **Museum of Western Art** features the work of classic painters of the West like Thomas Moran, Frederic Remington, Charles Russell and Georgia O'Keeffe. A few miles from downtown, in the Five Points area, the new **Black American West Museum** chronicles the role of black cowboys, soldiers, homesteaders and pioneers – many of them former slaves – in the settling of the Old West.

Farther afield, in suburban southwest Denver, **Four Mile Historic Park** is a restored 1860s stock ranch, stage stop and working farm, complete with draft horses and a stagecoach ride. In the southern suburb of Littleton, about 20 minutes from downtown Denver, the **Littleton Historical Museum** features living-history demonstrations at a frontier blacksmith shop, schoolhouse and smokehouse.

At **Lookout Mountain**, about 15 miles (24 km) west of the city off Interstate 70, is **Buffalo Bill's Memorial Museum and Grave**. Mythologized in countless dime novels and his own Wild West show, this legendary western figure died at his sister's Denver home in 1917 and was buried here despite protests from his home state of Wyoming. The exhibits and gift shop are a bit hokey, but the view is worth the visit.

Miners, merchants and scalawags: It's a short, scenic drive on **Lookout Mountain Road** to the town of **Golden**, founded in 1859 and the capital of Colo-

rado Territory from 1862 to 1867. You'll find a neighborhood of fine 19th-century buildings in the **Twelfth Street Historic District** and, just outside of town, an excellent collection of vintage narrow-gauge trains at the **Colorado Railroad Museum**. Golden's most popular attraction, however, is the **Coors Brewery**, established by Adolph Coors in 1873 shortly after the mining boom. Tours are offered Monday to Saturday.

Assorted scalawags: To the west, **Central City** and nearby **Black Hawk** are mining towns with an abundance of colorful history and well-preserved buildings. Gold was discovered here in 1859 and within a few months the place was crawling with thousands of miners, merchants and assorted scalawags.

Known as the "richest square mile on earth," Central City burned down in 1874 but was quickly rebuilt, this time with stone and brick. Among the old buildings that still stand is the **Central City Opera House**, which opened to packed houses in 1878. A jewel in this otherwise rugged country, its boards

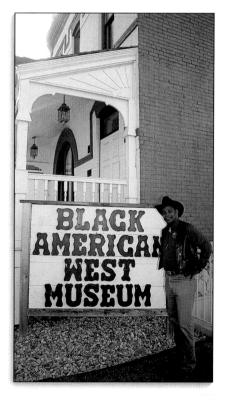

Denver pride: some historians say that one-quarter of all cowboys were black.

have been trod by Sarah Bernhardt, Edwin Booth and other actors of note. It is now the site of a popular summer opera festival. With the legalization of limited-stakes gambling in Colorado in 1990, these once-sleepy relics are undergoing yet another boom. These days, there's hardly a building in Central City that hasn't been taken over by slot machines and blackjack tables. If time allows, consider a heart-stopping drive along **Oh-My-God Road**, which passes abandoned mines in **Virginia Canyon** before reaching **Idaho Springs**, yet another 19th-century mining town.

Continuing west on Interstate 70, **Georgetown** is one of Colorado's best-preserved Old West towns. Brothers George and David Griffith were among the anointed few who actually struck pay dirt in this promised land. Their gold strike at the head of Clear Creek in 1859 lasted about two years and gave birth to what would become one of the territory's loveliest Victorian villages. When gold petered out, the townfolk switched to silver, which had been dis-covered just upstream at **Silver Plume**.

As always in these rugged mountains, there was a problem shipping the ore out of the mines. Although the mines at Silver Plume were only 638 feet (195 meters) higher than Georgetown, the grade was too steep for locomotives. The solution came in 1884 with the construction of the Georgetown Loop, a twisting railroad track that curves over itself on a high steel trestle. Today, interested visitors can ride the restored **Georgetown Loop Railroad** in a 1920s steam locomotive from the west edge of Georgetown to the **Silver Plume Depot**. A guided hard-hat tour of the old **Lebanon Mine** is available at the top. In Georgetown itself, the **Hamill House Museum** and **Hotel de Paris Museum** offer a glimpse of Victorian-era living.

Old Man Mountain: For a closer look at Colorado's natural beauty, consider a side trip north of Denver to **Rocky Mountain National Park**, one of the crown jewels of the National Park System. At the eastern gateway to the park is **Estes Park**, a tourist-friendly town

named after rancher Joel Estes, who settled here with his family in 1860. Lured by the writing of Isabella Bird (author of *A Lady's Life in the Rocky Mountains*), an eccentric Irish nobleman, Lord Dunraven, appeared on the scene in 1878 and launched a full-scale land-grab, snatching up some 15,000 acres (6,000 hectares) of prime real estate because he liked the hunting.

In the early 1900s, yet another colorful figure rolled into the valley – Freelan O. Stanley, inventor of the Stanley Steamer automobile. Stanley promptly bought up what was left of Dunraven's land and built the **Stanley Hotel**, whose handsome white clapboard exterior still shines against a backdrop of granite peaks. On fall evenings, herds of elk wander down the mountainside to graze on its lush green lawns. One of Stanley's pals was a naturalist named Enos Mills. Known as the "John Muir of the Rockies," Mills hatched the idea for a national park and spent years lobbying Congress, which gave approval in 1915.

The main route through the park is **Trail Ridge Road**. It winds through high-country meadows filled with summer wildflowers before climbing above the treeline into the fascinating but harsh world of alpine tundra, where gnarled whitebark pines, most no larger than a bush, may be 200 or 300 years old. You can pick up any number of trails along the way, including a 7-mile (11-km) round-trip hike to the old mining town of **Lulu City**, which drew its first and last breath in only three short years. The hike is the main point, since only a few foundation stones and some broken-down equipment remain.

Other attractions in this area include the **MacGregor Ranch Museum** (summer only), a working 19th-century cattle ranch in Estes Park. The **Homestead Meadows National Historic District** is also worth a visit, although it's much more difficult to find. Located off Highway 36 about 7 miles (11 km) east of Estes Park, the remains of these eight turn-of-the-century homesteads may be reached only by foot along the steep 2¾-mile (4.5-km) Lion Gulch Trail.

The Stanley Hotel, built in 1909 by Freelan O. Stanley, inventor of the Stanley Steamer.

Little London: About 60 miles south of Denver on Interstate 25, the city of Colorado Springs offers a few genuine glimpses into its genteel past. The Springs was established by Civil War General William J. Palmer, founder of the powerful Denver & Rio Grande Railway. Palmer intended his city to be an oasis of civility that would measure up to the standard of gentility set by his new English bride.

Alas, the experiment failed, and she returned to England. But Palmer's classy new burg attracted so many wealthy Englishmen that it became known as "Little London." The Renaissance-style **Broadmoor Hotel** reflects the wealth of the period – a stark contrast to the gritty mining shacks that once stood only a few miles west.

The **Colorado Springs Pioneers Museum** chronicles local history in a handsome stone structure that once served as the El Paso County Court-house. The **Pro Rodeo Hall of Fame and Museum of the American Cowboy** traces the evolution of rodeo from old-time cowpunchers to the present day. **The White House Ranch Historic Site** features demonstrations of ranch life in the late 19th century. And, just north of town, the **Western Museum of Mining and Industry** has exhibits on historic and modern mining equipment and techniques.

If time allows, there are several scenic drives: the curvy **Cheyenne Mountain Highway** to the **Will Rogers Shrine of the Sun**; a spin through the bizarre sandstone formations in the **Garden of the Gods**; or a spine-tingling ascent of 14,110-foot (4,300-meter) **Pikes Peak**. Better yet, hop aboard the **Manitou and Pikes Peak Cog Railway** for a 3-hour round-trip from nearby **Manitou Springs** to the summit.

West of Colorado Springs is the former gold-mining town of **Cripple Creek**, one of the wealthiest of its day. Visitors can get a feeling for the glory days at the **Cripple Creek District Museum**, or pick up the **Cripple Creek & Victor Narrow Gauge Railroad** for a 4-mile (6-km) ride past some of the mines that made the town rich.

You might also consider a side trip out to **Bent's Old Fort National Historic Site**, about 75 miles (120 km) west of Pueblo on Highway 50. Built in 1833, the fort was a vital trading center on the Santa Fe Trail and a haven for weary travelers. Mountain men like John Colter and Old Bill William passed through with loads of beaver pelts, and a young Kit Carson worked here as a hunter for three years. The Bents were particularly well known for dealing fairly with Indians, refusing to use whiskey to tip the trade in their favor.

Destroyed in 1848 (William Bent blew it up after the US Army commandeered the site during the Mexican War), the fort has been fully reconstructed, and guides in period costumes offer demonstrations of frontier living skills.

About 150 miles (240 km) to the west, at the foot of the soaring **Sangre de Cristo Mountains**, the country's tallest sand dunes (some standing as high as 700 feet/213 meters) are sculpted by the wind and can be seen at **Great Sand Dunes National Monument**.

Left, Ute Indian Bear dance. **Right**, modern pueblo-style buildings are common in the West.

WESTERN COLORADO

The Spanish called it *Colorado* for its red earth, but its palette includes tawny deserts, sage hills, slabs of naked sandstone and snowcapped peaks. Down the western slope of the Rockies come its streams and rivers, coursing through dense pine and juniper forests into a maze of slickrock canyons.

These canyons were occupied centuries ago by Anasazi Indians, who built their homes on the cliffs and farmed the fertile bottomlands. Much later, the Ute Indians moved in and hunted on the slopes of the San Juan Mountains, occasionally raiding Spanish villages in the San Luis Valley.

Then came the discovery of gold and silver, and the Indians' ancient tenure was disrupted. By the 1880s, the mountains were peppered with mining camps where fortunes were made and sometimes lost overnight and a motley cast of dreamers, schemers and confidence men played out one of the most colorful chapters in the Wild West.

Boom and bust: Start your tour at **Leadville**, the undisputed mining capital of 19th-century Colorado. Leadville's early history differs somewhat from other mining towns. A gold strike in the 1860s at nearby California Gulch petered out when sluice boxes became clogged with black sand. By the mid-1870s, only a few people remained, including a storekeeper named Horace Tabor. When a careful metallurgist figured out that the sand was rich in silver, a genuine boom swelled the town.

Among the newcomers were two German immigrants who blew into town penniless and began pestering Tabor to finance their adventure. He reluctantly traded a grubstake for a third of whatever they found. A month later, the silver vein discovered by the greenhorns was grossing $50,000 a month.

Tabor's fortunes grew almost as if by magic, but like so many rags-to-riches characters he and his flamboyant second wife, Baby Doe, died bankrupt (she was found dead in a shack next to one of her husband's failed mines). Only his prudent first wife, whom he had divorced to marry Baby Doe, hung onto her money. The **Tabor Opera House**, built by Tabor in 1879, and the **Tabor Home** (1877) are good places to learn more about the rise and fall of Leadville's favorite couple. Several museums are also worth a visit. In summer, the **Healy House** and **Dexter Cabin** reflect the life-style of the late 19th century. The **Heritage Museum** chronicles local history and the **National Mining Hall of Fame and Museum** offers an interesting look at the mining industry.

The **Route of the Silver Kings** is a self-guiding drive among the area's old mines (a guidebook is available at the **Chamber of Commerce** office), and on summer weekends costumed volunteers recreate life in the old mining camp at nearby **Oro City** where 5,000 prospectors scrambled for riches. In early August, Leadville's **Boom Days** fill the streets with music, dancing and general Wild West hell-raising.

Pick up Route 82 about 15 miles (24

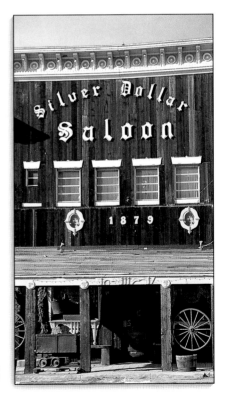

km) south of Leadville for the tortuous mountain drive across the Continental Divide to Aspen. The road tops out at 12,095-foot (3,686-meter) **Independence Pass** (closed in winter), where the abandoned mining camp of **Independence** once housed some 2,000 residents.

Aspen: Established in 1880 and now a glitzy winter getaway for well-heeled vacationers (including lots of Hollywood stars), Aspen has a rougher past than may first appear. In 1894, the streets echoed with the cries of drunken miners who pulled a silver nugget weighing more than a ton from Smuggler Mountain. Today, the precious boutiques that line these sleek streets echo with the jingle of a different kind of silver.

Several fine 19th-century buildings reflect Aspen's glory days, including the **Wheeler Opera House**, **Wheeler-Stallard House Museum** and **Jerome Hotel**, all built by Jerome B. Wheeler, a wealthy Easterner who sank his fortune in local mines only to go bust in the silver crash of 1893.

It's a breathtaking drive on Route 82

through valleys fringed with aspens and cottonwoods and framed by peaks soaring some 14,000 feet (4,260 meters) into the sky. At **Carbondale**, Route 133 runs south along the **Crystal River**. Here, in the last decades of the 19th century, settlers came to quarry white marble and black coal, and the Ute Indians were pushed out of the homeland they had been granted by treaty.

South of Carbondale, the tiny village of **Redstone** was founded by coal-mining magnate John Cleveland Osgood around the turn of the century. In an attempt to keep his workers from unionizing, Osgood built what he figured was the ideal company town, with cottages for married miners and a well-appointed dormitory for the bachelors (now the **Redstone Inn**). For his own home he erected **Cleveholm Manor**, a multimillion-dollar, 42-room Tudor mansion, now a bed-and-breakfast inn.

Both Osgood and his town eventually went bust, although the opening of the **Yule Marble Quarry** in 1905 in the nearby town of **Marble** helped give the area a second life. During its heyday, the town supplied sparkling white marble to the Tomb of the Unknown Soldier and Lincoln Monument in Washington, DC. East of Marble on an unimproved road (check conditions before leaving) is the sometimes-inhabited ghost town of **Crystal**, where the ruins of Sheep Mountain Mill and other buildings from the early 1880s repose beside the river.

Travel north to Interstate 70 and then head west to **Glenwood Springs**. Although the town was founded in 1882, it wasn't until 1887 that the Denver & Rio Grande Railway blasted through the canyon and connected it directly to the outside world. By that time, engineer Walter Devereux, his pockets filled with Aspen mining profits, was busy turning Glenwood Springs into a world-class resort. After building the enormous hot springs-fed pool that still dominates the town, Devereux constructed the luxurious **Hotel Colorado** (where maids reputedly sewed the first teddy bear to console Theodore Roosevelt after he returned empty-handed from a bear hunt). You'll find the graves of notori-

Modern-day "gunfighter" at a Silverton shoot-out.

ous Old West figures at the town's **Pioneer Cemetery**, including John Henry "Doc" Holliday, who died here of tuberculosis in 1887 after surviving the legendary gunfight at the O.K. Corral, and Harvey Logan, better known as Kid Curry, who once rode and robbed with Butch Cassidy and the Wild Bunch.

Million dollar highway: Pick up the trail again far to the southwest where the **Gunnison River** snakes through the narrow gorge of the **Black Canyon of the Gunnison National Monument**; its sheer, dark, 2,000-foot (600-meter) walls are one of the most ominous sights in the West.

About 18 miles (29 km) outside the park, just south of **Montrose**, the **Ute Indian Museum** (closed in winter) details the culture and history of the people who were pushed from the San Juan Mountains by gold-hungry settlers and relegated to reservations near the Colorado–New Mexico border.

From Montrose, Highway 550 heads for the sky. The road climbs more than 5,000 feet (1,500 meters) in only 36 miles (58 km) before peaking at 14,150-foot (4,310-meter) **Mount Sneffels**. It then drops quickly into the town of **Ouray**, where a poor Irish immigrant named Thomas Walsh hit pay dirt in 1896; he later bought the Hope Diamond for his daughter. Several fine old buildings still stand in the **Ouray Historic District**, including the **Western Hotel**, **Beaumont Hotel** and **Wright's Opera House**. Visitors can ride an underground train into the **Bachelor-Syracuse Mine**, where a seasoned miner explains the differences between modern hardrock mining and the methods used a century ago. The town's history is detailed at the **Ouray Historical Museum**, housed in a former 19th-century hospital.

Silver was discovered around Ouray in 1875, but there was a problem: the rugged terrain made it too costly to ship all but ore of the highest quality. The solution came in the person of Russian-born Otto Mears, a man who recognized an opportunity when he saw one. Mears engineered and financed more than 450

Ghost town in the San Juan Mountains.

miles (725 km) of toll roads in the San Juans, including a narrow route south of Ouray that was literally chiseled into the side of **Uncompaghre Canyon** and over 11,118-foot (3,389-meter) **Red Mountain Pass**. After completing the trip by stagecoach, one traveler reputedly said he "wouldn't do it again for a million dollars."

Highway 550 follows Mears' **"Million Dollar Highway"** from Ouray to Silverton. This area is verging on the chic, as well-heeled nature enthusiasts roll in via **Telluride** airport and with the help of modems and computers, stay in touch with the modern world while in the midst of scenic splendor.

Silverton's unimproved streets, false-front buildings and old-fashioned boardwalks make it easy to imagine prospectors and petty hustlers crowding its 34 saloons. To help, gunfights are staged daily at 12th and Blair streets in summer. During the wild 1880s, when fights were common, citizens hired Bat Masterson to serve as their marshal and crack down on the gunslingers.

Silverton is the northern terminus of the coal-burning **Durango & Silverton Narrow Gauge Railroad**, which makes daily 90-mile (145-km) round-trips from **Durango** from May through October. This is the train that wouldn't die. In 1981, a Florida investor rescued the line and began restoring the trains to their former glory. Today, steam-powered locomotives pull old-fashioned coaches through a wild stretch of the **Animas River Canyon**.

Summer visitors to Durango can take in some of the West's best rodeos. The **Durango Pro Rodeo** series is held Tuesday and Wednesday evenings mid-June through August. The **Durango Cowgirl Classic** is scheduled around July 4, and the **Durango Ghost Dancer All-Indian Rodeo** is held on Labor Day weekend. The last rodeo of the season is the **Old West Rodeo** in early October.

About 40 miles (65 km) due west of Durango on Highway 160 is **Mesa Verde National Park**, where the Anasazi built a city of cliff dwellings with as many as 200 rooms in each. Native people in this region knew about the ruins, but it wasn't until 1888 that outsiders tripped over them. While searching for cattle in a snowstorm, two cowboys, Richard Wetherill and Charlie Mason, saw something strange through the curtain of falling snow.

It was **Cliff Palace**, the largest ruin in the park. You can easily spend a few days exploring the park, which ranges from the early Basketmaker period of about 1,400 years ago to the much later Pueblo period. The site was abandoned about 1300, although it's not entirely clear why. For additional information, stop first at the **Far View Visitor Center** or the **Chapin Mesa Museum**.

Two other archaeological sites are well worth visiting, too. The **Ute Mountain Tribal Park** about 15 miles (24 km) south of **Cortez** offers guided tours (reservations required) of Anasazi ruins. And on the Colorado–Utah border, **Hovenweep National Monument** protects six Anasazi villages in the remote canyons west of Cortez. The road to Hovenweep is unpaved; check driving conditions before departing.

Anasazl cliff dwelling at Mesa Verde National Park.

ARCHITECTURE

When it comes to the architecture of the Old West, Hollywood movies and Disneyland's Frontierland taught many Americans most of what they know. Take one main street almost as wide as Texas and twice as dusty. Flank it with low, false-front buildings. Add boardwalks, a hitching post and *voila*! One Old West town.

Such rough-and-tumble towns are indeed part of the West's architectural heritage. But only part. The real story is far more complex.

The West's first great builders were Native Americans. In the Southwest, the Anasazi and Pueblo people created some of the world's great architectural treasures. In New Mexico, the "Sky City" of Acoma sprawls magnificently across a soaring mesa. And certainly no one who has seen the cliff dwellings of Colorado's Mesa Verde will ever forget them.

The Spanish were the first Europeans to put their architectural mark on the country. Santa Fe's Palace of the Governors (completed in 1612) has the low adobe walls and protruding *vigas* (tree trunks used as roof beams) that typify the architecture of Spanish New Mexico.

But the true Spanish genius lay in ecclesiastical architecture. The greatest of all its glories is Mission San Xavier del Bac, near Tucson. Built from 1776 to 1797, San Xavier boasts a domed interior in the ornate style called Churrigueresque.

The first American builders were less ambitious. The earliest structures were outposts like Fort Laramie, Wyoming: simple log or adobe buildings, sometimes protected by a stockade. As for housing, scarcity of building materials became the mother of invention. Settlers in the Nebraska and Dakota prairies lacked the trees to build log cabins – so they built homes from thick blocks of prairie sod. These "soddies," as the houses were called, were inherently ephemeral: of the thousands built in the 19th century, only a handful survive today.

When gold was struck, or when a railroad reached a cattle trail, western towns sprang up so quickly their buildings were hardly buildings at all. One California traveler noted gold camps where hovels were "formed of pine boughs and calico shirts."

The next step up for a western town was to erect more permanent structures, generally simple wood-frame buildings. Here was where the false front came in handy: a tall, decorated parapet made even a shack look grander than it was. Such classic western architecture has been restored or reproduced in towns like Dodge City, Kansas, and Tombstone, Arizona; it can be seen decaying picturesquely in ghost towns like Bodie, California, and Berlin, Nevada.

But false-front, wooden-sidewalked towns were themselves just a phase. To prosper, western cities had to appear substantial enough to attract eastern investors: this meant building in the same Greek and Renaissance revival styles popular in Boston and New York. Up in Leadville, Colorado, mining baron Horace Tabor drew nationwide attention with his sumptuous Tabor Opera House. In San Francisco, tents were replaced by the Italian Renaissance mansions of railroad robber barons.

The style that had the strongest influence on the rest of the country was a simple one: the ranch house. Descended from adobe *ranchos*, it became the model for mass housing from coast to coast after World War II.

Finally, no discussion of western architecture can ignore the fantasy West. As the 19th century turned into the 20th, eastern visitors discovered the glories of western scenery. They wanted to experience the West – but in comfort. And so rose the West's great national park hotels. Most awe-inspiring of all is Yellowstone's Old Faithful Inn. Built in 1904, it holds a five-story lobby decked with log balconies and dominated by a massive stone fireplace. Here is western architecture as wild and vast in scale as the land it graces. ∎

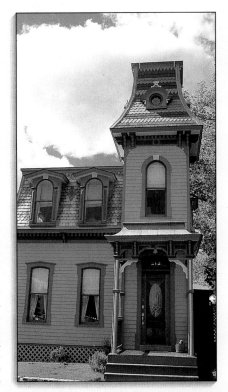

A gingerbread Victorian home in Leadville, Colorado.

NORTHERN UTAH

Two clues to understanding northern Utah: First, explore the Wasatch Range. Second, look for the beehive.

The **Wasatch Range** runs like a spine down the middle of the state. To the east are the canyonlands of the Green and Colorado rivers. To the west is the vast geological province known as the Great Basin. Explorer John C. Fremont was the first to observe that the rivers of the Great Basin flow not to the ocean but, instead, drain inland, into dry lakebeds baked by the sun.

It was from Fremont that the Mormon leader Brigham Young learned of the Great Salt Lake. Persecuted in Missouri and Illinois, where their prophet, Joseph Smith, was dragged from jail and fatally shot, the Mormons wanted a new home far from the disapproval of "Gentiles," a place that, in Young's words, "nobody else wanted."

The first party of Mormons reached the Great Salt Lake in 1847 and immediately started building their new Zion. Young called the territory Deseret, a word from the *Book of Mormon* meaning "honeybee." The symbol he chose for the new state was the beehive, signifying industry, community and the spiritual hierarchy that ties heaven and earth.

The faithful came by the thousands, many of them pulling simple hand carts over the rugged 1,300-mile (2,010-km) trail. By the mid-1850s there were more than 50,000 Mormons in Salt Lake City, with smaller colonies spread throughout the territory.

But even in this western no-man's land, the Mormons weren't left alone. President Franklin Pierce, afraid that they might secede from the Union, sent Federal troops to keep an eye on them. The practice of polygamy only inflamed opinion against the Mormons, as did the activities of a secret vigilante group known as the Danites, who were implicated in a number of violent incidents. A standoff between the Mormon militia and federal soldiers came to a head in 1857 when Brigham Young, then gov-

ernor of Utah Territory, was removed from office, provoking a tense, though mostly bloodless, confrontation.

Violence was in the air, however, and as often happened in the Old West, innocent people were the victims. In September 1857, a party of emigrants bound for California passed through southern Utah. Among them were a gang known as the Missouri Wild Cats whose cursing and thieving quickly made enemies of local Mormons and Paiute Indians, who later attacked the party at Mountain Meadows and massacred all but the youngest children.

But it was polygamy rather than violence that was the sticking point in Utah's attempts to become a state. It was not until 1896, six years after the Mormons officially renounced polygamy, that Utah was accepted into the Union.

This is it: Start your tour at the same place where Brigham Young and his followers first set eyes on the Promised Land, on July 24, 1847. As the pioneers made their way down **Emigration Canyon**, Young stopped and gazed over

the valley. "It is enough. This is the right place," he proclaimed.

The **This Is The Place Monument** sits atop the highest knoll of **This Is The Place State Park**. Here the life-size figures of Young and his councilors look out over the city from a tall granite pedestal. The view is quite lovely and gives an opportunity to see just how logically the city is laid out. The plan was designed by Joseph Smith, a carpenter by trade, who had envisioned his "City of Zion" with wide streets dividing the town into 10-acre blocks.

At the north end of the valley, under a copper dome, is the **State Capitol**, built in 1915. To the south, looking something like a fairy-tale castle, is the **Mormon Temple**, the center of the city plan and the very heart of the Mormon world. Before leaving the park, stroll through **Old Deseret**, a reconstruction of a frontier Mormon village, including an original farmhouse built by Brigham Young in the 1850s.

Leave the park and head directly to **Temple Square**. One hears a great deal about the Mormon imperative to "make the desert bloom," and that's certainly what has been done here. Set off from the city by walls 15 feet (4.5 meters) high, the 10-acre (4-hectare) square is an oasis of green lawns and trees. The Temple itself is an imposing granite structure capped with a gold statue of Moroni, the angel who, in Mormon doctrine, appeared to Joseph Smith; it is decorated with carved figures of all-seeing eyes, clasped hands and – of course – beehives. Started in 1853, the building took 40 years to complete. And as with all Mormon temples, only Mormons in good standing may enter.

The **Tabernacle**, on the other hand, is open to all visitors. Known for its marvelous acoustics and grand organ, it has been the home of the world-famous **Mormon Tabernacle Choir** since its completion in 1857. When asked how to build the Tabernacle, Brigham Young advised modeling the ceiling on the roof of the mouth since God, the greatest architect, would have designed it for the best acoustics. The choir offers free

A Mormon family celebrates Christmas.

admission to its Thursday rehearsal and Sunday broadcast – the oldest continuous broadcast in the world.

City of saints: As you walk around the square, young, fresh-scrubbed guides explain the history of the Mormon church – properly known as the Church of Jesus Christ of Latter-day Saints. They will also ask about any interest you may have in theology, particularly Mormon theology. The pressure isn't great, but you may want to be prepared with a polite response.

On the west side of Temple Square is the prestigious **Family Library** – the largest genealogical library in the world – where visitors are welcome to research their family histories at no charge. A few steps away, you can peek through the windows of the tiny **Deuel Log Cabin**, the oldest house in Salt Lake City. The modern building next door is the **Museum of Church History and Art**, which chronicles the Mormon experience from the founding to the present day with an impressive collection of Mormon artifacts, photographs and art.

To the east of Temple Square, the **Joseph Smith Memorial Building** (featuring a giant-screen IMAX film about the Mormon odyssey) is housed in the old **Hotel Utah**, built in 1911 and once the grandest hostelry in the state. Farther east, the handsome **Lion House** was built in 1856 to house some of Brigham Young's huge family, which numbered well over 15 wives and 44 children. Next door, visitors may tour the fully restored **Beehive House**, which served as Young's official residence from 1854 until his death in 1877.

To the north of the square, on North Main Street near the State Capitol, is the **Daughters of Utah Pioneers Museum**, where you'll find hundreds of frontier artifacts painstakingly exhibited in a jam-packed style that curators sometimes call "visual storage."

In the **Capitol** itself, the marble-clad rotunda features murals of four early trailblazers: the Domínguez–Escalante expedition of 1776, mountain man Peter Skene Ogden, explorer John C. Fremont, and Brigham Young. Across

Golden Spike National Historical Site, where America's first transcontinental railroad was completed.

the street, the handsome **Council Hall** was completed in 1866 and served as the home of the territorial legislature. It was dismantled and moved to this spot in 1963 and now houses a visitor information center and bookstore.

The golden spike: About 35 miles (56 km) north of Salt Lake City via Interstate 15, the city of **Ogden** was the site of the first permanent white settlement in Utah. A mountain man and trader named Miles Goodyear established Fort Buenaventura on the spot in 1846, only to be bought out by the Mormons shortly after. The fort's stockade and log buildings have been reconstructed at **Fort Buenaventura State Park**, open from March through November.

It wasn't until after1869, however, that Ogden really began to grow. That's when the Union Pacific and Central Pacific railroads chose the town as their transfer station – a place where passengers and cargo switched from one line to the other. The railroad brought big changes to Utah. Non-Mormons poured into the territory and began challenging the church's monopoly on power. Many newcomers came to seek their fortune in the silver mines, a pursuit that Brigham Young regarded as wholly unfit for church members.

Built in 1924 and now fully restored, the lavish **Ogden Union Station** houses a fine collection of vintage locomotives, automobiles and Browning firearms. You'll find other structures dating to the late 19th and early 20th centuries in the **25th Street Historic District**. The most unusual is **Peery's Egyptian Theater**, completed in 1924 and decorated in an ornate faux-Egyptian style. If time allows, you might also consider a visit to the **Daughters of Utah Pioneers Museum** which, like the main branch in Salt Like City, features a collection of frontier artifacts.

Continue north on Interstate 15 about 20 miles (32 km) to **Brigham City**, where the striking **Box Elder Tabernacle**, completed in the 1890s, stands before the rolling foothills of the Wasatch Range.

From here a 30-minute drive to the northeast on Route 89/91 takes you to the town of **Logan** in the **Cache Valley**. Several interesting buildings here date to the late 19th century. The **Logan LDS Temple** – a formidable-looking stone structure with three towers on either end – took seven years to build and was completed in 1884. Only church members may enter.

In town, the **Logan LDS Tabernacle** and **Saint John's Episcopal Church** are also well worth a look; both are open to visitors. About 5 miles (8 km) southwest of town on Route 89, the **Ronald V. Jensen Living Historical Farm** (open spring through autumn) recreates farm life in the early 19th century.

About 32 miles (52 km) west of Brigham City is **Golden Spike National Historic Site**. Here on May 10, 1869, the final spike was driven into America's first transcontinental railroad.

Trains no longer pass through Promontory, but the park does include a visitor center and replicas of the Union Pacific's *Number 119* and the Central Pacific's *Jupiter* which met here for the spike-driving ceremony.

Cactus blossom.

One of the 19th century's most romantic enterprises, the Pony Express galloped across the western landscape and into the history books in just over 18 months. From April 1860 through October 1861, Express horsemen formed a record-setting, trans-Mississippi relay team that won over the hearts of the American people, if not the pocketbooks of the US Congress. The daring young mail carriers braved rain, snow, sleet, dead of night and Indian attacks between St Joseph, Missouri, and Sacramento, California, to deliver 35,000 letters, telegrams and newspapers. The riders tallied up 650,000 miles on the 1,966-mile-long Pony Express Trail. And they lost only one mailbag.

William Hepburn Russell, the irrepressible risk-taker of the Russell, Majors & Waddell freighting firm, boldly announced on January 27, 1860, that a Pony Express would begin service between the Missouri River and Sacramento, with the trip to take 10 days each way.

Russell worked fast, buying good horses, establishing relay stations (horses were changed every 10 to 15 miles, riders every 75 miles), and hiring station-keepers and riders. His newspaper ads didn't mince words: "WANTED – Young, skinny, wiry fellows not over 18. Must be expert riders willing to risk death daily. Orphans preferred."

Eighty riders, almost all weighing less than 125 pounds, were hired initially, including a fatherless 15-year-old named William F. Cody, later known as Buffalo Bill. The pay was attractive, at least $50 a month, plus free lodging and food.

Each rider took an oath, agreeing not to use profane language, not to get drunk, and not to fight with other employees. That was Majors' idea. He also made sure each horseman received a copy of the Bible to go along with his weapons – two Colt revolvers, a knife and a carbine.

The first Express riders took off on April 3. Enthusiastic crowds bid the lead riders farewell – eastbound James Randall and westbound Johnny Fry. The rejoicing resumed on April 13 in both St Joseph and Sacramento when the "last" riders arrived. Russell's bold "10-day" forecast had come true.

The Pony Express riders turned in many a valiant performance. Because of Paiute Indian trouble in May 1860, "Pony Bob" Haslam's usual 75-mile (120-km) run in Nevada turned into a 380-mile (612-km) round-trip, completed within 36 hours (including an eight-hour nap). Jack Keetley, the "joyous jockey of the Pony Express," pulled off the longest continuous ride, going 340 miles in about 24 hours. Cody himself pulled off a 322-miler. After covering his assigned 76-mile stretch, Cody found that his relief had been killed and rode on with the mail another 85 miles. And then, with hardly any rest, he rode back the way he came.

At least the riders could usually count on fast horses to keep them alive. The stationmaster's job was more hazardous. The Paiutes, hoping to drive the white man from their hunting grounds, killed some 17 of them and cost the Pony Express about $75,000 worth of horses, supplies and equipment. More damaging to the operation were more mundane financial difficulties. Congress never authorized the mail subsidy, and a desperate Russell became involved in a scandal in which $3 million in bonds was "borrowed" from the Department of the Interior. Charges against Russell were eventually dismissed, but his company was finished. The Pony Express was all but dead by the time a transcontinental telegraph line was completed on October 24, 1861. Even a financially sound Pony Express couldn't have kept riding along in the face of such progress. ∎

SOUTHERN UTAH

A newspaper in 1861 dismissed southern Utah as "measurably valueless, excepting for nomadic purposes, hunting grounds for Indians, and to hold the world together." It looked altogether different a century later to the wilderness enthusiast Edward Abbey. He called it "the most beautiful place on earth."

The rainbow cliffs, dreaming spires and maze-like canyons of southern Utah have served as the backdrop to countless Western movies. But nothing can prepare you for the sheer physicality of this torrid desert, where waves of bare rock are wrenched from the earth. People have come and gone, but the land itself remains the most powerful and enduring presence.

The area was first occupied more than 6,000 years ago by Indians, who left an abundance of rock art and hundreds of well-preserved ruins. White explorers began passing through in the late 18th century, but they rarely stayed for more than a look. The people who made the most lasting mark on the region were the Mormons, with their European-style irrigation and neatly built towns.

The last shoot-out: Determined to settle every corner of the Mormon empire, Brigham Young dispatched several parties of colonists to southern Utah, including the Iron Mission of 1851, which was sent to mine and manufacture iron in the hills around Cedar City, and the Cotton Mission of 1861, which established a community at St George.

The remote southeastern corner of Utah wasn't settled until 1880, when the courageous members of the Hole-in-the-Rock Expedition labored 180 treacherous miles across cliffs and canyons. When they came to the Colorado River, they had to search for a notch in the sheer wall of Glen Canyon (the so-called Hole-in-the-Rock) in order to let down their disassembled wagons. The pilgrims settled near the San Juan River at a tiny village named **Bluff**. Today, a short historic loop leads past the old pioneer cemetery and several original houses, some of which have been taken over by artists.

When floods wiped out their crops in 1905, some Hole-in-the-Rockers established a second town, now named **Blanding**, about 25 miles (40 km) north of Bluff at the base of the **Abajo Mountains**. Blanding was the scene of the Old West's last gun battle in 1923, when a couple of Indian rustlers broke out of jail with the help of a Ute chief named Old Posey. A posse chased them for two days before Posey was shot and killed.

Blanding is also the site of the excellent **Edge of the Cedars State Park**, which preserves the ruins of six Anasazi pueblos (only one of which is excavated) and a rare great *kiva*, probably used as a regional ceremonial center. The park museum houses an extensive collection of Anasazi pottery, sandals, baskets and other artifacts excavated in southeastern Utah. State-of-the-art exhibits discuss archaeology and rock art, and offer an overview of the area's Indian and Anglo history.

About 40 miles (75 km) west of

Blanding, **Natural Bridges National Monument** protects three spectacular sandstone bridges carved by tributaries of the Colorado River as well as fine examples of prehistoric rock art and ruins. One of these spans – **Sipapu** – is second in size only to nearby **Rainbow Bridge**, the world's largest natural bridge. The flat-topped formations were first seen by white men in 1883, when prospector Cass Hite and several companions explored the area with a Paiute guide. Ancient Anasazi Indians used these sheltered, well-watered canyons from about 100 AD to 1300, occupying small dwellings like **Horse Collar Ruin**, hunting game, and farming the mesa tops. A 9-mile (14-km) scenic drive winds past the bridges, and hiking trails lead into the backcountry.

Return to Highway 191 and head north about 80 miles (130 km) to **Moab**, a dandified Old West town set in southern Utah's slickrock country just south of the Colorado River. The Mormons' first attempt to settle the area ended in failure in 1855, when members of the Elk Moun-

tain Mission were driven off by angry Ute Indians. A second attempt in the late 1870s was successful, although trouble with Indians – including the killing of eight settlers in 1881 – continued for several years.

Moab exploded in the 1950s when Charlie Steen struck it rich at his Mi Vida uranium mine, setting off an intense but short-lived boom that swelled the town's population. Steen built a mansion on a hill just north of town that is now occupied by the **Mi Vida Restaurant**. Nowadays, Moab is experiencing a boom of a different sort. The area's slickrock trails and extraordinary scenery have made Moab the "mountain biking capital of the world." Hardly a weekend goes by without a horde of bikers flocking into town.

In downtown Moab, you'll find the **Dan O'Laurie Museum**, with exhibits on local geology, archaeology and history. A visitor center on Main Street has information on outdoor recreation, Jeep tours, horseback riding, movie locations, river trips, historic walking tours, and other attractions.

Canyon country: Five miles (8 km) north of Moab, **Arches National Park** is famous for the geologic formations for which it is named. More than 2,000 sandstone arches have been discovered in the park, one of which – **Landscape Arch** – is the longest in the world. "This is a landscape that has to be seen to be believed," marveled the late writer Ed Abbey, one of the Southwest's most passionate advocates, "and even then, confronted directly by the senses, it strains credulity."

Park rangers recommend that you drive at least as far as the **Windows Section**, for it is here that you can see single and double arches, windows, buttes and the gravity-defying **Balanced Rock**. Just beyond the Windows, you can stop and take in much of the park at **Panorama Point**. The canyon of the **Colorado River** is visible on the southeast border. The green belt of willows, tamarisks and cottonwoods that grows along the waterway seems like a mirage on the other side of this sparsely vegetated valley. Travelers on the Spanish

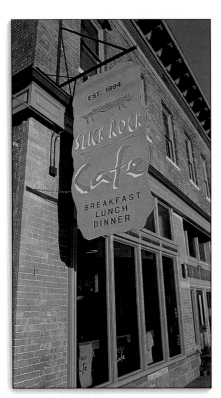

Informal dining in Moab's slick rock country.

Trail in the 1830s and 1840s forded the river nearby.

After Panorama Point, a road turns northeast for three miles to a viewpoint overlooking **Delicate Arch**, the world-famous symbol of Utah's red rock country. Delicate Arch is actually not very tall – only 45 feet (13 meters) high – but its location on the lip of a slickrock bowl gives it a dramatic bearing. For a close-up look, climb the steep trail to the arch – one of the most rewarding hikes in the park. The trail begins at a tiny log cabin built by a crusty Civil War veteran named John Wesley Wolfe, who eked out a meager living as a rancher around the turn of the century.

Five miles north of Arches, a left turn onto Highway 313 leads to the Island in the Sky District of **Canyonlands National Park**. Along the way, you can stop at **Dead Horse Point State Park** for a spectacular view of the goosenecks of the Colorado River 2,000 feet (610 meters) below. This landlocked peninsula earned its name after cowboys used the neck of the mesa to corral wild horses, taking the best and leaving the others to starve. The 6,000-foot (1,830-meter) **Island in the Sky Plateau** was carved by the confluence of the Colorado and Green rivers. The view of the 527-sq.-mile (1,365-sq.-km) park from **Grand View Point** is stunning. The 100-mile (160-km) **Shafer Trail**, an old ranchers' and prospectors' trail, follows the sandstone rim above the river and is popular among back-country campers.

Rest up for the next leg of your journey: a long scenic drive west on Interstate 70, then south on Route 24. You may want to stop along the way at the **John Wesley Powell River History Museum** on Main Street in Green River, which recounts the history of the region with a special emphasis on Powell's epic journeys through the Grand Canyon on the Colorado River.

Pick up Route 24 about 13 miles (21 km) from Green River and head south, skirting the big, empty country of the **Maze**, Canyonlands' wildest section. To evade the law, Butch Cassidy, the

Another eaterie in Moab, "mountain biking capital of the world."

Sundance Kid and the Wild Bunch all holed up at **Robbers Roost** in the Maze. Desert Archaic Indians and later Fremont Indians wandered through these canyons centuries ago, leaving ghostly paintings on pale sandstone walls.

The Wild Bunch were well known in the nearby community of **Hanksville**, founded by fugitive Mormons following the 1882 Edmunds Act outlawing polygamy. Hanksville is the gateway to the **Henry Mountains**, the last range to be named in the United States.

Continue west on Route 24 along the winding **Fremont River** through the ghost town of **Caineville** to **Capitol Reef National Park**. Capitol Reef preserves much of the unearthly-looking **Waterpocket Fold**, a 100-mile (160-km) long highly eroded bulge in the earth's crust that bisects south-central Utah. Route 24 traverses the park's north-central section with scenic views of the Behunin Cabin, Fremont Indian petroglyphs, Castle Rock, Chimney Rock and other geologic formations.

Park headquarters are in the 1880 Mormon community of **Fruita**, which was abandoned in the 1960s when the Park Service bought out the last residents. The 1896 Fruita schoolhouse, blacksmith shop, barn and pick-your-own fruit orchards sit close to the river. Though isolated, Fruita successfully supported itself and surrounding communities with produce and ranching. The 10-mile (16-km) scenic drive ends at **Capitol Gorge Trailhead**, a narrow canyon that was used as a highway from 1884 to 1962. Fremont Indians etched petroglyphs into the canyon walls; travelers later recorded their passage on the walls at the **Pioneer Register**.

To hell and back: Route 24 meets scenic Route 12 just below **Torrey**, the place closest to the park for food, gas and lodging. The drive south parallels the Waterpocket Fold through breathtaking high country, then drops down to **Boulder**, a ranching and farming community so remote that local residents had to get their mail by mule from Escalante until the 1940s.

Stop at **Anasazi Indian Village State**

Travelers stop at a down-home diner.

Park just beyond Boulder for a look at an excavated Anasazi pueblo and reconstructed buildings. Adventurous travelers may consider making a detour a bit farther on by turning right onto the unpaved **Hell's Backbone Road**, an old 38-mile (61-km) mule route to **Escalante** that skirts the **Box-Death Hollow Wilderness** (four-wheel-drive is recommended, although the road may be passable in a passenger car in good weather). The road climbs to an elevation of 9,200 feet (2,800 meters) and then crosses the **Hell's Backbone Bridge**, a tiny span built by the Civilian Conservation Corps in the 1930s and poised over a dizzying precipice. The ride, and the view, are spine-tingling.

From Escalante, continue west on Route 12 to **Tropic**, the gateway to **Bryce Canyon National Park**. The park's water-carved amphitheaters and colorful hoodoos can be seen in the cliffs 1,500 feet above the town. Before entering the canyon, stop at the **Water Canyon Trailhead** and hike the **Tropic Ditch**, one of southern Utah's historic irrigation canals. It was built by 19th-century Mormons to divert water from the East Fork of Sevier River.

To the Paiute people who have lived in the region for centuries, the remarkable geomorphic forms of Bryce Canyon came into being in legendary times, when the animal people so displeased powerful Coyote that he punished them by turning them to stone. Ebenezer Bryce, a Scottish Mormon who had a homestead in the **Paria Valley** below the cliffs in 1875–76, is said to have been somewhat more prosaic about the amphitheaters towering above him, complaining that it was "a hell of a place to lose a cow!"

You can view the park's highly eroded cliffs along the 18-mile scenic drive that follows the edge of the 8,000-foot (2,440-meter) Paunsaugant Plateau through forests of ponderosa pine and summer wildflowers. The drive takes in 13 overlooks whose names exude romance. Among them are **Fairyland Point**, **Sunrise Point**, **Sunset Point** and **Inspiration Point**. The highest spot in

Cowboy shack in Cathedral Valley, Capitol Reef National Park.

the park is **Rainbow Point**, at 9,105 feet (2,775 meters). If time allows, stop for a look at **Bryce Canyon Lodge**, built in 1923 by the Utah Pacific Railroad and now on the Register of Historic Places. Its log frame and green, wavy-shingled roof were designed by architect Gilbert Stanley Underwood to harmonize with the park's natural features.

Exit the park and continue on Route 12 through **Red Canyon** to Highway 89. Drive south about 20 miles (32 km) and then turn right on Route 14. The road climbs up through glorious sub-alpine scenery past wildflower-strewn **Cedar Breaks National Monument** and then descends into the Great Basin Desert toward **Cedar City**.

Cedar City was founded in 1852 by the members of the Iron Mission, mostly English, Scottish and Welsh miners who devoted themselves to "forting, fencing, ditching, farming, gardening, and prospecting, not forgetting the prime object to make iron." They mined the hills west of town (the ruins of **Iron Town** can still be seen there), but iron

production was short-lived. They eventually turned to ranching and farming.

Iron Mission State Park commemorates local history, with rather run-down displays about the mission, horse-drawn carriages and a number of lovely Paiute Indian baskets. Cedar City is also headquarters of the Southern Paiute Tribe, whose members now live on several small reservations and struggle to maintain their cultural identity within a largely Anglo society. The **Paiute Restoration Gathering**, which celebrates the 1980 reinstatement of the Paiute Tribe, takes place in Cedar City in June. Cedar City is also known for its nine-week summer **Utah Shakespeare Festival**. Other festivals include the statewide **Pioneer Day**, which commemorates the arrival of the first Mormon pioneers in Utah on July 24, 1847.

From Cedar City, head south on Interstate 15 past the tiny village of **New Harmony**, founded by pioneer John D. Lee. He was executed for his role in the Mountain Meadows Massacre of 1857, which took place in a little valley south-

The outlaw made this inscription at a hideout in what is now Capitol Reef National Park.

west of town. The Mormons feared government intervention in their polygamist way of life and were panicked by the arrival of federal troops. Fear turned to tragedy when a party of emigrants bound for California passed through southern Utah and harassed Mormon farmers and Indians. In anger, a group of Paiutes and Mormons led by Lee and other pioneers cornered the emigrants in **Mountain Meadows**, lured them out with a promise of safe passage, and then massacred 120 people, sparing only the youngest children. After evading capture for 20 years, Lee surrendered to authorities, was tried, found guilty, and executed atop his own coffin at the site of the massacre.

A marker beside the highway, farther south, commemorates the Spanish Domínguez-Escalante Expedition, which set out from New Mexico for California in 1776 but was forced to turn back when supplies ran out during the arduous journey. The men passed below the Markagunt Plateau at this point before heading toward the Grand Canyon. Although unsuccessful, the expedition was the first to record impressions of the region.

Nature's temple: Before crossing into Arizona, Interstate 15 passes through **St George**, the largest town in southern Utah. Founded in 1861 by members of the Cotton Mission and known as Utah's Dixie because of its moderate winters, St George was chosen by Brigham Young as the site of his **Winter Home**. Here, Young oversaw the construction of the dazzling white **St George Temple** and the sandstone **Tabernacle**, both completed in the 1870s. (Only Mormons in good standing may enter the Temple, while the Tabernacle is open to all visitors.) Artifacts from the town's pioneer days are exhibited at the **Daughters of Utah Pioneers Museum**. The museum, Winter Home, Temple, Tabernacle and other historic buildings are within walking distance of **Ancestor Square** in the town center. It's a short drive to Santa Clara, where you can visit the **Jacob Hamblin House**, built by a Mormon missionary in 1863.

About 40 miles (65 km) west of St George, **Zion National Park** preserves some of the most dramatic geologic formations in Utah. At its heart, the North Fork of the Virgin River knifes through **Zion Canyon**, which soars 2,000 feet (610 meters) high and, in places, is only 20 feet (6 meters) wide.

The first white man to see the canyon was probably Nephi Johnson, a Mormon missionary and translator. In 1858, he was guided as far as Oak Creek by a Paiute, who refused to venture farther into the canyon. The area later became home to Mormon colonists who farmed the flood plains, cut timber in the high country and raised livestock.

One Mormon settler, Isaac Behunin, was so taken by the landscape that he wrote: "These great mountains are natural temples of God. We can worship here as well as in the man-made temples in Zion." The name caught on with his religious brethren, although Brigham Young is said to have taken a dimmer view. After a particularly trying visit to the canyon, he remarked grumpily that it was definitely "not Zion."

NEVADA

Like moths to a flame, travelers out this way are drawn to the beckoning casinos of Las Vegas – only, you can bet, to get their wings burned. There's more to Nevada, however, than bright lights and poker chips. Beyond the neon palaces of glitzy Las Vegas, Nevada remains almost as raw and wild as during the glory days of the Wild West.

With fewer than 1.3 million people inhabiting its 110,000 sq. miles (285,000 sq. km), it is the most sparsely populated state in the continental US. There's an awful lot of dry, open country out there. Sagebrush flats. Isolated mountains. High, cold desert.

Starry sky: But not to worry: Nevadans are a tough-minded people. Who else, after all, would name the sagebrush as their state flower? They are proud to live in such an inhospitable land. The light is clear, the weather fierce and the night sky filled with stars. The old-time traditions of the rancher and buckaroo are still alive here. You may even bump into one of these folks in town. You can tell them by the flat-brimmed hats with braided rawhide "stampede strings" and by the bright silk bandannas known as "wild rags" tied around the neck.

Mining is still big business too, although now there's as much talk of putting waste *into* the mountains as taking minerals *out*. "Nevada is not a Wasteland," says a bumper sticker favored by environmentalists. Miners counter with a slogan of their own: "Earth First: We'll Mine Other Planets Later."

When mountain man Jedediah Smith first crossed the region in 1827, Nevada was occupied by the Paiute, Shoshone and Washoe Indians, who scraped together a living on the eastern slope of the Sierra Nevada and in the arid Great Basin Desert. After gold was discovered in the Sierra in 1849, miners swarmed through Nevada on the California Trail. The territory's first white settlement, a trading post named **Genoa**, was established along the trail the same year by Mormon colonists.

It wasn't until the discovery of the Comstock Lode on Mount Davidson in 1859, however, that Nevada really started to boom. Mining towns like Virginia City sprang up almost overnight. Miners poured in; railroads were built; fortunes were made. But the Big Bonanza was short-lived. Silver was demonetized in 1873, and the Comstock began to play out a few years later. Although the mines remained open until the 1940s, they never again produced the torrent of wealth of the early years.

Crude and brash: Start your tour in the far west of the state at **Reno**, Nevada's second largest city, known affectionately as the "biggest little city in the world." If you don't have time to visit the casinos in Las Vegas, Reno is the next best thing. Established as a railroad town when the Central Pacific rolled through in 1868, Reno is now home to the **University of Nevada**, whose **Mackay School of Mines Museum** chronicles the development of mining in the state. The **Nevada Historical Society** and the **Nevada Museum of Art** offer an interesting look at the region's art and history.

About 20 miles (32 km) south of Reno via Interstate 395 and Route 341 is **Virginia City**. David W. Toll said it was "as crude and as brash a city as ever rooted itself to a western mountainside." Established in 1859 after gold and, later, silver were discovered on **Mount Davidson**, Virginia City quickly became one of the biggest and liveliest cities in the West.

As often happened in other boom towns, the old wooden shanties burned down, in 1875, and were replaced by stately Victorian structures such as **Piper's Opera House** and the **Storey County Court House** (both on B Street). Several fine old homes from the earlier period are still standing, too, including the **Mackay Mansion**, **Chollar Mansion** and **Savage Mansion** on D Street and the lavish **Castle** on B Street.

In the 1870s, a tenderfoot from Missouri named Samuel Clemens came to town and began reporting for the *Territorial Enterprise* as Mark Twain. "Money was as plenty as dust," he wrote

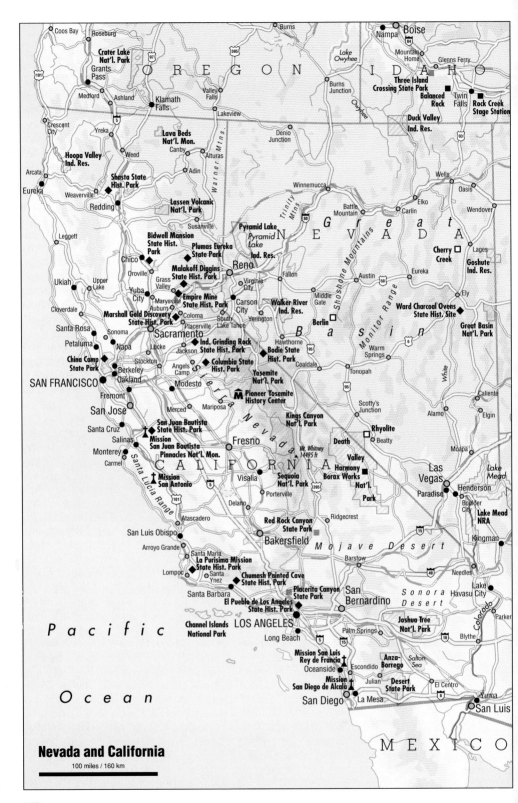

Nevada and California

100 miles / 160 km

of the "flush times" in Virginia City. And the town was no bastion of virtue: "There were… street fights, murders, inquests, riots, a whiskey mill every fifteen steps… and some talk of building a church."

The town itself was "roosted royally" on the slope of Mount Davidson, Twain wrote, adding with characteristic wryness that the "thin atmosphere" was beneficial for gunshot wounds: "to simply shoot your adversary through both lungs was a thing not likely to afford you any permanent satisfaction, for he would be nearly certain to be around looking for you within the month, and not with an opera glass, either."

The office where Sam Clemens launched his writing career is preserved at the **Mark Twain Museum** in the old *Territorial Enterprise* Building on C Street. If time allows, you may also want to consider taking a ride on the historic **Virginia & Truckee Steam Railroad**, one of the crookedest short lines in the world. Vintage trains make the 35-minute round-trip from the station on F Street to the old mining town of **Gold Hill** several times a day from late May to early October.

"Visibly our new home was a desert," Twain wrote of his approach to **Carson City**, about 15 miles (24 km) southwest of Virginia City. "[The town] nestled in the edge of a great plain and… [looked] like an assemblage of mere white spots in the shadow of a grim range of mountains overlooking it."

Carson City, set at the foot of the Sierra Nevada, is now much more than a few dots on the landscape. It was named the territorial capital in 1861 and chosen as the site of the **US Mint** only eight years later. Although no longer in operation, the Mint now houses the **Nevada State Museum**. It features a variety of exhibits ranging from pioneer artifacts to a 19th-century coin press that once transformed Comstock silver into the coin of the realm. Also in town is the **Warren Engine Company Museum**, with a fine collection of antique firefighting equipment. And the **Nevada State Railroad Museum** preserves vintage locomotives, rail cars and other equipment that once ran on the Virginia & Truckee Railroad.

High in the Sierra, about 14 miles (22 km) west of town, **Lake Tahoe**, a popular resort area, spills across the Nevada–California border. Nearby, Interstate 80 crosses the Sierra at **Donner Pass**, where the ill-fated Donner Party was trapped by an early snow in 1846. More than 30 members of the party died of cold and starvation; some of the survivors resorted to cannibalism *(see page 53)*.

The loneliest road: Gas up the car and stock up on supplies, because you're headed for the great frontier. Known as the "loneliest road in America," Highway 50 runs east out of Carson City across the wide-open heart of Nevada.

Turn right about 34 miles (55 km) east of Carson City onto Highway 95A and proceed about 8 miles (13 km) to **Fort Churchill Historic State Monument**. Only a few adobe walls remain of the old fort, built in 1860 after a posse was ambushed and 76 men killed while they were chasing a band of Paiute Indian raiders. The fort later served as a Pony

Express station before it was abandoned in 1869.

Return to Highway 50 and drive east another 73 miles (117 km) to Route 361. Continue south for 30 miles (50 km) and then turn left onto the 20-mile (32-km) access road to **Berlin Ichthyosaur State Park**. The fossils of giant sea dinosaurs called Ichthyosaurs were discovered here in 1954 near the old mining camp of **Berlin**, which was established in the late 1890s and is now a fairly well-preserved ghost town.

Continue east on Highway 50 to **Austin**, a 19th-century silver-mining camp that quickly grew into the second largest town in Nevada. Today, only about 300 folks live here. The town's old churches, cemeteries and tenacious commercial district cling to a steep slope beneath the austere face of the **Toiyabe Mountain Range**. Perched on a hillside just south of town is **Stokes Castle**, a three-story granite edifice built by an eccentric mining executive in 1897.

Proceed east another 70 miles (113 km) over craggy mountain passes and desolate sage-covered valleys to **Eureka**. This now-faded silver queen was established in the late 1860s, burned down twice in the 1880s, and then rebuilt in Victorian style. The town once boasted scores of saloons and whorehouses, two breweries, three opera houses and five volunteer fire brigades. Well-preserved 19th-century buildings like the **Eureka Opera House**, **Sentinel Newspaper Museum** and **Eureka County Courthouse** are handsome reminders of the past.

About 75 (120 km) miles east is **Ely**, a mining town that has seen both sides of the boom-and-bust cycle. The real treat here is the **Nevada Northern Railway Museum**, one of the best preserved short-line railroads in the country. Vintage locomotives take passengers on the 14-mile (23-km) Keystone or 22-mile (35 km) Hi-Line routes every Saturday during the summer months. About 20 miles (32 km) southeast of town, the six beehive-shaped charcoal ovens at **Ward Charcoal Ovens Historic State Monument** are all that remain of the

Shrine to the children of pioneers on the old California Trail.

264

mining town of **Ward**, which was born in the 1870s and died that same decade.

Continue about 65 miles (105 km) east on Highways 93 and 6/50 to **Great Basin National Park**, a 77,000-acre (31,200-hectare) nature preserve draped across the stunning **Snake Range**. The park's scenic drive leads visitors to the limestone passageways of **Lehman Caves** and then up the side of 13,063-foot (3,982-meter) **Wheeler Peak**, the second highest mountain in Nevada. A network of trails lead to the summit, remote alpine lakes, a glacier, and a grove of bristlecone pines, the oldest living trees in the world.

From the park, it's a long drive north to Interstate 80, which loops back to Reno through old railroad towns like Wells, Elko and Winnemucca. **Elko** is probably the most interesting. It's home to the **Western Folklife Center**, which offers year-round exhibits on western folk art and is host to the well-known **Cowboy Poetry Gathering** in January. While you're in town, visit **J.M. Capriola Co.**, a great western saddlery, **Elko General Merchandise**, a classic western general store, and one of the town's several Basque restaurants. The **Northeastern Nevada Museum** is also worth a visit, with an interesting collection of objects from the pioneer period.

To the south of the park, you can follow scenic Highway 93 to Las Vegas or make a long detour via Highway 6 to the old mining towns of **Tonopah** and **Goldfield** or to the impressive ruins at **Rhyolite**, a ghost town near the village of Beatty, east of **Death Valley National Monument**.

Las Vegas itself is about as far from the Old West as one can imagine – a neon oasis made possible by massive water-management projects like the nearby **Hoover Dam**. About the only thing that remains of Vegas's humble beginning as a dusty way station is the **Las Vegas Mormon Fort** (Las Vegas Boulevard), built by missionaries in 1855. You can get a more detailed look at the region's history at the **Nevada State Museum** in Lorenzi Park, which exhibits artifacts from prehistoric times to the mid-20th century.

Lonesome truckin'.

NORTHERN CALIFORNIA

On January 24, 1848, a man named James Marshall peered down into the silt of the South Fork of the American River, spotted glinting flecks in the water, stuck them in the crown of his hat, and cried, "Boys! By God I believe I have found a gold mine."

It was the start of the fabled Gold Rush. It spurred argonauts by the thousands to abandon mundane lives and flock to the Pacific shore. Some actually did find gold, while others found greater fortune selling jeans or groceries or rotgut liquor to the miners. Together they shaped a state. California had only been won from Mexico in 1848, but by 1850 it was part of the Union.

Competition: Today, Northern California's history has to compete with San Francisco skyscrapers, Silicon Valley office parks and Napa Valley wineries. But it's still there to be found – the world of mission fathers and Native Americans, Chinese immigrants and railroad tycoons, Mark Twain and Bret Harte, Lola Montez and Lotta Crabtree dancing for cheering miners.

San Francisco was the city that greeted the argonauts after their journey around Cape Horn. In its earliest incarnation, San Francisco was a sleepy little village concerned, for the most part, with God and war. In 1776 Father Junipero Serra dedicated **Mission San Francisco de Asis** (now usually called Mission Dolores), sixth in the chain of California missions. Today **Mission Dolores** is the anchor of the lively, largely Hispanic Mission District.

That same year the **San Francisco Presidio** was founded to defend the city's magnificent harbor. Only now – after more than 200 years of military use by Spain, Mexico and the United States – is the Presidio in civilian hands; it was recently taken over by **Golden Gate National Recreation Area**. It's a lovely place for strolling, jogging, and perusing historic structures like the **Presidio Army Museum**. Nearby **Fort Point**, beneath the southern end of the **Golden Gate Bridge**, is a mammoth brick fortress begun by the US Army Engineers in 1853; it now houses a museum guarded by a Civil War-era cannon, which can still deliver a satisfying roar.

Actual buildings from the Gold Rush era are rare in San Francisco, since so many were destroyed in the 1906 earthquake. One famous neighborhood that did survive is greatly changed: erstwhile haunt of 19th-century madams and cardsharps, the **Barbary Coast** (bounded roughly by Washington and Pacific streets, and Sansome Street and Columbus Avenue) is now a restored district called **Jackson Square**.

On Montgomery Street in the financial district, the **Wells Fargo History Room** holds Gold Rush memorabilia. The imposing **Old Mint** was built in 1874 and was chief depository for the gold and silver produced in local mines.

By far the liveliest historic neighborhood is **Chinatown**, centered along **Grant Avenue**. The Chinese first arrived in California during the Gold Rush; still more were brought over as laborers

for the railroads. Old Chinatown was destroyed in the earthquake of 1906 (only **Old St Mary's Church**, built in 1854, still stands). Even so, the district speaks eloquently of the cultural and gastronomic glories of 150 years of Chinese life in California.

San Francisco isn't the only northern California city with a Chinese heritage. Just to the north in Marin County, **China Camp State Park** contains the remnants of a Chinese fishing village that dates from the 1880s; the town of **Locke** is a picturesquely fading Chinese town in the Sacramento Delta; and, north of Sacramento, **Oroville, Marysville** and Weaverville boast beautifully restored 19th-century temples.

Gold Country: From San Francisco, the argonauts had to proceed east toward Gold Country by boat. You can simply cross the **Bay Bridge** to **Oakland**. **Jack London Square** harkens back to the youthful days of the city's most famous literary son. The **Oakland Museum**, one of the best in the state, holds fine exhibits on California art and history.

Heading east, you might consider stopping at **Benicia**. This charming little town on the **Carquinez Straits** had its moment of glory in 1853 when it briefly served as California's capital. Now its nicely restored downtown area has numerous antique stores, and the old capitol building is open for tours.

Two hours east of San Francisco is **Sacramento**. Its early history is inextricably linked with a larger-than-life Swiss-German immigrant named Johann Augustus Sutter, who sent John Marshall up to the American River to build a sawmill. Alas for Sutter, he was financially destroyed by the Gold Rush he inadvertently set in motion: his workers abandoned him for the gold fields, squatters occupied his lands, and he spent his last years futilely attempting to gain compensation from the US government for his lost fortune. All of this poignant history is on view at **Sutter's Fort State Historic Park**, now well-regarded for its living-history recreations of 19th-century California. Next door, the **State Indian Museum** fo-

Butch Marks, a Yurok Indian and salmon fisherman.

cuses on the state's large and diverse Native American population.

Most of Sacramento's other attractions are clustered on the east bank of the Sacramento River in **Old Sacramento** – a collection of handsomely restored 19th-century buildings that rise above wooden sidewalks and cobblestone streets. Touristy but fun, Old Sacramento's stand-out attraction is the **California State Railroad Museum**, the largest railroad museum in America and irresistible to train and history buffs of any age. You can even take an excursion in an antique passenger train along the Sacramento River.

East of Sacramento, the **Sacramento Valley** rises and rumples into the Sierra foothills, oak-dotted hills that shine vivid green in spring. This is California's **Gold Country,** which extends roughly 300 miles (480 km) from **Sierra City** in the north to **Mariposa** in the south. It's estimated that in the 50 years after the unbelievable strike at Coloma, some 125 million ounces/3.5 million kg of gold (worth $50 billion in present dollars) were pulled out of these foothills.

Gold Country is generally divided into two regions: the **Mother Lode**, from Coloma south, and the **Northern Mines**, from Auburn north. **Coloma,** where Marshall made his find, is a good place to start your tour. Marshall's strike immediately attracted gold seekers, and at its height Coloma boasted several thousand inhabitants. Today, however, it's a quiet hamlet on the banks of the South Fork of the American River. **Marshall Gold Discovery State Historic Park** holds a replica of **Sutter's Mill** and a good museum. Like many gold-country rivers, the South Fork American offers river-rafters a rollicking ride: check locally for the many companies that offer float trips.

Traveling south from Coloma you reach **Placerville**, once called Hangtown as a testament to its violent vigilante ways. Sites here include the **Gold Bug Park and Mine**, the only city-owned gold mine in the nation, and the **El Dorado County Museum**. If you hit town in fall, be sure to head up to nearby

All that glisters...

Apple Hill, famed throughout California for its cider and apple pies. Just below Placerville, **Sutter Creek** is one of the prettiest towns in Gold Country, its downtown a beautiful collection of tin-roofed, false-front buildings; its bed-and-breakfast inns make a good base for exploring Amador County's burgeoning wine country.

Jackson is noted for the **Kennedy Mine Tailing Wheels**, 58-foot (17-meter) diameter wheels that date from the early 20th century when the search for gold shifted to hardrock mines that were bored deep into the earth.

Also in Jackson, the **Amador County Museum** contains mining exhibits, and neighboring **Indian Grinding Rock State Historic Park** protects an immense grinding rock used by the Miwok Indians. Tucked into a nearby valley is **Volcano**, a charming little town with its balconied **St George Hotel** and fine general store.

As for **Angel's Camp,** it garnered literary immortality as the setting for Mark Twain's *The Celebrated Jumping Frog of Calaveras County,* and today many a ceramic or brass frog can be found for sale in town. Nearby **Murphys** has an air of 19th-century prosperity; the **Murphys Hotel**, which once accommodated Twain and Ulysses S. Grant, is well worth a visit.

If you have time to visit only one town in gold country, **Columbia** may be your best bet. Now enshrined as **Columbia State Historic Park,** this "gem of the southern mines" mixes genuine history with tourist-savvy entertainment. You can tour the town on an antique stagecoach, applaud a stage show at the **Fallon Theater** and savor a horehound drop bought at the **Nelson Candy Kitchen**. Nearby, in Jamestown, **Railtown 1897** is a shrine to traindom that has a six-stall roundhouse and three steam locomotives that offer weekend excursions from March through November.

The next town to the south, **Sonora**, was named by miners from Sonora, Mexico. One of the fastest-growing towns in Gold Country, it nevertheless retains a sense of the past, with a number of restored historic buildings lining Washington Street. Southernmost of the gold-country towns, Mariposa is home to the **California State Mining and Mineral Museum**, one of the best places in the area to learn how gold mining worked. Tour operators will also let you try your hand at panning on local streams.

Eureka!: As for the towns of the Northern Mines, **Auburn**, the largest, is rapidly becoming a Sacramento suburb, but its compact **Old Town** (presided over by the elaborately domed **Placer County Courthouse**) remains charming and walkable. A few miles north on Highway 49 lies **Grass Valley**. Home to famed dancers Lola Montez and Lotta Crabtree, Grass Valley was founded in 1850, allegedly when an argonaut tripped over a quartz outcropping while chasing a cow. Its true heyday came somewhat later, in the era of hard-rock mining. Because the mine companies needed laborers experienced in working in deep tunnels, they imported men from Cornwall, England.

By 1890, Grass Valley's population was 90 percent Cornish, and the Cor-

Engine No. 3 and roundhouse at Railtown 1897.

nish pasty was more or less the official town meal. You can still buy a meat pasty at a couple of places in town. As for the mines, **Empire Mine State Park** is one of the best places in Gold Country to get a feel for this tough business.

Next door, **Nevada City** has gotten downright chic of late. Many of its fine Victorians have been converted to bed-and-breakfasts, and the downtown buildings hold a number of good art and antique stores. But not far away you can see the gritty reality of the search for gold. **Malakoff Diggins State Park** demonstrates the lasting effects of hydraulic mining in which high-pressure hoses were used to rip through river banks and uncover precious deposits of gold. Efficient but ecologically disastrous, the practice was outlawed in 1884.

As you travel north from Nevada City on Highway 49, Gold Country becomes less traveled and more wild, and the road winds spectacularly along the **Yuba River**. **Downieville** is slow-paced and pretty, and **Sierra City** has as its backdrop the spectacular **Sierra Buttes**. It's home to the **Sierra County Historical Park and Museum**, the former Kentucky Mine now turned into a historic park, with a stamp mill and working water wheel. A little to the north, **Plumas Eureka State Park** is well worth a stop for mining buffs, not to mention hikers and campers. It too has a museum and stamp mill and 6,700 acres (2,700 ha) of lakes and forests.

A sea of sin: California's Gold Rush was not limited to the Sierra foothills. Rich finds were also made far to the north. **Shasta State Historic Park** (west of Redding), for example, is as genuine a gold town as any in the Sierra foothills, as is nearby **Weaverville**. Both sites are filled with historic treasures.

Way out on the eastern side of the Sierra, in Owens Valley near Nevada, **Bodie** sprang up after a gold strike in 1859. By 1879 the town had 10,000 inhabitants and a reputation for wickedness: one minister condemned it as "a sea of sin, lashed by the tempests of lust and passion." Now **Bodie State Historic Park**, it's one of California's most

Descendant of Gold-Rush immigrants in Weaverville, which has a 19th-century Chinese temple.

hauntingly lovely ghost towns. Between Bodie and Yosemite lies **Mono Lake**, said to be the oldest continuously existing body of water in North America.

California's Wild West heritage is not limited to gold hunting. Before John Marshall made his fortunate find, it was a land of mission fathers and *ranchos*. Perhaps the most lasting legacy of Spanish settlement was the chain of missions established by Father Serra and his successors. In Northern California they run north from **Mission San Antonio**, in southern Monterey County, to **Mission San Francisco Solano**, in Sonoma County. Among the most beautiful are **Mission San Antonio**, which is set against the **Santa Lucia Mountains**, and **Mission Carmel**, which is graced with an exceptionally lovely garden.

The richest concentration of Spanish California can be found at **Monterey**, where a marked "Path of History" leads past numerous 19th-century adobes, including **California's First Theater** – still used for melodramas today. **Cannery Row** has long supported more

tourists than fishermen, but here and there you can still get a taste of the 150-year-old fishing and whaling industry.

A little to the northeast of Monterey, **San Juan Bautista** is a charmingly preserved Spanish town, with its own graceful mission and a number of 19th-century buildings comprising **San Juan Bautista State Park**. North of San Francisco, the town of **Sonoma** was the center for the 1846 Bear Flag Rebellion that wrenched California away from Mexico and gave it to the United States. Today, Sonoma's plaza, mission and nearby vineyards make it a choice place to spend a day or weekend imbibing both history and wine.

Even farther north, in the upper Sacramento Valley, lie lands once owned by General John Bidwell, a bundle of energy who helped lead the first successful emigrant party from Missouri to California in 1841. Part of Bidwell's once-vast ranch is now the lively university town of **Chico**; his mansion is preserved at **Bidwell Mansion State Historic Park.**

Finally, one last sight must be counted among Northern California's must-sees: **Yosemite National Park.** Miwok and Yokut Indians lived in this part of the Sierra Nevada for thousands of years; Americans arrived in 1851 and quickly turned to herding sheep and logging redwoods. Appalled by the destruction of so beautiful a place, naturalist John Muir led a campaign to preserve Yosemite as a national park, which it became in 1890.

Yosemite's greatest glories are its glacier-carved landforms: Yosemite Valley, Half Dome, El Capitan. But its human history is also compelling. Near the park's visitor center in Yosemite Valley, the **Indian Cultural Museum** has a reconstructed Miwok village and a fine collection of basketry.

At Wawona, near the southern edge of the park, the **Pioneer Yosemite History Museum** holds log cabins, a blacksmith shop and other displays. Here, too, you can lodge in historic comfort at the charming **Wawona Hotel**, whose white-painted balconies seem to have changed little in the past 130 years.

SOUTHERN CALIFORNIA

Old-time jazz, said Jelly Roll Morton, had "that Spanish tinge." The same can be said of Southern California. You see signs of it everywhere. Red-tile roofs on mini-malls. Stuccoed subdivisions that sprawl across rolling hills once grazed by livestock. To be sure, there's a hollow ring to much of this. But if you are standing in the bougainvillea-draped gardens of a 200-year-old mission, the allure of the region's Spanish heritage is hard to resist.

There are other elements, of course. The stagecoach days. Gold rushes. Historic ranches. Cowboys and Indians. And thanks to all those movies filmed here, what we often envision as classic western landscapes are actually Southern California.

Around San Diego: If any city can rightfully stake a claim to Spanish heritage, it's **San Diego**. In 1542, Juan Rodriguez Cabrillo, a Portuguese navigator sailing for Spain, anchored in the protected harbor that he called the Bay of San Miguel. But it wasn't until more than 200 years later that the Spanish began to colonize the region; their first mission, **Mission San Diego de Alcalá**, was built on a hill overlooking the bay in 1769.

The mission was moved in 1774 to take advantage of a better water supply and to separate Indians from the soldiers who were stationed at the nearby *presidio*. The mission was restored in 1931 and has a small museum named for Father Luis Jayme, killed in the 1775 Indian uprising that destroyed most of the buildings.

North of San Diego on State Highway 76 is a much later mission, **San Luis Rey de Francia**. Much grander than San Diego de Alcalá, this Moorish-style mission was completed in 1815 and is one of only four still operated by the Franciscan order.

Near the original mission site, **Old Town State Historic Park** typifies Southern California's historic attractions – a mix of restored structures that don't betray their age and recreated buildings

that don't reveal their youth in a setting where the commercial and the historic vie for your attention. The 1829 **Casa de Bandini**, a former hacienda and hotel, now houses a Mexican restaurant, while the 1827 **Casa de Estudillo**, the home of a commander of the presidio, is open for daily tours.

East of San Diego, the Spanish influence gives way to more traditional Old West style. Now more famous for apple pie made from local orchards, **Julian**, a small town on Highway 79 in the **Cuyamaca Mountains**, experienced a major gold rush in the 1870s. Many 19th-century structures remain, and the **Eagle and High Peak Mines** offer daily tours into old mine shafts.

From Julian, Highway 78 continues over the **Volcan Mountains** and then drops into **Anza-Borrego State Park**. In 1774, Juan Bautista de Anza crossed this vast desert as he opened the first inland route into California. Later travelers, including miners seeking a winter route into California and the Butterfield Overland Stage between St

Preceding pages: Mesquite Flat Dunes, Death Valley National Park. Left, mission bells. Right, a cowgirl's best friend.

Louis and San Francisco, used a second route blazed by explorer Pedro Fages. Known as the **Southern Emigrant Trail**, it still provides one of the major routes through the desert; portions of Highway S2 follow the trail, with markers at old stagecoach stops and other historic sites. Ruts left by wagon wheels can still be seen just off the highway in the boulder-strewn **Blair Valley**, where you'll find several fairly easy trails to Kumeyaay Indian pictographs and an old village site.

Cow town queen: The city of **Los Angeles** slumbered for a long time after its founding in 1781. Through the early rancho era and the years of Mexican rule, it remained a small farming town. **El Pueblo de Los Angeles State Historic Park**, known to locals simply as **Olvera Street**, is considered the historic heart of the city, although it is actually the third town site, dating to the early 1800s. Mixed among the tourist shops and restaurants are several historic sites. For example, Nuestra Señora Reina de Los Angeles, also known as

Old Plaza Church, was completed in 1822 and still offers Mass.

Throughout the 19th century, outsiders knew Los Angeles as the rowdy "Queen of the Cow Towns." The trade in hides, tallow and beef kept the local range covered in cattle until a drought in the early 1860s devastated the herds.

Two former ranches in **Long Beach**, originally part of the largest land grant in California, preserve Southern California's ranching era. Once the center of a 28,000-acre (11,330-hectare) operation owned by Los Angeles pioneer Jonathan Temple, **Rancho Los Cerritos Historic Site** (4600 Virginia Road) is now surrounded by a country club. The two-story adobe and redwood structure dates to 1844 and was used as headquarters for American forces during the Mexican War. Views from the back balcony over a beautiful garden are grand.

Tucked away in a private residential development, the house at **Rancho Los Alamitos** (6400 Bixby Hill Road) includes an adobe built in 1806, although renovations make it appear more mod-

Left, truck stop markers. Below, red-hot chili peppers.

ern. The grounds and gardens retain the atmosphere of early California, and displays explain ranching operations that continued well into the 20th century.

In addition to these historic sites, the Los Angeles area has a trio of excellent museums. You might expect the **Gene Autry Museum of Western Heritage** (Western Heritage Way) to be filled with celebrity kitsch, but in fact it offers a thoughtful look at both the reality and myth of the Old West. Its collection of vintage Colt firearms shows off the art of 19th-century gunsmithing, while early landscape paintings and movie displays explain how images have long shaped the world's perception of the West.

A right turn at 14235 Sunset Boulevard leads around a long hill to the **Will Rogers Ranch**, a charming state park with a little museum devoted to the cowboy star-philosopher. The house with its funishings, Indian rugs and Western artifacts has been left as it was when Rogers occupied it.

And just off the Pasadena Freeway in **Highland Park**, a landmark 1907 Mis-

sion Revival building houses the **South-west Museum** (234 Museum Drive) and its excellent collection of Native American artifacts. **El Alisal**, the granite-and-timber home of the museum's founder, Charles Lummis, is nearby at 200 East Avenue 43.

Building a myth: The town of **Santa Barbara** is mythic California come to life, a city of red tile, palm trees, archways and whitewashed walls. That's no accident; after an earthquake in 1925, the city instituted a strict building code that restricted architectural styles.

The look certainly has a local precedent. **Mission Santa Barbara** (2201 Laguna Street) is generally considered the most beautiful of the 21 California missions. A meticulous renovation after the quake preserved the mission's aging grace and, fortunately, didn't over-restore it in an unrealistic way.

The downtown area has many adobes, including the second oldest building in California, **El Cuartel**, in **El Presidio de Santa Barbara Historical Park**. Maps for the 12-block **Red Tile**

Established in 1881, Calico ghost town has been fully restored.

Tour are your best bet for seeing this section; they are available at the **County Courthouse** information desk at Santa Barbara and Anapamu streets.

If you can tear yourself away from the ocean along Highway 101, take Route 154 for a historic route through **San Marcos Pass**. During the Mexican War in 1846, American Colonel John Fremont dodged Mexican forces massed at the Gaviota Pass, detoured inland, and took the settlement of Santa Barbara without bloodshed.

At Painted Cave Road north of the highway, **Chumash Painted Cave** harbors ancient pictographs of animal and human figures. The highway follows the route of the stagecoach line between Los Olivos and Santa Barbara. Two inns in Los Olivos – **Cold Spring Tavern** and **Mattei's Tavern** – date to the 1880s. They served passengers on the stage line. At nearby Santa Ynez, the **Parks-Janeway Carriage House** has a large collection of old-time carriages and stagecoaches.

If you haven't had your fill of missions,

head west about 25 miles (40 km) on Highway 246 toward Lompoc and **La Purísima Mission State Historic Park**. The most completely restored California mission, La Purísima is surrounded by 1,000 acres (400 hectares) of chaparral-covered hills that encompass the mission's old aqueducts and reservoirs.

The Mojave: Highway 14 leads into the **Mojave Desert**, a mix of rapid urbanization and hard-core wilderness. Cutting through the **San Gabriel Mountains**, the highway passes a turnoff for **Placerita Canyon County Park**, site of California's first gold rush. Legend has it that in 1842 Francisco López dreamt of gold all around him as he snoozed under an oak tree. When he woke, he gathered some wild onions and noticed gold stuck in the soil around the roots. Evidence of old mines can still be seen in nearby canyons.

Farther up the highway at Escondido Road, the tilted sandstone slabs of **Vásquez Rocks** not only appeared as the backdrop in countless Western movies but also starred in a real-life drama. The notorious outlaw Tiburcio Vásquez used this spot as a hideout in the 1860s and '70s. Nearby at Sierra Highway and Clampitt Road, **Beale's Cut Stagecoach Pass** was sliced through the mountains to improve north–south travel in 1859. Considered a great feat of engineering, the cut was often used as a movie location and appeared in John Ford's classic 1939 movie, *Stagecoach.*

Continue north on Highway 14 to **Mojave** and then east on Route 58. About 4 miles (6 km) east of **Barstow** on Interstate 15 is the turn-off for **Calico**, an old silver-mining town that boomed in 1881 and went bust in 1896. The ghost town has been restored for tourists but remains generally authentic.

Now return to Mojave and continue north on Highway 14 to **Red Rock Canyon State Park**. Best in early morning and late afternoon, Red Rock's eroded cliffs have served as dramatic backdrops for both science fiction and Western films.

Red Rock sits in an ecological transition zone between the Sierra Nevada and the desert. Your experience will

Scotty's Castle, Death Valley.

vary depending on which way you decide to drive. If you head west on Highway 178, you'll reach the groves of **Sequoia National Forest**. Early explorers told tales of the giant sequoias, the largest living things on the planet, and the big trees have come to symbolize the grandeur of the West. Stands of sequoias on the **Trail of a Hundred Giants** and in **Freeman Creek Grove** are easily reached from the highway, and tend to be less crowded than those in nearby **Sequoia National Park**.

To the east, Highway 178 leads into some of the most inhospitable terrain encountered by emigrants to the West. **Death Valley National Park** is the hottest place on earth and contains the lowest point in the Western Hemisphere – **Badwater**, 282 feet (86 meters) below sea level. This is a vast and unforgiving land, covered by salt flats, sand dunes and badlands and surrounded by bare mountains that rise more than 11,000 feet (3,350 meters).

This area's history is filled with tales of miners, doomed travelers and eccentrics. The latter include Death Valley Scotty, a con-artist-turned-miner and veteran of Buffalo Bill's famed Wild West Show who built a fairy-tale castle (with someone else's money) in the northern part of the park. Started in 1925 and never quite finished, **Scotty's Castle** is a 25-room, Spanish-style mansion lavishly appointed with antiques, chandeliers and a variety of imported furnishings. The Park Service offers daily tours.

The park is peppered with the ruins of mining camps and mines. The most impressive is the **Harmony Borax Works** near the **Furnace Creek Visitor Center**. Borax (a cleanser) was loaded onto 20-mule team wagons that rumbled out of the valley to the nearest rail line. The nearby **Borax Museum** chronicles the history of valley mining.

Other interesting sites are the beehive-shaped charcoal kilns of **Wildrose Canyon** and the ruins of several mining operations, including **Skidoo** (of "23 Skidoo" fame), the **Keane Wonder Mine** and **Ashford Mill**.

Cooking up
the evening
chow.

What is it about Montana and Idaho that seems so old? The log cabins built by the first white homesteaders began to appear little more than 125 years ago, recent history, even in a country as young as the United States.

Still, the setting hasn't changed much over the years. Sure, there are more fences, more roads, more towns. And, yes, the buffalo no longer roam freely. But you can still stand over the White Bird Battlefield in western Idaho and pick out the gullies and ravines where the Nez Perce surprised cavalry troops in 1877. There are no homes or shops here – nothing at all to distract you from the scene that sprawls below.

The same can be said of dozens of other historic sites in Montana and Idaho, as well as of hundreds of anonymous places like the broken-down "dog trot" cabin you may pass while driving along the Yellowstone River. Its roof caved in long ago, and its logs have weathered to a silvery gray, but it still overlooks the same meadow, the same treeline, the same bend in the river as it did decades ago. Who lived there? Were they starved out? Chased out by cattle barons? Do their descendants now live in the big white ranch house over the next rise?

Here in Big Sky country, history is written on broad open spaces. And the past is as vivid as the setting sun.

Custer's Last Stand: Start your journey on the Great Plains, south of **Hardin**, in **Montana**. On the **Crow Indian Reservation**, a footpath leads to the crest of a ridge and a cluster of white headstones. Other headstones jut from the prairie grass and lead down over dry hills to a thin green line of cottonwoods. The trees chart the course of the **Little Bighorn River**. The headstones chart the course of death in the most famous battle of all time between the US Army and the Plains Indians – the Battle of the Little Bighorn, better known as Custer's Last Stand (*see page 46*).

Desolate, evocative, raked by endless prairie winds, **Little Bighorn Battle-**field **National Monument** preserves the ground where Lt Col. George Armstrong Custer and 272 members of the Seventh Cavalry died on June 25, 1876, at the hands of their intended victims – Sioux and Cheyenne warriors. The battle came after whites openly violated an 1868 treaty that explicitly prohibited them from entering large tracts of buffalo country, including the **Black Hills**. When gold was discovered in 1874, the government failed to keep out prospectors. The tribes raided, and war followed. A museum at the **visitor center** displays weapons and other battle artifacts as well as a few uniforms that belonged to Custer. An auto tour leads through the battlefield.

If you're visiting this area in August, you may want to stick around for Crow Fair, a weeklong celebration of Plains Indian culture held at **Crow Agency**, with powwows, rodeos, hand games and traditional arts.

From the Custer battlefield, Interstate 90 curves northwest across the undulating plains to **Billings**, where it begins to

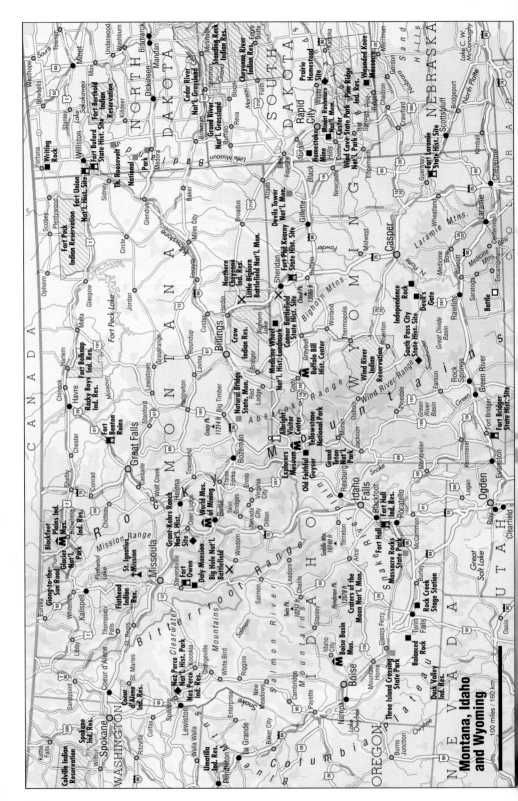

Montana, Idaho and Wyoming

100 miles / 160 km

trace the course of the **Yellowstone River**, a major travel corridor for generations of Indians and, later, for bands of fur trappers packing out beaver pelts. From **Three Forks**, follow Highway 287 south to Ennis, then west to the heart of Montana's frontier history – the restored 1860s gold-rush towns of Nevada City and Virginia City.

Here, in 1863, a dispirited band of six prospectors paused along **Alder Gulch** to eat antelope steaks and bemoan their rotten luck in being chased off the Yellowstone River by Indians. One man dipped a pan in Alder Creek's gravel and came up with gold. Lots of it. Word got out, and within two years 30,000 people lived along the gulch, all earning their keep in one way or another from Montana's richest deposit of placer gold. Famous for its diggings, the gulch was also the birthplace of Montana's Vigilantes, an ad hoc council of citizens who bypassed the sheriff (himself an outlaw) and suspended both judicial procedure and the accused in one swift, pretrial motion. Visit the resting place of the accused at **Boot Hill Cemetery**.

Most of **Virginia City**'s original buildings still stand along the town's main street, but you have to squint past the motor homes and tourists to get a sense of what the place looked like 100 years ago. **Nevada City**, just a mile west, maintains more of the feel of a ghost town, with several blocks of weathered log structures, all stuffed with period furnishings and merchandise. Don't miss the automated music contraptions at the Music Hall.

Copper and cattle: While gold initially drew miners to Montana, copper fueled a more enduring prosperity. **Butte** sputtered along as a small gold mining camp until the 1880s, when new technology made copper mining extremely profitable – especially for those who owned the mines. William Andrews Clark, one of Butte's Copper Kings, enjoyed a monthly income of $17 million. With a half-day's pay ($260,000), he built an opulent red-brick Victorian mansion with a castellated roof, 34 rooms, frescoed ceilings and ornately carved wood paneling. Now called the **Copper King**

Mansion, the house is open for tours and overnight guests.

While Clark grew rich, Butte grew into a thriving city of 100,000 people. Dozens of Victorian buildings grace Butte's West Side neighborhood. One, the **Arts Chateau**, serves as an art gallery. Reminders of the sweat-and-toil side of mining abound in Butte, but perhaps the most striking are the immense black headframes that loom over the entrances to underground mines. At the **Orphan Girl Mine**, one such frame marks the **World Museum of Mining** and Hell Roarin' Gulch. The museum sprawls over 12 acres (5 hectares) and includes a reconstructed frontier town, wagons, trucks and railroad cars and, of course, mining equipment.

Though miners were largely responsible for opening Montana's frontier, cowboys more often come to mind when we think about the West. Cowboys and the evolving cattle industry of the late 19th century take center stage at the **Grant-Kohrs Ranch National Historic Site**, just north of Deer Lodge. The

Custer's grave, Little Bighorn Battlefield.

ranch got its start during the 1850s when Johnny Grant, a former trapper, built up a large herd by trading for puny cattle along the Oregon Trail and fattening them on the grass of the Deer Lodge Valley. He got rich, built a large house in 1862 and sold out four years later to Conrad Kohrs. Kohrs and his half-brother expanded to became the richest ranchers in Montana. When Kohrs married, his bride kicked out the cowboys from the main house, extended it in 1890, and decorated the interior as if it were a Victorian mansion.

Today, the house and several out-buildings have been preserved to reflect the development of the northern plains cattle industry. You'll also see draft horses, cattle, chickens, farm machinery and perhaps a blacksmith at work.

At the south end of Deer Lodge, you can walk through the dreary cells of the **Old Montana Prison**, established in 1871 and used until 1979. Surrounded by a 24-foot (7-meter) sandstone wall, the prison includes an immense red-brick, Romanesque-style cell block.

Million-dollar town: From Deer Lodge, take Interstate 90 north to Garrison, then Highway 12 east to **Helena**, the state capital and another Montana city with roots in the gold-rush years. Here in 1864, four weary prospectors stopped to pan one last stream before calling it quits. Their discovery of a rich gold deposit launched the town. Helena prospered as a supply center for other mining towns and soon boasted 50 millionaires, a density of wealth said to rival any city in the world.

Today, the **Helena Historic District**, which winds through **Last Chance Gulch**, boasts ornate Victorian buildings as well as restored miners' houses that have been converted to stores, bars and eateries. Gold in its various forms – dust, nuggets, wire, leaf and coin – are on display in Norwest Bank's **Gold Collection**. The **Montana Historical Society Museum** houses an outstanding collection of regional pioneer artifacts that range from stone spear points to black-powder rifles, wagons and frontier veterinary tools.

Main Street, Virginia City.

Between Helena and Great Falls, Interstate 15 plunges into a canyon of bulbous rock outcroppings that burst from the flanks of the Missouri River. One of the most beautiful drives in Montana, it traverses the route of Lewis and Clark. For a better look, exit at Wolf Creek and follow **Recreation Road** north to Cascade.

In **Great Falls** you will not find quite the same grand cascades that gave the town its name and imposed two weeks of arduous portaging upon Lewis and Clark. **Ryan Dam**, built above the falls, now controls the flow of water. What you will find, however, is the world's most extensive collection of Charles M. Russell's paintings, sculptures and drawings at the **C. M. Russell Museum Complex**. The "cowboy artist" retired from active wrangling in his late twenties and moved to Great Falls to devote all his time to art. His oils and bronzes and even his illustrated letters celebrate the wrangler's life on the open range and mourn the demise of the Plains Indians. The complex includes Russell's log cabin studio and the house he shared with his wife, Nancy.

As you follow Highway 89 north across the plains, the ramparts of the Rocky Mountains rise to the west. The Blackfeet Indians controlled the buffalo country east of the mountains, but they were often fiercely challenged by the Kootenai and Flathead tribes who lived to the west. At Browning, the **Plains Indian Museum** honors the Northern Plains tribes by exhibiting marvelous articles of clothing, weapons, tools and ceremonial gear – all colorfully embellished with feathers, furs, beads, dyes and woven porcupine quills.

To the west, within the boundaries of **Glacier National Park**, stand two immense stone-and-log lodges built just before World War I by the Great Northern Railway. **Glacier Park Hotel** sprawls over manicured lawns in East Glacier. The other Glacier Hotel perches at the shore of Swiftcurrent Lake, surrounded by an amphitheater of stunning peaks. The park's spectacular **Going-to-the-Sun Road**, with its plunging

Tailgate party.

mountain vistas, climbs above timberline between St Mary and the McDonald Valley.

Missions and murder: From the park's west side, head south on Highways 2 and 93 past Flathead Lake to the **Mission Mountains**. In 1854, at the request of the Flathead tribe, Jesuit priests built a small log chapel and named it after the founder of their order, St Ignatius Loyola. The chapel still stands at **St Ignatius Mission**, but it is overshadowed by the Victorian Gothic church built nearby in 1891. In late afternoon, the red-brick exterior takes on an incandescent glow with the precipitous Mission Mountains as a backdrop. Inside, visitors crane their necks to admire 58 frescoes painted on the ceiling by the mission's cook and handyman, Brother Joseph Carignano. Nearby, **Flathead Indian Museum** displays the work of Flathead and Kootenai artists.

Continue south on Highway 93 through Missoula to the lovingly restored buildings of **St Mary's Mission** at Stevensville. The original mission, a

few miles down river, was established in 1841 by Father Pierre De Smet but was abandoned in 1850 under pressure from the Blackfeet. The present buildings date from 1866 and were built under the supervision of an ingenious man, Father Anthony Ravalli – physician, pharmacist, architect, artist and woodworker. The chapel and residence contain many of his clever works.

Major John Owen bought the original site of the mission in 1850 and established a trading post that prospered for about 20 years. The east barracks of **Fort Owen** survive and are open to visitors. In **Hamilton**, visit the 1890 **Daly Mansion**, a summer home for copper king Marcus Daly. The three-story, Georgian Revival structure has 24 bedrooms and 15 bathrooms.

After climbing south out of the Bitterroot Valley, follow Route 43 into the Big Hole Valley and the **Big Hole National Battlefield**. On this melancholy swath of ground, at least 100 people died in August 1877 during the fourth major battle of the Nez Perce War. A gold rush prompted whites to demand that the Nez Perce give up 75 percent of their reservation. This touched off the war and led to the tribe's epic but unsuccessful flight to Canada. After winning three major engagements with the Army, the Nez Perce felt safe enough to rest here without posting sentinels.

At dawn on August 9, 1862, soldiers crept out of the lodgepole-pine forest across the hollow and attacked the sleeping village. The troops killed at least as many women, children and elderly people as they did warriors before the Indians drove the bluecoats back into the forest. There, Nez Perce sharpshooters kept them pinned down while the rest of the village escaped. The site includes a **museum** and self-guiding trails to the village site and to the forested knoll where the soldiers were besieged.

Just east of the battlefield, follow Route 278 south to the unpaved turnoff for **Bannack State Park**. Now a ghost town, Bannack was the site of Montana's first big gold rush in 1862 and served briefly as its first territorial capital. Among its most intriguing citizens **Montana powwow.**

was Sheriff Henry Plummer, who was accused of leading a murderous gang of highwaymen and was later hanged with his bloodthirsty comrades. Several buildings still stand, including the **Hotel Meade**, **Bannack Jail**, **Skinner's Saloon** and **Methodist Church**. The town comes alive in July during Bannack Days when costumed guides recreate frontier life with a variety of living-history demonstrations.

Idaho: It's a short drive from Bannack to Interstate 15. The highway runs south into Idaho at Monida Pass and then drops into the **Snake River Plain** – a broad expanse of lava, sagebrush and prairie grass that girdles southern Idaho and embraces the main route of the Oregon Trail.

The **Fort Hall Indian Reservation**, home of the Shoshone and Bannock tribes, includes the site of the original Fort Hall, an important stopover on the Oregon Trail. It was built by a Yankee entrepreneur in 1834 who hoped to strike it rich in the fur trade. Instead, he went broke and sold out to the Hudson's Bay Company, which ran the fort during the height of westward emigration. None of the buildings remain, but wagon ruts still mark the route of the Oregon Trail. Tours can be arranged through the **Shoshone-Bannock Tribal Museum**, where exhibits summarize life on the Snake River Plain. The annual **Shoshone-Bannock Indian Festival**, held in August, offers dancing, traditional games, an all-Indian rodeo, art exhibit and a softball tournament.

The **Fort Hall Replica**, on the town of **Pocatello**'s south side, was built in the 1960s from Hudson's Bay Company plans of the original layout. It is a white-stucco enclosure with small blockhouses at diagonal corners. Inside the gates, log cabins and sheds line the walls. The buildings house a blacksmithy, carpenter's shop, trade room, dining hall, sleeping quarters and a lordly, two-room suite for the fort's factor. Nearby, exhibits at the **Bannock County Historical Society and Museum** track the area's frontier history.

Between 1841 and 1869, roughly

Indian pony.

300,000 people trudged across the gnarly surface of the Snake River Plain as they traveled the Oregon Trail. Bountiful evidence of their passage stretches from Pocatello to Oregon. Wagon ruts are visible about 30 miles (50 km) west of Pocatello at **Massacre Rocks State Park**, named for an 1862 fight with Indians that left 10 emigrants dead. Passing emigrants carved their names into a large basalt boulder called **Register Rock**, also in the park.

More ruts cut across the desert at the **Milner Interpretive Area** near Burley. The **Rock Creek Stage Station**, built in 1865, stands west of Hansen. At **Three Island Crossing State Park**, near Glenns Ferry, gaze across one of the most dangerous river crossings on the Oregon Trail. Every August, history buffs reenact the risky journey.

Continue west on Interstate 84 to **Boise**. Built among groves of shady trees at the foot of central Idaho's **Owyhee Mountains**, the town took root during the 1860s as a rough-and-tumble mining town and military post. Today it

enjoys as cosmopolitan an atmosphere as is possible in Idaho, thanks in large part to its being the state capital. At the site of **Fort Boise** stand some of the city's oldest buildings: two sandstone houses on officers' row and the quartermaster's building, *circa* 1864.

The **Idaho State Historical Museum** offers a walk-through tutorial of state history, starting with the migration of nomads over the Bering land bridge that once connected North America with Asia. Packed with artifacts, the museum includes a magnificent back bar, Victorian parlor and dining room, firearms, stone spear and arrow points, opium pipes and band instruments.

Self-guided tours of the **Old Idaho Penitentiary** lead through cell blocks built 100 years ago and used until the 1970s. Here you can step into a solitary-confinement cell and learn about tattoos, tunneling and how to convert butter knives into daggers.

Tough town: From Boise, Route 21 climbs off the desert floor into the shade of a ponderosa pine forest. Soon, heaps of gravel and cobblestones appear among the trees. These are what gold dredges left behind as they worked the creek bed around **Idaho City**. Prospectors discovered gold here in 1862. Soon, Idaho City became a mining town of 20,000 people, most of them packing sidearms and bowie knives. Violence was commonplace and often unavenged by the law or even the victim's buddies – they were too busy making money.

On average, the gold in one panful of dirt was worth $1 – at a time when Union Pacific track-layers thought themselves well-paid at $3 a day. The easy money played out quickly, and the town's population plummeted. Many claims were taken over by Chinese immigrants, who accounted for 45 percent of the county's population by 1870.

Today, many of Idaho City's buildings date to the 1860s and include miners' homes, a church, meat market, mercantile center, newspaper office, Masonic lodge, schoolhouse, the homes of various wealthy merchants and even the hand-hewn walls of the territorial penitentiary. A self-guided tour bro- **Western wrangler.**

chure is available at the **Boise Basin Museum**, a fine place to start.

The slow drive north from Boise to **Riggins** goes a long way toward explaining why the Oregon Trail broke away from the Snake River rather than following it to the Columbia. The land was simply too rugged for wagon travel, and the river, which plunges into North America's deepest gorge, was too wild to cross. Today's roads avoid the Snake for similar reasons. The only route north, Highway 95, leads instead into the continent's second deepest gorge, the **Salmon River Canyon**.

From Riggins, the highway climbs to **White Bird Summit**. Partway up, a small interpretive center overlooks the **White Bird Battlefield**, where 60 to 80 Nez Perce warriors wiped out one-third of a 100-member cavalry unit that was about to attack their village. It was the first battle of the 1877 Nez Perce War, which began after whites demanded that the Nez Perce accept a drastic reduction of their reservation. An auto tour winds through the battlefield.

Cowboy cuisine.

The site is part of the **Nez Perce National Historic Park**, which preserves 38 sites in five states. Headquarters are in **Spalding**, where Henry and Eliza Spalding established their mission in 1836. The **visitor center** houses a good collection of Nez Perce artifacts.

Continuing north, Idaho's oldest building, the lovely **Old Mission** at **Cataldo**, stands on a small grassy knoll overlooking the forest east of **Coeur d'Alene**. Father Anthony Ravalli built the cream-colored, Greek Revival church in 1850–53 with a crew of Coeur d'Alene Indians, a pocket knife, ax, rope and pulleys. Ravalli carved the altars and painted them to resemble Italian marble.

He fashioned chandeliers from tin cans and used berry juice to paint the ceiling the color of the sky. The Indians called it the House of the Great Spirit and left reluctantly in 1877 when they were forced onto a reservation farther south. On August 15, members of the tribe return to celebrate the Feast of the Assumption, and visitors are welcome.

Wyoming

DUDE

ntennial . 1990

WYOMING

It's been nearly 200 years since the first Anglos roasted buffalo hump ribs under Wyoming's magnificent night sky. As they carved slice after slice of tender meat and washed it down with mugs of melted kidney fat, did they think that a country so vast and wild and free might never change?

Certainly they, or other trappers like themselves, knew better by 1834, when there was already talk of the decline of the buffalo. The Plains Indians knew better, too. They were the first to detect changes in the buffalo's migration patterns. And indeed change came – profound and inexorable. Hundreds of thousands of emigrants crossed Wyoming on the Oregon Trail between 1841 and 1868. The discovery of gold sparked Indian wars in the 1860s and 1870s. At about the same time, the nation's first transcontinental railroad laid tracks across southern Wyoming and opened a huge eastern market for the region's coal and cattle. The railroad, and the highways that have followed it in our own century, laid the groundwork for settlements and cities. And yet, in spite of the transformation, much of Wyoming still feels vast and wild and free. Its history is as tangible as a stalk of prairie grass between the teeth.

Hell on wheels: As it curves through southern Wyoming from Pine Bluffs to **Evanston**, Interstate 80 roughly parallels the course of America's first transcontinental railroad, the Union Pacific. As the building crews shoveled and hammered their way over the mountains and across the desert in 1867–69, they played the central role in three of the most exciting years of Wyoming history. They drew a flock of low-lifes, gamblers and whores who inadvertently founded Wyoming's principal cities on the dubious proposition that all men needed a place to get drunk, beat the living pulp out of one another, and find a woman willing to help them out of their trousers. Cheyenne, Laramie, Rawlins, Rock Springs, Evanston – all owe their existence to the arrival of the Union Pacific and the tireless efforts of the Hell-on-Wheels crowd.

Cheyenne: The tracks arrived in Cheyenne in November 1867 and they soon opened a vast market for open-range cattle. During the Black Hills gold rush, the city became the jumping-off point for prospectors and other entrepreneurs headed for Deadwood via stagecoach. The railroad, cattle and gold, as well as Cheyenne's standing as the state capital, ensured its place in the world.

Each July Cheyenne throws the state's biggest rodeo bash, which is enshrined at the **Cheyenne Frontier Days Old West Museum** in Frontier Park. During the 1870s and 1880s, wealthy citizens built spectacular mansions, now mostly demolished, as well as beautiful churches and commercial buildings, many of which survive downtown on Capitol Avenue. One elegant residence still opens its doors to visitors: the **Historic Governor's Mansion**, a large Georgian-style house decorated with eclectic furnishings. Displays at the **Wyoming State Museum** summarize state history. Restoration of Cheyenne's magnificent 1886 **Union Pacific Depot** provides another glimpse of the past.

Cheyenne may have been the capital of the territory, but **Laramie** was, in its early years, the capital of eye-gouging, robbery, garroting and shoot-em-ups. So lawless was the town that it was put under the jurisdiction of federal courts until 1874. Small wonder that the territory's first prison was built here.

Today, the **Wyoming Territorial Prison** has been restored to its 1890s condition and then some. Buffed up, polished and stuffed with excellent interpretive exhibits, the prison offers guided and self-guided tours through the cell blocks, dining hall, warden's office and infirmary. Inmates, including Butch Cassidy, did their time here from 1872 to 1901, when a new prison opened in Rawlins.

The large stone structure anchors the **Wyoming Territorial Park**, which also includes the **National US Marshals Museum**, a frontier-town replica with a working 1860s steam train and living-history demonstrations. Elsewhere in town, the **Laramie Plains Museum** presents a more genteel picture of the past with a collection of memorabilia at the **Ivinson Mansion**, a stone-and-shingle Queen Anne-style house.

Boom and bust: From Laramie, Highway 130 barrels straight into the **Medicine Bow Mountains**, also called the Snowy Range because of the heavy winter storms that bury the peaks and close the road half the year. This spectacular highway climbs to **Snowy Range Pass**, elevation 10,847 feet (3,306 meters), before descending into one of the state's oldest cattle-ranching areas.

Most of the Medicine Bow's history traces the boom and bust of disappointing mining ventures, beginning with Centennial, where interest in gold, platinum, silver and copper all came to nought between 1876 and the 1930s. **Encampment**, west of the pass off Route 230, enjoyed about 25 years of copper-mining prosperity beginning in the early 1880s. A smelter and 16-mile (26-km) aerial tramway were built, but copper prices plummeted in 1907 just as the ore played out. The **Grand Encampment Museum** preserves articles from the era as well as ghost-town buildings and a section of the aerial tram. The ghost town of **Battle** lies about 15 miles (24 km) west on Route 70.

Highway 130 runs north over sagebrush flats to **Saratoga**, site of free municipal hot springs and the red brick **Wolf Hotel**, in continuous operation for more than 100 years. At Walcott, take Interstate 80 west to Rawlins. Founded during the Hell-on-Wheels era, **Rawlins** blossomed as an embarkation point for the gold-rush towns of Atlantic and South Pass. From 1901 to 1981, robbers, murderers and other convicts were confined at the **Frontier Prison**, far gloomier and perhaps truer to prison life than Laramie's restored territorial prison. Daily tours visit the gas chamber, gallows and cell blocks.

Two of the Oregon Trail's most notable landmarks stand about 60 miles (97 km) northeast of Rawlins via Highways 287 and 220. At **Devil's Gate**, the

Sizing up the land sale near Cody.

Sweetwater River plunges through a gorge 370 feet (113 meters) deep and, in some spots, only 50 feet (15 meters) across. Emigrants scaled the bluffs for a dizzying view of the gorge. Some fell in. Farther east, the oblong hump of **Independence Rock** rises from the windswept prairie. From 1841 to 1868, thousands of travelers stopped here to clamber over the rocks and add their names to those who had come before. Inscriptions date to the early 1840s.

Across the great divide: Pick up the trail again far to the west at **Fort Bridger State Historic Site**, about 70 miles (110 km) west of Rock Springs off Interstate 80. Before the arrival of the railroad and the first wagons on the Oregon Trail, small bands of fur trappers, often called mountain men, combed the streams and rivers of the Rockies for beaver pelts. In the late 1830s, their trade began to dwindle and the trappers looked for other work. Some turned to prospecting. Others ferried emigrants across rivers or guided them through the mountains.

Jim Bridger, the best-known of that singular breed, built a trading post in 1842 with his partner Louis Vasquez. Called **Fort Bridger**, it was located on Black's Fork of the Green River, on the main branch of the Oregon Trail. Thousands of pilgrims stopped here to buy food, repair wagons and replace footsore draft animals. But as the tide of travelers rose, many favored a more northerly route and bypassed the fort.

The partners' fortunes sank further as they fought with Mormon colonists during the 1850s. They finally sold out in 1855 to a church representative. The Mormons burned the fort two years later, when President Buchanan sacked Brigham Young as governor of Utah and sent in the Army. After the Utah War fizzled, the Army occupied and rebuilt the fort. The Pony Express and Overland stage line kept things hopping through the 1860s, but once Union Pacific trains started rolling the importance of the outpost diminished.

Today, several structures have been restored, including Wyoming's first schoolhouse, the commanding officer's

Wyoming architecture.

quarters, guardhouse and Pony Express barn. A replica of Bridger's stockaded fort also stands on the grounds.

From Rock Springs, Highway 191 heads up the dry side of the Green River Valley and intersects the Oregon Trail at **Farson**. There, Route 28 breaks off to the northeast and climbs to **South Pass**, the key to the wagon route through the Rockies. It marked the halfway point for emigrants who were heading to the Pacific Coast and acted as principal gateway to the Far West, just as the Cumberland Gap had opened up Kentucky and the first western frontier.

The pass inclined so gently that many travelers did not realize they had crossed the **Continental Divide** until they spotted the first stream flowing west. A roadside exhibit marks the pass, which still bears Oregon Trail wagon ruts.

In 1867, prospectors struck gold near South Pass. Their discovery and other promising claims launched the boomtowns of South Pass City and **Atlantic City**. During the height of the gold rush, two stage lines ferried passengers and freight from the Union Pacific to **South Pass City**, which boasted five hotels, 13 saloons, a newspaper, bowling alley and beer garden.

The town also made history in 1869 by sending to the territorial legislature a saloon keeper who introduced a bill calling for women's suffrage, the first such law in the world. The next year, South Pass City elected the first woman justice of the peace, Esther Morris. By the early 1870s, mining profits dwindled and so did the population. Today, the **South Pass City State Historic Site** preserves 24 of the original buildings, including a hotel, saloon, stamp mill and an 1870s jail. The site includes an excellent museum. You'll find more old buildings and relics of the gold rush in nearby Atlantic City.

Though prospectors, cowboys, settlers and missionaries left their mark along the Green River, the history of this beautiful valley really centers around one group – the mountain men. Tough, independent, ruthless and supremely adaptable, this rugged breed of early

The grounds of Buffalo Bill Historical Center, Cody.

westerner ranged throughout the Rocky Mountains from the 1820s to the 1840s, trapping beaver for the felt-hat industry.

The **Green River Valley** became the trappers' favorite site for their summer rendezvous, at which hundreds of trappers and Indians gathered to trade their furs with a St Louis supply caravan bearing powder, lead, knives, rifles, traps, coffee, sugar, fabric, trinkets and plenty of whiskey. It was an event so drunk and disorderly as to make a rally of motorcycle gangs seem like an accounting seminar. In Pinedale, the **Museum of the Mountain Man** offers excellent interpretation of the fur-trapping era. Exhibits include one of Jim Bridger's rifles and items from the trapper's basic kit – hide shirt, powder flask, bullet pouch, traps and rifle. Each July, modern buckskinners meet in **Pinedale** for the **Green River Rendezvous Pageant**, a recreation of the old mountain-man gathering.

Jackson Hole and Yellowstone: Continue north on Highway 191/189 into the valley of Jackson Hole. Ringed with peaks, including the awesome Teton Range, and drained by the emerald waters of the Snake River, the valley has provided a haven for Indians, fur trappers, homesteaders, horse thieves and cattle ranchers.

The center of activity is the town of **Jackson**, an old ranching town now dominated by the tourist trade. **Town Square**, with its boardwalks and elk-antler archway, still retains something of an old-time feeling, although much of it is now given over to fancy boutiques and art galleries. You can watch a staged shoot-out on summer evenings, ride around town in a stagecoach, or have a shot of red-eye at the Million Dollar Cowboy Bar, where patrons sit on saddles instead of barstools.

Lately Jackson has been undergoing an invasion of sorts as wealthy out-of-towners, including high-profile celebrities, government officials and corporate giants, move into the valley and build enormous estates. Long-time residents fear that, like Aspen, Jackson is being transformed into a glitzy western play-

Antler arch at Christmas in Jackson town square.

ground. There are still a few genuine cowboys ambling along the boardwalks, but you may have to look hard to find them. Both the **Jackson Hole Museum** and the **Teton County Historical Center** offer a look at life in the valley as it really was, from prehistoric times to the frontier era.

Just north of Jackson, in a fine naturalistic setting, is the **National Wildlife Art Museum**. Around 100 artists, including Russell and Catlin, are represented in this museum, which celebrates the animals of the West.

Jackson Hole embraces most of **Grand Teton National Park**, a relatively small but sensational preserve established in 1929 and expanded after World War II. In the park, you'll find two homesteads from the 1890s: **Menor's Ferry**, which was the site of a cable ferry across the Snake, and the **Cunningham Cabin**, a two-room, dogtrot cabin where two suspected horse thieves were murdered in the early 1890s. The **Colter Bay Indian Arts Museum** concentrates on Plains Indian artifacts.

First explored by Indians and fur trappers and later by scientists anxious to document all the wild talk about geysers and petrified forests, **Yellowstone** became the world's first national park in 1872. The product of a massive volcanic explosion, the park contains two-thirds of the world's geysers, including perhaps the most famous, **Old Faithful**. Nearby, you can walk into the six-story grand hall of **Old Faithful Inn** and admire its fussy logwork and immense stone fireplaces. Probably the world's largest log structure, the inn took 25 years to build, from 1903 to 1928. A few miles away at Madison Junction, the **Explorers' Museum** presents the history of Yellowstone and the stories of those who explored it.

Army troops were posted at Yellowstone during its early years to manage the park, fight fires and discourage poaching. At **Mammoth** in 1891, the Army built **Fort Yellowstone**, today one of the best-preserved cavalry outposts of the late 19th century and still in use as park headquarters. Some of the troops' gear is on display at the **Albright Visitor Center** in Mammoth, along with paintings by Thomas Moran and photos by W.H. Jackson.

Cody country: Just east of the park boundary on Highway 14, look for **Pahaska Teepee**, a two-story hunting lodge built in 1904 for William H. "Buffalo Bill" Cody. Constructed of hand-hewn logs, the lodge is a princely retreat in rustic guise, where Cody entertained high-powered guests.

A Pony Express rider, scout and buffalo hunter turned showman, Buffalo Bill came to the Yellowstone area in 1895 to boost land sales in the town that bears his name. **Cody** preserves Bill's boyhood home, shipped in from Iowa, as well as the **Irma Hotel**, which he built for his daughter. More important, Cody is the site of the outstanding **Buffalo Bill Historical Center**, which includes the **Whitney Collection of Western Art**, one of the finest collections of western painting and sculpture in the world. The center also houses a fine Plains Indian museum, a huge collection of firearms and a treasure trove

Young rancher and friend.

of Buffalo Bill memorabilia. Another good stop: **Old Trail Town**, a collection of frontier-era buildings.

The route then glides across the plains of the **Big Horn Basin** via Highway 14A, which climbs into the precipitous red-rock cliffs of the Big Horn Mountains. It passes **Medicine Wheel National Historic Landmark**, site of a mysterious stone pattern resembling a large, spoked wheel (still regarded as sacred by some Native Americans).

As the road descends onto the sprawling plains of the **Powder River Basin**, take a moment to consider all that grass. It once supported huge herds of buffalo, a resource the Plains Indians fought two bloody wars to protect. Later, cattle and sheep fattened on the grass, and their owners killed one another in disputes over who got to graze their stock on which portions of the open range. The place looks deserted, but it's the bloodiest region in Wyoming history.

During the 1860s, the Army tried to secure the Bozeman Trail, which ran through Powder River country to Montana's gold fields. As part of a major campaign in 1865, General Patrick E. Connor attacked an Arapaho village of 1,500 people camped at what is now the city park in **Ranchester**. It made no difference to Connor that the village wasn't hostile. His troops killed dozens of warriors and destroyed the village. Elsewhere, the 1865 Army campaign was an utter failure.

In 1866, the Army tried again, this time with a series of three forts, including **Fort Phil Kearny**, south of **Sheridan**. There, on a cold December day, a reckless officer named William Fetterman fell for a classic Plains Indian tactic and chased a decoy party over a hill where he and 80 other soldiers were wiped out by Lakota warriors. But the following summer, thanks in part to new breach-loading rifles, troops beat back a major Indian attack. Even so, the Indians strangled the Bozeman Trail and won the war. As the troops withdrew, the Lakota burned the fort. Today at the site, an excellent museum examines the battles and describes military life on the

Once a vital way station on the Oregon Trail, Fort Laramie is now a national historical site.

plains. Self-guided trails lead through the battlefields near the fort.

Range war: In Sheridan, some of the high life of the great cattle boom is preserved at **Trail End Historic Center**, a Flemish-style brick mansion built for John B. Kendrick, cattle baron, governor and three-term US senator. Also in town: the **Sheridan Inn**, an 1890s gambrel-roof hotel with many dormers. The air of prosperity belies the murderous atmosphere that existed between cattle barons and small-time ranchers during the 1880s and '90s.

Lynchings, shootings and other forms of harassment culminated in the infamous Johnson County War in 1892, an invasion of north-central Wyoming by a small private army financed by the state's wealthiest ranchers. Their object was to kill upwards of 20 Johnson County men, including, perhaps, the sheriff, his deputies and the mayor of **Buffalo**. Just four men were killed in two battles – one south of Buffalo on the TA Ranch, the other in Kaycee. Details about the war, along with artifacts from the battles, can be found in Buffalo at the **Jim Gatchell Memorial Museum of the West.**

From Buffalo, head south on Interstate 25 to **Casper**. The highway crosses the North Platte River at roughly the same point where hundreds of thousands of Oregon Trail emigrants crossed the river from 1841 to 1868. At first, most of the travelers forded the river at Red Buttes, west of town on Highway 220. Starting in 1847, though, various ferry services sprang up, and during the 1850s emigrants drove their teams over one of two bridges.

The Army assigned a cavalry troop to what was known as Platte Bridge Station in 1859. It was named **Fort Caspar** in 1865, after a large force of Lakota and Cheyenne killed Lt. Caspar Collins and 26 others in a nearby battle. Abandoned and burned down in 1867, the fort was reconstructed in 1938 and now serves as an excellent pioneer museum.

Impressive evidence of the emigrant era survives farther south in the hills and cliffs outside of **Guernsey** off Highway 26. There, the Oregon Trail climbed over a ridge of soft sandstone. Passing wagons carved ruts several feet deep that can still be seen today. Nearby, emigrants stopped to carve their names in the sandstone of Register Cliff.

Brimming with history, **Fort Laramie National Historic Site** lies just 13 miles (21 km) east of Guernsey. Built in 1834 by fur trappers, the fort was one of the most important stopovers on the Oregon Trail and a major military outpost.

As the tide of emigration rose, the fort was dubbed Camp Sacrifice because it became a huge dumping ground where overburdened travelers disposed of surplus provisions and equipment. The fort was the site of two important treaties with the Plains Indians, as well as a staging area for troops when those treaties failed. Pony Express riders and stagecoach lines also used the fort as a relay point.

Today, Fort Laramie is a national historic site with an excellent museum, a dozen buildings restored to their original appearance, and living-history demonstrations throughout the summer.

Buddies on a bench.

THE OREGON TRAIL

Travel, travel, travel! Nothing else will take you to the end of your journey; nothing is wise that does not help you along. Nothing is good for you that causes a moment's delay.

Missionary Marcus Whitman directed this exhortation at the hardy band of pioneers making the first trek along the Oregon Trail. They followed his advice. So did tens of thousands more. Like wagon ruts on the prairies, the Oregon Trail, extending 2,000 miles from Missouri to the Pacific Northwest, left an indelible mark on the West.

As early as the 1830s, fur trappers and missionaries spread word of the Oregon Country – a vast region of rich river valleys and snowy mountains from Russian Alaska to Spanish California. Never mind that the United States and Great Britain disputed who owned it. By Manifest Destiny, Americans felt, Oregon was theirs.

Hurt by the economic panic of 1837, Midwestern farmers listened receptively to stories of the fertile Willamette Valley. Emigration societies lobbied Congress to encourage western settlement. Missouri Senator Thomas Hart Benton sent his son-in-law, the dashing explorer John Fremont, to survey the land between the Missouri River and the Rocky Mountains and publicize its potential as a western travel route.

In May 1843 that first pioneer party gathered near Independence, Missouri: an estimated 1,000 men, women and children in 120 wagons accompanied by 2,000 horses and cattle. Guided at points by missionary Whitman and then by Whitman's Indian pupil, Stickus, the party arrived in Oregon six months later, effectively doubling the territory's American population.

The die was cast. In the spring of 1845, some 3,000 pioneers were pointing their covered wagons toward Oregon. The trail the pioneers followed began at Independence, forded the Kansas River and then cut west with the Platte River across Nebraska and into Wyoming. Pioneers crossed the Rockies at low, relatively gentle South Pass, but then had to brave the rugged terrain and river crossings of Idaho's Snake River country before following the Columbia River west toward the Willamette Valley.

Fort Laramie, Wyoming, was the first place where wagon trains could obtain supplies, albeit at inflated prices. Fort Laramie was also where some pioneers reconsidered and turned their wagons back toward home. The most formidable terrain lay near the trail's end, along the Columbia River. As the trail disappeared into the river gorge, the pioneers were forced to float their wagons, their livestock and themselves downstream on homemade rafts – a rapid-filled journey that not all survived.

Within a few years, the Oregon Trail journey grew easier. In 1846 the Barlow Road was blazed across the flanks of Mount Hood, making the dangerous Columbia River voyage unnecessary. Toll bridges eased other river crossings. By the 1860s, the time required to travel the trail had been cut from six months to three. By then, some 330,000 emigrants had made the epic journey.

Was it worth it? One member of the pioneer band of 1843, James Nesmith, wondered. "Then it may be asked why did such men peril everything, exposing their helpless families to the possibilities of massacre and starvation, braving death – and for what purpose? I am not quite certain that any rational answer will ever be given to that question."

But in 1846 another trail traveler, Virgil Pringle, viewed his new Willamette Valley home contentedly: "The handsomest valley I ever beheld. All [are] charmed with the prospects and think that they will be well paid for their suffering. ∎

Prairie schooner."

L DRUG

XIT →

PEN

M - 10:00 PM

THE DAKOTAS

When pioneers first set out across the prairie, Dakota Territory was the land of the great Sioux nation. One of the most powerful tribes on the Great Plains, the Sioux dominated their Indian enemies, frustrated the US Army, and held back western expansion for more than 50 years. Their leaders – Red Cloud, Sitting Bull, Crazy Horse – are stock figures in the lore of the Wild West. Their victories and defeats are chapters in American history.

But not even the mighty Sioux could hold back the tide of western migration. With the discovery of gold in 1874, miners swarmed the Black Hills, sparking an epic confrontation between whites and Indians that reached a climax in 1876 at the Battle of the Little Bighorn and ended tragically in 1890 at Wounded Knee. In the intervening years, Dakota Territory saw the likes of such Wild West legends as Wild Bill Hickok, Calamity Jane, George Armstrong Custer and Theodore Roosevelt.

Ancestral ground: Start your tour in the very heart of Sioux country – **Paha Sapa**, the sacred **Black Hills**. Little wonder that the Sioux revere these ancient peaks. They are the most unlikely mountains in America, rising like an island of granite in a sea of grass. Famous Sioux mystics like Crazy Horse and Black Elk came here seeking visions, as do Indians today.

In 1868, Sioux chief Red Cloud signed a treaty guaranteeing the Black Hills to the Indians: "No white person shall be permitted to settle upon or occupy any portion of the territory, or... pass through the same." But when gold was discovered just six years later, the treaty proved as flimsy as the paper it was written on.

The discovery was made by none other than Lt. Col. George Armstrong Custer, a Civil War hero and experienced Indian fighter. His announcement of gold "from the grass roots down" lured prospectors by the thousands and, in one of the great ironies of frontier history, hastened his own destruction.

The government tried to buy the Black Hills, but most Sioux leaders weren't interested in mere money. "One does not sell the earth upon which all living things walk," said Crazy Horse. Nor were they shaken by the threat of war. "If the whites try to take them, I will fight," Sitting Bull warned.

War came quickly enough. In 1876, Custer led the elite Seventh Cavalry against the "hostiles" in the unceded territory west of the Black Hills. On June 25, his scouts sighted a large encampment on the Little Bighorn River. Rather than wait for reinforcements, the brash young officer rushed to the attack. They were never seen alive again.

But the Indian victory at the Little Bighorn didn't save the Black Hills. If anything, it increased the pressure on the Sioux and their Cheyenne and Arapaho allies. Within a year, Sitting Bull retreated to Canada, most of the Cheyennes surrendered, and Crazy Horse laid down his arms – only to be killed while in custody. The struggle for the Black Hills was finally over.

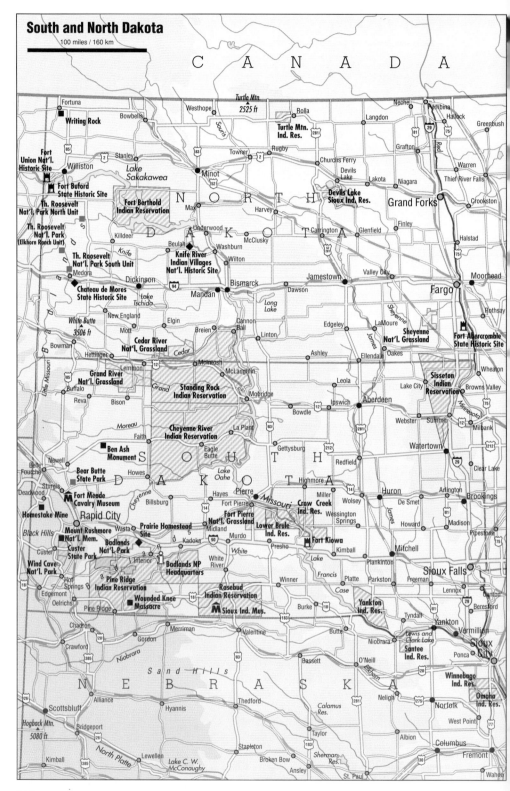

South and North Dakota

100 miles / 160 km

CANADA

Fortuna
Bowbells
Westhope
Turtle Mtn.
2525 ft
Rolla
Neche
Pembina
Hallock
Greenbush

Writing Rock
Turtle Mtn.
Ind. Res.
Langdon
Grafton
Warren

Fort
Union Nat'l.
Historic Site
Williston
Stanley
Towner
Rugby
Churchs Ferry
Devils
Lake
Lakota
Niagara
Thief River Falls

Fort Buford
State Historic Site
Lake
Sakakawea
Minot
Harvey
Devils Lake
Sioux Ind. Res.
Grand Forks
Crookston

Th. Roosevelt
Nat'l. Park North Unit
NORTH
Max
Underwood
Carrington
Glenfield
Finley
Halstad

Th. Roosevelt
Nat'l. Park
(Elkhorn Ranch Unit)
Killdeer
Beulah
Washburn
McClusky
DAKOTA
Valley City
Moorhead

Th. Roosevelt Nat'l. Park South Unit
Knife
Knife River
Indian Villages
Nat'l. Historic Site
Wilton
Bismarck
Jamestown
Fargo

Medora
Dickinson
Mandan
Dawson
Edgeley
Sheyenne
LaMoure
Rothsay

Chateau de Mores
State Historic Site
Lake
Tschida
94
New England
Elgin
Breien
Long
Lake
Linton
Edgeley
LaMoure
Sheyenne
Nat'l. Grassland
Fort Abercrombie
State Historic Site

White Butte
3506 ft
Mott
Cannon
Ball
Ashley
Ellendale
Oakes
Wheaton

Bowman
Hettinger
Cedar River
Nat'l. Grassland
Cedar
McIntosh
Leola
Ipswich
Lake City
Sisseton
Indian
Reservation
Browns Valley

Buffalo
Reva
Bison
Grand River
Nat'l. Grassland
Grand
Lemmon
McLaughlin
Mobridge
Bowdle
Aberdeen
Webster
Summit
Milbank

Standing Rock
Indian Reservation
Moreau
Faith
Cheyenne River
Indian Reservation
La Plant
Gettysburg
281
Watertown

Ben Ash
Monument
Eagle
Butte
Lake
Oahe
Redfield
212
Clear Lake

Bear Butte
State Park
Howes
SOUTH
DAKOTA
Highmore
114
Huron
Arlington
Brookings

Newell
Belle
Fourche
Sturgis
Deadwood
Fort Meade
Cavalry Museum
Cheyenne
Billsburg
Hayes
Pierre
Fort Pierre
Crow Creek
Ind. Res.
Miller
Wolsey
De Smet
Madison
81

Homestake Mine
Rapid City
Wasta
Prairie Homestead
Site
Midland
Fort Pierre
Nat'l. Grassland
Lower Brule
Ind. Res.
Wessington
Springs
Howard
Pipestone

Mount Rushmore
Nat'l. Mem.
Custer
State Park
Kadoka
90
Murdo
Presho
Fort Kiowa
Kimball
Mitchell
75

Wind Cave
Nat'l. Park
Hot
Springs
Interior
Badlands
Nat'l. Park
White
White River
Lake
Plankinton
Sioux Falls

Edgemont
Oelrichs
Pine Ridge
Indian Reservation
Badlands NP
Headquarters
Winner
Francis
Platte
Parkston
Freeman
Lennox
Canton
Beresford

Chadron
Wounded Knee
Massacre
Rasebud
Indian Reservation
Sioux Ind. Mus.
Burke
18
Yankton
Ind. Res.
Tyndall
Yankton
Vermillion
Sioux City

Crawford
Gordon
Merriman
Valentine
Butte
183
Niobrara
Lewis and
Clark Lake
Santee
Ind. Res.
Ponca
Winnebago
Ind. Res.

NEBRASKA
Sand Hills
Thedford
Calamus
Res.
Neligh
Norfolk
Omaha
Ind. Res.

Scottsbluff
Alliance
Hyannis
West Point
Albion
Columbus

Hogback Mtn.
5080 ft
Bridgeport
Taylor
Sherman
Res.
Fremont

Kimball
Lewellen
Lake C. W.
McConaughy
North Platte
Stapleton
Broken Bow
Ansley
St. Paul
Wahoo

Head for the hills: In the Black Hills today, the new tenants have carved an entire mountainside into a portrait of their leaders – the colossal presidential faces of **Mount Rushmore National Monument**, sculpted by Gutzon Borglum. An even larger sculpture is being made of Crazy Horse at the **Crazy Horse Memorial**, where the **Indian Museum of North America** specializes in Plains Indian art and culture.

But the biggest attraction here is the landscape itself. A short drive on the stunning **Needles Highway**, **Rim Rock Drive**, **Nemo Road** or into the rugged backcountry is proof of that. Bear Butte, Harney Peak and the soaring granite mass of Devils Tower in Wyoming are still revered by the Sioux. The rolling grasslands, bison herds and prairie-dog towns at **Custer State Park** and **Wind Cave National Park** are a peaceful refuge from the tourist traps and a potent reminder of what this country looked like before white settlement.

There are also plenty of old mining towns that haven't lost the look or feel of the Wild West. In the southern Black Hills, for example, you'll find **Hot Springs**, a turn-of-the-century spa town, and **Custer**, where the main street is wide enough for a team of oxen to make a U-turn. Farther north, you can catch a ride on the 1880 train between **Hill City** and Keystone, where visitors can pan for gold at the **Big Thunder Mine**.

Nestled on the eastern front of the Black Hills, **Rapid City** is the largest town in the area. Its historic Main Street still has an Old West feel, and the **Sioux Indian Museum** and **Minnilusa Pioneer Museum**, housed in the same building on West Boulevard, have fine collections of frontier artifacts.

From Rapid City, head north on Highway 385 into the heart of gold-rush country. Established in 1875 after the discovery of gold, **Deadwood** quickly grew into a wild and wicked mining camp known for its brothels, saloons and colorful personalities like Calamity Jane and Potato Creek Johnny.

The infamous gunfighter Wild Bill Hickok came to town in 1876, hoping to be elected marshal. "I never allowed a man to get the drop on me," Hickok boasted. Not until August 2, anyway, when a "common gunslinger" named Jack McCall burst into Saloon #10 and shot Hickok in the back of the head as he sat playing poker. Hickok was holding black eights and aces, known thereafter as the "Deadman's Hand." McCall was acquitted by a miners' court in Deadwood but was later convicted, hanged and buried – with the noose still around his neck – in Yankton, South Dakota. You can visit a replica of Saloon #10 and watch a dramatization of the capture and trial of Jack McCall at **Old Town Hall** on historic Main Street.

The entire town of Deadwood is designated a National Historic Landmark, and with the recent legalization of gambling, many turn-of-the-century buildings now house working casinos. Among the most interesting structures is the **House of Roses Museum** on Forest Avenue, which was built in 1879 and has been restored with period furnishings. The **Adams Memorial Museum** on Sherman Street features gold-rush

Wounded Knee Monument.

memorabilia. On the eastern slope of Deadwood Gulch is **Mount Moriah Cemetery**, also known as Boot Hill, the final resting place of several well-known figures. One of them is Calamity Jane, who asked to be buried next to the object of her unrequited affection, Wild Bill Hickok, "the only man I ever loved." Just outside of town on Highway 14A, the **Broken Boot Gold Mine** offers underground tours led by miners.

Three miles to the south, a 19th-century boom town named **Lead** (pronounced *Leed*) is the site of the **Homestake Mine**, started in the 1870s and still one of the biggest in North America. The **Black Hills Mining Museum** on West Main Street chronicles the development of mining in the region.

About 16 miles (26 km) to the northeast is **Sturgis**, founded in 1878 as a military camp charged with maintaining order in the mining towns. It was once known as "Scooptown" because soldiers from nearby Fort Meade were "scooped" (cleaned out) by characters like Poker Alice Tubbs, a cigar-chomping Englishwoman who ran a brothel and casino in what is now the **Poker Alice House** on North Junction Street. Sturgis was also the home of Annie Tallent, the first female settler in the Black Hills. The little stone **Annie Tallent House** was built on Main Street in 1898.

To the east of town, the **Fort Meade Museum** – home of the Seventh Cavalry after the Battle of the Little Bighorn – recounts life at a frontier outpost. A few miles north, the volcanic mass of **Bear Butte** is considered sacred by the Sioux; stay on the trail while hiking to the summit, and don't disturb the medicine bags and prayer ribbons that have been left as offerings.

The last stop in the Black Hills is **Spearfish**, about 20 miles (32 km) northwest of Sturgis via Interstate 90. It stands at the terminus of **Spearfish Canyon Highway**, a tortuous 26-mile (42-km) drive through a stunning granite gorge. About 10 miles (16 km) north, **Belle Fourche** is host to the Black Hills Roundup, a rowdy, annual rodeo.

Twilight in the mountains.

Ghost dance: While the Black Hills were booming, the Indians who once occupied them were struggling for survival. Most were confined to reservations, living on government handouts. Then, in 1890, a shred of hope came their way. Rumors had reached them of an Indian prophet who claimed that whites would soon be swept away and that the buffalo would return to the plains. He taught them a sacred dance, the ghost dance, and promised that all who performed it would be reborn in this new world.

By December 1890, the ghost dance had reached such a fever pitch that reservation officials were getting panicky about an uprising. "Indians are dancing in the snow and are wild and crazy. We need protection and we need it now," the agent at Pine Ridge Reservation wrote. Reinforcements were sent to Pine Ridge, but the sight of so many soldiers scared the Indians away. Little by little, they fled into the Badlands, where several hundred gathered on an isolated mesa called Stronghold Table.

Meanwhile, at the Standing Rock Agency, the order had gone out to arrest Sitting Bull. On December 15, 1890, a contingent of Indian police came to take Sitting Bull away. As they led the old chief from his cabin, a group of angry followers surrounded them, screaming for his release. A shot was fired from the crowd and a policeman was mortally wounded. As he fell, he shot Sitting Bull in the side. From behind, a second policeman shot Sitting Bull in the head.

Terrified by the killing, Sitting Bull's people fled the reservation. Some joined the ghost dancers in the Badlands; others joined a small band of Sioux led by Chief Big Foot camped near the Cheyenne River.

Big Foot was also on the army's list of "troublemakers," and when he heard of Sitting Bull's death, he decided to seek refuge on the **Pine Ridge Reservation**. Soldiers caught up with the band just south of the Badlands, however, and ordered them to make camp near Wounded Knee Creek.

The next morning, a contingent of

Deadwood's historic main street.

soldiers was sent to disarm Big Foot's people. As the soldiers ransacked the tepees, someone, somewhere, fired a shot. And that was all it took to start the killing. A hail of shrapnel fell on the camp, cutting down everything that moved. When the smoke cleared, the camp was littered with bodies.

You can trace the events leading up to **Wounded Knee** about 60 miles (100 km) east of Rapid City in the Badlands, where the prairie has been eroded into an unearthly tableau of deep ravines and crooked spires.

In the early 19th century, French fur traders called the area *les mauvaises terres à traverser* – "bad lands to cross." Many years later, American surveyors compared the fantastic landscape to the remains of "some ancient city in ruins." John Evans, a government geologist dispatched to Dakota Territory in 1849, likened the area to a "magnificent city of the dead, where the labor and genius of forgotten nations had left… a multitude of monuments of art and skill." Today, much of the region falls within **Badlands National Park**, which includes a designated wilderness area where antelope, buffalo and prairie dogs live much as they did when the Sioux roamed the territory in search of game.

Among the many turnouts along the park's 40-mile (65-km) loop is the **Journey to Wounded Knee Overlook**, where Chief Big Foot led his people through the Badlands. To the southeast, in the park's south unit, is **Stronghold Table**, a slender finger of high ground where ghost dancers gathered in December 1890. The only access to the Stronghold is a gravel road about 7 miles (11 km) off County Road 589, and then a long hike to the "narrows," the eroding land-bridge that connects the table with the "mainland." You can get directions and ask about road conditions at the **White River Visitor Center**, open only in summer.

Farther south on Route 27, in a little cemetery near **Wounded Knee Village**, a granite monument marks the mass grave where some 250 victims of the Wounded Knee Massacre are buried.

Bisons roam freely in several Dakota parks.

316

North Dakota: Ambitious travelers can pick up the trail again far to the north in the North Dakota badlands near the little town of **Belfield**. Here in 1883 a young New Yorker named Theodore Roosevelt came to hunt buffalo and ended up taking part in one of the great episodes of western ranching.

During his hunting trip, Roosevelt became absorbed with the cattle industry and, being well-off financially, invested in the **Maltese Cross Ranch**. When he returned the following year, he set up his own operation, the Elkhorn Ranch, on the banks of the Little Missouri River. It was a short-lived affair. The range was exhausted by overgrazing and couldn't sustain the herds through the devastating winter of 1886–87.

Like those of so many other ranchers, Roosevelt's herd was wiped out and the Elkhorn failed. Nevertheless, the brief time spent "among the barren, fantastic and grimly picturesque deserts of the so-called Bad Lands" left a deep impression on him. "If it had not been for what I learned during those years here in North Dakota," he later said, "I would never in the world have been President of the United States."

Today, much of the land Roosevelt knew and loved is protected in the three units of **Theodore Roosevelt National Park**. General Alfred Sully, who conducted campaigns against the Plains Indians, described the area as "Hell with fires out." It is a harsh and unforgiving land, where the prairie is broken into countless ridges and coulees and covered by isolated stands of juniper and ash and thick patches of cactus, sage and spiky yucca.

A leisurely driving tour of either of the main units takes about half a day and features breathtaking views of the landscape and, more often than not, a close-up look at bison, pronghorn and prairie dogs. Starting in the south unit, the **Medora Visitor Center** has modest exhibits on natural history as well as a collection of artifacts left by Roosevelt during his ranching days. The tiny **Maltese Cross Cabin**, occupied by Roosevelt during his first stab at ranching life,

Modern-day "cavalrymen" relive the past.

is restored with period furnishings; it was moved to this spot behind the visitor center in 1959.

The first leg of the 36-mile (58-km) **Scenic Loop Drive** takes you to the Medora Overlook, with a grand view of the tiny western town founded by the Marquis de Mores, a French aristocrat who came to the Badlands in 1883 with the intention of establishing a cattle empire. The marquis built his home, the Chateau de Mores, on a bluff overlooking **Medora**, which he named after his wife. His house and the remains of his meat-packing plant are preserved at **Chateau de Mores State Historic Site**. In summer, an Old West variety show called the Medora Musical is held at an outdoor amphitheater nearby. In Medora itself, boardwalks are lined with shops, saloons and the **Roughrider Hotel**, where young Teddy Roosevelt stayed.

About 65 miles (105 km) north, the park's north unit is even farther off the beaten path and offers wonderful seclusion during the off-season. The 14-mile (22-km) **Scenic Drive** runs roughly par-allel to the Little Missouri River for the first 5 miles (8 km) or so. Just beyond the visitor center, you may see a few head of Texas longhorns, maintained by the park as a reminder of the area's ranching history. An excellent network of hiking trails is available at both units; horseback excursions are offered by the historic **Peaceful Valley Ranch** in the south unit.

To the east, travelers can follow a string of historic forts and Indian villages along the Missouri River. Across the river from **Bismarck**, for example, is **Fort Abraham Lincoln State Park**, where Custer launched his fateful campaign against the Sioux and Cheyenne at the Little Bighorn. Farther upstream, near Washburn, is **Fort Mandan Historic Site**, established in 1804 by the members of the Lewis and Clark expedition who spent the winter here in makeshift shelters. This is also where trader Toussaint Charbonneau and his Shoshone wife, Sacajawea, joined the expedition. Across the river, **Fort Clark Historic Site** preserves the remains of an early fur-trading post and a nearby Mandan village.

A bit farther upstream, at the confluence of the Knife and Missouri rivers, is the **Knife River Indian Villages National Historic Site**, the locale of the Mandan and Hidatsa villages visited by Lewis and Clark in 1804.

About 24 miles (38 km) miles southwest of Williston near the Montana border is **Fort Union Trading Post National Historic Site**, active from 1829 to 1867 and perhaps the finest fur-trading fort on the Upper Missouri River. The Park Service has rebuilt much of the fort, including the palatial (by prairie standards) home of the chief trader, which now serves as a visitor center and museum. Thousands attend the annual **Mountain Men Rendezvous** during the Fourth of July weekend. The post was dismantled in 1867 and the lumber was used to expand **Fort Buford**, now a state historic site about a mile downriver. Black "buffalo soldiers" were stationed at the fort in the 1880s; Sitting Bull surrendered here in 1881 after returning to the United States from Canada.

Left, Native American traditions linger on. **Right**, the long ride home.

INSIGHT GUIDES
Travel Tips

FOR THOSE
WITH MORE THAN
A PASSING INTEREST
IN TIME...

Before you put your name down for a Patek Philippe watch *fig. 1*, there are a few basic things you might like to know, without knowing exactly whom to ask. In addressing such issues as accuracy, reliability and value for money, we would like to demonstrate why the watch we will make for you will be quite unlike any other watch currently produced.

"Punctuality", Louis XVIII was fond of saying, "is the politeness of kings."

We believe that in the matter of punctuality, we can rise to the occasion by making you a mechanical timepiece that will keep its rendezvous with the Gregorian calendar at the end of every century, omitting the leap-years in 2100, 2200 and 2300 and recording them in 2000 and 2400 *fig. 2*. Nevertheless, such a watch does need the occasional adjustment. Every 3333 years and 122 days you should remember to set it forward one day to the true time of the celestial clock. We suspect, however, that you are simply content to observe the politeness of kings. Be assured, therefore, that when you order your watch, we will be exploring for you the physical—if not the metaphysical—limits of precision.

Does everything have to depend on how much?

Consider, if you will, the motives of collectors who set record prices at auction to acquire a Patek Philippe. They may be paying for rarity, for looks or for micromechanical ingenuity. But we believe that behind each $500,000-plus

bid is the conviction that a Patek Philippe, even if 50 years old or older, can be expected to work perfectly for future generations.

In case your ambitions to own a Patek Philippe are somewhat discouraged by the scale of the sacrifice involved, may we hasten to point out that the watch we will make for you today will certainly be a technical improvement on the Pateks bought at auction? In keeping with our tradition of inventing new mechanical solutions for greater reliability and better time-keeping, we will bring to your watch innovations *fig. 3* inconceivable to our watchmakers who created the supreme wristwatches of 50 years ago *fig. 4*. At the same time, we will of course do our utmost to avoid placing undue strain on your financial resources.

Can it really be mine?

May we turn your thoughts to the day you take delivery of your watch? Sealed within its case is your watchmaker's tribute to the mysterious process of time. He has decorated each wheel with a chamfer carved into its hub and polished into a shining circle. Delicate ribbing flows over the plates and bridges of gold and rare alloys. Millimetric surfaces are bevelled and burnished to exactitudes measured in microns. Rubies are transformed into jewels that triumph over friction. And after many months—or even years—of work, your watchmaker stamps a small badge into the mainbridge of your watch. The Geneva Seal—the highest possible attestation of fine watchmaking *fig. 5*.

Looks that speak of inner grace *fig. 6*.

When you order your watch, you will no doubt like its outward appearance to reflect the harmony and elegance of the movement within. You may therefore find it helpful to know that we are uniquely able to cater for any special decorative needs you might like to express. For example, our engravers will delight in conjuring a subtle play of light and shadow on the gold case-back of one of our rare pocket-watches *fig. 7*. If you bring us your favourite picture, our enamellers will reproduce it in a brilliant miniature of hair-breadth detail *fig. 8*. The perfect execution of a double hobnail pattern on the bezel of a wristwatch is the pride of our casemakers and the satisfaction of our designers, while our chainsmiths will weave for you a rich brocade in gold *figs. 9 & 10*. May we also recommend the artistry of our goldsmiths and the experience of our lapidaries in the selection and setting of the finest gemstones? *figs. 11 & 12*.

How to enjoy your watch before you own it.

As you will appreciate, the very nature of our watches imposes a limit on the number we can make available. (The four Calibre 89 time-pieces we are now making will take up to nine years to complete). We cannot therefore promise instant gratification, but while you look forward to the day on which you take delivery of your Patek Philippe *fig. 13*, you will have the pleasure of reflecting that time is a universal and everlasting commodity, freely available to be enjoyed by all.

Should you require information on any particular Patek Philippe watch, or even on watchmaking in general, we would be delighted to reply to your letter of enquiry. And if you send us

fig. 1: The classic face of Patek Philippe.

fig. 4: Complicated wristwatches circa 1930 (left) and 1990. The golden age of watchmaking will always be with us.

fig. 6: Your pleasure in owning a Patek Philippe is the purpose of those who made it for you.

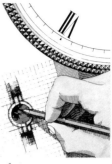

fig. 9: Harmony of design is executed in a work of simplicity and perfection in a lady's Calatrava wristwatch.

fig. 10: The chainsmith's hands impart strength and delicacy to a tracery of gold.

fig. 5: The Geneva Seal is awarded only to watches which achieve the standards of horological purity laid down in the laws of Geneva. These rules define the supreme quality of watchmaking.

fig. 7: Arabesques come to life on a gold case-back.

fig. 11: Circles in gold: symbols of perfection in the making.

fig. 2: One of the 33 complications of the Calibre 89 astronomical clock-watch is a satellite wheel that completes one revolution every 400 years.

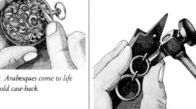

fig. 8: An artist working six hours a day takes about four months to complete a miniature in enamel on the case of a pocket-watch.

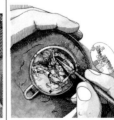

fig. 12: The test of a master lapidary is his ability to express the splendour of precious gemstones.

fig. 3: Recognized as the most advanced mechanical regulating device to date, Patek Philippe's Gyromax balance wheel demonstrates the equivalence of simplicity and precision.

PATEK PHILIPPE
GENEVE
fig. 13: The discreet sign of those who value their time.

your card marked "book catalogue" we shall post you a catalogue of our publications. Patek Philippe, 41 rue du Rhône, 1204 Geneva, Switzerland, Tel. +41 22/310 03 66.

THOMAS COOK
MasterCard
TRAVELLERS CHEQUES...

...HOLIDAY ESSENTIALS

Travel money from the travel experts

THOMAS COOK MASTERCARD TRAVELLERS CHEQUES ARE
WIDELY AVAILABLE THROUGHOUT THE WORLD.

TRAVEL TIPS

Getting Acquainted

Telephone numbers preceded by 800 are toll free in the US. Do not use a prefix for calls within the same area code.

Time Zones

The continental US is divided into four time zones. From east to west, later to earlier, they are Eastern, Central, Mountain and Pacific, each separated by 1 hour. Thus, when it is 8pm in London, in the US it is 3pm in New York City, 2pm in Chicago, 1pm in Denver and 12pm in Los Angeles.

The following regions are in the **Central Time Zone**: eastern North Dakota, eastern South Dakota, eastern Nebraska, eastern Kansas, Oklahoma, all but the westernmost tip of Texas.

Mountain Time Zone: Montana, southern Idaho, Wyoming, Colorado, Utah, Arizona, New Mexico, the western tip of Texas.

Pacific Time Zone: California, Nevada, Oregon (with the exception of a portion of east central Oregon bordering Idaho), northern Idaho.

Climate

Climate in the western states varies dramatically by region, season and elevation. Bad weather, including violent rain, snow, lightning or dust storms, can kick up unexpectedly. A change in elevation can cause temperatures to fall or rise by 20˚F (-7˚C) or mor e. It may be warm in low-lying areas but frigid in the mountains. In some high-elevation areas, daytime temperatures can top 90˚F (32˚C) and then fall below freezing during the night. Similarly, a day may start clear and sunny but end with cold, soaking rain. Snowfall may close roads in some mountainous regions as much as 10 months a year. Flash floods may temporarily close roads in desert areas and can make walking or driving in canyons, arroyos and other low-lying areas very unsafe.

Best Visiting Times

Summer offers the best choice of outdoor events such as powwows and rodeos, although this is when parks, monuments and other attractions tend to be most crowded. Remember, too, that summer temperatures in desert areas routinely exceed 100˚F (38˚C).

Winter offers great skiing, but roads – especially in remote or high-elevation areas – may sometimes be closed by snow. Consider visiting popular ski areas such as Jackson Hole, Taos and Aspen in late spring or early fall, when attractions tend to be less crowded and accommodations less costly.

Planning the Trip

Clothing

Weather can change unpredictably in any season, so be prepared for just about anything. The best plan is to dress in layers that can be peeled off or put on as conditions dictate. Bringing rain gear is always a good idea. A high-SPF sunblock, wide-brimmed hat and sunglasses are a good idea, too, even if the day starts out cloudy. The sun can be merciless, especially in deserts or prairies where there is little shade.

If you plan on doing a lot of walking or hiking, it's worthwhile to invest in a sturdy pair of hiking shoes or boots. Consider buying them a half or full size larger then usual and be sure to break them in properly before arriving. A thin, inner polypropylene sock and a thick, outer sock will help keep your feet dry and comfortable. If blisters or sore spots develop, quickly cover them with moleskin, available at just about any pharmacy or camping supply store.

With few exceptions, western dress is informal. A nice pair of jeans or slacks, a polo or button-down shirt, and boots or shoes are appropriate at all but the fanciest places and events.

Electrical Adapters

Standard American electric current is 110 volts. An adapter is necessary for European appliances, which run on 220–240 volts.

Film

A variety of 35mm, 110 and cartridge films are available in most grocery stores, pharmacies and convenience stores. If you need professional-quality photographic equipment or film, consult the local telephone directory for the nearest camera shop. If you don't have a camera, consider the inexpensive disposable cameras that are now available at many supermarkets, pharmacies and convenience stores.

Maps

Accurate maps are indispensable when traveling in the West. You can usually find a good selection at bookstores, convenience stores and many gas stations.

Free maps may be available by mail from state or regional tourism bureaus (see listing below). Free city, state and regional maps as well as up-to-date road conditions and other valuable services are also available to members of the Automobile Association of America. If you plan on driving any distance, the service is well worth the price of membership.

Maps of national parks, forests and other natural areas are usually offered by the managing agency (see listing below). High-quality topographical maps are available from **Trails Illustrated**, PO Box 3610, Evergreen, CO 80439, tel: 800-962-1643 or 303-670-3457. Topographical maps are also available from the **US Geological Survey**, PO Box 25286, Denver Federal Center, Denver, CO 80225, tel: 303-236-7477.

Entry Regulations
Passports & Visas

A passport, a visitor's visa and evidence of intent to leave the US after your visit are required for entry into the US by most foreign nationals. Visitors from the United Kingdom and several other countries (including but not limited to Japan, Germany, Italy, France,

Switzerland, Sweden and the Netherlands) staying less than 90 days may not need a visa if they meet certain requirements. All other foreign nationals must obtain a visa from the US consulate or embassy in their country. An international vaccination certificate may also be required depending on your country of origin.

Exceptions are Canadians entering from the Western Hemisphere, Mexicans with border passes, and British residents of Bermuda and Canada. Normally, these travelers do not need a visa or passport, although it's always a good idea to confirm visa requirements before leaving your home country.

Once admitted to the US, you may visit Canada or Mexico for up to 30 days and re-enter the US without a new visa, but be sure to take your passport with you. If you lose your visa or passport, arrange to get a new one at your country's nearest consulate or embassy. For additional information, contact the US consulate or embassy in your country or the **US State Department**, tel: 202-663-1225

Customs

All people entering the US must go through Customs. Be prepared to have your luggage inspected and keep the following guidelines in mind:

● There is no limit to the amount of money you can bring into the US. If the amount exceeds $10,000 (in cash and other negotiable instruments), however, you must file a special report.

● Any objects brought for personal use may enter duty-free.

● Adults may enter with a maximum of 200 cigarettes or 50 cigars or 2 kilograms of tobacco and/or 1 liter of alcohol duty-free.

● Gifts valued at less than $400 can enter duty-free.

● Agricultural products, meat and animals are subject to complex restrictions. In order to avoid delays, leave these items at home unless absolutely necessary.

● Illicit drugs and drug paraphernalia are strictly prohibited. If you must bring narcotic or habit-forming medicines for health reasons, be sure that all products are properly identified, carry only the quantity you will need while traveling, and have either a prescription or a letter from your doctor.

For additional information, contact **US Customs**, 1301 Constitution Ave. NW, Washington, DC 20229, tel: 202-927-6724.

Extensions of Stay

Visas are usually granted for 6 months. If you wish to remain in the country longer than 6 months, you must apply for an extension of stay at the **US Immigration and Naturalization Service**, 2401 E St, Washington, DC 20520, tel: 202-514-4330.

Money
Currency & Exchange

American money is based on the decimal system. The basic unit, a dollar ($1), is equal to 100 cents (¢). There are 4 basic coins, each worth less than a dollar. A penny is worth 1 cent (1¢). A nickel is worth 5 cents (5¢). A dime is worth 10 cents (10¢). And a quarter is worth 25 cents (25¢).

In addition, there are several denominations of paper money. They are: $1, $5, $10, $20, $50, $100 and, rarely, $2. Each bill is the same color, size and shape, so be sure to check the amount on the face of the bill.

It's advisable to arrive with at least $100 in cash (in small bills) in order to pay for ground transportation and other incidentals. It's always a good idea to carry internationally recognized traveler's checks rather than cash. Traveler's checks are usually accepted by retailers in lieu of cash. They can also be exchanged for cash at most banks. Bring your passport with you to the bank.

Foreign currency is rarely accepted in the US. You can exchange currency at major big-city banks, hotels, international airports and currency-exchange offices.

Credit Cards

Major credit cards are widely accepted at shops, restaurants, hotels and gas stations, although not all cards are accepted by every vendor. To be safe, try to carry at least two kinds. Major credit cards include American Express, Visa, MasterCard, Carte Blanche, Discover and Diners Club. Some credit cards may also be used to withdraw cash from automatic teller machines (ATMs) located in most larger towns and cities. Out-of-town ATM cards may also work. Check with your bank or credit-card company for the names of the systems your card will operate.

Money may be sent or received by wire at any **Western Union** office (tel: 800-325-6000) or **American Express Money Gram** office (tel: 800-543-4080).

Public Holidays

Government offices, banks and post offices are closed on public holidays. Public transportation usually runs less frequently on these days.

January 1: New Year's Day
January 15: Martin Luther King, Jr's Birthday
Third Monday in February: Presidents Day
March/April: Easter Sunday
Last Monday in May: Memorial Day
July 4: Independence Day
First Monday in September: Labor Day
Second Monday in October: Columbus Day
November 11: Veterans Day
Fourth Thursday in November: Thanksgiving Day
December 25: Christmas Day

Getting There
By Air

If driving out west is impractical because of distance, the next best way to get there is to fly to a nearby city and rent a car. The major airports in the western states are:
Arizona: Phoenix Sky Harbor International, Tucson International.
California: San Diego International, Los Angeles International, San Jose International, Oakland International, Ontario International, San Francisco International.
Colorado: Denver International, Colorado Springs Airport.
Idaho: Boise Airport.
Montana: Logan International (Billings), Missoula International, Great Falls International, Bozeman International.
Nevada: McCarran International (Las Vegas), Reno-Cannon International.
New Mexico: Albuquerque International.
North Dakota: Bismark Airport.
Oklahoma: Will Rogers International.
South Dakota: Rapid City Regional.

Texas: Dallas-Fort Worth International, Houston Intercontinental, San Antonio International, El Paso International.
Utah: Salt Lake City International.
Wyoming: Jackson Airport, Casper Airport.

By Train

Amtrak offers more than 500 destinations across the US. Generally speaking, the trains are comfortable and reliable, with lounges, restaurants, snack bars and, in some cases, movies and live entertainment. Amtrak trains include:

The *Southwest Chief*, which runs from Chicago to Los Angeles. Stops include Dodge City, Kansas; La Junta, Colorado; Albuquerque and Gallup, New Mexico; Winslow, Flagstaff (Amtrak Thruway bus service to Grand Canyon) and Kingman, Arizona; and Barstow, California.

The *Sunset Limited* runs from Miami to Los Angeles. Stops include Alpine and El Paso, Texas; Deming, New Mexico; and Tucson and Phoenix, Arizona.

The *Texas Eagle* runs from Chicago to San Antonio or Houston. Stops include St Louis, Missouri; Little Rock, Arkansas; Dallas and Ft Worth, Texas.

The *California Zephyr* runs from Chicago to San Francisco. Stops include Denver and Grand Junction, Colorado; Thompson and Salt Lake City, Utah; Elko and Reno, Nevada; and Sacramento and Oakland, California.

The *Pioneer* runs from Chicago to Seattle. Stops include Denver, Colorado; Ogden, Utah; Pocatello, Idaho; and Tacoma, Washington.

The *Empire Builder* also runs from Chicago to Seattle. Stops include Williston, North Dakota; Glacier Park, Montana; Spokane and Seattle, Washington.

The *Desert Wind* runs from Chicago to Los Angeles. Stops include Denver and Grand Junction, Colorado; Thompson and Salt Lake City, Utah; Las Vegas, Nevada; and Barstow, California.

The *Coast Starlight* runs from Seattle to Los Angeles. Stops include Tacoma, Washington; Klamath Falls, Oregon; Redding and Sacramento, California.

Be sure to ask about two- or three-stopover discounts, senior citizens and children's discounts, and also Amtrak's package tours. To obtain detailed scheduling information, tel: 800-USA-RAIL.

By Bus

One of the least expensive ways to travel in America is by bus. The biggest national bus company is Greyhound (tel: 800-231-2222). The company routinely offers discounts such as a $99 go-anywhere fare and a $1 ticket for moms on Mother's Day. Call the Greyhound office nearest you for information on special rates and package tours. However, Greyhound generally does not service remote areas. A car or another mode of transportation will be necessary from the major air hubs.

By Car

Driving is by far the most flexible and convenient way of traveling in the West. The major roads are well-maintained, although back-country roads may be unpaved. If you plan on driving into remote areas or will be encountering heavy snow, mud or severe weather, it's a good idea to use a four-wheel-drive vehicle with high chassis clearance. (*See Getting Around*.)

(*See Getting Around*.)

Special Facilities
Traveling with children

Two words of advice about traveling with children: first, be prepared and, second, don't expect to cover too much ground.

Be sure to take everything you need. Western towns may be quite small and remote; supplies may be limited. If you need baby formula, special foods, diapers or medication, carry them with you. It's also a good idea to bring a general first-aid kit for minor scrapes and bruises. Games, books and crayons help kids pass the time in the car. Carrying snacks and drinks in a day pack will come in handy when kids (or adults) get hungry and there are no restaurants nearby.

Give yourself plenty of time. Remember, kids don't travel at the same pace as adults. They're a lot less interested in traveling from point A to point B than in exploring their immediate surroundings. What you find fascinating (an art museum), they may find boring. And what they think is "really cool" (the game room at the hotel), you may find totally uninteresting.

Inquire about special children's programs at parks, museums and other attractions. Be sure that wilderness areas, ghost towns and other back-country places are suitable for children. Are there abandoned mine shafts, steep stairways, cliffs, other hazards? Are there special precautions in regard to wildlife? Is a lot of walking necessary? If so, will it be too strenuous for a child? May visitors use baby carriages? Are food, water, shelter, bathrooms and other essentials available at the site?

Avoid dehydration by having children drink plenty of water before and during outdoor activities, even if they don't seem particularly thirsty. Put a wide-brimmed hat and high-SPF (at least 30 SPF) on children in order to protect them from the sun. Don't push children beyond their limits. Rest often, provide plenty of snacks, and allow for extra napping.

Disabled Travelers

For general information on travel for the handicapped, contact the **Moss Rehabilitation Hospital Travel Information Service**, 1200 West Tabor Road, Philadelphia, PA 19141, tel: 215-456-9600, TDD 215-456-9602, or **The Information Center for Individuals with Disabilities**, 27-43 Wormwood St, Boston, MA 02210, tel: 617-727-5540.

Practical Tips

Business Hours

Standard business hours are 9am–5pm, Mon–Fri. Many banks open a little earlier, usually 8.30am, and nearly all close by 3pm. A few have Saturday morning hours. Most stores are open weekends and may stay open late one or more nights a week.

Tipping

Service personnel depend on tips for a large part of their income. With few exceptions, tipping is left to your discretion; gratuities are not automatically added to the bill. In the majority of cases, 15–20 percent is the going rate for tipping waiters, taxi drivers, bartenders, barbers and hairdressers. Porters and bellmen usually get about 75¢–$1 per bag, but never less than $1 total.

Media

Magazines

The following magazines often feature articles concerning the historic and contemporary West, ranch life and Indian cultures:

American Cowboy, 650 Westdale Drive, Suite 100, Wichita, KS 67209. Tel: 316-946-0600.
American Indian Art, 7314 E. Osborn Drive, Scottsdale, AZ 85251. Tel: 602-994-5445.
Arizona Highways, 2039 West Lewis St, Phoenix, AZ 85009. Tel: 602-258-6641
Native Peoples, PO Box 36820, Phoenix, AZ 85067-6820. Tel: 602-277-7852.
New Mexico Magazine, 1100 Saint Francis Drive, Joseph Montoya Building, Santa Fe, NM 87503. Tel: 505-827-0220.
Range, 43 Bellevue Road, Carson City, NV 89704. Tel: 702-882-0121.
Wild West, Cowles History Group, 741 Miller Drive, SE, Suite D-2, Leesburg, VA 22075. Tel: 703-771-9400.

Postal Services

Even the most remote towns are served by the US Postal Service. Smaller post offices tend to be limited to business hours (9am–5pm, Mon–Fri), although central, big-city branches may have extended weekday and weekend hours.

Stamps are sold at all post offices and at some convenience stores, filling stations, hotels and transportation terminals, usually in vending machines.

For reasonably quick delivery at a modest price, ask for first-class or priority mail. Second- and third-class mail is cheaper and slower. For expedited deliveries, often overnight, try **US Express Mail** or one of several international courier services: **Fedex** (tel: 800-238-5355), **DHL** (tel: 800-345-

2727), **United Parcel Service** (tel: 800-272-4877) or other local services listed in the telephone directory.

Telecoms

Public telephones are located at many highway rest areas, service stations, convenience stores, bars, motels and restaurants. The quickest way to get assistance is to dial 0 for the operator; or if you need to find a number, call information at 555-1212. Local calls cost 25¢ and can be dialed directly. Rates vary for long-distance calls, but they can also be dialed directly with the proper area and country code. If you don't know the codes, call information or dial 0 and ask for the international operator.

Make use of toll-free numbers whenever possible. For information on toll-free numbers, dial 800-555-1212. For personal calls, take advantage of lower long-distance rates on weekends and after 5pm on weekdays.

Western Union (tel: 800-325-6000) can arrange telegrams and mailgrams. Check the local phone directory or call information for local offices. Fax machines are available at most hotels and even some motels. Printers, copy shops, stationers and office-supply shops may also have them, as well as some convenience stores.

Weights and Measures

Despite efforts to convert to metric, the US still uses the Imperial System of weights and measures:
   1 inch = 2.54 centimeters
   1 foot = 30.48 centimeters
   1 mile = 1.609 kilometers
   1 quart = 1.136 liters
   1 ounce = 28.4 grams
   1 pound = 0.453 kilograms
   1 yard = 0.9144 meters

Emergencies

Security and Crime

A few common-sense precautions will help keep you safe while traveling in the American West. For starters, know where you are and where you're going. Whether traveling on foot or by car, bring a map and plan your route in advance. If you get lost, ask a passerby, shopkeeper or police officer for directions. Most people are happy to help.

Don't carry large sums of cash or wear flashy or expensive jewelry. Keep them locked in your trunk or in a hotel safe. Lock unattended cars and keep your belongings in the trunk. If possible, travel with a companion, especially after dark.

If you are a witness to or victim of a crime, or need to report an emergency situation of any kind, immediately contact the police (dial 911 or 0 for an operator). If you are involved in a traffic accident, remain at or very near the site. It is illegal to leave the scene of an accident. Find a nearby telephone or ask a passing motorist to call the police, and then wait for emergency vehicles to arrive.

If you plan on drinking, ask a companion to be a "designated driver," a person who forgoes alcohol and drives the others home. Otherwise, plan on using public transportation or a taxi. Driving under the influence of alcohol is extremely dangerous and carries stiff penalities, including fines, jail, community service and suspension of your driver's license.

Buckle up! Wearing seatbelts is required in most states. Children under 4 must be in a child's seat or (depending on age and size) in a seatbelt.

Useful Addresses

State Tourism Offices

ARIZONA

Arizona Office of Tourism, 1100 W. Washington St, Phoenix, AZ 85007, tel: 602-542-8687 or toll free 800-842-8257.
Flagstaff Convention and Visitors Bureau, 211 W. Aspen Ave, Flagstaff, AZ 86001. Tel: 520-779-7611.
Grand Canyon Chamber of Commerce, PO Box 3007, Grand Canyon, AZ 86023. Tel: 520-638-2901.
Navajo Nation Tourism Office, PO Box 663, Window Rock, AZ 86515. Tel: 520-871-6436.
Phoenix & Valley of the Sun Convention and Visitor Bureau, 400 E. Van Buren #600, Phoenix, AZ 85004. Tel: 602-254-6500.
Prescott Chamber of Commerce, 117 W. Goodwin St, Prescott, AZ 86302. Tel: 520-445-2000.
Tombstone Office of Tourism, PO Box 917, Tombstone, AZ 85638. Tel: 520-457-3929 or toll free 800-457-3423.

Tucson Convention & Visitors Bureau, 130 S. Scott Ave, Tucson, AZ 85701. Tel: 520-624-1817.

CALIFORNIA

California Tourism, 801 K St, Suite 1600, Sacramento, CA 95814. Tel: 916-322-2881 or toll free 800-462-2543.

Calaveras Lodging and Visitors Center, 1301 S. Main St, Angels Camp, CA 95222. Tel: 209-736-0049.

California Deserts Tourism Association, 37-115 Palm View Road, PO Box 364, Rancho Mirage, CA 92270. Tel: 619-328-9256.

Los Angeles Convention and Visitors Bureau, 633 W. 5th St, Suite 6000, Los Angeles, CA 90071. Tel: 213-624-7300.

San Diego Convention and Visitors Bureau, 1200 Third Ave, Suite 824, San Diego, CA 92101. Tel: 619-232-3101.

San Francisco Convention and Visitors Bureau, 201 Third St, Suite 900, San Francisco, CA 94103. Tel: 415-974-6900.

COLORADO

Colorado Tourism Authority, 1625 Broadway, Suite 1700, Denver, CO 80202. Tel: 800-265-6723.

Aspen Chamber of Commerce, 425 Rio Grande Place, Aspen, CO 81611. 303-925-1940.

Colorado Springs Convention and Visitors Bureau, 104 S. Cascade, Suite 104, Colorado Springs, CO 80903. Tel: 719-635-7506 or toll free 800-368-4748.

Cortez Chamber of Commerce, PO Box 968, Cortez, CO 81321. Tel: 970-565-3414 or toll free 800-346-6528.

Denver Metro Convention and Visitors Bureau, 225 W. Colfax, Denver, CO 80202. Tel: 303-892-1112.

Durango Chamber Resort Association, 111 S. Camino del Rio, Durango, CO 81301. Tel: 970-247-0312.

Estes Park Chamber of Commerce, 500 Big Thompson Ave, Estes Park, CO 80517. Tel: 970-586-4431 or toll free 800-443-7837.

Georgetown Visitor Information Center, 613 Sixth St, Georgetown, CO 80444. Tel: 303-569-2888.

Pueblo Chamber of Commerce, 210 N. Santa Fe Drive, Pueblo, CO 81002. Tel: 719-542-1704 or toll free 800-233-3446.

Silverton Chamber of Commerce, PO Box 565, Silverton, CO 81433. Tel: 970-387-5654 or toll free 800-752-4494.

IDAHO

Idaho Travel Council, 700 W. State St, Boise, ID 83720, tel: 800-635-7820.

Boise Convention and Visitors Bureau, 2739 Airport Way, Boise, ID 83705. Tel: 208-385-0362 or toll free 800-635-5240.

North Central Idaho Travel Committee, 2207 E. Main St, Suite G, Lewiston, ID 83501. Tel: 208-743-3531 or toll free 800-473-3543.

North Idaho Travel Committee, PO Box 928, Sandpoint, ID 83864. Tel: 208-263-2161.

Southeastern Idaho Travel Council, PO Box 668, Lava Hot Springs, ID 83246. Tel: 208-776-5273 or toll free 800-423-8597.

Sun Valley-Ketchum Chamber of Commerce, PO Box 2420, Sun Valley, ID 83353. Tel: 208-726-3423.

MONTANA

Travel Montana, Department of Commerce, 1424 9th Ave, Helena, MT 59620, tel: 406-444-2654 or toll free 800-541-1447.

Charlie Russell Country, PO Box 3166, Great Falls, MT 59403. Tel: 406-761-5036 or toll free 800-527-5348.

Custer Country, Route 1, Box 1206A, Hardin, MT 59034. Tel: 406-665-1671.

Glacier Country, 945 4th Ave East, Kalispell, MT 59901. Tel: 406-756-7128 or toll free 800-338-5072.

Gold West Country, 1155 Main St, Deer Lodge, MT 59722. Tel: 406-846-1943.

Yellowstone Country, PO Box 1107, Red Lodge, MT 59068. Tel: 406-446-1005 or toll free 800-736-5276.

NEVADA

Nevada Tourism, Capital Complex, Carson City, NV 89710. Tel: 702-687-4322 or toll free 800-237-0774.

Las Vegas Chamber of Commerce, 711 E. Desert Inn Road, Las Vegas, NV 89104. Tel: 702-735-1616.

Las Vegas Convention and Visitors Authority, Convention Center, 3150 Paradise Road, Las Vegas, NV 89109. Tel: 702-892-0711 or toll free 800-332-5333.

Greater Reno Chamber of Commerce, 405 Marsh Ave, Reno, NV 89505. Tel: 702-686-3030.

Reno-Sparks Convention and Visitors Authority, 4590 S. Virginia St, Reno, NV 89504. Tel: 702-827-7667 or toll free 800-367-7366.

NEW MEXICO

New Mexico Tourism, Lamy Building, 491 Old Santa Fe Trail, Santa Fe, NM 87503. Tel: 505-827-7400 or toll 800-545-2040.

Alamogordo Chamber of Commerce, PO Box 518, Alamogordo, NM 88311. Tel: 505-437-6120.

Albuquerque Convention and Visitors Bureau, PO Box 26866, Albuquerque, NM 87125. Tel: 505-243-3696 or toll free 800-284-2282.

Fort Sumner Chamber of Commerce, PO Box 28, Fort Sumner, NM 88119. Tel: 505-355-7705.

Gallup Convention and Visitors Bureau, PO Drawer Q, Gallup, NM 87305. Tel: 505-863-3841.

New Mexico North, PO Box 547, Angel Fire, NM 87710. Tel: 505-377-6353.

Old West Country, 1103 N. Hudson, Silver City, NM 88061. Tel: 505-538-0061 or toll free 800-548-9378.

Santa Fe Convention & Visitors Bureau, PO Box 909, Santa Fe, NM 87501. Tel: 505-984-6760.

Taos County Chamber of Commerce, PO Drawer I, Taos, NM 87571. Tel: 505-758-3873 or toll free 800-732-8267.

NORTH DAKOTA

North Dakota Tourism, Liberty Memorial Building, State Capitol Grounds, 604 E. Blvd, Bismark, ND 58505. Tel: 701-328-2525 or toll free 800-435-5663.

Theodore Roosevelt-Medora Foundation, PO Box 1696 Bismark, ND 58502. Tel: 701-223-4800.

OKLAHOMA

Oklahoma Travel and Tourism, 505 Will Rogers Building, Oklahoma City, OK 73105-4492. Tel: 405-521-2409.

Frontier Country, PO Box 187, Oklahoma City, OK 73101. Tel: 405-272-9443.

Green Country, 616 S. Boston, Suite 402, Tulsa, OK 74119. Tel: 918-599-7546.

Kiamichi Country, PO Box 638, Wilburton, OK 74578. Tel: 918-465-2367 or toll free 800-722-8180.

Oklahoma City Convention and Visitors Bureau, 123 Park Ave, Oklahoma City, OK 73102. Tel: 405-297-8912 or toll free 800-225-5652.

Red Carpet Country, Drawer B, Alva, OK 73717. Tel: 405-327-4918 or toll free 800-447-2698.

Tulsa Convention and Visitors Bureau, 616 S. Boston, Tulsa, OK 74119. Tel: 918-585-1201.

SOUTH DAKOTA

South Dakota Tourism, 221 S. Central, Pierre, SD 57501. Tel: 605-773-3301.

Black Hills, Badlands and Lakes Association, 900 Jackson Blvd, Rapid City, SD 57702. Tel: 605-341-1462.

Deadwood-Lead Chamber of Commerce, 735 Main St, Deadwood, SD 57732. Tel: 605-578-1876.

TEXAS

Texas Tourism, PO Box 12728, Austin, TX 78711. Tel: 512-478-0098 or toll free 800-888-8839.

Amarillo Convention and Visitors Bureau, 1000 Polk St, Amarillo, TX 79105. Tel: 806-374-1497.

Austin Convention and Visitors Bureau, PO Box 1088, Austin, TX 78769. Tel: 512-478-0098.

Dallas Convention and Visitors Bureau, 1201 Elm St, Suite 2000, Dallas, TX 75270. Tel: 214-746-6600.

El Paso Convention and Visitors Bureau, 1 Civic Center Plaza, El Paso, TX 79940. Tel: 915-534-0658.

Fort Worth Convention and Visitors Bureau, 415 Throckmorton, Fort Worth, TX 76102-7410. Tel: 817-336-8791 or toll free 800-433-5747.

Houston Convention and Visitors Bureau, 3300 Main St, Houston TX 77002. Tel: 713-523-5050 or or toll free 800-231-799.

Lubbock Visitors and Convention Bureau, 14th and K Ave, Lubbock, TX 79408. Tel: 806-763-4666.

San Angelo Convention and Visitors Bureau, 500 Rio Concho Drive, San Angelo, TX 76903. Tel: 915-653-3162.

San Antonio Convention and Visitors Bureau, 121 Alamo Plaza, PO Box 2277, San Antonio, TX 78298. Tel: 210-270-8700.

UTAH

Utah Travel Council, Council Hall, Capitol Hill, Salt Lake City, UT 84114. Tel: 801-538-1030 or toll free 800-200-1160.

Bridgerland, 160 N. Main, Logan, UT 84321. Tel: 801-752-2161 or toll free 800-882-4433.

Canyonlands, 117 S. Main, Monticello, UT 84535. Tel: 801-587-3235.

Color Country, 906 N. 1400 West, St George, UT 84771. 801-628-4171 or toll free 800-233-8824.

Golden Spike Empire, 2501 Wall Ave, Ogden, UT 84401. Tel: 801-627-8288 or toll free 800-255-8824.

Great Salt Lake Country, 180 S. West Temple, Salt Lake City, UT 84101. Tel: 801-521-2822.

Mountainland, 2545 N. Canyon Road, Provo, UT 84604. Tel: 801-377-2262.

Panoramaland, 250 N. Main, Richfield, UT 84701. Tel: 801-896-9222 or toll free 800-748-4361.

WYOMING

Wyoming Division of Tourism, I-25 at College Drive, Cheyenne, WY 82002. Tel: 307-777-7777 or toll free 800-225-5996.

Casper Chamber of Commerce, 500 N. Center, Casper, WY 82601. Tel: 307-234-5311.

Cheyenne Chamber of Commerce, 301 W. 16th, Cheyenne, WY 82001. Tel: 307-638-3388.

Cody Country Visitors & Conventions Council, 836 Sheridan Ave, Cody, WY 2777. Tel: 307-587-2297.

Jackson Chamber of Commerce, 532 N. Cache St, Jackson, WY 83001. Tel: 307-733-3316.

Laramie Chamber of Commerce, 800 S. 3rd St, Laramie, WY 82070. Tel: 307-745-7339.

Pinedale Chamber of Commerce, PO Box 176, Pinedale, WY 82941. Tel: 307-367-2242.

Sheridan Chamber of Commerce, PO Box 707, Sheridan, WY 82801. Tel: 307-672-2485.

National Parks and Wilderness Areas

National Park Service, Office of Public Inquiries, PO Box 37127, Washington, DC 20013, tel: 202-208-4747. Information is also available from the appropriate regional offices:

Midwest Region, National Park Service, 1709 Jackson St, Omaha, NE 68102-2571. Tel: 402-221-3471.

Rocky Mountain Region, National Park Service, 12795 Alameda Parkway, Lakewood, CO 80228. Tel: 303-969-2000.

Southwest Region, National Park Service, PO Box 728, Santa Fe, NM 87504-0728. Tel: 505-988-6016.

Western Region, National Park Service, 600 Harrison St, Suite 600, San Francisco, CA 94107. Tel: 415-744-3929.

National Trails System Branch, National Park Service, 1800 N. Capitol St, Suite 490, Washington, DC 20013-7127. Tel: 202-343-3780.

Other wilderness areas are administered by:

Bureau of Land Management, US Department of the Interior, 1849 C St NW, Washington, DC 20240. Tel: 202-208-5717.

Fish and Wildlife Service, US Department of the Interior, 1849 C St NW, Washington, DC 20240. Tel: 202-208-5634.

Forest Service, US Department of Agriculture, 14th and Independence Ave SW, S. Agriculture Building, Washington, DC 20250. Tel: 202-205-8333.

Embassies

Australia: 1601 Massachusetts Ave NW, Washington, DC 20036, tel: 202-797-3000.

Canada: 501 Pennsylvania Ave NW, Washington, DC 20001, tel: 202-682-1740.

Denmark: 3200 Whitehaven St NW, Washington, DC 20008, tel: 202-234-4300.

France: 4101 Reservoir Road NW, Washington, DC 20007, tel: 202-944-6000.

Germany: 4645 Reservoir Road NW, Washington, DC 20007, tel: 202-298-4000.

Great Britain: 3100 Massachusetts Ave NW, Washington, DC 20008, tel: 202-462-1340.

Israel: 3514 International Drive NW, Washington, DC 20008, tel: 202-364-5500.

Italy: 1601 Fuller St NW, Washington, DC 20009, tel: 202-328-5500.

Japan: 2520 Massachusetts Ave NW, Washington, DC 20008, tel: 202-939-6700.

Mexico: 1911 Pennsylvania Ave NW, Washington, DC 20006, tel: 202-728-1600.
New Zealand: 37 Observatory Circle NW, Washington, DC 20008, tel: 202-328-4800.
Singapore: 3501 International Place NW, Washington, DC 20008, tel: 202-537-3100.
Spain: 2375 Pennsylvania Ave NW, Washington, DC 20037, tel: 202-452-0100.

Getting Around
Transportation Tips
By Car

Your greatest asset as a driver is a good road map. They can be obtained from state tourism offices, filling stations, supermarkets and convenience stores. Although roads are maintained even in remote areas, it is advisable to listen to local radio stations and to check with highway officials or police officers for the latest information on weather and road conditions, especially if you plan on leaving paved roads. Driving conditions vary dramatically depending on elevation. During fall, winter and early spring, your car should be equipped with snow tires or chains, a small collapsible shovel, and an ice scraper. Also, be prepared for the extra time required to drive along winding, narrow mountain roads.

If you plan to drive in desert areas, carry extra water – at least 1 gallon per person per day. It's a good idea to take along some food, too. Flash floods may occur during the rainy season, from early summer to fall. Stay out of arroyos, washes and drainage areas.

Service stations can be few and far between in remote areas. Not every town will have one, and many close early. Check your gas gauge often. It's always better to have more fuel than you think you will need.

A word of caution: If your car breaks down on a back road, do not attempt to strike out on foot, even with water. A car is easier to spot than a person

and gives shelter from the elements. Sit tight and wait to be found.

Finally, if you intend to do a lot of driving, it's a good idea to join the **American Automobile Association**. The AAA offers emergency road service, maps, insurance, bail bond protection and other services (AAA, 1000 AAA Drive, Heathrow, FL 32746, tel: 407-444-4300)

CAR RENTALS

National car rental agencies are located at all airports, cities and large towns. In most places, you must be at least 21 years old (25 in some states) to rent a car, and you must have a valid driver's license and at least one major credit card. Foreign drivers must have an international driver's license. Be sure that you are properly insured for both collision and personal liability. Insurance may not be included in the base rental fee. Additional cost varies depending on the car and the type of coverage, but usually ranges between $10 and $20 per day. You may already be covered by your own auto insurance or credit-card company, so be sure to check with them first.

It is also a good idea to inquire about an unlimited mileage package. If not, you may be charged an extra 10¢–25¢ or more per mile over a given limit. Rental fees vary depending on time of year, location, how far in advance you book your rental, and if you travel on weekdays or weekends. Be sure to inquire about discounts or benefits for which you may be eligible, including corporate, credit-card or frequent-flyer programs.

Alamo	
US	(800) 327-9633
International	+1-305-522 0000
Avis	
US	(800) 331-1212
International	+1-918-664 4600
Budget	
US	(800) 527-0700
International	+1-214-404 7600
Dollar	
US	(800) 800-4000
International	+1-813-877 5507
Enterprise	
US	(800) 325-8007
International	+1-314-781 8232
Hertz	
US	(800) 654-3131
International	+1-405-749 4424

National	
US	(800) 227-7368
International	+1-612-830 2345
Thrifty	
US	(800) 331-4200
International	+1-918-669 2499

RV RENTALS

No special license is necessary to operate a motor home (or recreational vehicle – RV for short), but they aren't cheap. When you add up the cost of rental fees, insurance, gas and campsites, you may find that renting a car and staying in motels or camping is less expensive. Keep in mind, too, that RVs are large and slow and may be difficult to handle on narrow mountain roads. If parking space is tight, driving an RV may be extremely inconvenient. Access to some roads may be limited. For additional information about RV rentals, call the **Recreational Vehicle Rental Association**, tel: 800-336-0355.

Hitchhiking

Hitchhiking is illegal in many places and ill-advised everywhere. It's an inefficient and dangerous method of travel. Don't do it!

Where to Stay

All major western cities and towns offer accommodation ranging from luxurious to inexpensive. The following are included either because they are convenient or because they have a particularly Western flavor. For information on camping, see "Outdoor Activities."

Hotels

The price guide indicates approximate room rates:

$	$50 or less
$$	$50 – $100
$$$	$100 – $150
$$$$	$150+

Arizona

Bisbee Grand Hotel, 61 Main St, Bisbee, AZ 85603, tel: 520-432-5900. An elegantly restored Victorian with period decor in a small southern Arizona mining town. Amenities: parking, saloon, billiard room, free breakfast; no in-room telephones or televisions. Credit cards: American Express, Discover, MasterCard, Visa. $$

Copper Queen Hotel, 11 Howell Ave, Bisbee, AZ 85603, tel: 520-432-2216. A turn-of-the century Victorian landmark built during the heyday of the Copper Queen Mine; guests in the past have included John Wayne and Teddy Roosevelt. Amenities: parking, television, restaurant, saloon, pool. Credit cards: all major. $$

El Tovar Hotel, Grand Canyon National Park Lodges, PO Box 699, Grand Canyon, AZ 86023, tel: 520-638-2401. A rustic lodge built in 1905 on the edge of the South Rim of the Grand Canyon. Amenities: air conditioning, television, parking, restaurant, bar, gift shop, some rooms with balcony. Credit cards: all major. $$$$

California

The Ahwahnee, Yosemite National Park, The Yosemite Concessions Services Corp., 5410 East Home Ave, Fresno, CA 93727, tel: 209-252-4848. A grand rustic lodge built in the 1920s in the beautiful Yosemite Valley. Guests have included John F. Kennedy, Queen Elizabeth II, Winston Churchill and Gertrude Stein. Amenities: pool, tennis courts, horseback riding, parking, restaurant, bar, some rooms with fireplace. Credit cards: all major. $$$$

Amargosa Hotel, Highway 127 and 190, Death Valley Junction, CA 92328, tel: 619-852-4441. A small, historic hotel built in 1923 by the Pacific Coast Borax Company. Offers simple but comfortable accommodations. Amenities: air conditioning, parking; no in-room television or telephone. Credit cards: MasterCard, Visa. $

Julian Hotel, 2032 Main St, Julian, CA 92036, tel: 619-765-0201. A small Victorian bed and breakfast built in 1897 that recalls this boom town's colorful past. Amenities: free breakfast, afternoon tea, one room with fireplace, period decor; no in-room television or telephone. Credit cards: American Express, MasterCard, Visa. $$–$$$

Murphys Historic Hotel, 457 Main St, Murphys, CA 95247, tel: 209-728-3454. Opened in 1856, this property is on the Register of Historic Places;

guests have included Horatio Alger, Ulysses S. Grant, Mark Twain and J.P. Morgan. Amenities: 20 modern rooms with television, telephone, private bath; 9 period rooms with antique furnishings, shared bath, no television or telephone; restaurant, saloon, free breakfast, parking. Credit cards: all major. $$

Wawona Hotel, Yosemite Concessions Services Corp., 5410 East Home Ave, Fresno, CA 93727, tel: 209-252-4848. Originally built in 1856, this fully restored Victorian-style hotel offers simple but comfortable accommodations in Yosemite National Park. Amenities: parking, pool, golf course, tennis courts, horseback riding, restaurant, stagecoach rides. Credit cards: all major. $$

Colorado

Alps Boulder Canyon Inn, 38619 Boulder Canyon Drive, Boulder, CO 80302, tel: 303-444-5445. This small, charming, historic inn was once a stagecoach stop. Amenities: parking, fireplaces, some rooms with Jacuzzi, free breakfast, hiking; no in-room television. Credit cards: all major. $$–$$$$

Broadmoor Hotel, One Lake Ave, Colorado Springs, CO 80906, tel: 719-634-7711 or toll free 800-634-7711. Set on 3,000 acres at the foot of Cheyenne Mountain, this luxurious Renaissance-style resort reflects the extraordinary wealth of the 1920s and is one of the great hotels of the West. Amenities: air conditioning, television, parking, golf courses, tennis courts, fitness club, peddle boats, movie theater, nightclub, restaurants, bars. Credit cards: All major. $$$$

Brown Palace Hotel, 321 17th St, Denver, CO 80202, tel: 303-297-3111 or toll free 800-321-2599. This stately Victorian landmark recalls the glory days of the late 19th century. Amenities: air conditioning, television, parking, restaurants, bars, live entertainment, fitness room, gift shop. Credit cards: all major. $$$$

General Palmer Hotel, 567 Main Ave, Durango, CO 81301, tel: 970-247-4747 or toll free 800-523-3358. A gracious, mid-sized Victorian now fully restored with period furnishings. Amenities: air conditioning, television, parking, library, restaurant, bar, one room with Jacuzzi. Credit cards: all major. $$–$$$

Hotel Boulderado, 2115 13th St, Boulder, CO 80302, tel: 303-442-4344 or toll free 800-433-4344. A Victorian gem with well-appointed rooms and public areas. Amenities: air conditioning, television, parking, restaurants, bars, nightclub. Credit cards: all major. $$$–$$$$

Hotel Jerome, 330 E. Main St, Aspen, CO 81611, tel: 970-920-1000 or toll free 800-331-7213. A beautifully restored hotel with period furnishings and first-rate service; built in 1889 and listed on the National Register of Historic Places. Amenities: air conditioning, television, some rooms with Jacuzzi, parking, pool, fitness club, restaurants, bar, ski shop. Credit cards: all major. $$$$

Oxford, 1600 17th St, Denver, CO 80202, tel: 303-628-5400 or toll free 800-228-5838. An elegant little hotel built in 1891 and fully restored in Victorian style. Amenities: air conditioning, television, parking, fitness club, restaurant, bar. Credit cards: all major. $$$

Stanley Hotel, 333 Wonderview Ave, Estes Park, CO, tel: 970-586-3371 or toll free 800-976-1377. Set at the foot of the Rocky Mountains, this grand hotel was built in 1909 by Freelan O. Stanley, inventor of the Stanley Steamer automobile; it is listed on the National Register of Historic Places. Amenities: television, parking, pool, restaurant, bar. Credit cards: all major. $$$–$$$$

Strater Hotel, 699 Main Ave, Durango, CO 81301, tel: 970-247-4431 or toll free 800-247-4431. A fine Victorian built in 1887 with authentic period furnishings and an Old West saloon. Amenities: air conditioning, television, parking, restaurant, saloon. Credit cards: all major. $$–$$$

Montana

Glacier Park Lodge and Many Glacier Hotel, Glacier Park, Inc., PO Box 147, East Glacier, MT 59434, tel: 406-226-5551 or (in winter) 602-207-6000. Set in Glacier National Park, these chalet-style lodges were built by the Great Northern Railway between 1912 and 1915 and feature grand central lobbies. Amenities: restaurant, bar, gift shop. Credit cards: Discover, Visa, MasterCard. $$–$$$

Prince of Wales Hotel, Glacier Park, Inc., PO Box 147, East Glacier, MT

59434, tel: 406-226-5551 or (in winter) 602-207-6000. This glorious chalet-style lodge was built in 1927 between Upper and Middle Waterton lakes in Canada's Waterton National Park near the Montana border. Amenities: restaurant, bar, gift shop. Credit cards: Visa, MasterCard. $$$–$$$$

Nevada

Gold Hill Hotel, Highway 341, Virginia City, NV 89440, tel: 702-847-0111. Built in 1859, this small, charming hotel is the oldest in Nevada; it is fully renovated and features period furnishings. Amenities: some rooms with air conditioning, television and fireplaces, free continental breakfast, parking. Credit cards: MaterCard, Visa. $–$$$

New Mexico

La Fonda, 100 E. San Francisco St, Santa Fe, NM 87501, tel: 505-982-5511 or toll free 800-523-5002. Historic Pueblo Revival-style hotel on the Plaza rebuilt in 1919. Amenities: air conditioning, television, parking, pool, restaurant, bars, nightclub, some rooms with fireplaces, shops. Credit cards: all major. $$$–$$$$

Mabel Dodge Luhan House, PO Box 3400, Taos, NM 87571, tel: 505-758-9456. This lovely bed and breakfast inn is the former home of Mabel Dodge Luhan, socialite and patron of the arts whose guests included D.H. Lawrence and Georgia O'Keeffe. Amenities: parking, free breakfast, hot tub, fireplaces; no in-room televisions or telephones. Credit cards: MasterCard, Visa. $$–$$$$

North Dakota

Roughrider Hotel, 1 Main St, Medora, ND 58645, tel: 701-623-4422. Teddy Roosevelt stayed at this small, restored Old West hotel constructed in the 1880s and filled with western furnishings and paraphernalia; located near Theodore Roosevelt National Park. Amenities: air conditioning, television, restaurant, bar, horseback riding, sleigh rides, hay rides. Credit cards: American Express, Discover, MasterCard, Visa. $

South Dakota

Bullock Hotel, 633 Main St, Deadwood, SD 57732, tel: 605-578-1745. Built in 1895, Deadwood's oldest hotel is a fine Victorian on historic Main Street. Amenities: Air conditioning, television, parking, casino, restaurant. Credit cards: all major. $$–$$$

Franklin Hotel, 700 Main St, Deadwood, SD 57732, tel: 605-578-2241. Located on Deadwood's historic Main Street, this lovely old hotel was built in 1903 and is now thoroughly restored. Amenities: air conditioning in most rooms, television, parking, restaurant, bars, casino. Credit cards: all major. $$

State Game Lodge, Highway 16A, Custer, SD 57730, tel: 605-255-4541 or toll free 800-658-3530. A well-appointed rustic lodge built in the 1920s and set in the Black Hills in Custer State Park, renowned for its buffalo herd and other wildlife. Amenities: parking, restaurant, fishing, Jeep tours. Credit cards: American Express, Discover, MaterCard, Visa. $$–$$$$

Texas

Fairmount Hotel, 401 S. Alamo St, San Antonio, TX 78205, tel: 210-224-8800 or toll free 800-345-3457. A small, elegant Victorian home built in 1906 and renovated in period style. Amenities: air conditioning, television, parking, restaurant, bar. Credit card: all major. $$$$

Hotel Blessing, Box 142, Blessing, TX 77419, tel: 512-588-9579. Built in 1906 by Jonathan Pierce, brother of colorful rancher Shanghai Pierce, this little hotel features period furnishings and excellent home-cooked meals. Amenities: air conditioning, television, parking, restaurant, shared baths. No credit cards. $–$$

Gage Hotel, PO Box 46, Marathon, TX 79842, tel: 915-386-4205. Built as a private lodge by rancher Alfred Gage in the 1920s, this charming little hotel, a Texas Historical Landmark, is replete with western antiques; a modern adobe building was added in the early 1990s. Amenities: air conditioning, restaurant, pool, shared baths, some rooms with fireplaces; no in-room televisions or telephones. Credit Cards: Discover, MasterCard, Visa. $–$$

Menger Hotel, 204 Alamo Plaza, San Antonio, TX 78205, tel: 210-223-4361 or toll free 800-345-9285. Built in 1859 and located across from the Alamo, this historic hotel welcomed Sam Houston, Ulysses S. Grant, Robert E. Lee and other illustrious figures. Theodore Roosevelt recruited

members of the Rough Riders at the bar. Amenities: Air conditioning, television, parking, pool, fitness club, restaurant, bar, gift shop. Credit cards: all major. $$$

St Anthony Hotel, 300 E. Travis St, San Antonio, TX 78205, tel: 210-227-4392 or toll free 800-338-1338. A landmark hotel built in 1909 with comfortable rooms and elegant period furnishings. Amenities: air conditioning, television, parking, pool, fitness club, restaurant, bar, nightclub. Credit cards: all major. $$$

Stockyards Hotel, 109 E. Exchange Ave, Fort Worth, TX 76106, tel: 817-625-6427 or toll free 800-423-8471. This renovated 1902 hotel set in the Stockyards Historic District is full of Old West ambiance. Amenities: air conditioning, television, parking, restaurant, bar. Credit cards: all major. $$–$$$.

Utah

Bryce Canyon Lodge, TW Services, PO Box 400, Cedar City, UT 84720, tel: 801-586-7686. Built in 1923 by the Utah Pacific Railroad and now on the Register of Historic Places, this rustic lodge is set in the heart of Bryce Canyon National Park. Amenities: some rooms with air conditioning, television, parking, pool, horseback riding, restaurant. Credit cards: all major. $$$

Zion Lodge, TW Recreational Services, Cedar City, UT 84720, tel: 801-586-7686 or 801-772-3213. Rustic but comfortable amenities surrounded by the glorious scenery of Zion National Park. Amenities: Air conditioning, parking, restaurant, horseback riding, bus tours. Credit cards: all major. $$

Wyoming

Irma Hotel, 1192 Sheridan Ave, Cody, WY 82414, tel: 307-587-4221 or toll free 800-745-IRMA. Built in 1902 by Buffalo Bill Cody for his daughter, Irma, the hotel still retains the flavor of the Old West. Amenities: air conditioning, television, restaurant, parking. Credit cards: all major. $–$$

Old Faithful Inn, TW Services, Inc., PO Box 528, Yellowstone National Park, WY 82190, tel: 307-344-7311. An impressive chalet-style lodge built in Yellowstone National Park in 1902. Amenities: Parking, bar, and restaurant. Credit cards: American Express, MasterCard, Visa. $$$

Chain Hotels and Motels

Chain hotels and motels are reliable and convenient but tend to lack character. You can usually depend on a clean, comfortable room for a reasonable cost. In general, prices range from $25 to $75 a room depending on location and additional amenities such as a pool, lobby or restaurant.

Concerning the majority of hotels listed below, if you are unable to get through by using these toll-free numbers then you should phone the local reservation center of that particular hotel chain in the region or country you happen to be in. Telephone numbers will be available either from the telephone directory or from the operator.

MODERATE

Best Western	800-528-1234
Hilton	800-HILTONS
Holiday Inn	800-HOLIDAY
Hyatt	800-228-9000
ITT Sheraton	800-325-3535
La Quinta	800-531-5900
Marriott	800-228-9290
Radisson	800-333-3333
Ramada	800-2-RAMADA
Westin	800-228-3000

The following motels can only be contacted by dialing the numbers listed below. If you are unable to get through on these numbers, then you can make your reservations once you are in the United States.

INEXPENSIVE

Comfort Inn	800-228-5150
Days Inn	800-325-2525
Econo Lodge	800-553-2666
Howard Johnsons	800-654-2000
Motel 6	800-466-8356
Quality Inn	800-228-5151
Red Lion Inn	800-733-5466
Super 8	800-800-8000
Travelodge	800-578-7878

Bed & Breakfast Inns

Unlike their European counterparts, American B&Bs can be pricey. Most are, however, small and individually furnished, often with antiques. Smoking is sometimes prohibited.

Information about bed and breakfast inns can be obtained from the following associations:

Arizona Association of Bed & Breakfast Inns, 3101 N. Central #560, Phoenix, AZ 85012. Tel: 602-277-0775.

California Association of Bed and Breakfast Innkeepers, 2715 Porter Street, Soquel, CA 95073. Tel: 408-462-9191.

Bed and Breakfast Innkeepers of Colorado Association, 1102 W. Pikes Peak Ave, Dept. T, Colorado Springs, CO 80904. Tel: 800-756-2242.

Montana Bed and Breakfast Association, 480 Bad Rock Drive, Columbia Falls, MT 59912. Tel: 406-892-2829 or toll free 800-453-8870/800-270-7515.

Bed and Breakfast of New Mexico, PO Box 2805, Santa Fe, NM 87504. Tel: 505-982-3332.

Bed and Breakfast Texas Style, 4224 W. Red Bird Lane, Dallas, TX 75237. Tel: 214-298-8586.

Dude Ranches

Staying in a Dude Ranch isn't cheap – charges for one day can easily work out to be at least $200. Always be sure to find out what the ranch's minimum stay requirements are as many ranches ask that you stay for at least a week. Also, as horseback riding is such an important component of the experience, find out what kind of lessons are given, how long the trial rides usually last, and whether you keep the same horse throughout your visit. If you're making this a family vacation, find out if the ranch offers riding lessons and other activities for children.

For additional information and an extensive list of dude ranches contact: **Dude Ranchers Association**, PO Box 471, LaPorte, CO 80535. Tel: 303-223-8440.

The price guide below indicates weekly rates per person for lodging, meals and activities. Rates may vary depending on season and size of party. Some ranches offer daily rates and family or children's rates:

$	$500 – $1,000
$$	$1,000 – $1,500
$$$	$1,500 – $2,000
$$$$	$2,000 – $2,500
$$$$$	$2,500+

Arizona

Circle Z Ranch, PO Box 194, Patagonia, AZ 85624, tel: 520-287-2091. Guests stay in adobe cottages 60 miles south of Tucson at the foot of the Patagonia and Santa Rita mountains. Amenities: Horseback riding and instruction, swimming pool, tennis courts, cookouts, pack trips. No credit cards. $

Grapevine Canyon Ranch, PO Box 302, Pearce, AZ 85625, tel: 520-826-3185 or toll free 800-245-9202. Located in southern Arizona's Dragoon Mountains, this is a working cattle ranch with guest cabins and *casitas*. Amenities: horseback riding and instruction, pool, hot tub, cookouts, fishing, entertainment. Credit cards: American Express, MasterCard, Visa. $–$$

Lazy K Bar Guest Ranch, 8401 N. Scenic Drive, Tucson, AZ 85743, tel: 520-744-3050 or toll free 800-321-7018. Guests stay in cabins in the Tucson Mountains overlooking the Santa Cruz Valley. Amenities: horseback riding and instruction, pool, spa, tennis courts, volleyball, basketball and other activities, ranch store, entertainment. Credit cards: MasterCard, Visa. $

Tanque Verde Guest Ranch, 14301 E. Speedway Blvd, Tucson, AZ 85748, tel: 520-296-6275 or 800-234-3833. Guests are housed in *casitas* at this former stagecoach station situated at the base of the Rincon Mountains. Amenities: horseback riding and instruction, pools, tennis, cookouts, outdoor sports, entertainment. Credit cards: American Express, MasterCard, Visa. $$$–$$$$

White Stallion Ranch, 9251 W. Twin Peaks Road, Tucson, AZ 85743, tel: 520-297-0252 or toll free 800-782-5546. A 3,000-acre cattle ranch bordering Saguaro National Park in southern Arizona. Amenities: horseback riding, pool, tennis, hot tub, petting zoo, hayrides, cookouts. No credit cards. $$–$$$$

California

Coffee Creek Ranch, HC 2, Box 4940, Trinity Center, CA 96091, tel: 916-266-3343 or toll free 800-624-4480. Secluded cabins on 127 acres surrounded by the Trinity Alps Wilderness Area in northern California. Amenities: horseback riding and lessons, sleigh rides, cross-country skiing, hunting, fishing, hayrides, pool, entertainment. Credit cards: American Express, Discover, MasterCard, Visa. $

Hunewill Circle "H" Ranch, PO Box 368, Bridgeport, CA 93517, tel: 619-932-7710 or (winter) 702-465-2201. This working cattle ranch was founded in 1861 and is set on 4,400 acres near Yosemite National Park. Amenities: horseback riding and instruction, fishing, children's programs, cookouts, volleyball. No credit cards. $

Colorado

Cherokee Park Ranch, PO Box 97, Livermore, CO 80536, tel: 970-493-6522 or toll free 800-628-0949. The ranch features a historic lodge and cabins on the North Fork of the Cache La Poudre River in north-central Colorado. Amenities: horseback riding and instruction, children's programs, guest rodeo, rafting, fishing, shooting, pool, hot tub. $$

Colorado Trails Ranch, 12161 County Road 240, Durango, CO 81301, tel: 970-247-5055 or toll free 800-323-3833. Guests stay in cabins in the San Juan Mountains of southwestern Colorado. Amenities: horseback riding and instruction, tennis, pool, shooting, water skiing, river rafting, fishing, children's counselors. Credit cards: all major. $$$$–$$$$$

North Fork Ranch, Box B, Shawnee, CO 80475, tel: 303-838-9873 or toll free 800-843-7895. The ranch's log cabins, stone mansion and main lodge are set on the North Fork of the South Platte River about 50 miles from Denver. Amenities: horseback riding and instruction, children's program, fishing, shooting, rafting, cookouts, pool, spa. No credit cards. $–$$

Powderhorn Guest Ranch, Powderhorn, CO 81243, tel: 970-641-0220 or toll free 800-786-1220. The ranch offers log cabins in the historic Powderhorn Valley near Gunnison and is surrounded by wilderness areas. Amenities: horseback riding and lessons, fishing, swimming pool, spa, rafting, cookouts, entertainments. No credit cards. $

Idaho

Moose Creek Ranch, PO Box 350, Victor, ID 83455, tel: 208-787-2784 or toll free 800-676-0075. The ranch is set in the Teton Mountains near Yellowstone and Grand Teton national parks. Amenities: horseback riding and instruction, wagon rides, float trips, fishing, indoor pool, sauna, hot tub. Credit cards: American Express, Discover, MasterCard, Visa. $–$$

Twin Peaks Ranch, PO Box 774, Salmon, ID 83467, tel: 208-894-2290 or toll free 800-659-4899. This 2,850-acre ranch offers guest cabins in the scenic Salmon River in central Idaho. Amenities: horseback riding, rafting, fishing, entertainment, pool, hot tub, cookouts. Credit cards: MasterCard, Visa. $$

Montana

Mountain Sky Guest Ranch, Box 1128, Bozeman, MT 59715, tel: 406-587-1244 or toll free 800-548-3392. The ranch overlooks the lovely Paradise Valley about 30 miles from Yellowstone National Park in southwestern Montana. Amenities: horseback riding and instruction, children's counselors, fishing, tennis, pool, hot tub, entertainment. Credit cards: Visa, MasterCard. $$$

63 Ranch, Box 979, Livingston, MT 59047, tel: 406-222-0570. Founded in 1929, this working ranch is set on 2,000 acres in the Absaroka Mountains about 50 miles north of Yellowstone National Park and is listed on the National Register of Historic Places. Amenities: horseback riding and instruction, fishing, overnight trips. No credit cards. $

Nevada

Spurs Cross Ranch, PO Box 38, Golconda, NV 89414, tel: 800-651-4567. A working horse and cattle ranch situated near Winnemucca in northwest Nevada. Amenities: horseback riding and instruction, fishing, cattle drives, roundups, camping trips; no telephones, electricty provided by generator. No credit cards. $

Texas

Silver Spur Guest Ranch, PO Box 1657, Bandera, TX 78003, tel: 210-796-3037 or 210-460-3639. The ranch offers stone cottages in the Hill Country outside San Antonio. Amenities: horseback riding and instruction, hayrides, cookouts, pool, entertainment. Credit cards: Discover, MasterCard, Visa. $

Wyoming

Absaroka Ranch, Star Route, Dubois, WY 82513, tel: 307-455-2275. A small, rustic property situated at the headwaters of the Wind River in the Absaroka Mountains about 45 miles east of Grand Teton National Park. Amenities: horseback riding and instruction, fishing, pack trips, sauna. No credit cards. $

Crossed Sabres Ranch, Wapiti, WY 82450, tel: 307-587-3750. Rustic but modern cabins and a historic lodge about 9 miles east of Yellowstone National Park. Amenities: horseback riding, entertainment, cookouts, volleyball, pack trips, rafting, fishing, ranch store. No credit cards. $

High Island Guest Ranch, Box 71, Hamilton Dome, WY 82427, tel: 307-867-2374. A working cattle ranch east of Yellowstone National Park. Amenities: horseback riding, roundups, branding, cattle drives, fishing. Credit cards: Visa. $–$$

Lazy L and B Ranch, 1072 E. Fork Road, Dubois, WY 82513, tel: 307-455-2839 or toll free 800-453-9488. Guest cabins and lodge are set in the valley of the East Fork of the Wind River near Yellowstone and Grand Teton national parks. Amenities: horseback riding, fishing, shooting, pool, cookouts, entertainment. No credit cards. $

Moose Head Ranch, PO Box 214, Moose, WY 83012, tel: 307-733-3141. The ranch offers modern cabins on a property that is completely surrounded by Grand Teton National Park. Amenities: horseback riding and instruction, fishing, cookout. No credit cards. $$

R Lazy S Ranch, PO Box 308, Teton Village, WY 83025, tel: 307-733-2655. The ranch offers log cabins set at the foot of the Teton Mountains about 13 miles from Jackson. Amenities: horseback riding and instruction, children's riding program, fishing, pack trips. No credit cards. $

Triangle X Ranch, Moose, WY 83012, tel: 307-733-2183. The ranch sprawls over 1,600 acres of Grand Teton National Park bordered by the Snake River. Amenities: horseback riding and instruction, children's program, rafting, pack trips, fishing, hunting, entertainment, cookouts. No credit cards. $–$$

Attractions

Parks and Historic Sites

Arizona

Bird Cage Theater, 517 E. Allen, Tombstone, AZ 85638. Tel: 520-457-3421.

Canyon de Chelly National Monument, PO Box 588, Chinle, AZ 86503. Tel: 520-674-5436.

Casa Grande National Monument, 1100 Ruins Drive, Coolidge, AZ 85228. Tel: 602-723-3172.

Chiricahua National Monument, Dos Cabezas Route, Box 6500, Willcox, AZ 85643. Tel: 520-824-3560.

Coronado National Memorial, 4101 E. Montezuma Canyon Road, Hereford, AZ 85615. Tel: 520-366-5515.

Fort Bowie National Historic Site, PO Box 158, Bowie, AZ 85605. Tel: 520-847-2500.

Glen Canyon National Recreation Area, PO Box 1507, Page, AZ 86040. Tel: 520-645-2471.

Grand Canyon National Park, PO Box 129, Grand Canyon, AZ 86023. Tel: 520-638-7888.

Hubbell Trading Post National Historic Site, PO Box 150, Ganado, AZ 86505. Tel: 520-755-3475.

Jerome State Historic Park, PO Box D, Jerome, AZ 86331. Tel: 520-634-5381.

Montezuma Castle National Monument, PO Box 219, Camp Verde, AZ 86322. Tel: 520-567-3322.

Monument Valley Navajo Tribal Park, Box 93, Monument Valley, UT 84536. Tel: 801-727-3287.

Navajo National Monument, HC 71, Box 3, Tonalea, AZ 86044-9704. Tel: 520-672-2366.

Organ Pipe Cactus National Monument, Route 1, Box 100, Ajo, AZ 85321. Tel: 520-387-6849.

Petrified Forest National Park, PO Box 2217, Petrified Forest, AZ 86028. Tel: 520-524-6228.

Pipe Spring National Monument, HC 65, Box 5, Fredonia, AZ 86022. Tel: 520-643-7105.

Riordan State Historic Park, 1300 S. Riordan Ranch St, Flagstaff, AZ 86001. Tel: 520-779-4395.

Saguaro National Park, 3693 S. Old Spanish Trail, Tucson, AZ 85730. Tel: 520-296-8576.

San Xavier del Bac Mission, 1950 W. San Xavier, Tucson, AZ 85706. Tel: 520-294-2624.

Sunset Crater National Monument, Route 3, Box 149, Flagstaff, AZ 86004. Tel: 520-556-7042.

Tombstone Courthouse State Historic Park, 219 Toughnut St, Tombstone, AZ 85638. Tel: 520-457-3311.

Tonto National Monument, HC02, Box 4602, Roosevelt, AZ 85545. Tel: 520-467-2241.

Tumacacori National Historical Park, PO Box 67, Tumacacori, AZ 85640. Tel: 520-398-2341.

Tuzigoot National Monument, PO Box 68, Clarkdale, AZ 86324. Tel: 520-634-5564.

Walnut Canyon National Monument, Walnut Canyon Road, Flagstaff, AZ 86004-9705. Tel: 520-526-3367.

Wupatki National Monument, HC 33, Box 444A, Flagstaff, AZ 86004. Tel: 520-556-7040.

California

Anza-Borrego Desert State Park, 200 Palm Canyon Drive, Borrego Springs, CA 92004. Tel: 619-767-5311.

Bidwell Mansion State Historic Park, 525 Esplanade, Chico, CA 95926. Tel: 916-895-6144.

Bodie State Historical Park, PO Box 515, Bridgeport, CA 93517. Tel: 619-647-6445.

Calico Ghost Town, PO Box 638, Yermo, CA 92398. Tel: 619-254-2122.

California State Railroad Museum, 111 I St, Sacramento, CA 95814. Tel: 916-552-5252.

China Camp State Park, N. San Pedro Road, San Rafael, CA 94903. Tel: 415-456-0766.

Columbia State Historic Park, PO Box 151, Columbia, CA 95310. Tel: 209-532-0150.

Death Valley National Park, Death Valley, CA 92328. Tel: 619-786-2331.

Donner Memorial State Park, PO Box 9210, Truckee, CA 95737. Tel: 916-582-7894.

El Presidio de Santa Barbara State Historic Park, 123 E. Canon Perdido, Santa Barbara, CA 93101. Tel: 805-966-9719.

El Pueblo de Los Angeles Historic Monument, 622 N. Main St, Los Angeles, CA 90012. Tel: 213-628-1274.

Empire Mine State Park, 10791 E. Empire St, Grass Valley, CA 95945. Tel: 916-273-8522.

Gold Bug Park, 549 Main St, Placerville, CA 95667. Tel: 916-642-5232.

Golden Gate National Recreation Area, Fort Mason, Building 201, San Francisco, CA 94123. Tel: 415-556-0560.

Indian Grinding Rock State Historic Park, 14881 Pine Grove Volcano Road, Pine Grove, CA 95665. Tel: 209-296-7488.

Jack London State Historic Park, 20 E. Spain St, Sonoma, CA 95476. Tel: 707-938-5216.

John Muir National Historic Site, 4202 Alhambra Ave, Martinez, CA 94553. Tel: 415-228-8860.

Joshua Tree National Park, 74485 National Monument Drive, Twentynine Palms, CA 92277. Tel: 619-367-7511.

La Purisima Mission State Historic Park, 2295 Purisima Road, Lompoc, CA 93436. Tel: 805-733-3713.

Lassen Volcanic National Park, PO Box 100, Mineral, CA 96063. Tel: 916-595-4444.

Malakoff Diggens State Historic Park, 23579 N. Bloomfield Road, Nevada City, CA 95959. Tel: 916-265-2740.

Marshall Gold Discovery State Historic Park, 310 Back St, Coloma, CA 95613. Tel: 916-622-3470.

Mission Dolores, 3321 16th St, San Francisco, CA 94114. Tel: 415-621-8203.

Mission San Diego de Alcala, 10818 San Diego Mission Road, San Diego, CA 92108. Tel: 619-281-8449.

Mission San Francisco Solano, 20 E. Spain St, Sonoma, CA 95476. Tel: 707-938-1519.

Mission San Juan Capistrano, 31815 Camino Capistrano, Suite 16, San Juan Capistrano, CA 92675. Tel: 714-248-2048.

Mission San Luis Rey, 4050 Mission Ave, San Luis Rey, CA 92068. Tel: 619-757-3651.

Mission Santa Barbara, Laguna and Los Olivos Sts, Santa Barbara, CA 93105. Tel: 805-682-4149.

Monterey State Historic Park, 20 Custom House Plaza, Monterey, CA 93940. Tel: 408-649-7118.

Muir Woods National Monument, Mill Valley, CA 94941. Tel: 415-388-2595.

Old Sacramento, 917 Front St, Old Sacramento, CA 95814. Tel: 916-264-7031.

Old Town State Historic Park, 9609 Waples, San Diego, CA 92110. Tel: 619-220-5422.

Plumas Eureka State Park, 310 Johnsville Road, Blairsden, CA 96103. Tel: 916-836-2380.

Point Reyes National Seashore, Point Reyes, CA 94956. Tel: 415-663-1092.

Railtown 1897 State Historic Park, PO Box 1250, Jamestown, CA 95327. Tel: 209-984-3953.

Rancho Los Alamitos Historic Ranch, 6400 Bixby Hill Road, Long Beach, CA 90815. Tel: 310-431-3541.

Rancho Los Cerritos, 4600 Virginia Road, Long Beach, CA 90807. Tel: 310-570-1755.

Red Rock Canyon State Park, Abbot Drive and Highway 14, Cantil, CA 93519. Tel: 805-942-0662.

Redwood National Park, 1111 Second Street, Crescent City, CA 95531. Tel: 707-464-6101.

San Fernando Mission, 15151 San Fernando Mission Blvd, Mission Hills, CA 91345. Tel: 818-361-0186.

San Juan Bautista State Historic Park, PO Box 787, San Juan Bautista, CA 95045-787. Tel: 408-623-4881.

Santa Monica Mountains National Recreation Area, 30401 Agoura Road, Agoura Hills, CA 91301. Tel: 818-597-1036.

Sequoia and Kings Canyon National Parks, Three Rivers, CA 93271. Tel: 209-565-3134.

Shasta State Historic Park, PO Box 2430, Shasta, CA 96087. Tel: 916-225-2065.

Sierra County Historical Park, Highway 49, Sierra City, CA 96125. Tel: 916-862-1310.

Sutter's Fort State Historic Park, 2701 L St, Sacramento, CA 95814. Tel: 916-324-0539.

Yosemite National Park, PO Box 577, Yosemite National Park, CA 95389. Tel: 209-372-0200.

Colorado

Bent's Old Fort National Historic Site, 35110 Highway 194 East, La Junta, CO 81050-9523. Tel: 719-384-2596.

Black Canyon of the Gunnison National Monument, 2233 E. Main St, Suite 2, Montrose, CO 81401. Tel: 970-249-7036.

Colorado National Monument, Fruita, CO 81521. Tel: 970-858-3617.

Dinosaur National Monument, 4545 Highway 40, Dinosaur, CO 81610. Tel: 970-374-2216.

Florissant Fossil Beds National Monument, PO Box 185, Florissant, CO 80816. Tel: 719-748-3253.

Four Mile Historic Park, 715 S. Forest, Denver, CO. Tel: 303-399-1859.

Great Sand Dunes National Monument, 11500 Highway 150, Mosca, CO 81146. Tel: 719-378-2312.

Hovenweep National Monument, McElmo Route, Cortez, CO 81321. Tel: 970-529-4465.

Mesa Verde National Park, PO Box 8, Mesa Verde National Park, CO 81330. Tel: 970-529-4465.

Rocky Mountain National Park, Estes Park, CO 80517. Tel: 970-586-1399.

Ute Mountain Tribal Park, Ute Mountain Ute Tribe, Towaoc, CO 81334. Tel: 970-565-3751.

Idaho

Craters of the Moon National Monument, PO Box 29, Arco, ID 83213. Tel: 208-527-3257.

Hagerman Fossil Beds National Monument, PO Box 570, Hagerman, ID 83332-0570. Tel: 208-733-8398.

Massacre Rocks State Park, 3592 Park Lane, American Falls, ID 83211. Tel: 208-548-2672.

Nez Perce National Historical Park, PO Box 93, Spalding, ID 83551-0093. Tel: 208-843-2261.

Old Idaho Penitentiary, 2445 Old Penitentiary Road, Boise, ID 83712. Tel: 208-334-2844.

Old Mission State Park, Box 30, Interstate 90, Cataldo, ID 83810. Tel: 208-682-3814.

Three Island State Park, PO Box 609, Glenns Ferry, ID 83623. Tel: 208-366-2394.

Montana

Bannack State Park, 4200 Bannack Road, Dillon, MT 59725. Tel: 406-834-3413.

Big Hole National Battlefield, PO Box 237, Wisdom, MT 59761. Tel: 406-689-3155.

Bighorn Canyon National Recreation Area, PO Box 458, Fort Smith, MT

59035. Tel: 406-666-2412 or 307-548-2251.

Copper King Mansion, 219 W. Granite, Butte, MT 59701. Tel: 406-782-7580.

Glacier National Park, West Glacier, MT 59936. Tel: 406-888-5441.

Grant-Kohrs Ranch National Historic Site, PO Box 790, Deer Lodge, MT 59722. Tel: 406-846-2070.

Little Bighorn Battlefield National Monument, PO Box 39, Crow Agency, MT 59022. Tel: 406-638-2621.

Old Montana Prison, 1106 Main St, Deer Lodge, MT 59722. Tel: 406-846-3111.

Virginia City (ghost town), Virginia City Chamber of Commerce, WY 59755. Tel: 406-843-5555.

Nevada

Berlin Ichthyosaur State Park, c/o Nevada State Parks, 123 W. Nye Lane, Carson City, NV 89710. Tel: 702-687-4384.

Great Basin National Park, Baker, NV 89311. Tel: 702-234-7331.

Lake Mead National Recreation Area, 601 Nevada Highway, Boulder City, NV 89005. Tel: 702-293-8907.

Las Vegas Mormon Fort, 908 N. Las Vegas Blvd, Las Vegas, NV. Tel: 702-486-3511.

Ward Charcoal Ovens Historic State Monument, c/o Nevada State Parks, 123 W. Nye Lane, Carson City, NV 89710. Tel: 702-687-4384.

New Mexico

Aztec Ruins National Monument, PO Box 640, Aztec, NM 87410. Tel: 505-334-6174.

Bandelier National Monument, HCR 1, Box 1, Suite 15, Los Alamos, NM 87544-9701. Tel: 505-672-3861.

Capulin Volcano National Monument, PO Box 40, Capulin, NM 88414. Tel: 505-278-2201.

Carlsbad Caverns National Park, 3225 National Parks Highway, Carlsbad, NM 88220. Tel: 505-785-2232.

Cathedral of St Francis of Assisi, 131 Cathedral Plaza, Santa Fe, NM 87501. Tel: 505-982-5619.

Chaco Culture National Historical Park, Star Route 4, Box 6500, Bloomfield, NM 87413. Tel: 505-786-7014.

Coronado State Monument and Park, PO Box 95, Bernalillo, NM 87004. Tel: 505-867-5351.

Cristo Rey Church, 1120 Canyon Road, Santa Fe, NM 87501. Tel: 505-983-8528.

El Malpais National Monument, PO Box 939, Grants, NM 87020. Tel: 505-285-4641.

El Morro National Monument, Route 2, Box 43, Ramah, NM, 87321. Tel: 505-783-4226.

Fort Selden State Monument, c/o New Mexico State Parks, 408 Galisteo, Santa Fe, NM 87501. Tel: 505-827-7465.

Fort Sumner State Monument, PO Box 356, Fort Sumner, NM 88119. Tel: 505-355-2573.

Fort Union National Monument, PO Box 127, Watrous, NM 87753. Tel: 505-425-8025.

Gila Cliff Dwellings National Monument, Route 11, Box 100, Silver City, NM 88061. Tel: 505-536-9461.

Jemez State Monument, Route 4, Jemez, NM. Tel: 505-829-3530.

Lincoln State Monument and National Landmark, PO Box 36, Lincoln, NM 88388. Tel: 505-653-4372.

Loretto Chapel, 211 Old Santa Fe Trail, Santa Fe, NM 87501. Tel: 505-984-7971.

Pancho Villa State Park, c/o New Mexico State Parks, 408 Galisteo, Santa Fe, NM 87501. Tel: 505-827-7465.

Pecos National Historical Park, PO Box 418, Pecos, NM 87552. Tel: 505-757-6414.

Petroglyph National Monument, PO Box 1293, Albuquerque, NM 87103. Tel: 505-768-3316.

Puye Cliff Dwellings, Santa Clara Pueblo, PO Box 580, Espanola, NM 87532. Tel: 505-753-7326.

Salinas Pueblo Missions National Monument, PO Box 496, Mountainair, NM 87036. Tel: 505-847-2585.

San Francisco de Asis Church, PO Box 72, Rancho de Taos, NM 87557. Tel: 505-758-2754.

San Miguel Mission, 401 Old Santa Fe Trail, Santa Fe, NM. Tel: 505-983-3974.

Santuario de Chimayo, PO Box 235, Chimayo, NM 87522. Tel: 505-351-4889.

Santuario de Guadalupe, 100 Guadalupe, Santa Fe, NM. Tel: 505-988-2027.

White Sands National Monument, PO Box 1086, Holloman Air Force Base, NM 88330. Tel: 505-479-6124.

North Dakota

Chateau de Mores State Historic Park, c/o North Dakota State Parks, 1835 Bismark Expressway, Bismark, ND 58501. Tel: 701-328-5357.

Fort Abraham Lincoln State Park, 401 W. Main St, Mandan, ND 58554. Tel: 701-663-9571.

Fort Union Trading Post National Historic Site, RR 3, Box 71, Williston, ND 58801. Tel: 701-572-9083.

Knife River Indian Villages National Historic Site, PO Box 9, Stanton, ND 58571. Tel: 701-745-3300.

Theodore Roosevelt National Park, PO Box 7, Medora, ND 58645. Tel: 701-623-4466.

Oklahoma

Fort Gibson Military Park, 110 E. Ash, Fort Gibson, OK 74434. Tel: 918-478-2669.

Old Post National Historic Landmark (Fort Sill Museum), 437 Quanah Road, Fort Sill, OK 73503. Tel: 405-351-5123.

Sequoyah's Home, Route 1, Box 141, Sallishaw, OK 74955. Tel: 918-775-2413.

Washita Battleground Historic Site (Black Kettle Museum), PO Box 252, Cheyenne, OK 73628. Tel: 405-497-3929.

Will Rogers Birthplace and Dog Iron Ranch, Route 2, Box 4800, Oologah, OK 74053. Tel: 918-275-4201.

South Dakota

Badlands National Park, PO Box 6, Interior, SD 57750. Tel: 605-433-5361.

Black Hills National Forest, RR 2, Box 200, Custer, SD 57730. Tel: 605-673-2251.

Custer State Park, HC83, Box 70, Custer, SD 57730. Tel: 605-255-4464.

Jewel Cave National Monument, RR 1, Box 60AA, Custer, SD 57730. Tel: 605-673-2288.

Mount Rushmore National Memorial, PO Box 268, Keystone, SD 57751. Tel: 605-574-2523.

Wind Cave National Park, Hot Springs, SD 57747. Tel: 605-745-4600.

Texas

The Alamo, 300 Alamo Plaza, San Antonio, TX 78205. Tel: 210-225-1391

Big Bend National Park, Big Bend National Park, TX 79834. Tel: 915-477-2251.

Caddoan State Historic Site, Box 85C, Alto, TX 75925. Tel: 409-858-3218.

Chamizal National Memorial, 800 S. San Marcial, El Paso, TX 79905. Tel: 915-532-7273.

Fort Concho National Historic Landmark, 630 S. Oakes St, San Angelo, TX 76903. Tel: 915-657-4441.

Fort Davis National Historic Site, PO Box 1456, Fort Davis, TX 79734. Tel: 915-426-3225.

Fort Leaton State Historical Park, PO Box 1220, Presidio, TX 79845. Tel: 915-229-3613.

Fort McKavett State Historical Park, PO Box 867, Fort McKavett, TX 76841. Tel: 915-396-2358.

Fort Parker State Historical Park, Route 3, Box 95, Mexia, TX 76667. Tel: 817-562-5751.

Fort Richardson State Historic Site, PO Box 4, Jacksboro, TX 76458. Tel: 817-567-3506.

Guadalupe Mountains National Park, HC 60, Box 400, Salt Flat, TX 79847. Tel: 915-828-3251.

King Ranch, W. Highway 141, Kingsville, TX 78363. Tel: 512-592-6411.

Log Cabin Village, 2100 Log Cabin Lane, Fort Worth, TX 76119. Tel: 915-926-5881.

Lyndon B. Johnson National Historical Park, PO Box 329, Johnson City, TX 78636. Tel: 210-868-7128.

Lyndon B. Johnson State Park, PO Box 238, Stonewall, TX 78671. Tel: 210-644-2252.

Mission Espiritu Santo, PO Box 727, Goliad State Park, Goliad, TX 77963. Tel: 512-645-3405.

Mission Tejas State Historical Park, Route 2, Box 108, Grapeland, TX 75844. Tel: 409-687-2394.

Palo Duro Canyon State Park, Route 2, Box 285, Canyon, TX 79015. Tel: 806-488-2227.

Presidio la Bahia, Goliad State Park, Goliad, TX 77963. Tel: 512-645-3405.

San Antonio Missions National Historical Park, 2202 Roosevelt Ave, San Antonio, TX 78210. Tel: 210-229-5701.

San Jacinto Battleground State Park, 3523 Highway 134, La Porte, TX 77571. Tel: 713-479-2019.

Seminole Canyon State Park, PO Box 820, Comstock, TX 78837. Tel: 915-292-4464.

Stephen F. Austin State Historical Park, PO Box 125, San Felipe, TX 77473. Tel: 409-885-3613.

Stockyards Historic Area, Visitor Center, 130 E. Exchange St, Fort Worth, TX 76106. Tel: 817-625-9715.

Thistle Hill, 1509 Pennsylvania Ave, Fort Worth, TX 76104. Tel: 817-336-1212.

Washington-on-the-Brazos State Historical Park, PO Box 305, Washington, TX 77880. Tel: 409-878-2214.

Utah

Anasazi Indian Village State Park, PO Box 1329, Boulder, UT 84716-1329. Tel: 801-335-7308.

Arches National Park, PO Box 907, Moab, UT 84532. Tel: 801-259-8161.

Bryce Canyon National Park, Bryce Canyon, UT 84717. Tel: 801-834-5322.

Canyonlands National Park, 2282 SW Resource Blvd, Moab, UT 84532. Tel: 801-259-7164.

Capitol Reef National Park, Torrey, UT 84775. Tel: 801-425-3791.

Cedar Breaks National Monument, 82 N. 100 East, Cedar City, UT 84720. Tel: 801-586-9451.

Dead Horse Point State Park, PO Box 609, Moab, UT 84532. Tel: 801-259-6511.

Edge of the Cedars State Park, 660 W. 400 North, Blanding, UT 84511. Tel: 801-678-2238.

Fort Buenaventura State Park, 2450 A Ave, Ogden, UT 84401. Tel: 801-621-4808.

Fremont Indian State Park, 11550 Clear Creek Canyon Road, Sevier, UT 84766. Tel: 801-527-4631.

Golden Spike National Historic Site, PO Box 897, Brigham City, UT 84302-0923. Tel: 801-471-2209.

Iron Mission State Park, 585 N. Main, Cedar City, UT 84720. Tel: 801-586-9290.

Mormon Tabernacle, Temple Square, Salt Lake City, UT 84114. Tel: 801-240-3171.

Natural Bridges National Monument, Box 1, Lake Powell, UT 84533. Tel: 801-259-5174.

This Is The Place State Park, 2601 Sunnyside Ave, Salt Lake City, UT 84108. Tel: 801-584-8391.

Timpanogos Cave National Monument, RR 3, Box 200, American Fork, UT 84003. Tel: 801-756-5238.

Zion National Park, Springdale, UT 84767-1099. Tel: 801-772-3256.

Wyoming

Devils Tower National Monument, PO Box 8, Devils Tower, WY 82714. Tel: 307-467-5283.

Fort Bridger State Historic Site, Po Box 35, Fort Bridger, WY 82933. Tel: 307-782-3842.

Fort Fetterman State Historic Site, Route 3, Box 6, Douglas, WY 82633. Tel: 307-358-2864.

Fort Laramie National Historic Site, PO Box 86, Fort Laramie, WY 82212. Tel: 307-837-2221.

Fort Phil Kearney, 528 Wagon Box Road, Banner, WY 82832. Tel: 307-684-7629.

Fossil Butte National Monument, PO Box 592, Kemmerer, WY 83101. Tel: 307-877-4455.

Grand Teton National Park, PO Drawer 170, Moose, WY 83012. Tel: 307-739-3300.

South Pass City State Historic Site, Wyoming Recreation Commission, Cheyenne, WY 82002. Tel: 307-332-3684.

Wyoming Frontier Prison, 5th and Walnut Sts, Rawlins, WY 82301. Tel: 307-324-4111.

Wyoming Territorial Prison, PO Box 1631, Laramie, WY 82070. Tel: 307-745-6161.

Yellowstone National Park, PO Box 168, Yellowstone National Park, WY 82190. Tel: 307-344-7381.

Historic Trails

Lewis and Clark National Historic Trail, National Park Service, 700 Rayovac Drive, Suite 100, Madison, WI 53711. Tel: 608-264-5610.

Mormon Pioneer National Historic Trail, Rocky Mountain Region, National Park Service, 12795 W. Alameda Parkway, Lakewood, CO 80225. Tel: 303-969-2875.

Nez Perce National Historic Trail, Forest Service, Region 1, Federal Building, PO Box 7669, Missoula, MT 59807. Tel: 406-329-3150.

Oregon National Historic Trail, Pacific Northwest Region, National Park Service, 83 S. King Street, Suite 212, Seattle, WA 98104. Tel: 206-553-5366.

Pony Express National Historic Trail, Bureau of Land Management, Salt Lake City District, 2370 South 2300 West, Salt Lake City, UT 84119. Tel: 801-977-4400

Santa Fe National Historic Trail, Southwest Region, National Park Service, PO Box 728, Santa Fe, NM 87504. Tel: 505-988-6888.

Historic Railroads

1880 Train, PO Box 1880, Hill City, SD 57745. Tel: 605-574-2222. Daily mid-May–Oct.

Cripple Creek & Victor Narrow Gauge Railroad, 520 E. Carr St, Cripple Creek, CO 80813. Tel: 719-689-2640. Daily late May–mid–Oct.

Cumbres & Toltec Scenic Railroad, PO Box 789, Chama, NM 87520. Tel: 505-756-2151. Daily late May–mid–Oct.

Durango & Silverton Narrow Gauge Railroad, 479 Main Ave, Durango, CO 81301. Tel: 303-247-2733. Daily year-round.

Georgetown Loop Railroad, 1106 Rose St, Georgetown, CO 80444. Tel: 303-569-2403. Daily late May–mid–Oct.

Grand Canyon Railway, 123 N. San Francisco St, Suite 210, Flagstaff, AZ 86001. Tel: 520-773-1976. Daily year-round.

Pikes Peak Cog Railway, 515 Ruxton Ave, Manitou Springs, CO 80829. Tel: 719-685-5401. Daily late-Apr–Oct.

Sad Monkey Railroad, Canyon, TX. Tel: 806-488-2222. Daily year-round.

Tarantula Railroad, 2318 Eighth Ave, Fort Worth, TX. Tel: 817-763-8394. Daily year-round.

Virginia & Truckee Steam Railroad, PO Box 467, Virginia City, NV 89440. Tel: 702-847-0380. Daily late-May–Sep.

Yosemite Mountain-Sugar Pine Railroad, 56001 Highway 41, Fish Camp, CA 93623. Tel: 209-683-7273. Mar–Oct, call for daily schedule.

Museums

Arizona

The Amerind Foundation, PO Box 400, Dragoon Road, Dragoon, AZ 85609. Tel: 520-586-3666. Daily 10am–4pm.

Arizona Historical Society, 949 E. Second St, Tucson, AZ 85719. Tel: 520-628-5774. Mon–Sat 10am–4pm, Sun 12pm–4pm.

Arizona Sonora Desert Museum, 2021 N. Kinney Road, Tucson, AZ 85743. Tel: 520-883-1380. Daily 8.30am–5pm.

Arizona State Museum, University of Arizona, Park Ave at University, Tucson, AZ 85721. Tel: 520-621-6281. Mon–Sat 10am–5pm, Sun 12pm–5pm.

Bisbee Mining and Historical Museum, 5 Copper Queen Plaza, PO Box 14, Bisbee, AZ 85603. Tel: 520-432-7071. Daily 10am–4pm.

Desert Caballeros Western Museum, 21 N. Frontier St, Wickenburg, AZ 85390. Tel: 520-684-2272. Mon–Sat 10am–4pm, Sun 1pm–4pm.

Fremont House Museum, Tucson Convention Center Complex, Tucson, AZ 85701. Tel: 520-622-0956. Wed–Sat 10am–4pm.

Heard Museum, 22 E. Monte Vista Road, Phoenix, AZ 85004. Tel: 602-252-8848. Mon–Sat 9.30am–5pm, until 9pm on Wed, Sun 12pm–5pm.

John Wesley Powell Memorial Museum, 6 Lake Powell Blvd, Page, AZ 86040. Tel: 520-645-9496. Mon–Fri 9am–5pm.

Mesa Southwest Museum, 53 N. Macdonald, Mesa, AZ 85201. Tel: 602-644-2230. Tue–Sat 9am–6pm, Sun 12pm–6pm.

Museum of the Forest, Gila County Historical Society, 1001 W. Main Street, Payson, AZ 85541. Tel: 520-474-3483. Wed–Sun 12pm–4pm.

Museum of Northern Arizona, Fort Valley Road, Route 4, Box 720, Flagstaff, AZ 86001. Tel: 520-774-5211. Daily 9am–5pm.

Museum of the Southwest, 1500 N. Circle I Road, Willcox, AZ 85643. Tel: 520-384-2272. Mon–Sat 9am–5pm, Sun 1pm–5pm.

Museum of the West, 109 S. Third St, Tombstone, AZ 85638. Tel: 520-457-9219. Daily 9.30am–5pm.

Old Tucson Studios, 201 S. Kinney Road, Tucson, AZ 85746. Tel: 520-883-0100. Reopening in 1996, call for schedule.

Phippen Museum of Western Art, 4701 Highway 89, Prescott, AZ 86301. Tel: 520-778-1385. Mon 10am–4pm, closed Tue, Wed–Sat 10am–4pm, Sun 1pm–4pm.

Sharlot Hall Museum, 415 W. Gurley, Prescott, AZ 86301. Tel: 520-445-3122. Tues–Sat 10am–4pm, Sun 1pm–5pm.

Tucson Museum of Art, 140 N. Main Ave, Tucson, AZ 85701. 520-624-2333. Mon–Sat 10am–4pm, Sun 12pm–4pm.

Zane Grey Museum, 408 W. Main St, Suite 8, Payson, AZ 85547. Tel: 520-474-6243. Mon–Sat 10am–4pm.

California

Amador County Museum, 225 Church St, Jackson, CA 95642. Tel: 209-223-6386. Wed–Sun 10am–4pm.

California State Mining and Mineral Museum, PO Box 1192, Mariposa, CA 95338. Tel: 209-742-7625. Wed–Sun 10am–4pm.

California State Railroad Museum, 2nd & I St, Sacramento, CA 95816. Tel: 916-448-4466. Daily 10am–5pm.

Craft and Folk Art Museum, 5814 Wilshire Blvd, Los Angeles, CA 90036. Tel: 213-937-5544. Tues–Sun 11am–5pm.

El Dorado County Historical Museum, 100 Placerville Drive, Placerville, CA 95667. Tel: 916-621-5865. Wed–Sat 10am–4pm, Sun 12pm–4pm.

Gene Autrey Western Heritage Museum, 4700 Western Heritage Way, Los Angeles, CA 90027. Tel: 213-667-2000. Tues–Sun 10am–5pm.

Gold Country Museum, 101 Maple St, Auburn, CA 95603. Tel: 916-889-6500. Tues–Fri 10am–3pm, Sat–Sun 11am–4pm.

Oakland Museum, 1000 Oak St, Oakland, CA 94607. Tel: 510-238-3401. Wed–Sat 10am–5pm, Sun 12pm–7pm.

Roy Rogers and Dale Evans Museum, 15650 Seneca Road, Victorville, CA 92392. Tel: 619-243-4547. Daily 9am–5pm.

San Buenaventura Mission Museum, 211 E. Main St, Ventura, CA 93001.

Tel: 805-643-4318. Mon–Sat 10am–5pm, Sun 10am–4pm.

Southwest Museum, 234 Museum Drive, Highland Park, Los Angeles, CA 90041. Tel: 213-221-2163. Tues–Sun 11am–5pm.

State Indian Museum, 2618 K St, Sacramento, CA 95816. Tel: 916-324-0971. Daily 10am–5pm.

Colorado

Black American West Museum and Heritage Center, 3091 California St, Denver, CO 80205. Tel: 303-292-2566. Mon–Fri 10am–5pm, Sat–Sun 12pm–5pm.

Buffalo Bill Cody Memorial Museum and Grave, Lookout Mountain Road, Route 5, Box 950, Golden, CO 80401. Tel: 303-526-0747. Tues–Sun 9am–4pm.

Byers-Evans House and Denver History Museum, 13th and Bannock Sts, Denver, CO 80203. Tel: 303-620-4933. Tues–Sun 11am–3pm.

Colorado History Museum, 13th and Broadway, Denver, CO 80203. Tel: 303-866-3682. Mon–Sat 10am–4.30pm, Sun 12pm–4.30pm.

Colorado Railroad Museum, 17155 W. 44th Ave, Golden, CO 80403. Tel: 303-279-4591. Daily 9am–5pm.

Colorado Springs Fine Arts Center, 30 W. Dale St, Colorado Springs, CO 80903. Tel: 719-634-5581. Tues–Fri 9am–5pm, Sat 10am–5pm, Sun 1pm–5pm.

Colorado Springs Pioneers Museum, 215 S. Tejon St, Colorado Springs, CO 80903. Tel: 719-578-6650. Tues–Sat 10am–5pm, Sun 1pm–5pm.

Cripple Creek District Museum, Bennet Ave, Cripple Creek, CO. Tel: 719-689-2634. May–Sep daily 9am–5pm, Oct–Apr Sat–Sun 12pm–5pm.

Denver Art Museum, 100 W. 14th Ave, Denver, CO 80204. Tel: 303-640-2793. Tues–Sat 10am–5pm, Sun 12pm–5pm.

Denver Museum of Natural History, 2001 Colorado Blvd, Denver, CO 80205. Tel: 303-370-6357. Sun–Wed 9am–5pm, Thur–Fri 9am–9pm.

Hamill House Museum, 305 Argentine St, Georgetown, CO 80444. Tel: 303-569-2840. Jun–Sep daily 10am–4pm, Oct–May Sat–Sun 12pm–4pm.

Heritage Museum, 102 E. 9th St, Leadville, CO 80461. Tel: 719-486-1878. May–Oct daily 10am–6pm.

Hotel de Paris Museum, 409 6th St, Georgetown, CO 80444. Tel: 303-569-2311. Jun–Sep daily 10am–5pm, Oct–May Sat–Sun 12pm–4pm.

Littleton Historical Museum, 6028 S. Gallup St, Littleton, CO 80120. Tel: 303-795-3950. Tues–Fri 8am–5pm, Sat 10am–5pm, Sun 1pm–5pm.

MacGregor Ranch Museum, 180 MacGregor Lane, Estes Park, CO. Tel: 303-586-3749. Jun–Sep Tue–Fri 10am–4pm.

Matchless Mine Museum, 414 W. 7th St, Leadville, CO 80461. Tel: 719-486-0371. Call for hours.

Molly Brown House Museum, 1340 Pennsylvania St, Denver, CO 80203. Tel: 303-832-4092. Tue–Sat 10am–3.30pm, Sun 12pm–3.30pm.

Museum of Western Art, 1727 Tremont Place, Denver, CO 80202. Tel: 303-296-1880. Tue–Sat 10am–4.30pm.

National Mining Hall of Fame and Museum, 120 W. 9th St, Leadville, CO 80461. Tel: 719-486-1229. Mon–Fri 9am–2pm.

Ouray Historical Museum, 420 6th Ave, Ouray, CO 81427. Tel: 970-325-4576. Jun–Sep daily 9am–6pm, Oct–May Fri–Mon 1pm–4pm.

Pro Rodeo Hall of Champions and Museum of the American Cowboy, 101 Pro Rodeo Drive, Colorado Springs, CO 80919. Tel: 719-593-8840. Daily 9am–5pm.

US Mint, 320 W. Colfax St, Denver, CO. Tel: 303-844-3582. Mon–Fri 8am–2.45pm.

Ute Indian Museum, 17253 Chipeta Road, Montrose, CO 81401. Tel: 970-249-3098. Call for hours.

Western Museum of Mining and Industry, 1025 N. Gate Road, Colorado Springs, CO 80921. Tel: 719-488-0880. Mon–Sat 9am–4pm, Sun 12pm–4pm (closed Sun Dec–Feb).

Idaho

Bannock County Historical Museum, 3000 Alzord, Pocatello, ID 83204. Tel: 208-233-0434. Tue–Sat 10am–2pm.

Fort Hall Replica, S. 4th St, Ross Park, Pocatello, ID. Tel: 208-234-6233. Apr–May Tue–Sat 10am–2pm, Jun–Aug daily 9am–7pm, Sep daily 10am–2pm.

Idaho State Historical Museum, 610 N. Julia Davis Drive, Boise, ID 83702. Tel: 208-334-2120. Mon–Sat 9am–5pm, Sun 1pm–5pm.

Montana

C.M. Russell Museum, 400 13th St North, Great Falls, MT 59401. Tel: 406-727-8787. Mon–Sat 10am–5pm, Sun 1pm–5pm.

Montana Historical Society, 225 N. Roberts St, Helena, MT 59620. Tel: 406-444-2694. Mon–Fri 8am–5pm, Sat 9am–5pm.

Museum of the Plains Indians, Highways 2 & 89, PO Box 400, Browning, MT 59417. Tel: 406-338-2230. Mon–Fri 10am–4.30pm.

Museum of the Rockies, Montana State University, Bozeman, MT 59717. Tel: 406-994-2251. Mon–Sat 9am–5pm, Sun 12.30pm–5pm.

World Museum of Mining and Hell Roarin' Gulch, W. Park St, Butte, MT 59701. Tel: 406-723-7211. Sep–May Tue–Sun 10am–5pm, Jun–Aug Tue–Sun 9am–9pm.

Nevada

Mackay School of Mines Museum, University of Nevada, Reno, NV 89501. Tel: 702-784-6987. Mon–Fri 8am–5pm.

Mark Twain Museum, *Territorial Enterprise* Building, 47 S. C Street, Virginia City, NV 89440. Tel: 702-847-0525. Daily 10am–5pm.

Nevada Historical Society, University of Nevada, 1650 N. Virginia St, Reno, NV 89501. Tel: 702-688-1190. Mon–Sat 10am–5pm.

Nevada State Museum, 600 N. Carson St, Carson City, NV 89701. Tel: 702-687-5160. Mon–Fri 8am–5pm.

Nevada State Museum and Historical Society, 700 Twin Lake Drive, Las Vegas, NV 89107. Tel: 702-486-5205. Daily 9am–5pm.

Nevada State Railroad Museum, 2180 S. Carson St, Carson City, NV 89701. Tel: 702-687-6953. Wed–Sun 8.30am–4.30pm.

Nevada Museum of Art, 160 W. Liberty St, Reno, NV 89501. Tel: 702-329-3333. Mon–Sat 10am–4pm, Sun 12pm–4pm.

Nevada Northern Railway Museum, PO Box 150040, East Ely, NV 89315. Tel: 702-289-2085. Daily Jun–Sep.

Northeastern Nevada Museum, 1515 Idaho St, Elko, NV 89801. Tel: 702-738-3418. Mon–Sat 9am–4pm, Sun 1pm–4pm.

Western Folklife Center, PO Box 888, Elko, NV 89801. Tel: 702-738-7508. Mon–Fri 8am–5pm.

New Mexico

Albuquerque Museum, 2000 Mountain NW, Albuquerque, NM 87102. Tel: 505-243-7255. Tues–Sun 9am–5pm.

Billy The Kid Museum, 1601 E. Sumner Ave, Fort Sumner, NM 88119. Tel: 505-355-2380. Mon–Sat 8.30am–5pm, Sun 11am–5pm.

El Rancho de las Golondrinas, 334 Los Pinos Road, Santa Fe, NM 87505. Tel: 505-471-2261. Jun–Sep Wed–Sun 10am–4pm, Apr–May & Oct by appointment.

Ernest L. Blumenschein Home, 222 LeDoux St, Taos, NM. Tel: 505-758-0330. Daily 9am–5pm.

Fleming Hall Museum, Western New Mexico University, Silver City, NM 88062. Tel: 505-538-6386. Mon–Fri 9.30am–4.30pm, Sat–Sun 10am–4pm.

Governor Bent Home and Museum, 117A Bent St, Taos 87571. Tel: 505-758-2376. Daily 10am–5pm.

Indian Pueblo Cultural Center, 2401 12th St NW, Albuquerque, NM 87102. Tel: 505-843-6950. Daily 9am–5.30pm.

Institute of American Indian Arts Museum, 108 Cathedral Place, Santa Fe, NM 87501. Tel: 505-988-6211. Mon–Sat 10am–5pm, Sun 12pm–5pm.

Kit Carson Home and Museum, 113 E. Kit Carson Road, Taos, NM 87571. Tel: 505-758-4741. Daily 9am–5pm.

Los Alamos County Historical Museum, 1921 Juniper St, Los Alamos, NM 87544. Tel: 505-662-4493, Mon–Sat 10am–4pm, Sun 1pm–4pm.

Maxwell Museum of Anthropology, University of New Mexico, Martin Luther King Blvd & Redondo Drive, Albuquerque, NM 87131. Tel: 505-277-4404. Mon–Fri 9am–4pm, Sat 10am–4pm, Sun 12pm–4pm.

Millicent Rogers Museum, 1504 Millicent Rogers Road, Taos, NM 87571. Tel: 505-758-2462. Nov–Mar Tue–Sun 10am–5pm, Apr–Oct daily 10am–5pm.

Museum of Fine Arts, 107 W. Palace Ave, Santa Fe, NM 87501. Tel: 505-827-4455. Mar–Dec daily 10am–5pm, closed Monday Jan–Feb.

Museum of Indian Arts and Culture, 710 Camino Lejo, Santa Fe, NM 87501. Tel: 505-827-6344. Daily 10am–5pm.

Museum of International Folk Art, 706 Camino Lejo, Santa Fe, NM

87503. Tel: 505-827-6350. Daily 10am–5pm.

Palace of the Governors, 105 W. Palace Ave, Santa Fe, NM 87501. Tel: 505-827-6483. Daily 10am–5pm.

Pinos Altos Museum, 33 Main St, Pinos Altos, NM 88053. Tel: 505-388-1882. Mon–Sat 9am–6pm, Sun 9am–5pm.

Santa Fe Trail Museum, Maxwell Ave, Springer, NM 87747. Tel: 505-483-2341. Jun–Sep Mon–Sat 9am–4pm.

Silver City Museum, 312 W. Broadway, Silver City, NM 88061. Tel: 505-538-5921. Tue–Fri 9am–4.30pm, Sat–Sun 10am–4pm.

Wheelwright Museum, 704 Camino Lejo, Santa Fe, NM 87501. Tel: 505-982-4636. Mon–Sat 10am–5pm, Sun 1pm–5pm.

Oklahoma

Cherokee Heritage Center, PO Box 515, Tahlequah, OK 74465. Tel: 918-456-6007. Mon–Sat 10am–5pm, Sun 1pm–5pm.

Chisholm Trail Museum, 605 Zellers Ave, Kingfisher, OK 73750. Tel: 405-375-5176. Tues–Sat 9am–5pm, Sun 1pm–5pm.

Dog Iron Ranch and Will Rogers Birthplace, Highway 169, Oologah, OK 74053. Tel: 918-275-4201. Daily 8am–5pm; the grounds are open dawn to dusk.

Five Civilized Tribes Museum, Honor Heights Drive, Muskogee, OK 74401. Tel: 918-683-1701. Mon–Sat 10am–5pm, Sun 1pm–5pm.

Fort Sill Museum, 437 Quanah Road, Fort Sill, OK 73503. Tel: 405-442-5123 or 442-8111. Daily 8.30am–4.30pm.

Gilcrease Museum, 1400 Gilcrease Museum Road, Tulsa, OK 74127. Tel: 918-596-2700. Tue–Wed & Fri 9am–5pm, Thu 9am–8pm, Sat 9am–5pm, Sun 1pm–5pm.

Harn Homestead and 1889er Museum, 313 NE 16th, Oklahoma City, OK 73102. Tel: 405-235-4058. Tue–Sat 10am–4pm.

Indian City USA, PO Box 695, Anadarko, OK 73005. Tel: 405-247-5661. Daily 9am–5pm.

Museum of the Great Plains, 601 Ferris Ave, Lawton, OK 73502. Tel: 405-581-3460. Mon–Fri 8am–5pm, Sat 10am–5.30pm, Sun 1pm–5.30pm.

Museum of the Western Prairie, 1100 Memorial, Altus, OK 73521. Tel: 405-482-1044. Tue–Fri 9am–5pm, Sat–Sun 2pm–5pm.

National Cowboy Hall of Fame and Western Heritage Center, 1700 NE 63rd St, Oklahoma City, OK 73111. Tel: 405-478-2250. Jun–Aug 8.30am–6pm, Sep–May 9am–5pm.

National Hall of Fame For Famous Indians, 115 Highway 62, Anadarko, OK 73005. Tel: 405-247-5555. Mon–Sat 9am–5pm, Sun 1pm–5pm.

Oklahoma Territorial Museum, 406 E. Oklahoma, Guthrie, OK 73044. Tel: 405-282-1889. Tue–Fri 9am–5pm, Sat 10am–4pm, Sun 1pm–4pm.

Pawnee Bill Museum, Highway 64, Pawnee, OK 74058. Tel: 918-762-2513. Tue–Fri 10am–5pm, Sat 10am–5pm, Sun–Mon 1pm–4pm.

Pioneer Woman Museum, 701 Monument Road, Ponca City, OK 74602. Tel: 405-765-6108. Tue–Sat 9am–5pm, Sun 1pm–5pm.

Sequoyah's Home Site, Highway 101, Sallisaw, OK 74955. Tel: 918-775-2413. Tue–Fri 9am–5pm, Sat–Sun 2pm–5pm.

Southern Plains Indian Museum, PO Box 749, Anadarko, OK 73005. Tel: 405-247-6221. Tue–Sun 9am–4.30pm.

State Museum of History, 2100 N. Lincoln, Wiley Post Building, Oklahoma City, OK 73105. Tel: 405-522-5244. Mon–Sat 8am–4.45pm.

Tom Mix Museum, 721 N. Delaware, Dewey, OK 74029. Tel: 918-534-1555. Tue–Sat 10am–4.30pm, Sun 1pm–4.30pm.

Will Rogers Memorial, 1720 W. Will Rogers Blvd, Claremore, OK 74017. Tel: 918-341-0719 or toll free 800-828-9643. Daily 8am–5pm.

South Dakota

Adams Memorial Museum, 54 Sherman St, Deadwood, SD 57732. Tel: 605-578-1714. Mon–Sat 10am–4pm.

Black Hills Mining Museum, PO Box 694, Lead, SD 57754. Tel: 605-584-1605. May–Sep daily 9am–5pm.

Broken Boot Gold Mine, 1200 Main St, Deadwood, SD 57732. Tel: 605-578-9997. Jun–Aug daily 8am–6pm; call for Sep hours.

Crazy Horse Memorial and Indian Museum of North America, Avenue of the Chiefs, Crazy Horse, SD 57730.

Tel: 605-673-4681. Jun–Sep 6.30am–10am, Oct–May 8am–5.30pm.

Homestake Gold Mine, 630 E. Summit St, Lead, SD 57754. Tel: 605-584-4653. Call for schedule.

Minnilusa Pioneer Museum, 515 West Blvd, Rapid City, SD 57709. Tel: 605-394-6099. Tue–Sat 10am–5pm, Sun 1pm–5pm.

Sioux Indian Museum, 515 West Blvd, PO Box 1504, Rapid City, SD 57709. Tel: 605-348-0557.

Texas

Amon G. Carter Museum of Western Art, 3501 Camp Bowie Blvd, Fort Worth, TX 76107. Tel: 817-738-1933. Tue–Sat 10am–5pm, Sun 12pm–5pm.

Buckhorn Hall of Horns, Lone Star Brewery, 600 Lone Star Blvd, San Antonio, TX 78204. Tel: 210-226-8301. Mon–Fri 7.30am–4.30pm.

Cattlemen's Museum, 1301 W. 7th St, Fort Worth, TX. Tel: 817-332-7064. Mon–Fri 8.30am–5.30pm.

Cowboy Artists of America Museum, 1550 Bandera Highway, Kerrville, TX 78028. Tel: 210-896-2553. Mon–Sat 9am–5pm, Sun 10am–5pm.

Cowboy Museum and Gallery, 209 Alamo Plaza, San Antonio, TX 78205. Tel: 210-229-1257. Daily 10am–7pm.

Fire Station No. 1, Second and Commerce Sts, Fort Worth, TX 76102. Tel: 817-732-1631. Daily 9am–7pm.

Institute of Texas Cultures, 801 S. Bowie, HemisFair Park, San Antonio, TX 78205. Tel: 210-558-2300. Tue–Sun 9am–5pm.

Judge Roy Bean Visitor Center, PO Box 160, Langtry, TX 78871. Tel: 915-291-3340. Daily 8am–5pm.

King Ranch Museum, PO Box 1090, Kingsville, TX 78364-1090. Tel: 512-592-8055. Mon–Sat 12pm–4pm, Sun 1pm–5pm.

Millard's Crossing, 6020 North St, Nacogdoches, TX 77963. Tel: 409-564-6631. Mon–Fri 9am–4pm, Sat–Sun 1pm–4pm.

Miss Hattie's Museum, 18 E. Concho Ave, San Angelo, TX 76903. Tel: 915-658-3735. Mon–Fri 10.30am–5.30pm, Sat 1pm–5.30pm.

National Cowgirl Hall of Fame and Western Heritage Center, 515 Avenue B, Hereford, TX 79045. Tel: 806-364-5252 or 817-626-4475. Mon–Fri 9am–5pm; the museum plans to move to Fort Worth after 1998.

Panhandle-Plains Museum, West Texas A & M University, 2401 4th Ave, Canyon, TX. Tel: 806-656-2244. Mon–Sat 9am–5pm, Sun 1pm–6pm.

Ranching Heritage Center, 4th and Indiana, Lubbock, TX 79409. Tel: 806-742-2498. Tue–Sat 10am–5pm, Sun 1pm–5pm.

Sam Houston Memorial Museum Complex, 13310 Westheimer, Suite 150, Houston, TX 77077. Tel: 713-493-6386. Tue–Sat 9.30am– 6pm.

Sid Richardson Collection of Western Art, 309 Main St, Fort Worth, TX 76101. Tel: 817-332-6554. Tue–Wed 10am–5pm, Thu–Sat 10am–8pm, Sun 1pm–5pm.

Stark Museum of Art, 712 Green Ave, Orange, TX 77630. Tel: 409-883-6661. Wed–Sat 10am–5pm, Sun 1pm–5pm.

Star of the Republic Museum, PO Box 317, Washington, TX 77880. Tel: 409-878-2461. Daily 10am–5pm.

Stockyards Museum, 131 E. Exchange Ave, Fort Worth, TX 76106. Tel: 817-625-5087. Daily 10am–5pm.

Texas Memorial Museum, 2400 Trinity St, Austin, TX 78705. Tel: 512-471-1604. Mon–Fri 9am–5pm, Sat 10am–5pm, Sun 1pm–5pm.

Texas Ranger Hall of Fame and Museum, Fort Fisher Park, PO Box 2570, Waco, TX 76702. Tel: 817-754-1433. Daily 9am–5pm.

Utah

Beehive House, 67 E. South Temple, Salt Lake City, UT 84111. Tel: 801-240-2671. Mon–Sat 9.30am–4.30pm, Sun 10am–1pm.

Brigham Young Winter Home, 200 N. 100 West, St George, UT 84770. Tel: 801-673-2517. Daily 9am–5pm.

Dan O'Laurie Museum, 118 E. Center St, Moab, UT 84532. Tel: 801-259-7985. Mon–Thu 3pm–7pm, Fri–Sat 1pm–7pm.

Daughters of the Utah Pioneers Museum-Ogden, 2148 Grant Ave, Ogden, UT 84401. Tel: 801-393-4460. Mon–Sat 10am–5pm.

Daughters of the Utah Pioneers Museum-Salt Lake City, 35 E. Vine St, Salt Lake City, UT 84150. Tel: 801-882-0982. Mon–Sat 10am–5pm.

Daughters of the Utah Pioneers Museum-St George, 145 N. 100 East, St George, UT 84770. Tel: 801-628-7274. Mon–Sat 10am–5pm.

Family Library, 50 E. North Temple, Salt Lake City, UT 84150. Tel: 801-240-3435. Mon 7.30am–6pm, Tue–Sat 7.30am–10pm.

Jacob Hamblin House, Route 91, Santa Clara, UT 84765. Tel: 801-673-2161. Daily 9am–5pm.

John Wesley Powell River History Museum, State Road 91, Green River, UT 84525. Tel: 801-564-3427. Daily 9am–5pm.

Museum of Church History and Art, 45 N. West Temple, Salt Lake City, UT. Tel: 801-240-3310. Mon–Fri 9am–9pm, Sat–Sun 10am–7pm.

Ronald V. Jensen Living Historical Farm, 4025 S. Highway 89/91, Wellsville, UT 84339. Tel: 801-245-4064. Jun–Aug Tue–Sat 10am–4pm; call for information on special events throughout the year.

Utah State Historical Society, 300 S. Rio Grande, Salt Lake City, UT 84101. Tel: 801-533-3501. Mon–Fri 8am–5pm, Sat 10am–3pm.

Wyoming

Buffalo Bill Historical Center, 720 Sheridan Ave, PO Box 1000, Cody, WY 82414. Tel: 307-587-4771. Summer daily 7am–7pm, Winter Tue–Sun 10am–3pm; schedule changes monthly, contact center for information.

Colter Bay Indian Arts Museum, Grand Teton National Park, Moose, WY 83012. Tel: 307-739-3594. May–Oct 8am–5pm, extended hours in summer.

Explorers' Museum, Madison Junction, Yellowstone National Park, WY 82190. Tel: 307-344-7381. May–Oct 8am–5pm, extended hours in summer.

Grand Encampment Museum, 7th St and Barnett Ave, Encampment, WY 82325. Tel: 307-327-5308. May–Sep Mon–Fri 10am–5pm, Sat 1pm–5pm.

Historic Governor's Mansion, 300 E. 21st St, Cheyenne, WY 82002. Tel: 307-777-7878. Tue–Sat 9am–4pm.

Jackson Hole Museum, 105 N. Glenwood, Jackson, WY 83001. Tel: 307-733-9605. Jun–Sep Mon–Sat 9.30am–6pm, Sun 10am–5pm.

Jim Gatchell Memorial Museum of the West, 100 Fort St, Buffalo, WY 82834. Tel: 307-684-9331. May & Oct Mon–Sat 9am–5pm, Jun–Sep daily 8am–8pm.

Laramie Plains Museum, 603 Ivinson Ave, Laramie, WY 82070. Tel: 307-742-4448. Winter 11am–3pm; call for summer hours.

Museum of the Mountain Man, 700 E. Hennick, Pinedale, WY 82941. Tel: 307-367-4101. May–Oct daily 10am–6pm, winter hours by appointment.

Old Trail Town, 1831 DeMaris Drive, Cody, WY 82414. Tel: 307-587-5302. May–Sep daily 9am–6pm.

Pioneer Museum, 630 Lincoln St, Lander, WY 82520. Tel: 307-332-4137. Jul–Aug Mon–Fri 10am–5pm, Sat 1pm–5pm; Sep–Jun Mon–Fri 1pm–5pm, Sat 1pm–4pm.

Teton County Historical Center, 105 Mercill, Jackson, WY 83001. Tel: 307-733-9605. Mon–Fri 9am–5pm.

Trail End Historic Center, 400 Clarendon Ave, Sheridan, WY 82801. Tel. 307-672-1729. Apr–May daily 1pm–4pm, Jun–Aug daily 9am–6pm, Sep–Dec daily 1pm–4pm; closed Jan–Mar.

Wyoming State Museum, Barret Building, 24th and Central, Cheyenne, WY 82002. Tel: 307-777-7024. Call museum for schedule.

Indian Tribes

A note about visiting Indian communities and events:
Cultural sensitivity is absolutely vital in Indian Country. Because some Indian people may feel uncomfortable or ambivalent about the presence of outsiders, it is very important to be on your best behavior. Here are a few "dos" and "don'ts" to keep in mind:

● Don't use racist terms. Calling an American Indian chief, redskin, squaw, buck, Pocahontas, Hiawatha or any other off-color term is highly offensive.

● Abide by all rules and regulations while on Indian land and at Indian events. These may include prohibitions on photography, sketching, taking notes, video and audio recording. In some cases a photography fee may be required. If you wish to take an individual's picture, you must ask permission first (a gratuity of $2 or $3 may be appropriate).

● Respect all restricted areas. These

are usually posted, but it is advisable to ask permission before hiking into wilderness or archaeological areas, driving on back roads, wandering around villages, and entering churches or other ceremonial structures.

• Try to be unobtrusive. Remember that you are a guest at Indian communities and events. Be polite and accommodating. In general, it is better to be too formal than too casual.

• Don't ask intrusive questions or interrupt during Indian ceremonies or dances. Even if an Indian event is not explicitly religious (such as a powwow), it may have a spiritual component. Show the same respect at Indian ceremonies that you would at any other religious service. At all events, try to maintain a low profile. Do not talk loudly, push to the front of a crowd, block anyone's view, or sit in chairs that do not belong to you.

• Keep in mind that many Indian people have a looser sense of time than non-Indians. You may hear jokes about "Indian time." Don't be surprised at long delays in the start of ceremonies, powwows, etc.

Arizona

Ak Chin Indian Community, Route 2, Box 27, Maricopa, AZ 85239. Tel: 520-568-2227.

Colorado River Indian Tribes, Route 1, Box 23B, Parker, AZ 85344. Tel: 520-669-9211.

Havasupai Tribe, PO Box 10, Supai, AZ 86435. Tel: 520-448-2961.

Hopi Tribe, PO Box 123, Kykotsmovi, AZ 86039. Tel: 520-734-2445.

Hualapai Tribe, PO Box 179, Peach Springs, AZ 86434. Tel: 520-769-2216.

Kaibab Band of Paiute Indians, Tribal Affairs Building, HC 65, Box 2, Fredonia, AZ 86022. Tel: 520-643-7245.

Navajo Nation, PO Box 308, Window Rock, AZ 86515. Tel: 520-871-6352.

Pascua Yaqui Tribe, 7474 S. Camino de Oeste, Tucson, AZ 85746. Tel: 520-883-5000.

San Carlos Apache Tribe, PO Box 0, San Carlos, AZ 85550. Tel: 520-475-2361.

Tohono O'odham Nation, PO Box 837, Sells, AZ 85634. Tel: 520-383-2221.

Tonto Apache Tribe, Tonto Reservation No. 30, Payson, AZ 85541. Tel: 520-474-5000.

White Mountain Apache Tribe, PO Box 700, Whiteriver, AZ 85941. Tel: 520-338-4346.

California

Agua Caliente Band of Cahuilla Indians, 960 E. Tahquitz Way No. 106, Palm Springs, CA 92262. Tel: 619-325-5673.

Bishop Tribe, PO Box 548, Bishop, CA 93515. Tel: 619-873-3584.

Chemehuevi Tribe, PO Box 1976, Chemehuevi Valley, CA 92363. Tel: 619-858-4531.

Hupa Tribe, PO Box 1245, Hoopa, CA 95546. Tel: 916-625-4110.

Karuk Tribe, PO Box 1016, Happy Camp, CA 96039. Tel: 916-493-5305.

Timbi-Sha Shoshone Indian Tribe, PO Box 206, Death Valley, CA 92328. Tel: 619-786-2374.

Yurok Indian Tribe, Klamath Field Office, PO Box 789, Klamath, CA 95548. Tel: 707-482-6421.

Colorado

Southern Ute Tribe, PO Box 737, Ignacio, CO 81137. Tel: 970-563-4525.

Ute Mountain Ute Tribe, Towaoc, CO 81334. Tel: 970-565-3751.

Idaho

Coeur d'Alene Tribe, Route 1, Box 11FA, Plummer, ID 83851. Tel: 208-686-1800.

Kootenai Tribe, PO Box 1269, Bonners Ferry, ID 83805. Tel: 208-267-3519.

Nez Perce Tribe, PO Box 305, Lapwai, ID 83540. Tel: 208-843-2253.

Shoshone-Bannock Indian Tribe, PO Box 306, Fort Hall, ID 83203. Tel: 208-238-3700.

Montana

Blackfeet Tribal Council, PO Box 850, Browning, MT 59417. Tel: 406-338-7522.

Confederated Salish and Kootenai Tribes, PO Box 278, Pablo, MT 59855. Tel: 406-675-2700.

Crow Tribal Council, PO Box 159, Crow Agency, MT 59022. Tel: 406-638-2601.

Fort Belknap Indian Community, Route 1, Box 66, Harlem, MT 59526. Tel: 406-353-2205.

Fort Peck Tribe, PO Box 1027, Poplar, MT 59255. Tel: 406-768-5155.

Northern Cheyenne Tribe, PO Box 128, Lame Deer, MT 59043. Tel: 406-477-8283.

Nevada

Duckwater Shoshone Tribe, PO Box 68, Duckwater, NV 89314. Tel: 702-863-0227.

Las Vegas Paiute Tribe, 1 Paiute Drive, Las Vegas, NV 89106. Tel: 702-386-3926.

Lovelock Paiute Tribe, PO Box 878, Lovelock, NV 89419. Tel: 702-273-7861.

Paiute-Shoshone Tribe, 8955 Mission Road, Fallon, NV 89406. Tel: 702-423-6075.

Pyramid Lake Paiute Tribe, PO Box 256, Nixon, NV 89424. Tel: 702-574-0140.

Summit Lake Paiute Tribe, PO Box 1958, Winnemucca, NV 89445. Tel: 702-623-5151.

Te-Moak Tribe of Western Shoshone Indians, 525 Sunset St, Elko, NV 89801. Tel: 702-738-9251.

Walker River Paiute Tribe, PO Box 220, Schurz, NV 89427. Tel: 702-773-2306.

Washoe Tribe of Nevada, 919 Highway 395, Garnerville, NV 89410. Tel: 702-265-4191.

New Mexico

Acoma Pueblo, PO Box 309, Acomita, NM 87034. Tel: 505-552-6604.

Jemez Pueblo, PO Box 100, Jemez, NM 87024. Tel: 505-834-7359.

Jicarilla Apache Tribe, PO Box 507, Dulce, NM 87528. Tel: 505-759-3242.

Laguna Pueblo, PO Box 194, Laguna Pueblo, NM. Tel: 505-552-6654.

Mescalero Apache Tribe, PO Box 176, Mescalero, NM 88340. Tel: 505-671-4495.

San Ildefonso Pueblo, PO Box 315-A, Santa Fe, NM 87501. Tel: 505-455-2273.

San Juan Pueblo, PO Box 1099, San Juan, NM 87566. Tel: 505-852-4400.

Santa Clara Pueblo, PO Box 580, Espanola, NM 87532. Tel: 505-753-7326.

Santo Domingo Pueblo, PO Box 99, Santo Domingo, NM 87052. Tel: 505-465-2214.

Taos Pueblo, PO Box 1846, Taos, NM 87571. Tel: 505-758-8626.

Tesuque Pueblo, Route 11, Box 1, Santa Fe, NM 87501. Tel: 505-983-2667.

Zuni Pueblo, PO Box 339, Zuni, NM 87327. Tel: 505-782-4481.

North Dakota

Devils Lake Sioux Tribe, Sioux Community Center, PO Box 359, Fort Totten, ND 58335. Tel: 701-766-4221.
Fort Berthold Tribe, PO Box 220, New Town, ND 58763. Tel: 701-627-4781.
Standing Rock Sioux Tribe, PO Box D, Fort Yates, ND 58538. Tel: 701-854-7231.
Turtle Mountain Band of Chippewa Indians, PO Box 900, Belcourt, ND 58316. Tel: 701-477-6451.

Oklahoma

Apache Tribe of Oklahoma, PO Box 1220, Anadarko, OK 73005. Tel: 405-247-9493.
Cherokee Nation of Oklahoma, PO Box 948, Tahlequah, OK 74465. Tel: 918-456-0671.
Cheyenne-Arapaho Tribe, PO Box 38, Concho, OK 73022. Tel: 405-262-0345.
Chickasaw Nation of Oklahoma, PO Drawer 1548, Ada, OK 74820. Tel: 405-436-2603.
Choctaw Nation of Oklahoma, PO Drawer 1210, Durant, OK 74702. Tel: 405-924-8280.
Comanche Tribe, PO Box 908, Lawton, OK 73502. Tel: 405-492-4988.
Creek Nation of Oklahoma, PO Box 580, Okmulgee, OK 74447. Tel: 918-756-8700.
Fort Sill Apache Tribe, Route 2, Box 121, Apache, OK 73006. Tel: 405-588-2298.
Kiowa Tribe, PO Box 369, Carnegie, OK 73015. Tel: 405-654-2300.
Pawnee Tribe, PO Box 470, Pawnee, OK 74058. Tel: 918-762-3624.

South Dakota

Cheyenne River Sioux Tribe, PO Box 590, Eagle Butte, SD 57625. Tel: 605-964-4155.
Crow Creek Sioux Tribe, PO Box 50, Fort Thompson, SD 57339. Tel: 605-245-2221.
Flandreau Santee Sioux Tribe, Flandreau Field Office, PO Box 283, Flandreau, SD 57028. Tel: 605-997-3891.
Lower Brule Sioux Tribe, PO Box 187, Lower Brule, SD 57548. Tel: 605-473-5561.
Oglala Sioux Tribe, PO Box H, Pine Ridge, SD 57770. Tel: 605-867-5821.

Rosebud Sioux Tribe, PO Box 430, Rosebud, SD 57570. Tel: 605-747-2381.
Yankton Sioux Tribe, PO Box 248, Marty, SD 57361. Tel: 605-384-3804.

Utah

Paiute Indian Tribe of Utah, 600 North 100 East, Cedar City, UT 84720. Tel: 801-586-1111.
Ute Tribe, PO Box 190, Fort Duchesne, UT 84026. Tel: 801-722-5141.

Wyoming

Arapaho Tribe, PO Box 396, Fort Washakie, WY 82514. Tel: 307-332-6120.
Shoshone Tribe, PO Box 217, Fort Washakie, WY 82514. Tel: 307-332-4932.

Calendar of Events

Contact the following organizations for information on rodeos:

Professional Rodeo Cowboys Association, 101 Pro Rodeo Drive, Colorado Springs, CO 80919. Tel: 719-593-8840.
International Professional Rodeo Association, 2304 Exchange Ave, Oklahoma City, OK 73108. Tel: 405-235-6540.
Women's Professional Rodeo Association, Route 5, Box 698, Blanchard, OK 73010. Tel: 405-485-2277.

JANUARY

Arizona National Livestock Show, 1826 W. McDowell Road, Phoenix, AZ 85007. Tel: 602-258-8568.
Cowboy Poetry Gathering, Western Folklife Center, PO Box 888, Elko, NV 89801. Tel: 702-738-7508.
National Western Stock Show Festival, 1325 E. 46th Ave, Denver, CO 80216. Tel: 303-297-1166.
Parada del Sol and Rodeo, Scottsdale Chamber of Commerce, 7343 Scottsdale Mall, Scottsdale, AZ 85251. Tel: 602-945-8481.

San Ildefonso Feast Day, San Ildefonso Pueblo, PO Box 315-A, Santa Fe, NM 87501. Tel: 505-455-2273.
Southwestern Exposition and Livestock Show, Fort Worth Convention and Visitors Bureau, 415 Throckmorton, Fort Worth, TX 76102-7410. Tel: 817-336-8791 or toll free 800-433-5747.
Southwestern Livestock Show and Rodeo, PO Box 10239, El Paso, TX 79993. Tel: 915-532-1401.
Turtle Dance, Taos Pueblo, PO Box 1846, Taos, NM 87571. Tel: 505-758-8626.

FEBRUARY

Houston Livestock Show and Rodeo, PO Box 20070, Houston, TX 77225. Tel: 713-791-9000.
Los Comanches Dance, Taos Pueblo, PO Box 1846, Taos, NM 87571. Tel: 505-758-8626.
O'odham Tash Indian Celebration, Tohono O'odham Nation, PO Box 837, Sells, AZ 85634. Tel: 520-383-2221.
San Antonio Stock Show and Rodeo, PO Box 200230, San Antonio, TX 78296-0230. Tel: 210-225-5851.
Tucson Rodeo – La Fiesta de los Vaqueros, Tucson Convention & Visitors Bureau, 130 S. Scott Ave, Tucson, AZ 85701. Tel: 520-624-1817.
Tulsa Indian Art Festival, Expo Square, Tulsa Convention and Visitors Bureau, 616 S. Boston, Tulsa, OK 74119. Tel: 918-585-1201.

MARCH

Calico Hullabaloo, Calico Ghost Town, PO Box 638, Yermo, CA 92398. Tel: 619-254-2122.
Cowboy Poetry Gathering, Alpine Chamber of Commerce, PO Box 209, Alpine, TX 79831. Tel: 915-837-8191.
Great Train Robberies of the Old West, Roaring Camp, PO Box G-1, Felton, CA 95018. Tel: 408-335-4484.
Heard Museum Indian Fair and Market, 22 E. Monte Vista Road, Phoenix, AZ 85004. Tel: 602-252-8848.
National Circuit Finals Rodeo, Pocatello Frontier Rodeo Association, 1553 E. Center, Pocatello, ID 83201. Tel: 208-233-1546.
San Jose Feast Day, Laguna Pueblo, PO Box 194, Laguna Pueblo, NM. Tel: 505-552-6654.
Texas Independence Day Celebration, Star of the Republic Museum, PO Box

317, Washington, TX 77880. Tel: 409-878-2461.

World's Largest Rattlesnake Round-Up, Sweetwater Chamber of Commerce, 18 E. Broadway Ave, Sweetwater, TX 79556. Tel: 915-235-5488.

APRIL

Clovis Rodeo, 961 W. Shaw, Clovis, CA 93612. Tel: 209-299-8838.

Cowboy Poetry Gathering, National Cowboy Hall of Fame and Western Heritage Center, 1700 NE 63rd St, Oklahoma City, OK 73111. Tel: 405-478-2250.

Gathering of Nations Powwow, Albuquerque Convention and Visitors Bureau, PO Box 26866, Albuquerque, NM 87125. Tel: 505-243-3696 or toll free 800-284-2282.

Institute of American Indian Arts Powwow, 1369 Cerillos Road, Santa Fe, NM 87501. Tel: 505-988-6463.

Rendezvous Fair and Yahoo! Barbecue, Gilcrease Museum, 1400 Gilcrease Museum Road, Tulsa, OK 74127. Tel: 918-596-2700.

MAY

Buckskinner Rendezvous, Arizona Office of Tourism, 1100 W. Washington St, Phoenix, AZ 85007. Tel: 602-542-8687 or toll free 800-842-8257.

Calaveras County Fair and Jumping Frog Jubilee, Calaveras Lodging and Visitor Association, 1211 S. Main, Angels Camp, CA 95222. Tel: 209-736-0049.

Dakota Cowboy Poetry Gathering, Theodore Roosevelt-Medora Foundation, PO Box 1696, Bismark, ND 58502. Tel: 701-623-4444.

Cinco de Mayo Celebration, Albuquerque Convention and Visitors Bureau, PO Box 26866, Albuquerque, NM 87125. Tel: 505-243-3696 or toll free 800-284-2282.

Fiesta de Santa Fe Baile de Mayo, Santa Fe Convention & Visitors Bureau, PO Box 909, Santa Fe, NM 87501. Tel: 505-984-6760.

Gold Rush Days Extravaganza, Roaring Camp, PO Box G-1, Felton, CA 95018. Tel: 408-335-4484.

Mountain Man Living History, Chisholm Trail Museum, 605 Zellers Ave, Kingfisher, OK 73750. Tel: 405-375-5176.

Santa Cruz Feast Day, Taos Pueblo, PO Box 1846, Taos, NM 87571. Tel: 505-758-8626.

Stanford University Powwow, Native American Students Association, PO Box 2990, Stanford, CA 94305. Tel: 415-723-4078.

JUNE

Big Wind Powwow, Shoshone Business Council, Northern Arapaho Business Council, Fort Washakie, WY 82514. Tel: 307-332-4932.

Bozeman Trail Days, Fort Phil Kearney, 528 Wagon Box Road, Banner, Wy 82832. Tel: 307-684-7629.

Chisholm Trail Round-Up, Stockyards Historic Area, Visitor Center, 130 E. Exchange St, Fort Worth, TX 76106. Tel: 817-625-9715.

Durango Pro Rodeo Series (through August), Durango Chamber Resort Association, 111 S. Camino del Rio, Durango, CO 81301. Tel: 970-247-0312.

Fiesta del Concho, Convention and Visitors Bureau, 500 Rio Concho Drive, San Angelo, TX 76903. Tel: 915-653-1206.

Fort Union Trading Post Rendezvous, Fort Union Trading Post National Historic Site, RR 3, Box 71, Williston, ND 58801. Tel: 701-572-9083.

Indian Fair, San Diego Museum of Man, 1350 El Prado, Balboa Park, San Diego, CA 92101. Tel: 619-239-2001.

Massacre Rocks Rendezvous, Massacre Rocks State Park, 3592 Park Lane, American Falls, ID 83211. Tel: 208-548-2672.

National Cowgirl Hall of Fame and Western Heritage Center Rodeo, 515 Avenue B, Hereford, TX 79045. Tel: 806-364-5252 or 817-626-4475.

National Oldtime Fiddlers' Contest, 8 E. Idaho St, Weiser, ID 83672. Tel: 208-549-0452.

Old Fort Days, Fort Sumner State Monument, PO Box 356, Fort Sumner, NM 88119. Tel: 505-355-2573.

Old Miners Day, Chloride, Arizona Office of Tourism, 1100 W. Washington St, Phoenix, AZ 85007. Tel: 602-542-8687 or toll free 800-842-8257.

Plains Indian Museum Powwow, Buffalo Bill Historical Center, PO Box 1000, Cody, WY 82414. Tel: 307-587-4771.

Red Earth Native American Festival, Myriad Convention Center, Oklahoma City Convention and Visitors Bureau,

123 Park Ave, Oklahoma City, OK 73102. Tel: 405-297-8912 or toll free 800-225-5652.

Reno Rodeo, Reno Livestock Event Center, PO Box 12335, Reno, NV 89510. Tel: 702-329-3877.

San Antonio Feast Day-Comanche Dance, San Ildefonso Pueblo, PO Box 315-A, Santa Fe, NM 87501. Tel: 505-455-2273.

San Felipe Fiesta, Albuquerque Convention and Visitors Bureau, PO Box 26866, Albuquerque, NM 87125. Tel: 505-243-3696 or toll free 800-284-2282.

San Juan Feast Day, Taos Pueblo, PO Box 1846, Taos, NM 87571. Tel: 505-758-8626.

Santa Fe Trail Rendezvous, Raton Chamber of Commerce, PO Box 1211, Raton, NM 87740. Tel: 505-445-3689.

Tulsa Powwow, Fairgrounds Pavilion, Tulsa Convention and Visitors Bureau, 616 S. Boston, Tulsa, OK 74119. Tel: 918-585-1201.

Woodchopper's Jamboree, Saratoga Chamber of Commerce, PO Box 1095, Saratoga, WY 82331. Tel: 307-326-8855.

JULY

Bannack Days, Bannack State Park, 4200 Bannack Road, Dillon, MT 59725. Tel: 406-834-3413.

Cheyenne Frontier Days, PO Box 2477, Cheyenne, WY 82003. Tel: 800-227-6336.

Cody Stampede Parade and Rodeo, Cody Country Visitors & Conventions Council, 836 Sheridan Ave, Cody, WY 2777. Tel: 307-587-2297.

Days of '47 Celebrations, Utah Travel Council, Council Hall, Capitol Hill, Salt Lake City, UT 84114, tel: 800-200-1160.

Durango Cowgirl Classic, Durango Chamber Resort Association, 111 S. Camino del Rio, Durango, CO 81301. Tel: 970-247-0312.

El Paso Festival, El Paso Arts Alliance, 333 E. Missouri St, El Paso, TX 79901. Tel: 915-533-1700.

Green River Rendezvous, Museum of the Mountain Man, 700 E. Hennick, Pinedale, WY 82941. Tel: 307-367-4101.

Mescalero Festival, Mescalero Apache Tribe, PO Box 176, Mescalero, NM 88340. Tel: 505-671-4495.

Mountain Man Rendezvous, Fort Union Trading Post National Historic Site, RR 3, Box 71, Williston, ND 58801. Tel: 701-572-9083.

Mountain Man Rendezvous-Pioneer Days Celebration, Lava Hot Springs Chamber of Commerce, PO Box 55, Lava Hot Springs, ID 83246. Tel: 208-776-5221.

North American Indian Days, Blackfeet Tribal Council, PO Box 850, Browning, MT 59417. Tel: 406-338-7522.

Sitting Bull Stampede, Mobridge Chamber of Commerce, Mobridge, SD 57601. Tel: 605-845-2387.

Snake River Stampede, PO Box 231, Nampa, ID 83653. Tel: 208-466-8497.

Soldiering on the Santa Fe Trail, Fort Union National Monument, PO Box 127, Watrous, NM 87753. Tel: 505-425-8025.

Spanish Market, Spanish Colonial Arts Society, PO Box 1611, Santa Fe, NM 87504. Tel: 505-983-4038.

Taos Fiesta, Taos County Chamber of Commerce, PO Drawer I, Taos, NM 87571. Tel: 505-758-3873 or toll free 800-732-8267.

Taos Pueblo Powwow, Taos Pueblo, PO Box 1846, Taos, NM 87571. Tel: 505-758-8626.

Texas Cowboy Reunion, Chamber of Commerce, PO Box 1206, Stamford, TX 79553. Tel: 915-773-2411.

Western Days, Chamber of Commerce, PO Box 2519, Billings, MT 59103. Tel: 406-252-4016.

West of the Pecos Rodeo, Pecos Chamber of Commerce, PO Box 1127, Pecos, TX 79772. Tel: 915-445-2406.

Wolf Horse Stampede, Wolf Point Chamber of Commerce, PO Box 237, Wolf Point, MT 59201. Tel: 406-653-2012.

AUGUST

American Indian Exposition, PO Box 908, Anadarko, OK 73005. Tel: 405-247-2733.

Boom Days, Leadville Chamber of Commerce, PO Box 861, Leadville, CO 80461. Tel: 719-486-3900.

Cherokee National Holiday, Cherokee Heritage Center, PO Box 515, Tahlequah, OK 74465. Tel: 918-456-6007.

Coeur d'Alene Indian Pilgrimage, Old Mission State Park, PO Box 30, Interstate 90, Cataldo, ID 83810. Tel: 208-682-3814.

Crow Fair, Crow Tribal Council, PO Box 159, Crow Agency, MT 59022. Tel: 406-638-2601.

Days of '76 Parade and Rodeo, Deadwood-Lead Chamber of Commerce, 735 Main St, Deadwood, SD 57732. Tel: 605-578-1876.

Indian Market, Santa Fe Convention & Visitor Bureau, PO Box 909, Santa Fe, NM 87501. Tel: 505-984-6760.

Lewis and Clark Reenactment, Knife River Indian Villages National Historic Site, PO Box 9, Stanton, ND 58571. Tel: 701-745-3300.

National Cowgirl Hall of Fame Rodeo, 515 Avenue B, Hereford, TX 79045. Tel: 806-364-5252 or 817-626-4475.

Nez Perce Cultural Days, Nez Perce National Historical Park, PO Box 93, Spalding, ID 83551. Tel: 208-843-2261.

Oglala Nation Powwow and Rodeo, Oglala Sioux Tribe, PO Box H, Pine Ridge, SD 57770. Tel: 605-867-5821.

Old Lincoln Days, New Mexico Tourism, Lamy Building, 491 Old Santa Fe Trail, Santa Fe, NM 87503, tel: 800-545-2040.

Old West Days, Convention and Visitors Bureau, PO Drawer 9480, Amarillo, TX 79105-9480. Tel: 806-378-4297.

Palace Mountain Man Rendezvous and Buffalo Roast, Museum of New Mexico, Palace of the Governors, 105 W. Palace Ave, Santa Fe, NM 87501. Tel: 505-827-6483.

Powwow of Champions, Expo Square, Tulsa Convention and Visitors Bureau, 616 S. Boston, Tulsa, OK 74119. Tel: 918-585-1201.

Shoshone-Bannock Indian Festival, Shoshone-Bannock Indian Tribe, PO Box 306, Fort Hall, ID 83203. Tel: 208-238-3700.

Santa Clara Feast Day, Santa Clara Pueblo, PO Box 580, Espanola, NM 87532. Tel: 505-753-7326.

Three Island Crossing Rendezvous, Oregon Trail, Three Island State Park, PO Box 609, Glenns Ferry, ID 83623. Tel: 208-366-2394.

US Team Roping Championship, Northwest Finals, Caldwell Chamber of Commerce, 300 Frontage Road, Caldwell, ID 83606. Tel: 208-459-7493.

SEPTEMBER

Cheyenne River Labor Day Powwow, Cheyenne River Sioux Tribal Council,

PO Box 590, Eagle Butte, SD 57625. Tel: 605-964-4155.

Fiesta de Santa Fe, **Santa Fe Convention & Visitor Bureau**, PO Box 909, Santa Fe, NM 87501. Tel: 505-984-6760.

Fort Bridger Rendezvous, Fort Bridger State Historic Site, PO Box 35, Fort Bridger, WY 82933. Tel: 307-782-3842.

Ghost Dancer All-Indian Rodeo, Durango Chamber Resort Association, 111 S. Camino del Rio, Durango, CO 81301. Tel: 970-247-0312.

Heart O'Texas Fair, Chamber of Commerce, 108 W. Denison, Waco, TX 76706. Tel: 817-752-6551.

Navajo Nation Fair, Navajo Nation Tourism Office, PO Box 663, Window Rock, AZ 86515. Tel: 520-871-6436.

New Mexico State Fair and Rodeo, New Mexico Tourism, Lamy Building, 491 Old Santa Fe Trail, Santa Fe, NM 87503, tel: 800-545-2040.

Old Taos Trade Fair, Taos County Chamber of Commerce, PO Drawer I, Taos, NM 87571. Tel: 505-758-3873 or toll free 800-732-8267.

Pendleton Round-Up, PO Box 609, Pendleton, OR 97801. Tel: 503-276-2553.

Pioneer Days in Fallbrook, San Diego Convention and Visitors Bureau, 1200 Third Ave, Suite 824, San Diego, CA 92101. Tel: 619-232-3101.

Pioneer Days Celebration and Rodeo, Stockyards Historic Area, Visitor Center, 130 E. Exchange St, Fort Worth, TX 76106. Tel: 817-625-9715.

Pioneer Woman Living History, Pioneer Woman Museum, 701 Monument Road, Ponca City, OK 74602. Tel: 405-765-6108.

San Esteban Feast Day, Acoma Pueblo, PO Box 309, Acomita, NM 87034. Tel: 505-552-6604.

San Geronimo Feast Day, Taos Pueblo, PO Box 1846, Taos, NM 87571. Tel: 505-758-8626.

Texas State Fair, PO Box 26010, Dallas, TX 75226. Tel: 214-421-8716.

OCTOBER

Apache Days, Globe, San Carlos Apache Tribe, PO Box O, San Carlos, AZ 85550. Tel: 520-475-2361.

Cherokee Fall Festival, Cherokee Nation of Oklahoma, PO Box 948, Tahlequah, OK 74465. Tel: 918-456-0671.

Four Nations Powwow, Nez Perce Tribe, PO Box 305, Lapwai, ID 83540. Tel: 208-843-2253.
Grand National Rodeo, Horse and Livestock Exhibition, Cow Palace, PO Box 34206, San Francisco, CA 94134. Tel: 415-469-6000.
Northern Navajo Fair, Shiprock, Navajo Nation Tourism Office, PO Box 663, Window Rock, AZ 86515. Tel: 520-871-6436.
Old West Rodeo, Durango Chamber Resort Association, 111 S. Camino del Rio, Durango, CO 81301. Tel: 970-247-0312.
World Championship Chili Cook-off, International Chili Society, PO Box 2966, Newport Beach, CA 92663. Tel: 714-631-1780.

NOVEMBER

Death Valley Encampment, Death Valley Chamber of Commerce, PO Box 157, Shoshone, CA 92384. Tel: 619-852-4524.
Fall Encampment at Red River Trading Post, Museum of the Great Plains, 601 Ferris Ave, Lawton, OK 73502. Tel: 405-581-3460.
Indian National Finals Rodeo, New Mexico Tourism, Lamy Building, 491 Old Santa Fe Trail, Santa Fe, NM 87503, tel: 800-545-2040.
World Championship Chili Cook-Off, Texas Tourism, PO Box 12728, Austin, TX 78711, tel: 800-888-8839.

DECEMBER

Candlelight Christmas at the Ranch, Ranching Heritage Center, 4th and Indiana, Lubbock, TX 79409. Tel: 806-742-2498.
Christmas at Old Fort Concho, Fort Concho National Historic Landmark, 630 S. Oakes St, San Angelo, TX 76903. Tel: 915-657-4441.
Christmas Powwow, Expo Square, Tulsa Convention and Visitors Bureau, 616 S. Boston, Tulsa, OK 74119. Tel: 918-585-1201.
Gilcrease Rendezvous, Gilcrease Museum, 11400 Gilcrease Museum Road, Tulsa, OK 74127. Tel: 918-596-2700.
National Finals Rodeo in Las Vegas, Nevada, Pro Rodeo Cowboys Association, 101 Pro Rodeo Drive, Colorado Springs, CO 80919. Tel: 719-593-8840.

Shopping

Where to Shop

Saddles, chaps, hats, belt buckles, boots and other western gear, art and collectibles are available in specialty shops throughout the West. Here are a few recommendations:

Arizona

Bacon's Boots and Saddles, 290 N. Broad St, Globe, AZ 85501. Tel: 520-425-2681.
Harry Thurston Saddlemaker, 3144 E. Bell Road, Phoenix, AZ 85032. Tel: 602-992-4414.
Herron's Cowboy Shop, PO Box 1207, Chino Valley, AZ 86323. Tel: 520-636-5461.
Paul Bond Western Boot Company, 915 W. Paul Bond Drive, Nogales, AZ 85621. Tel: 520-281-0512.
Rocky's Custom Saddlery, 120 E. Park Ave, Gilbert, AZ 85234. Tel: 602-926-4137.
Stewart Boots, 30 W. 28th St, South Tucson, AZ 85713. Tel: 520-791-9973.
Yippie-ei-o!, 7014 E. Camelback, Scottsdale, AZ 85251. Tel: 602-994-4416.

California

Federico, 1522 Montana Ave, Santa Monica, CA 90403. Tel: 310-458-4134.
High Noon, 9929 Venice Blvd, Los Angeles, CA 90034. Tel: 310-202-9010.
Sonrisa Folk Art, 7609 Beverly Blvd, Los Angeles, CA 90067. Tel: 213-935-8438.

Colorado

Rusty May Saddlery, 6239 W. Highway 34, Loveland, CO 80538. Tel: 303-663-4036.

Miller Stockman, 1600 California St, Denver, CO 80202. Tel: 303-825-5339.

Montana

Grizzly Boot Company, 814 S. Higgins Ave, Missoula, MT 59801. Tel: 406-549-1555.

Nevada

Elko General Merchandise, 416 Idaho St, Elko, NV 89801. Tel: 702-738-3295
J.M. Capriola Co., 500 Commercial St, Elko, NV 89801. Tel: 702-738-5816
Tip's Western Wear and Custom Saddles, 185 Melarkey St, Winnemucca, NV 89445. Tel: 702-623-3300.

New Mexico

Caballo, 727 Canyon Road, Santa Fe, NM 87501. Tel: 505-984-0971.
Jackalope, 2820 Cerrillos Road, Santa Fe, NM 87505. Tel: 505-471-8539.
Streets of Taos, 200 Canyon Road, Santa Fe, NM 87501. Tel: 505-983-8268.

Oklahoma

G.C. Blucher Boot Company, 350 N. Main, Fairfax, OK 74637. Tel: 918-642-3205.

Texas

Catalena Hatter, 203 N. Main, Bryan, TX 77803. Tel: 409-822-4423.
Eddie Kimmel Custom Boots and Bags, Route 1, Box 36, Comanche, TX 76442. Tel: 915-356-3197.
Homestead, 223 E. Main, Fredericksburg, TX 78624. Tel: 210-997-5551.
Jabberwocky Antiques, 207 E. Main, Fredericksburg, TX 78624. Tel: 210-997-7071.
Spriggs, Boot Maker, 608 E. Holland, Alpine, TX 79830. Tel: 915-837-7392.
Donaho Saddle Shop, 8 E. Concho Ave, San Angelo, TX 76903. Tel: 915-655-3270.
Resistol Hat Shop, 2300 N. Simmons Freeway, Dallas, TX 75258. Tel: 214-631-2211.
Rocketbuster Boots, 115 S. Anthony St, El Paso, TX 79901. Tel: 915-541-1300.
Stanley Boot Shop, 1112 N. Chadbourne, San Angelo, TX 76903. Tel: 915-655-8226.

The Turquoise Door, 316 Colorado St, Austin, TX 78701. Tel: 512-480-0618. **Wild Bill's**, 603 Munger Ave, Dallas, TX 75202. Tel: 214-954-1050.

Wyoming

Unc's Boot Shop, 1025 S. Highway 89, Jackson, WY 83001. Tel: 307-733-5477.

Outdoor Activities

Horseback Riding, Roundups and Pack Trips

American Wilderness Experience, PO Box 1486, Boulder, CO 80306. Tel: 303-444-2622 or toll free 800-444-0099. Pack trips and other outdoor adventures.

Bar T Five Ranch, Cache Creek Road, Jackson, WY 83001. Tel: 307-733-3534 or 307-733-5386. Covered wagon and horseback trips in Bridger Teton National Forest.

Beartooth Plateau Outfitters, PO Box 1127, Cooke City, MT 59020, 406-838-2328 or 406-445-2293. Half-day rides, pack trips and other outdoor adventures.

Bitterroot Ranch, Route 66, Box 1402, Dubois, WY 82513. Tel: 307-455-3363 or toll free 800-545-0019. Pack trips on Wyoming's outlaw trail.

Canyon Trail Rides, PO Box 128, Tropic, UT 84736. Tel: 801-679-8665. Trail rides in the national parks and red-rock country of southern Utah and northern Arizona.

Cedar Grove Pack Station, PO Box 295, Three Rivers, CA 93271. Tel: 209-565-3464. Short rides and overnight pack trips in Sequoia and Kings Canyon National Parks.

Flint Hills Overland Wagon Train Trips, PO Box 1076, El Dorado, KS 67042. Tel: 316-321-6300. Re-create pioneer life on overnight covered-wagon trips.

Grant Grove Stables, Kings Canyon National Park, CA 93633. Tel: 209-335-2374. Short rides in Kings Canyon National Park.

Grand Teton Lodge Co., PO Box 240, Moran, WY 83013. Tel: 307-543-2855. Guided trail rides, fishing and raft trips in Grand Teton National Park.

Monument Valley Navajo Tribal Park, Box 93, Monument Valley, UT 84536. Tel: 801-727-3287. Inquire about horseback riding tours at visitor center.

Off the Beaten Path, 109 E. Main St, Suite 4, Bozeman, MT 59715. Tel: 406-586-1311. Wilderness pack trips and a whole host of other outdoor adventures.

Pack Creek Ranch, PO Box 1270, Moab, UT 84532. Tel: 801-259-5505. Pack trips in the La Sal Mountains.

Peaceful Valley Ranch, PO Box 197, Medora, ND 58645. Tel: 701-623-4496. Horseback riding in Theodore Roosevelt National Park.

Sombrero Ranch, 3300 Airport Road, Box A, Boulder CO 80301. Tel: 970-586-4577. Riding in and around Rocky Mountain National Park.

Yellowstone Adventure, Horse Creek Ranch, PO Box 3878, Jackson Hole, WY 83001. Tel: 307-733-6556. Short rides and pack trips in Yellowstone National Park.

Yosemite Concessions Services Corp., 5410 East Home Ave, Fresno, CA 93727. Tel: 209-252-4848. Riding in Yosemite National Park.

Camping

Most tent and RV sites in national and state parks and in national forests are available on a first-come, first-served basis. Arrive as early as possible to reserve a campsite. Campgrounds fill early during the busy summer season (spring, fall and winter in the desert parks). A limited number of campsites in the most popular parks may be reserved in advance. Contact the parks for information on availability. Fees are usually charged for campsites. Backcountry permits may be required for wilderness hiking and camping.

There are hundreds of private campgrounds, too, some with swimming pools, RV hookups, showers and other facilities. The largest network is **Kampgrounds of America (KOA)**, PO Box 30558, Billings, MT 59114, tel: 406-248-7444.

Hiking

Avoid solitary hiking. The best situation is to hike with at least two other partners. If one person is injured, one member of the party can seek help while the other two remain behind. If you must hike alone, be sure to tell someone your intended route and time of return. Back-country hiking may require a permit. Ask a ranger before setting out.

Use common sense on the trail. Don't attempt routes that are too strenuous for your level of fitness. Concentrate on what you're doing and where you're going. Even well-trod and well-marked trails can be dangerous. Be careful near cliffs, rocky slopes, ravines, rivers and other hazards. Don't attempt anything you're not comfortable with or anything that's beyond your level of skill.

Environmental Ethics

The old saw is good advice: "Take nothing but pictures, leave nothing but footprints." The goal of low-impact/no-impact backpacking is to leave the area in the same condition as you found it, if not better. If you're camping in the backcountry, don't break branches, level the ground or alter the landscape in any way. Make fires in designated places only. Otherwise, use a portable stove. When nature calls, dig a hole 6 inches deep and at least 100 feet from water, campsites and trails. Pack out all trash, including toilet paper.

Wildlife

Never approach wild animals. Don't try to feed or touch them, not even the "cute" ones like chipmunks, squirrels and prairie dogs (they may carry diseases). Some animals, such as bison, may seem placid and slow-moving but will charge if irritated. People who have tried to creep up on bison in order to get a better photograph have been seriously injured by the animals. If you want a close-up, buy a telephoto lens.

Store your food in airtight bags or containers, especially in bear country. Hang food at least 15 feet above the ground and 100 yards from camp. If you've been fishing, change clothes before bedding down for the night. Be careful with deodorants, colognes, perfumes and anything else that a bear might think has an interesting odor.

Health and Safety

Most accidents and injuries are caused by inattentive or incautious behavior. You may be on vacation but your brain shouldn't be. Pay attention to where you are and what you are doing. Keep your eyes on the road when driving. If you want to gaze at the scenery, use an overlook or pullout. Heed all posted warnings and, when in doubt, seek the advice of police officers, park rangers, highway officials or other authorities.

Ghost Towns

Travelers should exercise caution around old buildings and abandoned mines. Structures may be unstable and the ground may be littered with broken glass, nails and other debris. Mine shafts are particularly dangerous. Never attempt to enter a mine shaft or cave unless accompanied by a park ranger or other professional.

Fitness and altitude sickness

Remember that the air is thinner at higher elevations. Unless properly acclimated, you may feel uncharacteristically winded. If you experience nausea, headache, vomiting, extreme fatigue, lightheadedness or shortness of breath, you may be suffering from altitude sickness. Although the symptoms may be mild at first, they can steadily develop into a serious illness. Return to a lower elevation and try to acclimate gradually.

Water

It's always a good idea to carry a little more water than you think you'll need when hiking. The rule of thumb is a gallon a day per person, more in extreme conditions. Drink at least a quart at the start of a hike, and prevent dehydration by drinking at regular intervals while you're on the trail even if you don't feel particularly thirsty. Don't wait until you've become dehydrated before you start drinking!

All water taken from natural sources must be purified before drinking. *Giardia* is found in water (even crystal-clear water!) throughout the West and can cause severe cramps and diarrhoea. The most popular methods of purifying water are using a water-purification tablet, a water-purification filter (both available from camping supply stores) or by boiling water for at least 15 minutes.

Sunburn

There's a reason why cowboys wear big hats. The sun can be fierce, even on a cool day. Protect yourself by using a high-SPF sunscreen and wearing a wide-brimmed hat and sunglasses, even if the day starts out cloudy.

Further Reading

General

Across the Wide Missouri, by Bernard De Voto, Boston: Houghton Mifflin, 1947.

Age of the Gunfighter: The Taming of the West, by Joseph G. Rosa. New York: Smithmark Publishers.

The American Frontier: Pioneers, Settlers & Cowboys 1800-1899, by William C. Davis. New York: Smithmark Publishers.

The Arizona Rangers, by Bill O'Neal. Austin, TX: Eakin Press, 1986.

Art of the Golden West, by Alan Axelrod. New York: Abbeville Press, 1990.

The Best of the West: An Anthology of Classic Writing from the American West, edited by Tony Hillerman. New York: HarperCollins, 1991.

Beyond the Hundredth Meridian, by Wallace Stegner. New York: Penguin, 1953.

Billy the Kid: A Short and Violent Life, by Robert M. Utley. Lincoln: University of Nebraska Press, 1989.

Black Elk Speaks, by John Neihardt. Lincoln: University of Nebraska Press, 1961.

The Black West, by William Loren Katz. New York: Doubleday, 1971.

Buckaroo, edited by Hal Cannon and Thomas West. New York: Callaway, 1993.

Bury My Heart at Wounded Knee, by Dee Brown. New York: Bantam Books, 1971.

The Chroniclers, by Keith Wheeler. New York: Time-Life Books, 1976.

Custer Died For Your Sins, by Vine Deloria. New York: Avon, 1969.

Desert Solitaire: A Season in the Wilderness, by Edward Abbey. New York: McGraw-Hill, 1968.

Earthtones: A Nevada Album, by Ann Ronald and Stephen Trimble. Reno: University of Nevada Press, 1995.

Encyclopedia of Western Gunfighters, by Bill O'Neal. Norman: University of Oklahoma Press, 1979.

The Exploration of the Colorado River and Its Canyons, by John Wesley Powell. New York: Penguin, 1987.

The Expressmen, by David Nevin. New York: Time-Life Books, 1976.

500 Nations, by Alvin Josephy. New York: Knopf, 1994.

Fighting Men of the Indian Wars, by Bill O'Neal, Stillwater, OK: Barbed Wire Press, 1991.

Following the Guidon, by Elizabeth Custer. Norman: University of Oklahoma, 1966.

Ghost Towns of the American West, by Bill O'Neal. Lincolnwood, IL: Publications International, 1995.

Ghost Towns of the West, by William Carter. Menlo Park, CA: Lane Publishing, 1978.

Grand Canyon: An Anthology, by Bruce Babbitt. Flagstaff: Northland Press, 1978.

The Great West, by David Lavender. New York: American Heritage Publishing, 1985.

The Gunfighters, by Paul Trachtman. New York: Time-Life Books, 1976.

The Indians, by William Brandon. Boston: Houghton Mifflin, 1961.

Indian Villages of the Southwest, by Buddy Mays. San Francisco: Chronicle Books, 1985.

Its Your Misfortune and None of My Own, by Richard White. Norman: University of Oklahoma Press, 1991.

Killing Custer: The Battle of the Little Bighorn and the Fate of the Plains Indians, by James Welch. New York: Norton, 1994.

A Lady's Life in the Rocky Mountains, by Isabella L. Bird. Norman: University of Oklahoma, 1960.

The Legacy of Conquest, by Patricia Nelson Limerick. New York: Norton, 1987

The Long Death, by Ralph Andrist. New York: Collier Books, 1964.

My Life on the Plains, by George Armstrong Custer. Lincoln: University of Nebraska, 1966.

Native America, by Christine Mather, photographs by Jack Parsons. New York: Clarkson Potter, 1991.

The People: Indians of the American Southwest, by Stephen Trimble. Santa Fe: School of American Research Press, 1993.

An Overland Journey, by Horace Greeley. New York: Knopf, 1963.

Riding the White Horse Home, by Teresa Jordan. New York: Pantheon, 1993.

Roughing It, by Mark Twain. New York: Penguin, 1980.

Santa Fe Style, by Christine Mather, photographs by Jack Parsons. Rizzoli, 1986.

The Solace of Open Spaces, by Gretel Ehrlich. New York: Penguin Viking, 1985.

True West: Arts, Traditions, and Celebrations, by Christine Mather, photographs by Jack Parsons. New York: Clarkson Potter, 1992.

The West: A Treasury of Art and Literature, edited by T.H. Watkins and Joan Watkins. New York: Hugh Lauter Levin Associates, 1994.

The Westerners, by Dee Brown. New York: Holt, Rinehart and Winston, 1974.

The West of Buffalo Bill, edited by Patricia Gilchrest. New York: Abrams, 1974.

The West That Was, edited by Thomas W. Knowles and Joe R. Lansdale. New York: Wings Books, 1993.

Where the Bluebird Sings to the Lemonade Spring: Living and Writing in the West, by Wallace Stegner. New York: Random House, 1992.

Fiction and Poetry

All The Pretty Horses, by Cormac McCarthy. New York: Knopf, 1992.

Almanac of the Dead, by Leslie Marmon Silko. New York: Simon & Schuster, 1991.

Angle of Repose, by Wallace Stegner. New York: Doubleday, 1971.

Anything for Billy, by Larry McMurtry. New York: Simon & Schuster, 1988.

The Assassination of Jesse James by the Coward Robert Ford, by Ron Hansen. New York: Knopf, 1983.

The Big Rock Candy Mountain, by Wallace Stegner. New York: Penguin, 1991.

Blood Trails, by Rod McQueary. Dry Oak Press, 1993.

Bowdrie, by Louis L'Amour. New York: Bantam, 1983.

Buffalo Gals, by Larry McMurtry. New York: Simon & Schuster, 1990.

Ceremony, by Leslie Marmon Silko. New York: Viking, 1977.

Cowboy Curmudgeon, by Rod McRae. Salt Lake City: Gibbs Smith, 1992.

The Crossing, by Cormac McCarthy. New York: Knopf, 1994.

The Dance Hall of the Dead, by Tony Hillerman. New York: Harper & Row, 1973.

The Dark Wind, by Tony Hillerman. New York: Harper & Row, 1982.

Death Comes for the Archbishop, by Willa Cather. New York: Knopf, 1927.

The Death of Jim Loney, James Welch. New York: Norton, 1979.

Fool's Crow, James Welch. New York: Viking, 1986.

High Lonesome, by Louis L'Amour. New York: Bantam, 1962.

Horseman Pass By, by Larry McMurtry. New York: Penguin, 1984.

House Made of Dawn, by N. Scott Momaday. New York: Harper and Row, 1966.

Jubal Sackett, by Louis L'Amour. New York: Bantam, 1985.

Lonesome Dove, by Larry McMurtry. New York: Simon & Schuster, 1985.

Luck of Roaring Camp, by Bret Harte. Boston: Houghton Mifflin, 1903.

The Octopus, by Frank Norris. New York: Bantam, 1901.

O Pioneers, by Willa Cather. Boston: Houghton Mifflin, 1987.

The Ox-Bow Incident, by Walter Van Tilburg Clark. New York: Signet Classic, 1968.

Ramona, by Helen Hunt Jackson. New York: G&D, 1912.

Riders of the Purple Sage, by Zane Grey. New York: Penguin, 1990.

Roughstock Sonnets, by Paul Zarzyski. Kansas City: Lowell Press, 1989.

Skinwalkers, by Tony Hillerman. New York: Harper & Row, 1987.

Tales of the Gold Rush, by Bret Harte. New York: Heritage, 1944.

The Virginian, by Owen Wister. New York: G&D, 1929.

Other Insight Guides

The 190 books in the *Insight Guides* series cover every continent and include 40 titles devoted to the US. Companion books to this title include:

Insight Guide: Native America provides a unique blend of absorbing text about the Native Americans' culture and a detailed guide to Indian reservations, historic sites, festivals and ceremonies, from the arid deserts of the Southwest to the lush woodlands of the East Coast.

Insight Guide: American Southwest covers this culturally rich region in great detail, from Apache Junction to Albuquerque, from Los Alamos to Las Vegas, from ghost towns to the Grand Canyon.

Insight Guide: National Parks West. Ranging widely across the west, from Texas to North Dakota, from Colorado to California and then on to Washington state, the book also takes in the national parks of Alaska and Hawaii.

Index

Y–Z